Pearl Jam
FAQ

Pearl Jam FAQ

All That's Left to Know About Seattle's Most Enduring Band

Thomas Edward Harkins and Bernard M. Corbett

Backbeat
Books

An Imprint of Hal Leonard Corporation

Published in 2016 by Backbeat Books
An Imprint of Hal Leonard Corporation
7777 West Bluemound Road
Milwaukee, WI 53213

Trade Book Division Editorial Offices
33 Plymouth St., Montclair, NJ 07042

The FAQ series was conceived by Robert Rodriguez and developed with Stuart Shea.

Printed in the United States of America

Book design by Snow Creative Services

Library of Congress Cataloging-in-Publication Data

Names: Harkins, Thomas E., author. | Corbett, Bernard M., author.
Title: Pearl Jam FAQ : all that's left to know about Seattle's most enduring band / Thomas Edward Harkins and Bernard M. Corbett.
Other titles: Pearl Jam frequently asked questions
Description: Montclair : Backbeat Books, 2016. | Series: FAQ series | Includes bibliographical references and index.
Identifiers: LCCN 2015043404 | ISBN 9781617136122 (pbk.)
Subjects: LCSH: Pearl Jam (Musical group) | Rock musicians—United States—Biography.
Classification: LCC ML421.P43 H37 2016 | DDC 782.42166092/2—dc23
LC record available at http://lccn.loc.gov/2015043404

www.backbeatbooks.com

With love and respect to the memory and inspiration of legendary New York City disc jockey, musicologist, and author, Pete Fornatale. This one's for you, Uncle Pete. To paraphrase Sir Isaac Newton (1676): If we see further, it is because we have stood on the shoulders of giants.

Contents

Foreword

I never thought I'd be doing this. I've written and edited lots of books on music, especially punk rock and heavy metal, but this is the first foreword I've written for a book I didn't write or edit. But after reading it and seeing what an excellent job Tom Harkins and Bernard Corbett did in demonstrating why Pearl Jam is so important to so many people, I jumped at the chance to be a part of the project.

Something that gave me a moment's pause is that this is a book about Pearl Jam, one of the quintessential rock bands of the last three decades and a band with a dedicated and active audience. I'm sure that there are a *lot* of fans that own every bootleg, that can beat me at Pearl Jam trivia, and that have actually even surfed with Eddie Vedder (well, maybe). There are lots of people in the online Pearl Jam community who love the band more than me. Their dedicated posts and research show their involvement with, and love of, the band. But many groups have really dedicated fans. (Dead Heads, anyone?) Each band affects people in different ways. I think it's the emotional resonance that some music has with certain fans. Some people go completely bonkers over a band and dissect every lyric for minute particles of meaning the way Joyce scholars do over *Finnegans Wake*. Others just really enjoy the music. I fall into the latter category. So, why me?

Well, this is going to sound weird, but I *do* have something to say about Pearl Jam that a lot of critics won't give them credit for. The best way to describe my feelings for Pearl Jam is to say that I have a great deal of respect for them. The term "respect" has many different meanings to people, so let me explain what I mean.

I respect Pearl Jam not just as a band and as musicians; it's already obvious to everyone how good they are. Rather, when I say "respect," I mean that I respect them for their integrity and commitment to their fans. To their commitment to charity and fundraising, to which a hundred other bands I could mention never gave a second thought. To their fight against Ticketmaster, against corporate greed that screwed the real fans. Even though it was quixotic, they fought the corporate giant because someone needed to, and they stepped up to the plate.

I respect them in the way that I respect a group like Fugazi, a band that Pearl Jam looked up to and that shared their concern for the way a concert ticket should lead to an emotional, almost reverential bonding experience for everyone, not just for the 1 percent who can afford the front row of the MegaDome. I respect Pearl Jam even more for introducing their fans to punk legends like the Dead Boys, Avengers, the Buzzcocks, the Clash, Sleater Kinney, Dead Kennedys, Sonic Youth, X, and, of course, the Ramones, who were inducted into the Rock and Roll Hall of Fame in 2002 by none other than a freely drinking, freshly mohawked

Eddie Vedder. (The authors of this book don't think it was his finest moment, but I think it was punk as hell.)

Most of all, I respect Eddie (and the rest of the band) for one heroic, almost superhuman feat at Jones Beach during Lollapalooza 1992. The band, perhaps frustrated by their early daylight set or simply annoyed by the cavernous stage, seemed antsy and put on a ferocious set, one that culminated with Eddie Vedder climbing not up to a theater balcony this time, but instead climbing at least forty or fifty feet above the stage on the lighting rigging. As stagehands and security looked on, Vedder climbed methodically, hand over hand, until he crossed the top of the stage and came down on the other side. It was a magnificent feat of strength, daring, and sheer lunacy. And these are just a few of the reasons that I am honored to be a part of this book. The authors Tom Harkins and Bernard Corbett do a nifty (and meticulous) job in showing the reader why Pearl Jam is a great band. This may be the perfect book for both seasoned and new fans. Not all great bands care if the fans are with them or not, but Pearl Jam does care. I was convinced of this when I saw Eddie Vedder slowly reach out one arm after the other to move across the lighting rig, his legs dangling with no net below, and with no way of getting out of this other than going forward. At Lollapalooza 1992 Eddie Vedder took a leap of faith and launched himself into the air. For the last three decades, he and Stone and Jeff and Mike and Matt have asked fans to do the same thing, to follow them on leap of faith after leap of faith. This book is *the* book for those fans.

Brian Cogan
February 2016

Brian Cogan, PhD, is a professor, author, and gadfly about town. He's the author of (among other books) *The Encyclopedia of Punk* (2008), coauthor of *The Heavy Metal Encyclopedia* (2008) and the upcoming Backbeat Books publication *Monty Python FAQ* (2017), and, in the years between, he has authored lots of cool stuff about music, pop culture, the baby boomers, and Monty Python.

Acknowledgments

We would like to thank the following people for their support and enthusiasm. First of all, the wonderful staff at Backbeat Books, especially our (musically talented) project editor, Bernadette Malavarca, who was always available whenever we needed her; our publicity manager, Wes Seeley; and our copy editor, Micah White. Our agent, former coauthor, and (in Tom's case) cousin, Peter Thomas Fornatale, who came up with the idea for us to propose a Pearl Jam FAQ in the first place and who served as our "literary midwife" throughout the project, a task not unlike attempting to "herd cats," we are told. Pete, we could never, *ever* thank you enough, though that was also true *before* we began this project. Pete's wife, Susan Van Metre, executive vice president and publisher at Abrams Books, was a constant sounding board and source of professional wisdom and experience. Baby Perrin Tamar Fornatale (now *three*) was a constant source of delight with her toddler antics, and Muggsy the dog, "everybody's favorite Labrador!" vied for our attention and ate various things when we weren't looking.

We would also like to thank Bernie's immediate family, mother Fay and brother Mitchell, Boston University Men's Hockey, and Harvard University Football. We would like to thank Christina, a diehard Terriers fan from Boston University, for her timely secretarial support. Bernie would like to give a special shout out to his friend and fellow broadcaster, Rob "The Rob" Bleetstein, the program director, host, and producer of Sirius/XM Radio's all-Pearl Jam channel (22), Pearl Jam Radio. In a bit of poetic justice for Tom, "The Rob" is also a long-time host on Sirius/XM's the Grateful Dead Channel, just one notch down the dial at channel 23.

Tom would like to thank his parents, Thomas F. Harkins and Ann Marie Harkins, for their love, support (in spite of their still not really knowing who or *what* Pearl Jam is), and for *not* evicting him from the top floor apartment (I LOVE that place) while we wait for the royalty checks to start rolling in. Tom's sister, Andrea Harkins (whose favorite Pearl Jam song is "Release"), was an enthusiastic cheerleader for the project from day one and actively connected us with several valuable resources, such as: Joe Papeo, photographer, owner of iRockTheShot (irocktheshot.com; www.joepapeo.com), and a Pearl Jam enthusiast in his own right. Andrea also introduced her friend, Ten Club member, Daniel Miller. We would like to thank Matt Spitz, guitarist for the Pearl Jam tribute band, Lost Dogs: a Tribute to Pearl Jam, for being on board from the very beginning; indeed, the Lost Dogs were playing at Peggy O'Neill's, Coney Island, the day we got the news from Pete about the book deal, so Matt was among the very first to know. We would like to thank the Canny Brothers Band for their moral support, enthusiasm, and for continuing to employee Tom as a roadie/merchandise guy. Tom would like to thank his old friend Keith Fallon—sergeant of the New York City Court Officers, lead singer of the Canny Brothers Band, and long time Pearl Jam fan—for his friendship and for his touching anecdote about how a Pearl Jam concert ticket set off a chain of circumstances that ultimately helped him to win the hand of Kathleen Brady in marriage. Chef Russell Titland, of the Wicked Monk in Bay Ridge, has been a friend for a long time and has kept us fed at many different points along the way. Dean Russo, Joann Amitrano, and the friendly staff at Dean Russo Art provided creative inspiration and moral support. Some of Tom's old NYU friends, who are writers and rock and rollers in their own right, were a source of inspiration, including Robert Barry Francos, founder and publisher of *FFanzeen: Rock'n'Roll Attitude with Integrity*; Dr. Brian Cogan, PhD; and Dr. William Phillips, PhD. Robert and Tom both wrote for and edited the same college newspaper, Kingsborough Community College's *Scepter*, albeit twenty years apart—Robert in 1974, and Tom in 1994. Tom would also like to thank his friend and fellow music enthusiast, Mike Beitchman, of Mike Beitchman Photography and Bay Ridge Entertainment, for taking his publicity photos one hot summer day in Coney Island under the Parachute Jump. In addition to being an excellent photographer, Mike is a dedicated proponent of the local live music scene.

Finally, an extra special "Thank You" goes out to those dedicated members of the Ten Club, most of whom Tom met online through Facebook and who took time out of their busy schedules to share their Pearl Jam opinions, stories, and memorabilia photographs with us: Tanya Kang, proprietor of Tanya Kang Photography and creator of *Pearl Jam Fan Portraits*; Dustin M. Pardue, professional rock photographer and author of 2013's *A Fire That Wouldn't Go Out*, was very generous with his time, authorial empathy, and photograph submissions; Shawn Fitzgerald; Thomas Wegh of Strydhagen Antiques in Nijmegen, The Netherlands; Jen Manlove; Stephanie Huber, a volunteer for the Wishlist Foundation, for the photo of Eddie Vedder's lyric "cheat sheet" and the tattoo it inspired; Jeremy Mahn of Toronto, Canada; John Cafarella of Maynard, Massachusetts; Terri McNelly; Jeff Wilder of Sunrise, Florida; Jessica Seyfarth; Steven Tyler (not *that* one, no!); Sjaaj van den Berg; Jeremy "Crash" Crowley of Crashious Roadside; Jose R. Pava P; and last but certainly not least, Ryan Byrne, who just *may* have bragging rights when it comes to his voluminous Pearl Jam collection. Thank you all for talking and texting with us and for sharing your Pearl Jam experiences. You have all been most welcoming. Keep riding that wave where it takes you.

—Thomas Edward Harkins and Bernard M. Corbett

Introduction
Meanwhile, on the East Coast

When Pearl Jam (nee Mookie Blaylock) first hit the stage at the Off Ramp Café on October 22, 1990, I was 2,862 miles east, in Brooklyn, New York, far removed from the first rumblings of the so-called "Seattle Scene." I was living in a basement apartment on Tenth Avenue in Dyker Heights that my father only half-jokingly referred to as "the Spahn Ranch." My high school days were already more than five years in my own "Rearviewmirror." I was cooking at a Bay Ridge pub called Skinflints. Had I stayed there, I would have been eligible for the proverbial gold-watch retirement by now. But life had other plans. I had no way of knowing it at the time, but I'd be heading back to college in a couple of years, earning three degrees, teaching undergraduates as an adjunct at New York University and Adelphi University and achieving doctoral candidacy within NYU Steinhardt's Media Ecology program. Changes were imminent. You could feel it in the air, taste it in the water, and yes, hear it in the music.

Pearl Jam, Huh?

By the time I became aware of Pearl Jam—through a combination of MTV, VH1, *Rolling Stone* magazine, and word of mouth—*Singles* had been released, *Temple of the Dog* was a "thing," *Ten* was a hit, and people were beginning to use the word "grunge," a term I found puzzling. The new wave of music emanating from Seattle was being marketed as "alternative," but I was always on board with the Billy Joel message in "It's Still Rock and Roll to Me"; alternative to *what*, exactly?

In what Jeff Ament would surely regard as an irony, it was seeing the classic "Jeremy" video by Mark Pellington on MTV that finally prompted me to go out and buy Pearl Jam's debut album, *Ten*. I was captivated by the video, the story behind it, and by this band of earnest, endearing, longhaired rebels who were telling it. I can remember looking at the band members as my contemporaries, as people I could have very easily grown up and partied with had I only lived in Seattle.

I was a mere six months younger than Stone Gossard and nearly a year and a half older than Dave Abbruzzese (like most people, I had missed out on the brief Dave Krusen and Matt Chamberlain phases of the band's earliest days). We had all grown up listening to many of the same bands. The Who's *Quadrophenia* was often on my turntable, too, in spite of the fact that I was now only buying CDs.

And then, that was it. No, not *really* "it," but for many years Pearl Jam just became one of the hundreds of other bands on my CD shelves. I continued to buy their albums as they came out, but I never really went all-in on them. I didn't attend their shows or follow them around the way I had done with heavy metal bands or, later, the Grateful Dead. I suppose after a decade of attending hundreds of rock concerts I may have been feeling a bit jaded. Like Eddie Vedder once said at an awards show (you'll see), "There's too many bands, and you've heard it all before."

For the Love of Pete

Fast-forward about twenty years. Post-NYU, I was now in another transitional phase and looking to get into doing some writing that someone outside of the "Ivory Tower" of academia would actually *read*. My uncle, Pete Fornatale, a well-respected New York City disc jockey and musicologist, was working on a book for The Rolling Stones' fiftieth anniversary called *50 Licks: Myths and Stories from Half a Century of the Rolling Stones*. My cousin, Peter Thomas Fornatale, an experienced professional editor and prolific author, was my uncle's coauthor, along with a guy named Bernard M. Corbett, whom I had never met. That would change soon enough, albeit under unfortunate circumstances. Pete Fornatale passed away unexpectedly on April 26, 2012, shortly after completing his work on *50 Licks*.

I met Bernie Corbett for the first time at Pete's wake, and we became fast friends, bonding over music and the one professional sports team loyalty we share, the New York Giants. Like Pete, Bernie is a broadcaster by trade, though he is a sportscaster and not a disc jockey. He is the radio voice for Harvard University Football and Boston University's Men's Hockey. Bernie is a Boston University alumnus and essentially just stayed on after graduation as an employee who never left. This close connection to his alma mater was something he shared in common with the late, legendary disc jockey. And make no mistake about it; rock and roll is his abiding passion, too. As I would learn soon enough, Bernie had been a diehard Pearl Jam fan for nearly two decades and was a veteran of more than seventy shows.

Carry On

When *Fifty Licks* finally hit the shelves in the spring of 2013, Peter Thomas and Bernie worked together to promote it, and I helped them out here and there with a couple of blog posts. At the same time, there was the question of what comes *next?* A book for the Who's fiftieth anniversary seemed like the next logical project, and we're sure Eddie Vedder would have approved. At Peter's behest, Bernie and I drafted a proposal. We shopped it around to different publishers, but the idea didn't generate much interest.

Then one day, while browsing the Internet, Peter stumbled across the FAQ series by Backbeat Books. While looking through the available titles, he had his eureka moment. There was no Pearl Jam volume available. Suddenly, he knew. This was it. He called Backbeat Books and spoke to the series editor. Would they like to see a proposal for a *Pearl Jam FAQ*? As fate would have it, they were amenable to the idea.

And So It Began

From the day we began researching for the *Pearl Jam FAQ* proposal, I was on a journey of rediscovery. Whatever happened to that cool band of guys from Seattle with the thrift store wardrobes? Whatever happened to that basketball playing bass player with the funny hats, that skinny lead guitarist with the killer riffs, or that deathly serious looking lead singer? Pearl Jam . . . yeah. I always liked those guys.

For Bernie, the process was more like a journey of celebration, like looking through old photo albums with family members who haven't been around in awhile. To this day, Pearl Jam is *his* band, a sentiment that is clearly shared by many of the wonderful Ten Club members and Wishlist Foundation volunteers we have met during the past year or so. Pearl Jam speaks to them on some fundamental, human level that words can only hope to convey.

As the more objective, critical, and analytical member of the team, I could really only hope to understand the full scope of the Pearl Jam phenomenon vicariously, through Bernie and his fellow Ten Clubbers, and also by way of analogy. Having spent more than twelve years attending Grateful Dead shows, I naturally kept drawing analogies between Pearl Jam and the Grateful Dead, an idea that surely would have horrified many of Pearl Jam's Seattle contemporaries during the early 1990s.

Their music, obviously, is quite different, but there are many parallels to be drawn between the cultures that arose around each of these bands from different generations: the attentive fan clubs, the rampant bootlegging followed by the official release of live shows, the obsession over the set lists, and the groups of fans pooling resources to follow the bands from town to town, doing good works and forming communities along the way. It all began to feel very familiar.

To aid me in my part of the journey, the journey of rediscovery, Bernie brought me armloads of his Pearl Jam CDs, DVDs, and books to study, some of which I've even returned to him. Essentially, Pearl Jam became my homework assignment for the next year and a half, sort of like the doctoral dissertation I bailed out on back in 2009, only with much more compelling and enjoyable subject matter. The endless reading, listening, viewing, researching, and writing all proved instructive and satisfying, but it was the many connections I formed with Pearl Jam's most rabid fan base, the Ten Club members, that proved to be the most satisfying. Prior to undertaking this journey, I had always turned up my nose at social media like Facebook in favor of the formality and professionalism of LinkedIn. At Peter's urging, I forced myself to dive headlong into the world of Facebook on a quest to find the "Pearl Jam people." Find them I did, and that made all of the difference in this project—though I must admit that the addictive social medium has also sidetracked me on many an occasion. Like Deadheads, "Jammers" (as they are sometimes called) come from all walks of life, from every socioeconomic status, and from all over the world. It can honestly be said that the sun never sets on Pearl Jam fans. They are everywhere.

Pearls of Wisdom

By the time you read this, Pearl Jam will be gearing up for their twenty-fifth anniversary, and Bernie and I will no doubt be working on other projects. As you read this book and join us in celebrating the ongoing career of this unique and extraordinary band, make sure that you take a step back to appreciate the full scope of the Pearl Jam world. It isn't just about the music, though surely the music is the centerpiece. It is about the band's innumerable charitable works, the Vitalogy and Wishlist Foundations; it is about the sense of communal spirit, of celebration, of tribalism in the best sense of the word. In short, it is about *you*, the fans.

That is why Bernie and I wrote this book. Like you, we are grateful that Pearl Jam's journey will continue, and we are privileged to be a part of it. We have watched this band grow up before our eyes, and their most dedicated fans have grown and changed right along with them. Now that they have attained a healthy and productive maturity, we look forward to watching them continue to age gracefully, expanding the boundaries of rock and roll and social consciousness as they do. In closing, we leave you with a sentiment near and dear to Pearl Jam's hearts, a sentiment Bernie often uses as a salutation on letters and emails; in the words of Pearl Jam's dear old adopted uncle, Neil Young: "Keep on Rockin' in the Free World." We know that Pearl Jam certainly will.

—Thomas Edward Harkins

Pearl Jam
FAQ

Ride the Wave Where It Takes You

Life Before Pearl Jam

Let's Meet the Team

As difficult as it is to comprehend, as the band approaches its twenty-fifth anniversary, there was life before Pearl Jam. There was also a great deal of music, some of it made by the young men who would one day *become* Pearl Jam. While each of them had their own bands, notions, plans, and dreams of future success in the music industry, it is safe to say that none of them had the foresight to envision the band we celebrate today. Yet no one who knows or who has studied Pearl Jam in any detail seems at all surprised by the band's longevity. Apart from the fact that Pearl Jam did have a bit of a "revolving door" on their drum kit early on, the band as a whole has proven resilient and stable. It would surprise no one if, years hence, we find ourselves celebrating a Pearl Jam thirtieth, fortieth, or even fiftieth anniversary. With the clarity afforded by hindsight, the truly remarkable thing is that the band ever got together in the first place. As Cameron Crowe notes in the book version of *Pearl Jam Twenty*, "It all seems so unlikely: the blend of birth, death, joy, tragedy and coincidence that gave the world a band called Pearl Jam." He will get no argument here.

The members of Pearl Jam somehow managed to come together from the far corners of the United States, from a diversity of backgrounds, and from a dizzying array of earlier bands. Their prehistory is decidedly complex, as we will explore in the pages to come. In keeping with the spirit of the basketball-obsessed band, we will begin by taking a quick look at the guys who would become Pearl Jam's "starting five."

Dave Krusen, Drums

David Karl Krusen was born on March 10, 1966, in Tacoma, Washington, and began playing drums in the Seattle area as early as 1979, when he was only thirteen years old. Among his many pre-Pearl Jam bands were Outrigger, the Boibs, Agent Boy, Tramps of Panic, Liar's Club, and Hard Time. Krusen was not the band's first choice to man the drum kit.

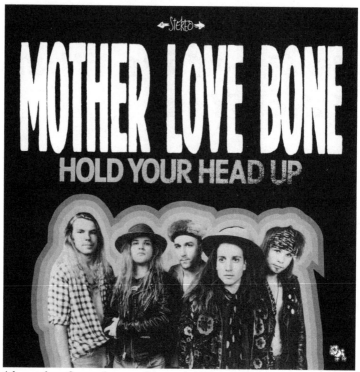

A heavy, bass-forward cover of Argent's 1972 smash hit, "Hold Your Head Up," a staple of FM classic rock radio to this day, became Mother Love Bone's first single. Jeff Ament, along with the ill-fated Andy Wood, earned a songwriting credit for the rollicking B-side, "Holy Roller." It was a promising start.   *Author's collection*

Jeff Ament, Bass

Jeffrey Allen Ament was born on March 10, 1963, in Havre, Montana. The family soon moved to Big Sandy, Montana; "big" being a relative term in this case. The population of the town was less than seven hundred, seven of whom comprised Ament's immediate family. His pre-Pearl Jam bands included Deranged Diction, Green River, and Mother Love Bone.

Stone Gossard, Rhythm/Lead Guitar

Stone Carpenter Gossard was born on July 20, 1966, in Seattle, Washington. The youngest of the founding members and the early leader of the band, Stone was the only Seattle native among the original members. His early bands included March of Crimes, the Ducky Boys, Green River, and Mother Love Bone.

Mike McCready, Lead Guitar

Michael David McCready was born on April 5, 1966, in Pensacola, Florida, and his family moved to Seattle, Washington, soon thereafter. His early bands included

Warrior, Shadow, and Love Chile. Interestingly enough, he knew Stone Gossard from middle school, but they wouldn't play music together until they were both part of the larval stages of a band that evolved first into Mookie Blaylock and then into Pearl Jam.

Eddie Vedder, Lead Vocals, Rhythm Guitar, Ukulele . . . (Yes, *ukulele*)

Edward Louis Severson III was born on December 23, 1964, in Evanston, Illinois. To make a *very* long and oft-told story short, his parents divorced while Eddie was still an infant, and he was renamed Edward Mueller when his mother married Peter Mueller shortly thereafter. He grew up believing that Mueller was his biological father, and that Edward Severson, whom he had met on a handful of occasions, was merely a friend of the family. Eddie only learned the truth about his lineage during his late teens, after his mother had divorced Mueller and after Severson had passed away from multiple sclerosis. Quite understandably, gaining this unexpected knowledge about his origins caused Eddie a great deal of emotional and psychological trauma. Eddie's early bands included Surf and Destroy, the Butts, India Style, and Bad Radio.

A Deep Bench (Especially for Drummers)

The drummer is the beating heart of any band, analogous to the center on a basketball team. It took Pearl Jam many years to attain the level of stability that they enjoy at that position today. In the interim, many different musicians have manned the skins for the band, all of them with different personalities and musical styles. As Pearl Jam's sound evolved to include more keyboards, they expanded their roster by employing a sixth man to come off the bench for live shows.

Matt Chamberlain, Drums

Born on April 17, 1967, in San Pedro, California, Matt was the drummer for Edie Brickell and the New Bohemians before that band broke up in1991. Chamberlain briefly joined Pearl Jam during the summer of 1991, after Dave Krusen was forced to leave the band in May of that year due to his alcohol abuse. Chamberlain filled in and toured with the band that year before *Ten* was officially released, when they were still driving around to their gigs in a van, and he actually appeared in the band's first video, for "Alive." Though the guys did ask him to join the band as a full-fledged member, Chamberlain wasn't into the idea and recommended a replacement, his friend, Dave Abbruzzese. All told, Chamberlain's tenure in Pearl Jam lasted about three weeks, but it was an eventful three weeks, and his post-Pearl Jam gig wasn't too shabby, either. He went on to join the prestigious *Saturday Night Live* house band for the 1991–1992 season.

Dave Abbruzzese, Drums

David James Abbruzzese was born on May 17, 1968, in Stamford, Connecticut. He was the man recommended by Matt Chamberlain to handle the skin duties for Pearl Jam. Abbruzzese, too, joined the band before the official release of *Ten*, though he did not play on the album. He would, however, go on to play on the next two albums, *Vs.* and *Vitalogy*, which remain among the best-selling albums of all time. Though he was, by most accounts, a happy-go-lucky guy and an accomplished musician, Abbruzzese was always something of an outsider in the band, and his tenure with Pearl Jam would come to an abrupt end with him sitting in a diner in 1994. Yes, sort of like the *Sopranos*, but . . . different; hold that thought.

Jack Irons, Drums

Jack Steven Irons was born on July 18, 1962, in Los Angeles, California. His early bands included Chain Reaction and Anthym. But his real claim to fame, and the reason Stone and Jeff were so eager to recruit him, was that he was a founding member of the Red Hot Chili Peppers, one of the hottest bands in the country. Their efforts are reminiscent of how a young Mick Jagger, Keith Richards, and Brian Jones went out of their way to recruit the experienced and respected Charlie Watts for their own drum slot. As we all know, Mick, Keith, and Brian got their man, and the fledgling Rolling Stones were off and running. Gossard and Ament were not as persuasive. They did *not* get their man—at least not at first. But it all worked out for the best. Jack Irons wound up playing an even more important role in Pearl Jam's origin story. It's a great story that involves a crazy camping trip, a demo tape, and games of pickup basketball with a young workaholic surfer punk named Eddie. You'll see.

Matt Cameron, Drums

Matthew David Cameron was born on November 28, 1962, in San Diego, California. Cameron's early bands included the dubiously named Kiss (Imitation), Bam Bam, and Skin Yard. And now for a fun factoid: Cameron attained B-movie fame in 1978 when, billed as "Foo" Cameron (the story goes that his older brother, Peter, used to mispronounce Matthew as "Ma-Foo," hence the ready-made nickname), he sang a song called "Puberty Love," which made the soundtrack of the film, *Attack of the Killer Tomatoes*. Cameron joined Soundgarden in 1986 and stayed with them until their breakup . . . er, lengthy hiatus, in 1997. Pearl Jam invited him aboard in 1998 for the *Yield* Tour, and he quickly became a permanent fixture behind the drum kit.

Boom Gaspar, Piano, Keyboards, Hammond B3 Organ

Kenneth E. Gaspar, aka "Boom," was born on February 3, 1953, in Waimānalo, Hawaii. He is the sixth man on the squad. Gaspar would not come on board until 2002, but the addition of keyboards to Pearl Jam's sound is a fascinating development in its own right. The idea no doubt would have been inconceivable to the grungy gaggle of surf and skateboard punks who made up the original Pearl Jam, but a lot can happen to a band in eleven years.

The Coach

Kelly Curtis worked for Heart, and he has been Pearl Jam's manager since pre-PJ times, in the Mother Love Bone days. Like the band members, he just grew into the role over time. Coach Curtis could never be mistaken for Led Zeppelin's Peter Grant, Elvis Presley's Colonel Tom Parker, or any of the other flamboyant talent managers of yore. Preferring the vantage point from the sidelines, Curtis continues to fly under the radar to this day. For all of the attention paid to Pearl Jam over the years, Curtis remains something of a mystery man.

Green River

What's in a name? Here's a macabre little factoid for you "true crime" enthusiasts: the band took their name from the infamous "Green River Killer," Gary Ridgway, one of the more prolific serial killers in the annals of American crime.

For those of you who thought that the band's name was inspired by the Creedence Clearwater Revival song of the same name, you are clearly showing your age, but your origin story is decidedly more family-friendly. "Green River," in Creedence's case, was the name of a soda syrup flavor, the favorite of young Tom Fogerty, which he regularly purchased from a soda fountain near his family's favorite vacation waterhole.

The significance of Green River, the *band*, in relation to the development of "grunge" and the so-called "Seattle scene" cannot be overstated. The original 1984 lineup included Jeff Ament, Mark Arm, Steve Turner, and Alex Vincent on drums. Stone Gossard and his guitar were added to the mix so that Arm could focus more on his preferred role as lead vocalist. Each of the members had, of course, appeared in earlier bands, and if you want a full and meticulously detailed accounting of the tangled webs of musicians crisscrossing Seattle in those days, you can do no better than to read Jo-Ann Greene's seminal 1993 publication: *Intrigue and Incest: Pearl Jam and the Secret History of Seattle*. With the thoroughness of a forensic detective, Greene traces the threads of the complex tapestry of Seattle musicians back to their origins and brings the scene into clearer focus as a result.

Green River was a serious band. Within a year of their formation, they had completed an EP, *Come on Down*. The record did not sell very well, but it is histori- cally significant because musicologists consider it to be the first concrete example of a "grunge" record. By and large the musicians on the scene did not embrace the term "grunge." Though the origin of the term was most likely in the form of an adjective, "grungy," the proliferation of the noun, "grunge," as though it were the name of a new sub-genre of rock and roll, seems largely to have been a creation of the mass media, which delights in the proliferation of such unnecessary categoriza- tion. The following year, Green River released more material on a C/Z Records compilation album called *Deep Six*. There were only two Green River songs on the compilation, but that project is far more significant for its roster of featured bands: Soundgarden, the Melvins, Malfunkshun, Skin-Yard, and the U-Men. As Stephen Stills might have opined, there was something happenin' here.

By June of 1986, Green River had completed work on a second EP, called *Dry as a Bone*, though it would not be released until July of 1987 on the small but locally influential Sub Pop label, run by Bruce Pavitt. While they were patiently awaiting the release of the EP, they put out a single, "Together We'll Never," on another label. Their patience was rewarded. *Dry as a Bone* was well received, and earned rave reviews. Thus encouraged, the band got right back to work, this time on a full-length LP, *Rehab Doll*. Almost predictably, this period of growing success and creativity was tempered by the onset of what would become serious infighting. Jeff and Stone had gotten a whiff of potential success, and they wanted the band to sign with a major label. Mark Arm, on the other hand, subscribed to the counter-intuitive ethos of the emerging scene and wanted the band to remain independent. For reasons that had yet to be analyzed in any depth at the time, the philosophy of the nascent "grunge" culture was that the conventional trappings and excesses of the rock and roll lifestyle—the big cars, the womanizing, the wild parties, and the megabucks record deals—were all verboten. Those ideas, of course, are nothing new and come straight out of the old punk rock playbook. Like Eddie Vedder, who—a few years later—would have been perfectly content to spend his days touring in a van, playing in small clubs to crowds of fifty people, Arm shunned the spotlight. He may have been a pioneer of this anti-fame attitude, but that did nothing to reconcile his point of view with that of his more ambitious bandmates. By the time the album was completed, they were at each other's throats, and the band essentially broke up. Jeff, Stone, and Bruce Fairweather called it quits on Halloween of 1987. *Rehab Doll* was "posthumously" released in June of 1988 to mixed reviews. This river had run dry.

Mother Love Bone

By the time *Rehab Doll* was released, Stone, Jeff, and Bruce had long put Green River in their collective rearview mirror. Within weeks of quitting the band, they were already on to their next project, a cover band called Lords of the Wasteland, with singer Andrew Wood and drummer Regan Hagar, formerly of Malfunkshun. As any self-respecting Kiss fan can tell you, the band's name references the lyrics of "God of Thunder," from Kiss's 1976 platinum smash, *Destroyer*. No matter. Lords of the Wasteland were not long for this world. Early in 1988 they changed their name to Mother Love Bone and got a new drummer, Greg Gilmore, formerly of Skin Yard and Ten Minute Warning. The wild card in this newly shuffled deck was, without question, the charismatic lead singer, Andrew Wood.

By way of a more formal introduction, Andrew Patrick Wood was born on January 8, 1966, in Columbus, Mississippi. As for his early bands, Wood seems to have been a bit more monogamous than many of his contemporaries, as this quick detour will illustrate.

Collaborating on Lords of the Wasteland with Stone, Jeff, Bruce, and Regan was a good way for Andrew to bridge his past and his future. When Gilmore was brought on board to replace Hagar on drums, and the band changed their name to Mother Love Bone, Andrew cut ties with his past and looked forward to a bright future. The same could be said for Jeff and Stone. The new band afforded them a perfect opportunity to achieve the success they had both dreamed of since grade school.

The band began writing original material, and within a year they signed a deal with PolyGram Records and released a six-song EP called *Shine*. Writing in the *Rocket* in early 1989, Richard T. White described Wood's stage presence, noting "his pouty outrageousness, balanced on the edge of pretension." The year 1989 saw the band out on the road as the supporting act for a British band, the Dogs D'Amour. Wood believed that he had been destined for the stage, and White quotes him as saying:

> I've been training for this all my life . . . I'd put Kiss [sic] *Alive* on really loud and I'd use my bed as a drum riser and a tennis racket for a guitar. And at the end of the album I'd smash my tennis racket, my guitar, start the album over for the encore, and walk out on stage with a brand new guitar. You should have seen it. The Andy Wood Band . . . we were really big in the '70s.

Wasting no time, Mother Love Bone headed right back into the studio after the tour ended to work on their debut album, *Apple*. The album was on schedule for a 1990 release, and morale was high. Unfortunately,

Malfunkshun

In 1980, at age fourteen, Andrew Wood put together the band Malfunkshun with his brother, Kevin, and the aforementioned drummer, Regan Hagar. Andrew affected an outrageous stage persona, L'Andrew the Love Child, which accentuated his natural androgyny. It was as if someone had taken the infectious "Hey, Dude!" enthusiasm of Skid Row's Sebastian Bach and blended it with the calculated freakishness of Ziggy-era David Bowie; a tough act to follow, any way you slice it. The other band members employed alter egos, too, but Andrew's was the only one that garnered any attention. They also enjoyed some longevity, relatively speaking. By Seattle standards, Malfunkshun had a pretty good run, lasting (almost) until 1988. They had two singles released on the *Deep Six* compilation, right alongside their colleagues in Soundgarden and Green River. Notably, those two songs, "With Yo' Heart (Not Yo' Hands)" and "Stars-n-You" were their *only* official releases. While that might not sound like much of a legacy for a band that lasted nearly eight years, this modest output was sufficient for music historians to consider them to be among the originators of the Seattle sound, or "grunge."

Tragically, but not altogether surprisingly, somewhere along the way Andrew discovered the deceptive allure of heroin, a powerful opiate that has been both muse and bane for generations of musicians. Evidence suggests that the addiction hit Andrew pretty hard. He entered a rehabilitation center for the first time at age nineteen, and the drug would continue to haunt him for the rest of his days. Malfunkshun had begun, for lack of a better term, to . . . well, *malfunction*, and they disbanded for good within two years.

so was Andrew, more often than not. To his credit, he was aware that he had a problem, and he made a concerted effort to overcome his addictions, entering rehab once more in 1989 after completing the studio work on *Apple*. He would not live to see *Apple* on record store shelves.

On March 16, 1990, heroin finally scored a decisive blow in its battle with Andrew Wood. As Kim Neely tells it in her lovingly detailed 1998 book, *Five Against*

One: The Pearl Jam Story, band manager Kelly Curtis was in his office waiting for Wood to show up for a meeting. They were going to be interviewing a "prospective road manager-substance abuse watchdog." Wood did not show up for that meeting. At 10:30 p.m., Wood's girlfriend, Xana La Fuente, found him facedown on the bed, a used needle nearby. Andy lingered between life and death at Harborview Medical Center for the next three days. He was brain dead and on life support. During that agonizing period of limbo, Andy's family, Xana, Kelly Curtis, and the other members of Mother Love Bone drifted about in a daze, praying and hoping for a miraculous recovery that would never come. Finally, the Woods accepted the horrible truth that the doctors had been preparing them for, and they agreed to remove their son from life support. As Neely tells it:

> On Monday afternoon, March 19, 1990, with the lights lowered and a tape of one of his favorite albums, Queen's *A Night at the Opera*, softly playing in the background, Andy's family, Xana, Curtis, and Mother Love Bone formed a close, loving circle around his bed, and let him go.

Like his childhood heroes Kiss, Andrew Wood was a larger-than-life performer. Here, clutching an "apple" in a promo shot for the debut album he would not live to see released, he appears to be the center of Greg, Bruce, Stone, and Jeff's world. Though largely unknown outside of his hometown, every time he stepped onto a stage he was playing in the Madison Square Garden of his mind.   *Mercury/Photofest*

The official cause of death was listed as an "accidental and acute overdose of heroin." He was just twenty-four years old. The needle had taken another man, and the world had lost another band.

Now What? Mother Love Bone, Post-Andy

When the person lying in the casket is as young, talented, and full of promise for a successful future as Andy, the tragedy gets magnified that much more. Loved by all who knew him, he was in many ways the spiritual center of the emerging scene. How do you even *begin* to move on? Such was the dilemma facing the surviving members of Mother Love Bone.

Beautiful and enigmatic, Xana La Fuente was Andrew Wood's love, frequent muse, and, ultimately, bereaved fiancé. He wrote the song "Crown of Thorns" about their stormy relationship, which was largely attributable to his dalliances with heroin. Tragically, La Fuente was the one who found Wood unresponsive after the overdose that would claim his life.

Steven Tyler

Greg Gilmore took the approach that the band should move forward without Andy. After all, he reasoned, they were signed to a record deal, and the first album was coming out soon. Stone and Jeff, however, were of a different mind. Andy was not the sort of lead singer who could easily be replaced. It wasn't any one thing about him in particular, either; it was the entire package: the voice, the looks, the stage presence, and the charisma. This truly was one of those cases where you *couldn't* find a better man.

And so, unable to reconcile their differences, the surviving members of Mother Love Bone drifted apart and quietly disbanded. *Apple* was released in July, 1990, and was positively reviewed. But with the grim words "In Memory Of Andrew Wood" plastered across the back cover, the album's release was bittersweet at best. The band was officially broken up, but within two years, perhaps because of all the attention garnered by Stone and Jeff's next project, *Apple* would reach number thirty-four on Billboard's Heatseeker's Chart.

Stone Gossard Demos 1990

Jeff and Stone had reached a moment of reckoning. They had already been playing music for a long time, and they weren't getting any younger. Stone, like Andy, was twenty-four; Jeff was twenty-seven. The two friends were wracked with uncertainty. Fairweather and Gilmore were already off and running on their next projects, but the way forward seemed less clear to Jeff and Stone. Had they missed their best shot? Would they ever play together again? Would either of them ever play again at *all*, for that matter? Shortly after Andy's passing, Jeff and Stone caught Mike McCready's band, Love Chile, at the OK Hotel, and the performance really resonated with them. Stone had started writing music again, and he thought that maybe he and Mike would sound really good together. Jeff started gigging around with some other local bands but wasn't doing anything too serious. In the meantime, all around them they could see friends of theirs, like Soundgarden and Alice

More than a quarter of a century after his untimely demise, Andrew Wood's haunting visage continues to peer out at the world from a seemingly endless parade of deluxe re-releases of *Apple*. His spirit looms large in Pearl Jam's near-mythic origin story and remains present in their hearts and minds to this day.   *Steven Tyler*

in Chains, begin to receive critical acclaim and commercial success. Even Tad and Mudhoney were keeping busy, being booked for gigs on a regular basis. Nirvana, too, had burst upon the scene, and was quickly gaining a solid reputation that would soon explode into international superstardom.

So Stone invited Mike over for a jam session, and they discovered that they did indeed have great musical chemistry. After jamming together for a period of time, Mike began to urge Stone to bring Jeff back into the fold. Stone, for reasons known only to him, was resistant to the idea at first, but Mike persisted in his vision. So Jeff began sitting in with them, and before long they realized that they just might have something worthwhile. Their friend Matt Cameron from Soundgarden came down to help out on the drums. The four went into the recording studio for a few days and jammed together. What they had those first few days were really just songs in their earliest stages of formation: ideas, riffs, licks, and a lot of jamming. Gradually, however, the jams began to take on recognizable forms and structures and became songs. They whittled away and edited until they came up with five solid instrumentals that they titled, *Stone Gossard Demos 1990*. The songs on this tape would eventually evolve into "Alive," "Once," "Footsteps," "Alone," and "Black." First, however, they needed something—several somethings, really, including a full-time drummer, lyrics for the instrumentals, and a lead singer.

You Don't Know Jack

The drummer they had in mind was Jack Irons. Jack, too, was still dealing with the effects of losing a close friend to heroin. Hillel Slovak, the Chili Peppers' founding guitarist, had lost his own battle with the insidious drug a few years earlier in June of 1988. The future Rock and Roll Hall of Famer was twenty-six years old. Irons was decidedly anti-drug and had been all along, so one can only imagine how difficult it must have been for him to function in a band in which the drummer, the bass player, *and* the lead singer, Anthony Keidis, were all nursing heroin habits at various times. He took Slovak's death very hard, quit the band, and suffered terribly from depression.

By the time Stone and Jeff came knocking, the death of their own bandmate still fresh in their minds, Jack was back in the music game full throttle, touring with Joe Strummer and Redd Kross, and putting together his own band, Eleven. As if all that were not enough, he and his wife were starting a family, so there was just no way he was going to be able to work with Stone and Jeff. Supposedly, Stone and

Jeff were *so* eager to recruit Jack that they were willing to leave Seattle and move down to California just to be near him. It just wasn't happening. But Jack played an even more important role in the prehistory of Pearl Jam. Stone and Jeff gave him a few cassette copies of the *Stone Gossard Demos 1990* and asked him to pass them on to potential drummers and lead singers. Of the latter, as quoted in the Neely book, Jack said, "I know this one guy down in San Diego who might be cool."

This One Guy Down in San Diego

The guy who Jack had in mind was, of course, Eddie Vedder. He had been the child model, the high school theater actor, and, as everyone in the free world knows by now, the troubled teenager. The 1990 incarnation of Eddie Vedder was clearly a driven, type-A personality and workaholic. The twenty-five-year-old aspiring musician, singer, and songwriter had already worked his way through a number of bands. When he wasn't pumping gas, waiting tables, working security, or volunteering as a roadie to get himself close to industry insiders, Eddie was busy promoting and gigging with his band, Bad Radio. In his "spare time," often while working at one of his many jobs, he wrote songs and lyrics. He was also an avid surfer and skateboarder who liked to play pickup basketball.

When you read through all that has been written and said about this phase of Eddie's life, you can't help but feel exhausted just thinking about it. That's when it hits you: You have read similar stories time and time again about highly successful people in other fields. These people all seem to share a quality that you do not find in the average person. They have an extra gear they can shift into or some other unknown attribute that the rest of us do not possess, or at least don't possess in such abundance. They are driven to succeed, and they pursue their art and their life's work with a clarity and relentless zeal that is nothing short of astonishing. Eddie was, and remains to this day, one of these exceptional people. It should come as no surprise to anyone that Eddie's ambitions and goals far outstripped those of his Bad Radio bandmates. He did everything for the band, from writing songs to negotiating gigs to going out and plastering the town with promotional posters. Eventually, he realized he'd taken the band as far as it was going to go, and he quit.

"Crazy Eddie" Goes Camping

The timing could not have been better. Jack Irons invited Eddie along on a ten-day Yosemite backpacking trip with Flea and some of his other friends from the music business. Lengthy camping excursions often have a cleansing, therapeutic effect on a person, and that seems to have been the case with Eddie on this trip. He really let his hair down, so to speak, in the company of his more successful traveling companions. Before long he was showing off, acting the daredevil, diving off cliffs, and performing all sorts of crazy stunts. By the end of the trip the other members of the group were referring to him as "Crazy Eddie." In a classic "oh, by the way" moment, Jack popped a Mother Love Bone tape into the car's cassette player on the drive home for Eddie to listen to.

"Posthumous" is one of the saddest words in the English language. *Mother Love Bone*, a compilation of the band's limited past glories, was released in the autumn of 1992 and gave us a sense of what might have been.   *Author's collection*

According to Neely, Jack didn't just hand Eddie a copy of the demo that day. It wasn't until September, a full two months after the camping trip, that Jack got around to playing matchmaker. He called Eddie and told him the whole tragic tale of Mother Love Bone and Andy Wood, and about how Stone and Jeff were putting together a new band and needed a drummer and a singer. Then he arranged for Eddie to meet Stone and Jeff when they came down to L.A. The meeting went well, with Eddie giving Stone and Jeff a tape of his own work, and with Stone and Jeff giving Eddie a copy of the demos. Stone and Jeff returned to Seattle, and Eddie went back to San Diego to see what he could do with the demo tape.

Where It Takes You

This part of the Pearl Jam origin story, which has nearly attained the status of classical mythology since its occurence, finds Eddie raw-nerved and emotionally vulnerable following a sleep-deprived night at work. He had taken the demos to work with him earlier that evening to familiarize himself with the music. While most people probably would have gone straight home to crash out and sleep, Eddie, being Eddie, decided to go surfing instead. Anyone who has spent time near the water knows that there is something primal and eternal about the ocean that can cut right to the core of our very existence. The rhythm of the waves is, in a sense, the heartbeat of the Earth. It is no coincidence that the ocean is a recurring theme in one of Eddie's all-time favorite albums, the Who's *Quadrophenia*. Having been a troubled youth himself, Eddie related to the protagonist of *Quadrophenia*, Jimmy Cooper. As a surfer, he related on an even more visceral level to the rhythms of the ocean. On the day in question, a perfect storm of conditions must have come together: the music from the demos playing in his head, the rhythm of the waves crashing around him, the emotional fragility from sleep deprivation settling in, and a collection of painful childhood memories bubbling to the surface. As he surfed, lyrics began to form in his mind. The muse was upon him. Eddie was riding the wave, but he had no idea where it was about to take him.

2

"Mookie Blaylock" Takes the Court

Will Mookie Blaylock Be Taking the Band to Court?

Momma-Son

When Eddie got home from Pacific Beach that foggy mid-September morning, he was still riding the crest of the only good wave he had caught that day, the wave of inspiration that fuels the creative process. He jotted down his lyrics, broke out his trusty 1984 Tascam four-track mixer, and began to lay down vocal tracks to accompany three of the five instrumentals on *Stone Gossard Demos 1990*. Eddie envisioned a mini-opera, a suite of thematically connected songs he dubbed "Momma-Son." Composing it was an act of soul-cleansing catharsis, and Eddie's lyrics allowed him to come to terms with many of the painful experiences of his youth. Best of all, those lyrics seemed to be a perfect fit for the demo songs.

Legend has it that with no blank cassettes lying around, he recorded over a copy of *Merle Haggard's Greatest Hits!* In short order, he wrapped the tape up and mailed it to Jeff, along with his contact info.

Jeff Ament, You've Got Mail

Meanwhile, 1,255 miles up the road to the north, Jeff and Stone were in Seattle, waiting. Cameron Crowe told the story in "Five Against the World," his 1993 *Rolling Stone* piece. "Sitting in his apartment in Seattle," Crowe wrote, "Ament listened to the tape three times and picked up the phone. 'Stone,' he said, 'you better get over here.'" In fellow *Rolling Stone* scribe Kim Neely's version of the events, Jeff said, "Stone, I may be totally whacked out, but I think this guy is amazing."

Listening to Eddie lay down those heavy lyrics in that unique voice of his was a revelatory experience. As Jeff told Jennifer Clay in her 1991 *Rip* magazine piece, "Life After Love Bone": "It was a kind of a sick, disturbed rock opera . . . if Nietzsche were to write a rock opera." Stone, too, had an almost visceral reaction to what Eddie had done with the demo tape. He told Clay:

We were blown. He was really the first that had it. We had a few other tapes of singers, but it was always people singing Mother Love Bone songs or trying to be like Andy. When we heard Eddie's tape, it was like, here's a guy who didn't really know anything about Mother Love Bone for the most part. He didn't have any preconceived notions about what it was. He just related to these non-vocal demos that we sent him.

Drumroll, Please

In hindsight it does seem a bit bizarre that Matt Cameron, Pearl Jam's (and Soundgarden's) current drummer, was the man behind the drum kit during the *Stone Gossard Demos 1990* sessions. But when you take Jo-Ann Greene's research into account, particularly her use of the term "incestuous" to describe the Seattle music scene at the time, it begins to make more sense. Perhaps it was the finite nature of the local talent pool that led Jeff and Stone to cast a wider net in their search for prospective band members. Their zealous pursuit of Jack Irons is understandable enough, given Irons's stature in the business. The truly remarkable thing about this story is that they were so focused on courting Irons to be their new drummer that their request that he pass along the tape to prospective *singers* seems to have been almost an afterthought at the time. Yet it led them to someone who would evolve into one of the greatest front men and lead vocalists of all time.

In the end, Greene tells us, it was a simple recommendation from a friend and fellow musician, Son of Man's Tal Goettling, which led them to Dave Krusen. The diminutive Krusen had been playing in Seattle for more than ten years, but he wasn't exactly a marquee name. No matter. He was exactly what the fledgling band needed at the time, a professional drummer. By all accounts the hiring process was fairly straightforward: Krusen auditioned for Jeff, Stone, and Mike, and they sent him home with a copy of the demo so he could learn the music. Within two weeks he was in the band, and the timing dovetailed perfectly with the travel plans Jeff had made with Eddie.

Workingman's Ed

With Krusen officially onboard, arrangements were made for Eddie to fly up to Seattle. He wasn't interested in sightseeing or other frivolities; true to form, he only wanted to get to work. He was, after all, just a working stiff from San Diego, "the guy who never sleeps," and he'd had to take time off from work in order to make this trip. Vedder insisted that he go directly from the airport to the band's rehearsal site, a cluttered basement studio beneath an art gallery. He didn't want to waste anyone's time, least of all his own. In fact, he arrived with lyrics he had already written for "Black" and two other songs ready to go.

Name Day

Gathered in the makeshift studio, the newly formed and still nameless band launched into "Alive," kicking off a grueling ten-hour day of rehearsals in a week that would soon be filled with ten-hour days. "Black," "Deep," and "Jeremy" evolved from these intense marathon sessions and added to the band's repertoire. The band had the presence of mind to record the rehearsal sessions on cassette. By the fifth day, they were ready to lay down the new tracks for an official demo.

According to the origin myth, somewhere along the way someone stuck Mookie Blaylock's basketball card into one of the cassette covers as a joke. The sight of Mookie Blaylock's basketball card led to one of those classic "eh, what the hell" moments, and suddenly the nameless were named.

Off Ramp, on Stage

And so it came to pass that on October 22, 1990—the sixth day of their collaboration—Jeff Ament, Stone Gossard, Mike McCready, Dave Krusen, and Eddie Vedder found themselves playing a hastily arranged, unannounced gig at the Off Ramp Café, billed under the name of the New Jersey Nets' point guard, Mookie Blaylock.

That night's performance caught a lot of people's attention. Kim Neely described the potentially awkward moment when the band was in the midst of their sound check, playing "Even Flow" to an empty room, when, unbeknownst to Eddie, who had his eyes tightly closed, the club opened its doors and the room began to fill. At the song's end, he opened his eyes to find a small but appreciative and growing audience.

1) Even Flow 2) Release 3) Alone 4) Alive
5) Once 6) Even Flow 7) Black 8) Breath
9) Girl

22-10-1990
off ramp cafe

It requires a great deal of courage to take the stage as a new band after only a week of rehearsals, yet that is precisely what the fledgling Mookie Blaylock did on October 22, 1990. Those in attendance at the Off Ramp Café for this brief and somewhat uneven set were treated to a glimpse of Pearl Jam in its larval form. Suffice it to say, things have improved somewhat since then.   *Ryan Byrne*

The show itself was far from a home run. There were still some rough edges to be smoothed out, but it did reveal a fledgling band with an enormous amount of potential. The set list for the forty-five minute debut included: "Release," "Alone," "Alive," "Once," "Even Flow," "Black," "Breath," and, for the encore, the first—and thus far *only*—performance of "Just a Girl."

Notables among the crowd included members of Soundgarden; Nancy Wilson of Heart (also known at the time as Mrs. Cameron Crowe); Mother Love Bone's manager, Kelly

Curtis (who still represented Stone and Jeff); Soundgarden's manager, Susan Silver; and the Seattle Mariners' 6'10" southpaw pitching ace, Randy Johnson. As Silver recalled for *Spin* magazine in August of 2001, the room was filled with a lot of good-will for Jeff and Stone's new project, if heavy with the memory of Andy Wood:

> And everyone was nervous, wanting to see the phoenix rise. There was such an intense connection among all of them. . . . So this was the first time that a lot of fans saw Eddie, and the feeling I was picking up from the audience was "Who is this guy? Is he good enough to fill Andy's shoes?" It felt like the place wholeheartedly accepted him.

And so Mookie Blaylock was born. Unlike in other creation myths, where the protagonists rest on the seventh day, the members of Mookie Blaylock spent their seventh day at London Bridge Studios, recording an official demo tape. Within forty-eight hours, Eddie would find himself back in San Diego, immersed in his usual routine. It was almost as though the whirl-wind trip to Seattle had been a dream. But soon enough the dream would recur and increase in intensity.

Go Ask Alice: Mookie Blaylock as a Supporting Player

By mid-December 1990, Eddie was back in Seattle, crashing at Kelly Curtis's home. On the sixteenth, the band appeared on KISW's *New Music Hour* to plug their upcoming tour in support of Seattle veterans Alice in Chains. They gave away free tickets and introduced Eddie, the new kid on the block, to the local listeners. During the show, lis-teners were calling in with suggested names for the band, but evidently none of them caught on.

Mookie Blaylock

Mookie Blaylock—the basketball player, not the band—was born in Garland, Texas, on March 20, 1967, and grew up to be a six-foot tall point guard known for his quick hands, defensive prowess, and enviable long-range jumpshot. He played ball at Garland High School, went on to play at Midland College, where he became an NJCAA All-American in 1987, and continued his collegiate career at the University of Oklahoma. Entering the NBA Draft in 1989, he was picked twelfth by the New Jersey Nets.

After three seasons with the Nets, Blaylock was traded to the Atlanta Hawks just prior to the start of the 1992–1993 season, and there he remained for the next seven years. While with Atlanta, under the guidance of future Hall-of-Fame Coach Lenny Wilkens, Blaylock enjoyed many of his greatest achieve-ments. He led the league in steals for two consecutive seasons (1996–97 and 1997–98), led the league in three-pointer attempts in 1996–97, and was second overall in terms of three-pointers made. Eventually he would become the Hawks' all-time leader in three-pointers attempted (3,023) and three-point-ers made (1,050), and, on the defensive end of the court, he became the Hawks' all-time leader in steals (1,321), among other impres-sive records. In 1994, he made his first and only NBA All-Star Game appearance. In 1999 he was traded to the Golden State Warriors, with whom he finished out his career, riding the bench as a reserve.

Pearl Jam's debut album, *Ten*, was named in honor of Blaylock's jersey number. For his part, Blaylock, in spite of that early weird-ness with the band naming itself after him, is reputed to be a Pearl Jam fan. Later on, as Jeff Ament told the *Missoulian*'s John Heaney during a 2008 interview for *Seattle Threads*, he got to meet Mookie and spend some time shooting hoops with him.

Alice in Chains

The incarnation of Alice in Chains that put Mookie Blaylock through their paces in 1990–1991 featured the original 1987 lineup: Layne Staley on lead vocals, Jerry Cantrell on guitar and vocals, Mike Starr on bass, and Sean Kinney on drums (an earlier incarnation, essentially Layne Staley with a different band, was known by the variant "Alice N' Chains," but that's another story). They were a Seattle band, so it should come as no surprise that the media labeled them "grunge." Putting aside for a moment the fact that *none* of the Seattle bands seem to have used, or approved, of the term "grunge," the word is, arguably, even less applicable in the case of AIC. Cantrell considered their music to be heavy metal. Many musicologists and rock historians consider them a hybrid band with some heavy metal and punk DNA. But perhaps the best description we've heard of the band's sound can be found in the "Grunge" episode of VH1's 2011 documentary series, *Metal Evolution*, wherein AIC is described as "the missing link" between grunge, punk, and heavy metal.

At the time of their tour with Mookie Blaylock, AIC's glory days still lay ahead of them. Their best-selling album, *Dirt*, would be released the following year, 1992, and they've racked up some impressive statistics in the years since: $14 million in U.S. sales, approximately $25 million in sales worldwide, five studio albums, two live albums, four EPs, four compilation albums, and two DVDs. They've managed to hit number one on the *Billboard* charts twice, and the Top Ten a total of fourteen times (so far), with twenty-one Top 40s. And although they've never actually *won*, they do have nine Grammy nominations under their belts, which means they must be doing something right.

Predictably, the band's history also contains a cautionary tale or two, as Staley suffered from the same addictive tendencies as Andy Wood. By the mid-1990s he was using heroin and smoking crack. The band's output from 1996 through 2002 is sporadic as a result. Staley passed away on April 19, 2002, with cocaine and heroin in his system, but the surviving members persevered.

The *Two Feet Thick* website's wonderful "Concert Chronology" feature suggests that Mookie Blaylock appeared at another Seattle venue, the Vogue, on December 19, in support of El Steiner and Bathtub Gin. And, yes, Pearl Jam's own official website also chronicles all of the band's live performances, and it is an invaluable research tool. The key difference is that *Two Feet Thick* features on-the-scene reporting from most of the shows. In keeping with our recurring basketball motif, one might say that Pearl Jam's official site gives you the play-by-play, while the dedicated staff of *Two Feet Thick* provides the color commentary.

The band's next scheduled gig remains a bit of a mystery. No one is quite sure what—if anything—happened two nights later, when the band was scheduled to appear at a "Seattle Musicians for the People" show at the New Melody Tavern. Though a poster does exist, advertising a long list of artists for the Toys for Tots and food bank benefit concert, there is no definitive evidence that the band actually *played*. Records indicate that inclement weather may have kept the bands away.

The next confirmed Mookie Blaylock sighting was the December 22 gig at the Moore Theatre, which featured the boys playing an eight-song set as the opening act for Alice in Chains. This was their final gig of 1990, and the first in a series of supporting gigs for AIC.

January 10 and 11, 1991, found Mookie Blaylock in the Great White North, supporting Alice in Chains at two gigs in Vancouver, British Columbia. Interestingly enough, an actual full-scale, headlining Temple of the Dog show had been scheduled for December 12, but the gig was cancelled a few days before. We'll get back to that in chapter three. In the meantime, Mookie Blaylock's supporting gig for Alice in Chains was about to swerve into the fast lane.

February 1 found the band back at the Off Ramp Café, supporting Alice in Chains before a capacity crowd just shy of three hundred. This Friday night show was a mere warm-up for the densely packed schedule of shows that began the following Thursday.

The Thursday, February 7, gig at LA's Florentine Gardens featured a few new additions to Mookie Blaylock's rapidly evolving repertoire, including "Porch" and "Garden." They also debuted one for the "serious collectors," "Brother," a song about "big brother," in the Orwellian sense. This was the first, and as far as anyone can tell, last time they played the song. Coincidence? No one can say for sure. But one thing is for certain, *someone* was watching. The band breezed through a brisk thirty-five minute set.

Alice in Chains was instrumental in helping Mookie Blaylock develop touring chops during those formative months in late 1990/early 1991, when they took the younger band out on the road as a supporting act at venues up and down the West Coast. By the time AIC's second full-length studio album, *Dirt*, was released at the end of September, 1992, their former opening act had a new name and was poised to become the biggest band in the world. *Author's collection*

This matches the length of the following night's set in Long Beach, California, at God Save the Queen. They played only seven songs on February 8, but at a more casual pace, leaving time for more interaction with the audience.

After a travel day, Mookie Blaylock and the Alice in Chains circus pulled into the Bacchanal in San Diego, familiar ground for Eddie, who had played some gigs there during his Bad Radio days. This was a banner night for Eddie, in particular, as he was asked up on stage to sing during AIC's set. These guest appearances, singing with other bands, would become something of a tradition in later years as Eddie, and Pearl Jam, became more prominent in stature. Fittingly enough, the tradition seems to have begun on Eddie's turf in San Diego on February 10. That evening also marked the beginning of an eight show run over eight straight nights, a respectably grueling schedule by most bands' standards.

The following evening's gig was at the cleverly named "Club with No Name" in Hollywood. Mookie Blaylock turned in a short set that night, only twenty-five minutes. One of the highlights had to be Eddie fretting publicly about their using the name "Mookie Blaylock." At one point he declares that the band's new name might be "Nuclear Love Frogs."

A name change would be coming soon enough, although not because of any legal action on the real Mookie Blaylock's part. But first there was this ambitious

MOOKIE BLAYLOCK
Guard

ROOKIE

NETS
10

NBA HOOPS

The band's name was in the cards—literally. Legend has it that Jeff Ament used part of his per diem from the record company to buy a pack of basketball cards along with his lunch. When he stuck this card into the cassette case of the band's demo tape, suddenly the nameless were named . . . albeit briefly.   *Author's collection*

run of shows to get through. The band played five more shows at California venues before heading north to Oregon.

In Portland, Oregon, at the Melody Ballroom, Eddie wore a T-shirt that read "Air Love Bone," which paid homage to basketball god Michael Jordan and Mother Love Bone. Here, perhaps, we saw the first of Eddie's many affectations to come, wearing odd, interesting, and provocative messages on his T-shirts, often without explanation and open to interpretation. As for our take on "Air Love Bone"? You have a native of Illinois, a basketball enthusiast and die-hard Chicago Bulls fan, playing a gig in Portland Trailblazers' territory with surviving members of Mother Love Bone. What could be more appropriate?

They enjoyed four days off after the Portland gig before regaining home-court advantage. The twenty-fifth found them back at the Off Ramp Café. This was also their last supporting gig for Alice in Chains, certainly a successful first run. But the workaholic Mookie Blaylock didn't rest on their laurels. The following night, on the twenty-sixth, they played another Seattle venue, the Vogue, in support of Bathtub Gin and El Steiner.

By the following Friday, they were back on the home court at the Off Ramp Café. Technically they may have been "supporting" Inspector Luv and the Ride Me Babies and Yellow Dog, but one can't help but notice that their name was, by far, the most prominent one on the handbill that night.

Benched

All good things must come to an end, and the same holds true for *strange* things, such as having an up-and-coming professional rock and roll band named after an up-and-coming professional basketball player. The band played only one more Seattle show as Mookie Blaylock, on Friday, March 8, 1991. And that was it for the name. Rumor has it that Jeff Ament had come up with a new name for the band during a trip to New York about two weeks earlier, and now the time was right to reveal it.

Ladies and Gentlemen, You Heard It Here First

The Sunday following the last Mookie Blaylock gig also happened to be Jeff Ament's twenty-eighth birthday. Jeff and Eddie stopped by KISW during DJ Damon Stewart's *New Music Hour* to do a little promotional work, spinning demos of their songs, "Once" and "Release." Then they revealed the new name of their band (spoiler alert).

According to Jessica Letkemann and John Reynolds in "How Did Mookie Blaylock Become Pearl Jam?"—their twentieth anniversary article from March 10, 2011, published on their astonishing treasure trove of a website, *Two Feet Thick*—Eddie and Jeff visited with Damon Stewart that day, and they joked around with one anoth-

193

Born: March 20, 1967
Garland, TX
Height: 6-0   Weight: 180
College: Oklahoma
Drafted: 1st Rd–Pick 12
New Jersey, 1989

DARON OSHAY BLAYLOCK

		College Record					
YEAR	TEAM	GP	FG%	FT%	REB	PTS	AVG
85-86	Midland	34	.566	.738	109	570	16.8
86-87	Midland	33	.516	.723	138	647	19.6
TOTALS		67	.540	.731	247	1217	18.2
87-88	Oklahoma	39	.460	.684	162	638	16.4
88-89	Oklahoma	35	.455	.650	164	700	20.0
TOTALS		74	.457	.668	326	1338	18.1

			NBA Record							
YEAR	TEAM	GP	FG%	FT%	REB	AST	STL	BLK	PTS	AVG
89-90	N. Jersey	50	.371	.778	140	210	82	14	505	10.1

"Mookie" led the Nets in assists through first half of 1990 season before missing two months with broken finger . . . Scored career high 24 points at Denver 2/1/90 . . . Set NCAA record at Oklahoma with career average of 3.8 steals per game . . . As a senior set school record with 90 three-pointers.

© 1990 NBA Properties, Inc.   The Official NBA Basketball Card

Imperfect "ten." Like the band that briefly adopted his name, Daron Oshay "Mookie" Blaylock showed a great deal of promise early on in his career. Pearl Jam's debut album, *Ten*, was named in honor of Blaylock's New Jersey Nets jersey number.   *Author's collection*

er for several minutes before making the big announcement. Stewart asked Jeff for the scoop, but Jeff passed the ball to Eddie, who countered Jeff's suggestion that the name change had anything to do with "legal issues;" it was really a matter of the band taking on the basketball star in—what else?—a game of five on one and getting their butts kicked in the process. Then Eddie let it drop: "So the name is, uh . . . Pearl Jam." You read that correctly, *Pearl Jam*—not to be confused with Nuclear Love Frogs.

What's in a Name?

So how, exactly, did Jeff come up with "Pearl Jam"? If anyone is still holding onto the quaint notion that the name was inspired by Eddie's great-grandma Pearl, who married a Native American and devised a recipe for hallucinogenic peyote jam, allow us to disabuse you of that belief once and for all. That was simply a story that Eddie used to tell interviewers, more for his own amusement than for their edification. A very "Dylanesque" move on Eddie's part, for sure, but it certainly led to a lot of confusion, as many people bought into the story and believe it to this day.

The truth is that the word "pearl" was one the guys had been kicking around for awhile, but they couldn't find anything to go with it. Apparently, Jeff had taken to heart the late Andy Wood's assertion that all bands should have names with two words in them, because all of the great bands had two-word names. Sounds reasonable enough at first blush (though I'm sure Nirvana may have disagreed). But the longer one ponders the logic of this Woodism, the more it unravels. After all, Malfunkshun was one word, and Mother Love Bone was three words. The best course of action is to give Andy and Jeff the benefit of the doubt, since we can now safely say that the formula, however illogical, has worked out in their favor.

Jeff's epiphany occurred while the boys were in the midst of a whirlwind trip to New York City—during a break in the Alice in Chains/Mookie Blaylock tour—to sort out their contract situation and sign papers with Epic Records. While there, they scored tickets to a Neil Young concert, courtesy of Epic. As reported in *Rolling Stone* and elsewhere, this was the February 22, 1991, show at Nassau Coliseum. However, there is a potential conflict. Pearl Jam's official website indicates that the band had a show scheduled at the Off Ramp Café on this same date, but there is no poster available, which raises a red flag. Either the band cancelled this show at the Off Ramp Café and attended Neil Young's Nassau Coliseum show, or they attended one of the other Neil Young shows in the area: Eisenhower Hall at West Point on February 23, or Brendan Byrne Arena on February 24. In spite of the conflicting evidence on the website, the preponderance of evidence points to the Nassau Coliseum show as the being the one.

There Jeff was, along with Stone and Eddie, on February 22, 1991, at Nassau Coliseum, watching Sonic Youth and Social Distortion open up for Neil Young and Crazy Horse. During Neil's set, Jeff was marveling at the fact that the band had played only a handful of songs, yet the show had been going on for quite some time. Why *was* that? It was because they stretched out every song into an extended, improvisational . . . (wait for it) . . . *JAM!*

Inspiration moved him (brightly). Pearl? Jam? *Pearl Jam!* At this point Jeff turned toward Stone and blurted out, "What about 'Pearl Jam'?" The name couldn't have been too hard a sell, considering that this was a group of guys who had no qualms about naming themselves after a living, breathing NBA player, two of whom were veterans of a band named Mother Love Bone (what the hell does *that* mean?). Yet they returned home as Mookie Blaylock to play the four remaining scheduled shows before making the name change official. Pearl Jam. It *is* kind of catchy, we must admit.

3

Dogs Before Pearls

Seattle's First Supergroup?

Roommates: A Rock and Roll "Odd Couple"

It all began the day that Soundgarden's lead singer, Chris Cornell, looked around his newly rented Seattle home and decided that he needed a roommate to replace his brother, who was moving out. In the *PJ20* film, Chris tells the story that he offered the space to Stone Gossard at first, but Stone declined, suggesting instead his friend Andy Wood, who had just gotten out of rehab. Stone, being six months Andy's junior, and two full years younger than Chris, evidently had it pretty good living at home with his well-to-do family, and he wasn't in any great hurry to leave the nest.

Upon completion of his rehabilitation program, Andy had initially planned to move back in with his family and lay low for a while. But Chris thought Stone's suggestion was an excellent one and reasoned that his new house could provide Andy with an environment more conducive to the creative process than his childhood bedroom. Left unsaid was the idea that the older, more stable Cornell would serve as a de facto role model and have a positive influence on Wood. So Chris made the call to see if Andy wanted to be his roommate.

The newly rehabbed Andy readily accepted the offer, and the two vocalists became fast friends. Thus began a period of intense creativity, collaboration, and healthy competition, which would enrich the lives of both men. They became, for a time, a real-life rock 'n' roll version of *The Odd Couple*.

Chris, a big believer in the communal spirit of his fellow Seattle musicians, enjoyed having Andy around and found himself inspired by the younger singer's drive and ambition. Famous or not, Andy *really was* a born rock star, and it was impossible not to get caught up in his enthusiasm.

The two singers fell into a routine where they'd each come up with a song every day, play it for one another, and compare notes: a sort of in-house music workshop. Like Eddie down in San Diego, both Chris and Andy used portable four-track mixers while they were working on their music at home. While Chris took a more thoughtful, analytical approach to his songwriting, Andy was more straightforward, letting the chips fall where they may. He was often satisfied with a single take of a song and not given to lengthy reflection. He was also in the habit of selling and/or giving away homemade cassette tapes of his work to anyone who cared to listen; he just wanted to get his music out there. Andy was like the Id to

Chris's Superego, and their divergent styles complemented one another very well. But it couldn't last forever.

Old Habits Die Hard

Eventually, Andy moved out of Chris's place and moved in with his new girlfriend, Xana La Fuente, but the two men's musical "bromance" and period of cohabitation would leave a lasting impression on Chris.

By this time Andy was back at work with his brother, Kevin, in their band, Malfunkshun, while all around them the Seattle scene began to gain some momentum. Within this odd little microculture of musicians, the members of Malfunkshun, Green River, Soundgarden, Skin Yard, the Melvins, etc. were all rooting for one another, supporting one another, and learning from one another, a comparatively rare occurrence in the competitive world of music.

As fate would have it, Chris was away on tour with Soundgarden when Andy suffered what would prove to be his fatal heroin overdose. It was St. Patrick's Day, 1990, and Soundgarden was playing a show with Faith No More and Voivod at Brooklyn's legendary club L'Amour. By the time Chris returned to Seattle two days later, heading directly to the hospital, his former roommate was on life support and would die shortly after. But because Soundgarden was leaving town again in a few days to embark on a European tour, Chris had no time to properly grieve. For him, Wood's death signaled a loss-of-innocence moment for the Seattle scene.

Far from Home: The Healing Begins

At first, Chris took an "out of sight, out of mind" approach to his grief, figuring that being away on tour was a good thing because there was nothing in Europe that would remind him of Andy. But it didn't exactly work out that way. He thought about him constantly. He couldn't really talk to anyone over there about his grief, so he channeled that energy into writing songs. But the songs he began writing were nothing like the songs Soundgarden normally played. They were more in the style of material that Andy had favored. Chris began to get an idea. What if he were to record a tribute single with Andy's bandmates, Jeff and Stone? That could be a really fun thing to do.

During the idea phase of the project, Chris had initially considered that they might cover some of Andy's own songs. They put the kibosh on that idea for a number of reasons, including potential legal hassles, but mostly out of respect for Andy's family. They wanted the spirit of the project to be a tribute, and they did not want it to seem exploitative in any way. Andy's death was still very recent at the time, and it was a very emotionally difficult period for those who knew and loved him.

Shall We Build a Temple?

The project really began with Chris's humble aspirations of putting out a tribute single—"Say Hello 2 Heaven" b/w "Reach Down"—with Stone and Jeff, the two surviving members of Mother Love Bone who were closest to Andy, along with their new lead guitarist, Mike McCready, and Soundgarden's drummer, Matt Cameron. Yet somehow the project evolved into a full-blown album after Chris scrapped his idea for the tribute single. Evidently, the circumstances just seemed to call for something more. They chose the hybrid band's name, Temple of the Dog, from the lyrics of one of Mother Love Bone's songs, "Man of Golden Words."

In the big picture, certainly, *Temple of the Dog* was only a minor, fifteen-day detour on the road from Mother Love Bone to Mookie Blaylock to Pearl Jam, but it was a significant detour, one which would have a profound and lasting impact on all of the participants, including newcomer Eddie Vedder, who found himself swept up in the project, almost by accident. Those fifteen days would also provide a foreshadowing of Matt Cameron's future as the drummer for Pearl Jam, following Soundgarden's 1997 breakup (and, later, for *both* bands, when Soundgarden reunited in 2010). Fittingly enough, the band turned to *Stone Gossard Demos 1990* for material, resulting in an unusual—perhaps even unprecedented—scenario in

Temple of the Dog began life humbly enough as a tribute to the fallen Andrew Wood. But when the "Seattle scene" exploded, the album was marketed anew as a collaborative effort between the surging Pearl Jam and Soundgarden. Attendance at this "temple" grew exponentially.   *Author's collection*

which the same base instrumental that would become "Footsteps" for Pearl Jam became "Times of Trouble" for Temple of the Dog.

Under My Wing?

And then there was the matter of that new kid from San Diego, Eddie. Mostly, he'd just been standing around with his hands jammed into his pockets, staring at his feet and by most accounts appearing shy and uncertain in these unfamiliar surroundings. But was he shy, *really*? Though Eddie's ambitious, take-charge approach during his San Diego days—and his rapid ascent to the helm of Pearl Jam—would seem to belie these initial impressions of timidity, that is how he was remembered by his colleagues during this period. In the spirit of acknowledging our own biases, it is our duty to say that we remain skeptical of this assessment. It seems to us that the preponderance of evidence suggests otherwise. But rather than psychoanalyze the man more than two decades after the fact, or question the others' judgment, we'll give the members of Temple of the Dog the benefit of the doubt and work with the notion of Eddie as the shy newcomer. They were there, after all, while we were not.

Bear in mind that Eddie had not known Andy Wood, had never even *met* him, in fact, and he was not in town to participate in the Temple of the Dog project. He was there specifically to audition for Stone and Jeff's new band, so he was really just along for the ride.

As fate would have it, Eddie was there during the recording session when Chris was having trouble finding the right approach for the lower register vocals on the song, "Hunger Strike." Eddie jumped in and instinctively sang it with the proper phrasing that Chris had been envisioning. Chris was extremely impressed, and he began to take more notice of Eddie. The finished version of the song features Eddie and Chris trading both choruses and verses.

One thing led to another: Eddie became an official member of Temple of the Dog, and "Hunger Strike" became a duet, a hit single, and a huge FM radio hit. More importantly, perhaps, Chris Cornell became a mentor for Eddie, a newcomer who had cut his first record on his very first day in Seattle. The immediate bonding was undeniable. Legend has it that the two singers went out for drinks one night during Eddie's initial visit, and the camaraderie really served to bolster his confidence.

Eddie was forever searching, whether consciously or not, for father figures and mentors, and the interest that Cornell showed in the younger singer was vitally important for Eddie's development as he acclimated to Seattle and went on to become one of the premier front men in the history of rock and roll. If ever there was an illustration of the unique camaraderie of the Seattle musical community, this was unquestionably the moment, and it was a testament to Chris Cornell in particular as a welcoming presence on every level. Truly he is an aberration in a world populated by monumental egos in general and among lead singers in particular. The Temple of the Dog experience helped Eddie to forge a lifelong friendship with Chris, and it solidified an unbreakable alliance between Pearl Jam and Soundgarden that survives to this day, as they share a drummer, Matt

Cameron, and occasionally a *former* drummer since ex-Pearl Jam drummer Matt Chamberlain manned the skins for Soundgarden during a recent tour, while Matt Cameron was busy touring with Pearl Jam.

Their new friendship was also beneficial for Chris because Eddie's presence helped to fill some of the void left by Andy's passing. Matt Cameron seems to suggest as much in the *PJ20* film, wherein he opines that it was good for Chris to have "another equally talented singer" around. Also in the film, Stone refers to the Temple of the Dog project—as a whole—as yet another example of Chris's generous nature, and he doesn't seem at all surprised that Chris reached out to Eddie and, essentially, took the younger singer under his wing. Stone and Jeff, for their part, were very happy and grateful to have been included, and they clearly enjoyed the whole stress-free recording process. They were still trying to figure out their next move, so this project was a positive and cathartic development for them. There was no recording company around to dictate terms, and the musicians picked up the tab for the recording studio. They didn't enter into the *Temple of the Dog* sessions with any real expectations, so that just made the experience all the more enjoyable for them.

In retrospect, one can consider Temple of the Dog on a number of different levels. It was a tribute to Andrew Wood; a shining example of Chris Cornell's generous nature; a welcoming party, or initiation, for Eddie; and an all-around act of catharsis, a type of renewal or purification rite, for the musicians who had known, worked with, lived with, and loved Andy.

The Tale of the Tape

Recorded: In just fifteen days, during November and December, 1990, at London Bridge Studios in Seattle, Washington

Produced By: Rick Parashar and Temple of the Dog

Released: April 16, 1991, on A&M Records; **re-released:** 1992, with a video for "Hunger Strike"

Singles: "Hunger Strike" on January 14, 1991; "Say Hello 2 Heaven" in 1991; "Pushin' Forward Back" in 1991

Billboard: Failed to chart, at *first*. Opening week sales of 70,000. It later became one of the Top 100 albums of 1992 and went on to sell over a million copies in the US alone; RIAA-certified Platinum album.

Into the Studio

For Mike McCready and Eddie Vedder, this was their first foray into a recording studio, so it was a special initiation on that level. Also fascinating, the assembled musicians provided a foreshadowing of the modern Pearl Jam lineup, with Matt Cameron on the drums. Timing, it is often said, is everything in life. The album, titled *Temple of the Dog*, recorded at London Bridge Studios and produced by Rick Parashar, was released on April 16, 1991. And while the reviews were generally favorable, no one was exactly breaking down the walls at their local record stores to buy a copy. Initial sales were around 70,000 units, not bad for a bunch of guys from Seattle but not good enough to hit the *Billboard* charts, either. Of course, the album was released right around the time that Mookie Blaylock became Pearl Jam, so not everyone knew who the guys were at the time. Temple of the Dog couldn't really gain any momentum as a band, either, because the newly christened Pearl Jam wanted to get their debut album out and hit the road, and Soundgarden was also heading back into the studio with a goal of putting out an album by September.

The Tunes

The final track listing of *Temple of the Dog* features ten original tracks, even though the project was stuck at nine tracks right up until the very end. And therein lies an important lesson about trusting your own instincts. Specifically, we are talking about Chris Cornell's instincts. As detailed below in the entry for the song, "Hunger Strike," Cornell was adamant that there be ten songs on the album. Lo and behold, that tenth track, "Hunger Strike," would turn out to be the album's signature song. Indeed, it proved to be the entire project's key to success.

"Say Hello 2 Heaven"

Hitting the high notes, both literally and figuratively, "Say Hello 2 Heaven," along with "Reach Down," was originally conceptualized as part of a tribute single to the memory of the late Andrew Wood. Certainly, there is nothing subtle about the song's title, which clearly mourns Wood's loss. The lyrics, too, are rife with grief, the first verse seemingly articulating Cornell's personal sense of grief and frustration about being unable to help a friend who steadfastly tried to hide his pain from others. The second and third verses both read more like a traditional lament, although there is a hint of a cautionary tale in the second verse. By the third verse, there is a sense of acceptance, loss, and a final farewell. Musically, the laid-back drumbeat and distorted guitars sound nothing at all like the bottom-heavy riffs of Soundgarden. Here they form a framework for Chris to flex his legendarily muscular voice, which is often reminiscent of Deep Purple's Ian Gillan in his heyday.

"Reach Down"

The same distorted guitar sound ushers in "Reach Down," the companion piece to "Say Hello 2 Heaven" in Chris Cornell's original vision for an Andrew Wood tribute single. But at more than eleven minutes in length, the final version of "Reach Down" is a long way from "single" territory.

The overall sound is reminiscent of a trippy, early 1970s acid rock song in the style of the Jimi Hendrix Experience. Others liken it to one of Neil Young's lengthier offerings, such as "Like a Hurricane," "Down by the River," "Cowgirl in the Sand," or "Southern Man," and you can definitely see, er, *hear* their point. To that we would just add that there is clearly a bit of gospel flavoring in the mix, which is appropriate enough, given the funereal overtones of the proceedings.

"Reach Down" certainly provided a vehicle for Mike McCready to showcase his considerable guitar playing skills. He and Chris Cornell did not know one another very well at this point, and Cornell kept pressing McCready to let it rip on his guitar solo. When he finally relaxed enough, he delivered a performance for the ages, earning the slack-jawed respect of his fellow musicians in the process.

"Hunger Strike"

Talk about "last but not least." "Hunger Strike," of course, became the signature song from the album and ultimately its best-selling single. It also received more radio play than any of the other songs on the album. In retrospect, the comical thing about all of this is that it was also the last song recorded and completed. According to legend, Chris has a "thing" about odd numbers, and he wanted the album to weigh in at an even ten tracks. Call it a touch of obsessive-compulsive disorder, call it a happy accident, or call it whatever else you like; the song is certainly a classic. And though we are sure the Pearl Jam contingent in particular would be loath to admit it, the corresponding video for the song is pretty darn good, too.

"Pushin' Forward Back"

"Pushin' Forward Back" gave Stone and Jeff an opportunity to get in on the action and cowrite a song, which also allowed Stone to flex his muscles at musical arrangement. Lyrically, the song seems to make vague allusions to teenaged angst and rebellion within a family dynamic. Musically, since Stone and Jeff cowrote it with Chris, this song adds a little more of the bottom end that was missing from many of the other guitar-forward tracks. And that bottom end is delightfully funky, thanks to Jeff Ament's bass.

"Call Me a Dog"

Though the title somehow manages to evoke images of Iggy Pop ("I Wanna Be Your Dog"), "Call Me a Dog" has an almost Lynyrd Skynyrd-esque, southern rock feel to it, albeit with a classic, hard rock Chris Cornell vocal delivery. Mike McCready delivers a brief but piercing guitar solo. But lyrically, the Cornell-penned song seems to deviate from the album's overarching theme as a tribute to Andrew Wood. While not quite as scathing as Bob Dylan's "Idiot Wind," the song sounds like a bitter diatribe to a lover in a troubled relationship. This led some to interpret the song as being meant for Alice in Chains' (and Soundgarden's future) manager, Susan Silver, also known in some circles as "Mrs. Cornell." But that interpretation doesn't make sense to us because Chris and Susan had just gotten married in 1990 and wouldn't be divorced until fourteen years later in 2004. However you choose to interpret it, it is arguably one of the best tracks on *Temple of the Dog*.

"Times of Trouble"

Musically, "Times of Trouble" dates back to the fabled *Stone Gossard Demos 1990*, the humble demo tape that was to become the foundation of *Ten*. Lyrically, from that single piece of music, Chris Cornell penned "Times of Trouble" for Temple of the Dog, and Eddie Vedder penned "Footsteps," which first saw life as a live-recorded B-side for the "Jeremy" single. It later saw life on the Japanese version of *Binaural* in 2000, and as a "lost dog" on *Lost Dogs* in 2003.

"Times of Trouble" makes explicit, graphic references to the logistics of heroin use and addiction. Though it was clearly too late to save Andy, the song comes across almost as a cautionary tale for those going down a similar path. There is still hope, at least in this song. The inclusion of a piano and a harmonica adds a layer of complexity and emotional depth to the music, giving it a Led Zeppelin-esque, electric blues feeling.

"Wooden Jesus"

"Wooden Jesus" has a nice, funky drums and percussion intro before Chris Cornell, clearly restraining his awesome power, comes in with his vocals. Mike McCready delivers one of his acid rock inspired guitar solos before Cornell returns and gives his voice free reign to soar and howl. Lyrically, because the words allude to spending money on one's future grave, there are those who take the easy way out and interpret the song to be about heroin. We think this is too simplistic of a leap of logic. To us, it reads more like a critique of the pervasive use of religious iconography, or even idolatry; in other words, a profaning of the sacred.

"Your Saviour"

"Your Saviour" continues the theme of songs with religious undercurrents. The song begins with a funky Matt Cameron drum intro bolstered by a Jeff Ament bass groove. McCready's guitar starts off subtly enough, but when he breaks in for his solo, it soars mightily. The underlying theme of religious skepticism evident in "Wooden Jesus" continues here, as Cornell seems to be rebuffing the efforts of proselytizers to show him their version of the proverbial "light."

"Four Walled World"

"Four Walled World" also has an odd southern rock undercurrent to it. Thematically, the lyrics are a fairly standard prisoner's lament, which was common fare among the blues and country set but a fresh sounding motif for the Seattle contingent. Though some Seattle scene purists might respond unkindly to the comparison, we cannot help but be reminded, atmospherically, of Bon Jovi's hit, "Wanted Dead or Alive," from five years earlier. "Four Walled World" has that same desperado sensibility to it, and it evokes the emotions of despair, longing, and regret. It is an excellent song on many levels, and though it remains relatively obscure, we believe it has withstood the test of time.

"All Night Thing"

If there were one song on *Temple of the Dog* that could fairly be called a "filler" song, "All Night Thing" is it. Ostensibly, it is a ballad from a bunch of guys who were unaccustomed to such restraint at the time. You can almost sense the musicians champing at the bit to cut loose with the power chords and crank the amps up high. Lyrically, the song reflects a carnally spoiled rock star's blasé attitude toward a potential one-night stand. But rather than dripping with Kiss-like swagger and eye-rolling innuendo, the protagonist of "All Night Thing" seems to say: hey, if it happens, it happens; if not, that's fine, too. What's interesting is that this sentiment reflects our own attitude about this track. It's a pity that an album with so many strengths does not end on a more powerful note.

Every Dog Has His Day

Due to what some people refer to as the "blowback effect," *Temple of the Dog* would later enjoy a new lease on life in the wake of the huge success of Pearl Jam's *Ten* and Soundgarden's *Badmotorfinger*. A&M's marketing geniuses decided to capitalize on this Soundgarden/Pearl Jam collaboration by reissuing the album and by re-releasing "Hunger Strike" as a single *and* as a music video, all of which served to ramp up sales figures. The single and the album both charted on *Billboard* in 1992, and *Temple of the Dog* made the Top 100 list in terms of album sales. Eventually, the

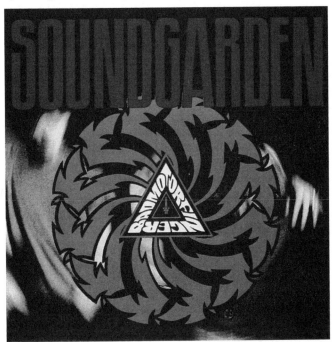

Released within weeks of Pearl Jam's *Ten, Badmotorfinger* was Soundgarden's third album, and it proved to be their commercial breakthrough. In anticipation of their friends' upcoming album, Pearl Jam performed the song "Outshined" on August 23 at Seattle's Mural Amphitheater, and thus began their longstanding tradition of playing select cover songs.   *Author's collection*

album sold more than a million copies and was certified Platinum in both the United States and Canada.

Temple of the Dog would also mark its territory in the world of film, if not always on the accompanying soundtrack albums. To date, songs from *Temple of the Dog* have appeared in three different Hollywood films, beginning with a favorite of rock and roll fans everywhere. Mike Myers and Dana Carvey's 1992 classic, *Wayne's World*—a love letter to rock and roll any way you look at it—featured the song, "All Night Thing," but it did not appear on the soundtrack album.

Johnny Depp's 1993 film, *Benny & Joon*, features the song, "Pushin Forward Back," which also appears on the official film soundtrack. Finally (so far), and most recently, "Hunger Strike" makes an appearance in Matt Damon's *We Bought a Zoo*, a 2011 film directed by the patron saint of the Seattle scene himself, Cameron Crowe. Alas, the song does not appear on the official soundtrack album.

Live Dogs: A Rare Breed

Temple of the Dog would go on to play only *one* actual concert, on November 13, 1990, at the same Off Ramp Café where Mookie Blaylock debuted three weeks earlier. For those of you keeping score at home, this one-off gig occurred after Eddie had returned to San Diego following his initial visit/audition, and he did not appear at this show. The one-hour gig took place on a Tuesday night, which is not exactly prime time for rock and roll shenanigans, but this *was* Seattle, after all, so the Off Ramp Café was soon filled with its usual capacity crowd of 299 souls, eager to hear what their friends were cooking up. Bathtub Gin served as the opening act that night. Temple of the Dog's set list included: "Hunger Strike," "Wooden Jesus," "Say Hello 2 Heaven," "Reach Down," "Call Me a Dog," "Times of Trouble," "Pushin' Forward Back," "Your Saviour," and "Four Walled World." As of this writing, this remains the first and only time Temple of the Dog has played a full, one-hour set of songs.

Corn Dogs

As the original top dog, leader of the pack, and elder of the temple, Chris Cornell began to work some of the *Temple of the Dog* material into his other projects. For example, during his Audioslave days following the breakup of Soundgarden—or during the twelve-year hiatus of the band (whichever you prefer)—Chris broke out "All Night Thing," "Call Me a Dog," and "Hunger Strike" (which was practically becoming a staple, by Temple of the Dog standards) for the 2005 tour. Chris gave the same material a workout during his frequent appearances as a solo artist, adding "Pushin' Forward Back," "Wooden Jesus," "Reach Down," and "Say Hello 2 Heaven." Clearly, this was material that still resonated with him, as it continues to do to this very day.

The next rare sighting took place more than a month later, with Eddie back in town for the Mookie Blaylock-Alice in Chains whirlwind tour. On December 20, 1990, it was Temple of the Dog, not Mookie Blaylock, who served as the opening act for Alice in Chains at the Moore Theatre. And that was it, as far as Temple of the Dog's live appearances in 1990.

By October 1991, Pearl Jam had been born and was gaining momentum, and Soundgarden was riding high, which didn't leave much time to even think about Temple of the Dog, much less schedule any shows for the hybrid band. On October 3, 1991, they performed one song, "Hunger Strike," at the Foundations Forum in LA. Three days later, at a fifth anniversary party for *RIP* magazine, they played three songs, coming on stage right after what had to be the surprise highlight of the evening, Spinal Tap, which means you had a hybrid band following a fictitious band.

By the following year, A&M had reissued the album and released a single and video of "Hunger Strike." The band would reconvene on two dates of the Lollapalooza Tour during the late summer of 1992, performing "Hunger Strike" at Lake Fairfax Park in Reston, Virginia, on August 14, and then performing "Hunger Strike" and "Reach Down" on September 13 at Irvine Meadows Amphitheater in Irvine, California. And that was it for the next eleven years.

The next TOTD reunion occurred at an October 28, 2003, Pearl Jam show, when Chris came out to join the band onstage (Matt Cameron, of course, was already *on* stage, as he had been manning the drum kit for Pearl Jam since 1998) for "Hunger Strike" and "Reach Down."

Chris joined Pearl Jam onstage again on October 6, 2009, for yet another rendition of "Hunger Strike." Nearly two years later, on Labor Day weekend of 2011, during the *PJ20* blowout in Alpine Valley, Wisconsin, Chris joined Pearl Jam onstage for a *true* hybrid set, beginning with one from the Mother Love Bone vault, "Star Dog Champion," with Chris assuming Andy's vocal duties, followed by "Say Hello 2 Heaven," "Reach Down," and, of course, the perennial favorite, "Hunger Strike." The scene played out again the following night, with "Reach Down" and "Hunger Strike" joining "Call Me a Dog" and "All Night Thing" in a full-blown hootenanny-style jam with several guest artists, including Beatles' progeny Dhani Harrison (son of George).

While the familiar idiom posits that you cannot teach an old dog new tricks, it would not surprise us in the least if we haven't seen the last of Temple of the Dog. Given the continuing bonds and camaraderie among the participants, the enduring legacy of Andy Wood now occupying a secure place in rock and roll mythology, and the impending twenty-fifth anniversaries of both Temple of the Dog and Pearl Jam, it is certainly conceivable that these dogs may run free once more. As fans, we certainly hope so.

4

The State of Love and Trust

The Singles Scene in Seattle

A Story Evolves as a Genius Comes of Age

When *Singles* began production in February of 1991, it had already evolved into a very different project from the one originally envisioned by writer and director Cameron Crowe, who had been kicking around ideas for the film as far back as 1984. Back then, the concept called for the film to be shot in Phoenix, Arizona, of all places. That was during the Reagan era, and the world was a very different place, if not necessarily a better place, as we're sure Eddie would be happy to point out. To gain a greater appreciation for the film, it is instructive to take a look back at the man behind the camera and see how it all came about.

As the Crowe Flies

The word "prodigy" is often overused and thrown about too casually, but there is no question that it is used appropriately in the case of Cameron Crowe. A native of Palm Springs, California, born on July 13, 1957, Crowe and his family bounced around a bit, first to Indio, and then to San Diego.

It was there that Crowe's school career was fast-forwarded. He skipped kindergarten altogether, and later advanced two additional grade levels. Writing for the school newspaper wasn't enough to satisfy the twelve-year-old freshman at the prestigious Catholic institution, University of San Diego High School. He began contributing pieces to a local underground newspaper, the *San Diego Door*, and reaching out to different writers, music critics, and editors he admired. Before long, he caught the attention of a former *San Diego Door* staffer named Lester Bangs, who was now the editor of *Creem*, a rock and roll magazine beloved by all music fans of the 70s and 80s. At an age when most of us were still navigating seventh grade and Little League, Crowe was submitting articles to *Creem* and their formidable competitor, *Circus*, both magazines which enjoyed nationwide distribution and, at times, gave *Rolling Stone* a real run for its money.

At the tender age of fifteen, the precocious Crowe graduated from high school and emerged from a lonely and often sickly childhood to become the youngest contributor ever for *Rolling Stone* magazine. During a post-graduation trip to Los Angeles, Crowe met senior editor Ben Fong-Torres, a giant of the industry, and he made a definite impression. His *Rolling Stone* career was off and running, as dramatized in his Academy Award-winning 2000 film, *Almost Famous.* This early start to his career made him a grizzled veteran by the time he turned twenty in 1977. He would rise swiftly through the ranks to contributing editor and then to associate editor.

During those first five years Crowe became the magazine's go-to guy for snagging the difficult interviews, which were comprised mostly of the newer generation of rockers who viewed *Rolling Stone*'s old guard with disdain. In many cases, the feeling was mutual. Though examples abound, a quick perusal of *Rolling Stone*'s reviews of Led Zeppelin's albums should suffice to help you understand why Crowe was considered a breath of fresh air. Clearly the magazine needed some young blood—guys who understood and appreciated Lynyrd Skynyrd, Bowie, Yes, and even the Eagles. Crowe was that man, in spite of the fact (or perhaps *because* of the fact) that he was technically still just a kid.

Stay West, Go North, Young Man

Rolling Stone experienced a watershed moment in 1977, as it moved its offices all the way across the country to Manhattan. It was also a turning point for Crowe, who decided to remain out west, where he gradually turned his attention toward his other love, filmmaking.

Crowe envisioned *Singles* as a west coast version of Woody Allen's *Manhattan.* He suffered many headaches dealing with the film studio, not only over the film's title, but also over just about every aspect of the production, from casting to the release date and almost everything else in between.

Over the years and through the rewrites, the story's locale drifted northward until it settled in Crowe's adopted hometown of Seattle. The erstwhile "boy wonder" of rock music journalism had long since turned his attention toward conquering the medium of film, and his aspirations were lofty indeed. In some ways, the death of Andrew Wood a few months earlier proved to be a catalyst for Crowe. Looking around that hospital room at the assembled grieving friends and family members, Crowe was struck by the all-too-human need for solidarity and connection. From that perspective, no one is ever truly "single," but part of a greater whole.

And . . . "Action!"

Filming for *Singles* began in February 1991. Matt Dillon stars in the role of rocker Cliff Poncier, leader of a band called Citizen Dick. While Citizen Dick is a fictional band, they have an air of authenticity, partly because Crowe chose Jeff, Stone, and Eddie to play Dillon's Citizen Dick bandmates. Crowe first met Stone and Jeff through his connections in Heart. After interviewing them, he decided to cast them, and later, Eddie, in the interest of adding that elusive sense of realism. The

Citizen Dick was a fictional band from the 1992 film *Singles*, which featured Jeff, Stone, and Ed, and was fronted by actor Matt Dillon as the dimwitted lead singer Cliff Poncier. In a hilarious cameo, Cameron Crowe appears as a music journalist asking Cliff to explain the deeper meaning behind Citizen Dick's single, "Touch Me, I'm Dick."   *Ryan Byrne*

three rockers also earned their keep by helping to land Dillon. Reportedly, the star was leery about accepting the role until he partied with Jeff, Stone, and Eddie and thought they were cool. So it seems the old adage proved true in this case: actors often want to be rock stars, just as rock stars often want to be actors. Jeff also generously opened his own closets to round out Dillon's wardrobe. And thus Citizen Dick was born.

Chris Cornell appears in the film as one of Cliff's neighbors, and later appears in his more familiar role as the lead singer of Soundgarden, playing music. Eric Stoltz, of *Mask* fame, is a traditional "that guy" in all of Crowe's films (who can ever forget the "No shirt, no shoes, no dice" scene from *Fast Times at Ridgemont High*?), and, true to form, he appears here in the ironic role of a mime who can't seem to honor the time-honored mime tradition of silence. Crowe, doing the old Alfred Hitchcock routine, dutifully appears in a cameo well within his comfort zone; he plays a rock journalist interviewing Cliff Poncier during a club scene. Alice in Chains also made the cut, playing the band in the bar.

A Complimentary Review

With all of the local yokels essentially playing themselves, or at least playing to type, nobody really had to do any "acting." Though there *is* that memorable scene where the members of Citizen Dick are seated in a booth discussing their live shows, and they happen upon a review of their record in a local newspaper. Lead singer Cliff (Dillon) urges Jeff [all of the Mookie Blaylock members were cast using their own names] to read the review aloud, with the caveat that he doesn't want to hear anything negative. Naturally, the review is almost *entirely* negative, slamming Cliff in particular. A moment of awkward silence ensues, as Jeff and Eddie, seated across the table from Cliff and Stone, scroll their fingers down the page, looking for something, *anything*, they can read aloud to him. Finally, in the last sentence of the review, the writer turns his attention to Jeff, Stone, and Eddie, and says that they do a good job of backing up Cliff. Jeff seizes the opportunity and reads this portion aloud, prompting Eddie to tell Cliff, "A compliment for us is a compliment for you." Cliff, emboldened and insistent that negative energy only bolsters him, proceeds to get the band members fired up for the coming weekend's gig in Portland, with high-fives all around.

A Cornell Cameo

In another memorable, comedic scene, Cliff arrives at Janet [Bridget Fonda]'s apartment, looking to make amends. He decides to surprise her with the fact that he has installed a powerful new stereo in her compact car. As he pushes the button to demonstrate the sound, neighbor Chris Cornell appears by their sides and stops to admire the heavy sounds emanating from the tiny vehicle. Cliff ups the ante by raising the volume, which, rather than having the desired effect of impressing Janet, only serves to shatter all of the car's windows. For Cliff, it was back to the old drawing board. Later, Chris appears in a more familiar guise, as lead singer of Soundgarden, belting out "Birth Ritual." The scene is less than a minute in length, but it serves its purpose by giving the viewer a sense of the Seattle sound in its purest form.

Alice Doesn't Live Here Anymore

Appropriately enough, since the first full cast meeting for *Singles* took place at a local club where Mookie Blaylock was opening for Alice in Chains, the veteran Seattle band appears in a club scene during the film. Crowe manages to capture the claustrophobic nature of these venues, complete with all of the familiar trappings, such as having your hand stamped by security as you enter the club, and finding it nearly impossible to carry on a conversation due to the sheer volume of the music. While Alice in Chains is on stage, Layne Staley and Jerry Cantrell remain the camera's focal point, but the action quickly shifts to other parts of the club. From a comedic standpoint, the best scene within the scene finds Cameron Crowe making his rock journalist cameo and engaging in an uncomfortable interview with Cliff, who comes across as a dim, ditzy rocker. Crowe's journalist asks Cliff to expound upon the deeper meaning of a song titled, "Touch Me, I'm Dick," which leads to some delightfully cringe-worthy attempts to answer the question without looking like a total imbecile.

The Musical and Sociological Significance of *Singles*

Singles had its theatrical release in September 1992. By that point in time the musical levee in Seattle had already broken. The musicians fleshing out the supporting cast are now household names. Soundgarden and Pearl Jam were soaring high, and Alice in Chains continued to be a star attraction. "Grunge," a term both denounced and despised by the inner circle of the scene, was the latest buzzword and cultural craze. Flannel shirts and other "grungy" articles of clothing became extremely trendy. As Mudhoney pointed out in a song, with tongues planted firmly in their cheeks: "Everybody Loves Our Town." Lest we forget, somewhere in there, with all of the excitement over the "Seattle Scene," there was a movie director who had been trying to tell this story for decades. Did the film get lost in the shuffle? Perhaps. The truth is that Cameron Crowe was never really that happy with the way *Singles* turned out. Ironically, the only thing the film really had going for it upon its release was the superstar status of the musicians who appear in the film. This begs

Masterfully curated by the Replacements' Paul Westerberg, *Singles: Original Motion Picture Soundtrack* is a wonderful primer for those looking to gain a broader perspective on the emerging Seattle scene. Indeed an argument can be made that this is one of those rare instances where a soundtrack album has proven to be more influential than the film itself.
Author's collection

the question: did the film make the scene, or did the scene make the film? The preponderance of evidence suggests it was the latter. Or perhaps the *music* deserves more of the credit.

The *Singles* Soundtrack: There Can Be No "Replacement"

Because the music was and still is such an important part of what makes *Singles* a cult classic, let's check out the tunes that make up its soundtrack. Scoring a film soundtrack, and then a soundtrack album, is not as easy of a task as many of us would like to imagine. It requires a true artist's eyes and ears. Paul Westerberg, former and future leader of the Replacements, was selected for this task. In addition to contributing "Dyslexic Heart" and the tenth track, "Waiting for Somebody," Westerberg is credited with scoring the entire *Singles* film soundtrack and putting together the soundtrack album. As you can clearly see below, Westerberg made some fine selections.

Alice in Chains' "Would"

In keeping with one of the tacit inspirations for *Singles*, "Would" is Jerry Cantrell's homage to the memory of Andrew Wood, lest anyone thought *Temple of the Dog* was the only project to cover that territory. This serves as another reminder just how loved the Mother Love Bone singer really was.

Pearl Jam's "Breath"

Considering that Pearl Jam was born as a band while *Singles* was being filmed, it is pretty impressive that they garnered the second slot on the soundtrack album, and the eighth slot, too. The song, "Breath" (not to be confused with the much later release "Just Breathe" from 2009's *Backspacer*), had its origins as "Doobie E," yet another instrumental from the famous *Stone Gossard Demos 1990* tape. Once adorned with Vedder's lyrics, the song became "Breath" and was recorded during the sessions that would become *Ten*. "Breath," or "Breath and a Scream," as it is called in an alternate title, did not make the cut for *Ten* but first saw the light of day in this version, rerecorded for the *Singles* soundtrack. By any name, the song is a hard rocker, and it remains somewhat lyrically mysterious and open for interpretation.

Chris Cornell's "Seasons"

Next we have a solo turn from Soundgarden front man Chris Cornell. The song begins with an almost Led Zeppelin-esque acoustic guitar intro, and that guitar goes on to form the basis of the entire song. Think of it as a little taste of Chris Cornell unplugged. Lyrically, the song is full of longing and regret, a lament for opportunities lost, and for not having the right words at the right time.

Paul Westerberg's "Dyslexic Heart"

Paul Westerberg's "Dyslexic Heart" is a fun, lighthearted tune that opens with an acoustic guitar and harmonica intro and is oddly evocative of Blues Traveler meets Joe Jackson. Westerberg, better known to many rock and roll fans as the lead singer and guitarist of the seminal alternative band the Replacements, was new to the solo artist game at the time. The Minnesota-based Replacements had just broken up in 1990 (they have since reunited and broken up again), and the Westerberg-penned "Dyslexic Heart" predated Westerberg's first solo album by a full year.

The Lovemongers' "Battle of Evermore"

This, for all intents and purposes, is a live Heart cover of Led Zeppelin's haunting "Battle of Evermore," but despite the familiar sound of Ann Wilson's powerful vocals, there is a distinction to be made. The Lovemongers are not Heart. Officially they were a four-piece side project that Ann and Nancy Wilson put together, along with their songwriting partner Sue Ennis and one-time Heart band member Frank Cox while Heart was on hiatus; the key difference being that the Lovemongers were an acoustic band, not a full-on rock and roll outfit like Heart. That distinction between Wilson projects aside, we would be remiss if we did not point out that the Lovemongers' version of "Battle of Evermore" may just be *the* best cover of a Led Zeppelin song by anyone, *ever*. It is, in fact, so powerful that it reportedly moved Led Zeppelin front man Robert Plant to the brink of tears. If anyone is wondering what a Led Zeppelin cover is doing on the soundtrack of a film set in the Seattle scene of the early 1990s, we must remind you that Nancy Wilson was married to Cameron Crowe at the time. But save your grumblings about nepotism; this version of the song is nothing short of phenomenal, as even hardcore Led Zeppelin fans can agree.

Mother Love Bone's "Chloe Dancer/Crown of Thorns"

Rounding out the sixth spot, and arguably the spiritual centerpiece of the soundtrack, not to mention the project as a *whole*, is Mother Love Bone's "Chloe

Dancer/Crown of Thorns." Stone and Jeff's post-Green River, pre-Mookie Blaylock and Pearl Jam band, led by local scene martyr Andrew Wood, envisioned these songs as a couplet, with one segueing into the other almost seamlessly. This recording presents the songs as they first appeared on *Shine*, Mother Love Bone's 1989 EP. Curiously, when the full album, *Apple*, was finally released (posthumously for Andrew Wood) on July 19, 1990, "Crown of Thorns" stood on its own, with "Chloe Dancer" nowhere to be found. The *Singles* soundtrack presents the pair as Mother Love Bone originally conceptualized them.

Soundgarden's "Birth Ritual"

A mere snippet of Soundgarden's live performance of "Birth Ritual" appears during a club scene in the film, so it is only fitting that we get to appreciate the entire song in all its ragged glory on the soundtrack. Like many of Soundgarden's best offerings, "Birth Ritual" kicks into a pummeling high gear from the opening note—a dense, galloping sound reminiscent of Black Sabbath's best work nearly two decades earlier. The lyrics defy most conventional attempts at meaningful interpretation, though many suggest it has something vaguely to do with Paganism (trees, rituals?) and, of course, sex. While we are often fascinated with discussions of song meaning, we'll give "Birth Ritual" a pass. When you have a riff this killer, with those ear-splitting Cornell vocals, what more meaning do you need? This song has all the essence of a classic hard rock, even heavy metal, song.

Pearl Jam's "State of Love and Trust"

Making their triumphant return in the eighth spot, Pearl Jam offers up "State of Love and Trust." The song opens with a delightfully distorted electric guitar intro before galloping off to the races. A break toward the middle allows for some tasteful Jeff Ament bass fills. McCready finally gets to break free with a solo in the final thirty seconds. The version of "State of Love and Trust" that appears here was recorded with Dave Abbruzzese in 1992, but there was also an earlier version recorded during the *Ten* sessions with Dave Krusen. The Krusen version saw the light of day later on in Pearl Jam's history with the 2009 reissue of *Ten*. Interestingly, both from a psychological perspective and a songwriting workshop perspective, Eddie wrote the lyrics *after* watching the completed film. So, yes, this is what he got out of it. Though the film is ostensibly a comedy, the song lyrics clearly contain suicidal imagery, guns, etc. Even early on, Eddie could be a pretty heavy, serious guy.

Mudhoney's "Overblown"

In the ninth spot, and continuing in the "old home week" tradition of the assembled artists, we find Mudhoney's "Overblown." Like Mother Love Bone, Mudhoney arose from the ashes of Green River. The Jeff and Stone faction went on to form Mother Love Bone, while the Mark Arm and Steve Turner faction went on to form Mudhoney. Importantly, there was no longer any bad blood between the former members of Green River; they had all moved on to bigger and better things by this point. Green River, if you'll forgive the analogy, was so much water under the bridge.

The song "Overblown" is a blistering, three-minute tongue-in-cheek commentary on the hysteria of the "Seattlemania" then sweeping the nation. Now, all of a sudden, everybody seemed to love Mudhoney's hometown, a circumstance they find most amusing, or, as the title suggests, overblown. The lyrics suggest a level of annoyance with the hype sufficient to make them contemplate leaving town, much as the Grateful Dead bailed out of Haight-Ashbury in the late 1960s when they discovered that their house had become an attraction on the local sightseeing bus tours. Mudhoney weathered the storm and stayed put. Suffice it to say, their colleagues in fellow Seattle bands shared their sentiment.

Paul Westerberg's "Waiting for Somebody"

The former and future Replacements' front man returns in the number ten slot with "Waiting for Somebody." The veteran "alternative" rocker offers up yet another bouncy rocker with a more mainstream sensibility than many of the other assembled songs. Almost instinctively, Westerberg seems to capture the ethos of the film with the go-it-alone spirit of the lyrics. While some have interpreted the line about sleeping alone to be a cryptic reference to suicide, we interpret the song overall as being more about self-sufficiency and independence.

The Jimi Hendrix Experience's "May This Be Love"

Though Mike McCready doesn't appear in the film, you can bet he was thrilled to find this song on the soundtrack album. After all, just how often does one get to appear on an album alongside one of your childhood guitar heroes? Let us not forget that the late, great James Marshall Hendrix was also a native of Seattle, a pioneering figure on the scene while most of the future members of "The Scene" were still in diapers.

"May This Be Love" is a comparatively mellow, vaguely psychedelic ballad from the classic 1967 album, *Are You Experienced?* The song showcases just how versatile Hendrix could be. It wasn't all about his speed and dexterity, there was room for pretty melodies, too. Westerberg no doubt included this in the film to remind everyone of their local musical roots.

Screaming Trees' "Nearly Lost You"

Screaming Trees were veterans of the scene, dating back to 1985. "Nearly Lost You," from 1992, is one terrific rock and roll song. It has a distinctively "classic rock" or "hard rock" sound to it, in spite of its so-called "alternative" roots. While thematically it sounds like a typical rock and roll relationship song, bassist Van Connor told *Alternative Nation* that the song's origins were much more mundane: "It's basically about being on acid, and how you can lose control of your mind." Well, folks, let's just say that the creative process tends to be a very personal sort of journey. If you are the type whose illusions are easily shattered, it is often best *not* to ask an artist about a song's meaning.

Long before he became a wizened bard and settled down to his wine and ever-expanding array of musical instruments, volatile young front man Eddie Vedder was literally climbing the walls, or swinging from the rafters, at every early Pearl Jam show. Now in their fifties, the members of Pearl Jam are still quite energetic on stage by most standards, though you aren't likely to witness a scene like this again anytime soon.   *Photofest*

The Smashing Pumpkins' "Drown"

Finally, rounding out the soundtrack is the Smashing Pumpkins' "Drown," which also happens to be the longest piece on the album. Alternative rock's perennial "Debbie Downer," Billy Corgan adorns the grimly titled song with sparse lyrics that seem to indicate a sense of loss and regret without saying anything remotely specific. Part of the song's length stems from the fact that it devolves into a full blown acid rock guitar feedback solo about halfway through; nothing that would impress the late Mr. Hendrix, though he would certainly understand the sentiment. The haunting, psychedelic guitar feedback is accompanied only by a gentle, marching drumbeat. And that's it. The *Singles* soundtrack fades out in a wall of distorted feedback notes, leaving an almost hypnotic effect on the listener.

Making the "Scene"

Collectively, the thirteen songs on the *Singles* soundtrack serve to flesh out the spiritual center of the film and extend that spirit to people who may not have been particularly impressed by what they saw on the screen. Certainly the soundtrack album was more successful commercially. The film version of *Singles* at least managed to double its $9 million dollar budget by taking in nearly $18-and-a-half million at the box office. It was barely a blip on the radar. The soundtrack album, however, cracked the *Billboard* Top Ten and was certified Platinum. On the socio-cultural level, the popularity of the soundtrack album certainly helped to reify the notion that there existed such a thing as the "Seattle Scene." Mudhoney's (and Pearl Jam's) worst nightmare had become a reality.

5

Release Me

The Countdown to *Ten*

The Tale of the Tape

Recorded: Between March and April of 1991* at London Bridge Studios in Seattle

Produced By: Pearl Jam and Rick Parashar

Released: August 27, 1991, on Epic Records

Singles: "Alive," "Even Flow," and "Jeremy"

Billboard: A late bloomer, *Ten* didn't chart until January 1992. It cracked the *Billboard* 200 Top Ten at number eight on May 30, 1992, and topped out at number two, where it remained for two weeks. *Ten* spent 256 weeks on the chart, putting it, at the time, in the top fifteen all-time albums. With over ten million copies sold to date, it has been certified Platinum by the RIAA *thirteen* times over!

*"Alive" was recorded during the January demo sessions.

It's Still Rock and Roll to Me

Here is a philosophical question for you to ponder. If a band releases an album and no radio station program director in the country seems to know what to make of it, will anyone ever get to hear it? Such was the nature of the uncertainty surrounding the release of Pearl Jam's debut album, *Ten*. The album was named, as many of you are no doubt aware, for Mookie Blaylock's New Jersey Nets jersey number. To be fair, we have heard more compelling stories about the naming of albums, but not everything needs to be imbued with a deeper meaning. Perhaps this was just Pearl Jam's way of telling us that, ultimately, it is the *songs* that matter, not the album titles or even the name of the band. How much does the music matter? Just ask the hardcore fans, the Ten Clubbers. For Jessica Seyfarth, *Ten* marked a turning point in her life. She told us:

> It inspired me to go ahead and like things that I wanted to like instead of what the majority was into. I was ten years old when this album came out, and the first copy I had was given to me by my older cousin in 1994. Listening to this album helped me cope with the struggles I had going through adolescence, including peer pressure and bad relationships with guys.

Across gender lines and generations, her words capture the ethos of the band perfectly. John Cafarella, a Ten Clubber from Maynard, Massachusetts, also loves the album, which he bought in 1992 while attending UMASS Lowell. He said, "The songs on the album flow together, and I love that the beginning of 'Once' is the end of 'Release.' It brings the album together."

And those positive feelings about *Ten* endure. As Texas Ten Clubber Terri McNelly put it, "Every song speaks to my thoughts, feelings, and life experiences; when I was in my early twenties, when it was first released, and in my mid-forties, as I listen to it now."

But *Ten* faced other sorts of challenges, and, in truth, most people probably didn't give a second thought to the album title. We must take into account that this was back in 1991, a period of rock and roll history when MTV aired more than music videos; they were also, arguably, the dominant cultural force shaping the landscape of popular music. The influence of MTV and VH1 cannot be discounted when discussing the history of Pearl Jam, for they add a layer of complexity and complication to the story, in spite of the band's resistance to the music video medium. Pearl Jam felt strongly that their songs should stand on their own merit, without the narrative being controlled by a music video director's vision. They wanted their fans to forms their own impressions and images of the songs, rather than having those images provided for them. And while they did yield to pressure from their label to create music videos from time to time, they did so reluctantly, in spite of the commercial success it brought them. Their area code may have been 206, but Pearl Jam's sound was different than the triumvirate of heavyweights that had defined the "grunge explosion"—Alice in Chains, Nirvana, and Soundgarden. *Ten* was clearly more "classic" rock than "alternative" rock, initially confounding critics and disc jockeys alike. With a big assist from MTV, along with the band's relentless touring, the record slowly gained momentum and broke out on the FM rock stations that ruled the day.

Into the Studio

The groundwork for Pearl Jam's epochal debut album, *Ten*, began the moment that Eddie Vedder arrived in Seattle on October 13, 1990. For the soon-to-be lead singer of Pearl Jam, this journey north from San Diego was unquestionably a business trip. Now with Dave Krusen on drums, the fledgling band proceeded to write eleven songs in one week. It was a once-in-a-lifetime perfect storm to behold. From the long since dried up bed of Green River and the skeletal remains of Mother Love Bone and out of the Shadow to the sounds of Bad Radio emerged a force of nature.

As the time-honored music business adage goes, you have twenty years to write your first album and six *months* to write your second. Eddie poured a lifetime of dysfunction and alienation into his lyrics. Indeed, Edward Louis Severson had more than a "little story" for what would become a mass audience. Lyrically, the songs would focus on a myriad of dark subjects: depression, suicide, loneliness,

And they're off! The somewhat unusual circumstances surrounding the album's title notwithstanding, *Ten* was a solid debut by any standard of excellence. In later years, the band would see fit to have the album remixed for a re-release, but we've always been perfectly satisfied with *Ten* in its original form.

Author's collection

homelessness, and murder. Upon its release in August 1991, *Ten* suffered, as we have suggested, from an identity crisis.

In retrospect, there was no other album for Pearl Jam to make. This was a group of unabashed disciples of 1970s rock icons, such as Alice Cooper, Kiss, and Queen, with tastes reaching back further into the 1960s to the Rolling Stones, Led Zeppelin, Pink Floyd, and, of course, the Who, Eddie's Vedder's all-time favorite band. His personal obsession with *Quadrophenia* prompted him to tell interviewers early on that he should have been sending Father's Day cards to Pete Townshend.

The producer and engineer selected for the band's debut album, the late Rick Parashar, had handled *Temple of the Dog* and was brought on board to produce by Jeff and Stone. His addition of time-tested, old school 70s rock elements—Fender Rhodes piano, organ, additional percussion, and the reverb layering of Mike and Stone's dual guitar attack—proved to be defining in the creation of the band's overall sound.

British engineer Tim Palmer took the project's final mix to his home turf at Ridge Farm Studios in Surrey, England, on the site of a converted farm. Palmer was responsible for extending Mike's guitar solo on "Alive," reworking the intro for "Black," and overdubbing the sounds of a pepper shaker and fire extinguisher to enhance the background on "Oceans." In addition, Parashar cowrote vocal harmonies and the album's instrumental intro/outro.

Despite the fact that the band, in later years, expressed some disappointment with the production and mixing, Parashar and Palmer were the one-two punch that the band needed at this nascent moment. To this day, there is no denying that the record sounded great on the radio and provided some absolutely killer signature material for their live performances. It must also be noted that the band's most frequent career collaborator, Brendan O'Brien, was brought in years later to remix the *reissue* of *Ten*, which was released on March 24, 2009.

The Tunes

As for the songs, the thematic centerpiece of *Ten* was a mini-opera in the spirit of the Who's "A Quick One While He's Away." Known as "Momma-Son," the mini opera consisted of "Alive," "Once," and "Footsteps," the latter of which did not make it onto the final track listing but was instead released as the B-side of the "Jeremy" single.

"Once"

The tone is set right out of the gate with "Once," which Stone Gossard considers to be among the band's heaviest songs. The descent is precipitous, and, since the lyrics give us the point of view of a serial killer, the song would have been right at home with the Doors' "L.A. Woman."

"Even Flow"

The subject of "Even Flow" is a homeless man, and this was the first of many Pearl Jam acknowledgments of those who inhabit the fraying fringes of society. Like "Once," the music of "Even Flow" is credited to Stone Gossard. The recording process for this song created quite a degree of frustration, and it required more than fifty takes to get it just right. Ultimately, the successful coupling of a Gossard funk guitar riff with a McCready "Stevie Ray Vaughan" sendup creates a classic song, a concert staple that allows Mike to take his solo just about anywhere he chooses (and allows Eddie to take a cigarette break).

"Alive"

Eddie's quasi-autobiographical masterpiece was nailed down during the demo sessions of January, 1991, and that is the version that appears on the album. "Alive" tells the story of Eddie's personal revelation that his biological father, Edward Louis Severson Jr., died of multiple sclerosis in 1981 and was not the "family friend" he had been led to believe. Never having the opportunity to see his real father again, "Alive" had a cathartic, yet cursed implication for Vedder's teenaged protagonist, who was condemned to still be alive after suffering through an abusive childhood. In a poignant moment during Pearl Jam's episode of *VH1's Storytellers* in 2006, Eddie talks about how the fans changed the meaning of the song for him and lifted the curse by making the song seem survivalist and life affirming. This was a heartfelt observation from an artist to his fans.

"Why Go"

"Why Go" was originally written on acoustic guitar and adapted by Jeff Ament for his twelve-string bass. The song tells the true story of a thirteen-year-old girl from Chicago who, after her mother caught her smoking marijuana, was remanded to a mental institution against her will for two years. Her parents were looking for an easy solution to detach themselves from their child, rather than accepting the responsibilities of parenting. The anger that comes across in the lyrics is palpable, as Eddie snarls and rails against the horrific injustice.

"Black"

Another Stone composition, "Black" deals with more conventional subject matter, a heartbroken man lamenting his lost lover. Epic Records smelled a hit and wanted the band to release it as a single. Pearl Jam steadfastly refused, citing the personal nature of the song's lyrics. Single or not, and in spite of the band's protests, the song became a hit on the radio. The power of this track was evident from the very beginning, and many Pearl Jam fans continue to allude to that power. According to Ten Clubber Jessica Seyfarth, "It helped me get through bouts of depression and emotional pain that I dealt with as a teenager. This song is my favorite, also, because when Eddie sings it you can hear, feel, and see his pain as well."

"Jeremy"

"Jeremy" is reminiscent of the Boomtown Rats' "I Don't Like Mondays," which chronicles the words and murderous deeds of sixteen-year-old Brenda Lee Spencer. She fired upon students and staff at San Diego's Grover Cleveland Elementary School with a semiautomatic .22 caliber rifle from her bedroom window across the street on January 29, 1979, killing two and wounding nine. "Jeremy," too, grew out of a tragic real-life news story.

The song describes the Texas high school suicide of fifteen-year-old Jeremy Wade Delle on January 8, 1991. Upon arriving late for his second period English class, Jeremy was sent to the office to get an admittance slip. But he returned armed with a .357 magnum instead, saying, "Miss, I got what I really went for." He then placed the barrel of the gun into his mouth and fired, blowing his brains out in front of his horrified teacher and classmates.

The story moved Vedder, who recalled a former San Diego classmate who shot up the oceanography room at their school. As he observed in 2009, "The world goes on and you're gone. The best revenge is to live on and prove yourself; be stronger than those people." The song became a cultural phenomenon, fueled in large part by director Mark Pellington's award-winning video. "Jeremy" had a captivating, aching quality that was highlighted by Eddie's impassioned, tortured

pearl jam jeremy

When fifteen-year-old Jeremy Wade Delle placed the barrel of a .357 magnum into his mouth and pulled the trigger in front of his horrified classmates on January 8, 1991, he had no way of knowing that in less than two years he would become a household name. As to whether knowledge of his impending, macabre immortality would have stayed his hand that day, one can only speculate.   *Author's collection*

vocals and a turn on cello by Rick Parashar. After all these years, "Jeremy" remains firmly entrenched in the Pearl Jam pantheon.

"Oceans"

Eddie wrote this one while he was locked out of the recording studio, stuck in the rain and able only to hear the sound of Jeff's bass from inside the building. Despite these less-than-ideal conditions, he managed to perfectly synch his vocals with Jeff's bass line. "Oceans" is a testament to just how sympatico everyone was during this musical maiden voyage. Tim Palmer even contributed some improvised percussion elements, a most welcome addition. It also marked the first of Vedder's many homages to surfing.

"Porch"

"Porch" began as a byproduct of one of Eddie's creative late night/early morning solo interludes, in the middle of the marathon recording sessions. As he told a Seattle audience about the song just days before *Ten's* release, "If you love someone, tell them." The slow-burning intensity of the song has made it a centerpiece of any

"Jeremy," a Tale of Two Videos

During the summer of 1991, Ed got to know the photographer Chris Cuffaro. The band suggested that he film a music video for a song of his choice from *Ten*. Cuffaro chose "Jeremy," but Epic Records refused to finance the project because the song was not scheduled for release as a single.

Undaunted, Cuffaro took out a loan and sold almost everything he owned to bankroll the project. Combining footage of a young actor named Eric Shubert as Jeremy with ghostly black and white images of Pearl Jam performing on a revolving platform, the finished product has never been officially released, but it can be readily seen on YouTube. In Cuffaro's video, the protagonist is a subtle presence, coloring with crayons and bouncing on his bed. There is only a hint of classroom imagery, in the form of a chalkboard, but we do see a handful of bullets and an image of a gun with the hammer pulled back and ready to fire. The band is the primary visual focus, and they are lit from above, giving them an ethereal glow.

Meanwhile, Epic Records had a change of heart and decided to release "Jeremy" as a single. The combination of video director Mark Pellington and editor Bruce Ashley resulted in a big budget production starring teenage actor Trevor Wilson in the titular role.

The impact of the video, which premiered on MTV on August 1, 1992, was immense. One critic described "Jeremy" as "an After School Special from Hell." As the story unfolds, Jeremy is the only character in motion; everything else that he encounters in his video world is stationary, save for the classroom teacher, who reaches out to catch the apple Jeremy tosses her just before the climactic scene. The film follows the lyrics mainly through the eyes of Vedder as the singer/narrator, juxtaposed with Wilson acting out the tale of the classroom tragedy, and climaxing with the suicide and the blood-splattered students.

The visual montage is fast-moving, with images of Jeremy acting out in frustration at home, isolated and uncomfortable among his motionless classmates (who at one point are depicted giving a Nazi-esque salute), wrapped in the American flag, and wreathed in flames. Eerily lit images of Jeremy are intercut with images of Pearl Jam, all of whom, save for the omnipresent Vedder, appear fleetingly amid the haunting imagery and flashes of spooky, biblical quotations.

MTV guidelines prevented Pellington from airing the scene of Jeremy placing the gun into his mouth and firing, which created a firestorm when some viewers misinterpreted the censored scene as implying that Jeremy had murdered his classmates instead of committing suicide. Pellington was frustrated by this misinterpretation, and he often took pains to point out to people that it is Jeremy's blood that appears spattered on his classmates, who are frozen in shock and horror at the violent suicide before them.

The video claimed four MTV Video Music Awards and remains one of the most iconic ever. For Pearl Jam, ever the contrarians, it solidified their position that, going forward, videos would *not* be a part of their overall promotional campaigns. The band would not release another video until the animated "Do the Evolution" in 1998. However, an absence from video would not kill these radio stars.

Pearl Jam concert. The fact that Eddie is still alive to sing "Porch" is a story unto itself.

During the lengthy instrumental breaks the band featured during live performances of "Porch," Eddie began to take death-defying risks. Every night the song would find him climbing the stage scaffolding, stage diving, crowd surfing, and, at the Pinkpop Festival in 1992, diving from a TV camera boom into the crowd. Later that same year, he scaled a scaffolding 40-feet high above the stage. Needless to say, these antics made Stone and Jeff *very* nervous because they had already experienced firsthand the tragedy of losing one lead singer. Losing Eddie would have been more than they could have handled, as Stone has suggested on more than one occasion.

"Garden"

"Garden" is one of the band's more enigmatic songs, and it is certainly open to interpretation. It is almost like a dirge, and we hear it as a statement of disillusionment with the modern world and—when placed in the context of that moment in time—an indictment of the first Gulf War. Others have more personal, emotional reactions. Ten Clubber John Carafella told us, "My favorite song has always been 'Garden.' That song's always had a special feel for me since I first heard it and still to this day it gives me goose bumps hearing it, especially in concert."

"Deep"

The hard rockin' grooves run accordingly in "Deep." Jeff Ament provides us with the paradox of his enjoying a beautiful, sunny day in often-gloomy Seattle, and then observing a man in the window of an abandoned apartment building shooting heroin. This grim juxtaposition of nature's beauty with the human squalor and debasement of the junkie was the indelible image that provided Jeff with the inspiration he needed to write this song. No matter how deep he sinks that needle into his arm, he will never fill that void in his soul.

"Release" (with hidden track, "Master/Slave")

The finale, "Release," with its instrumental "hidden" track, "Master/Slave," takes the listener full circle with Eddie's haunted protagonist desperately seeking the closure that he knows he will never find with his departed father. It's a cathartic track, and Stone and Jeff's recent loss of Andrew Wood was not lost on Eddie, either. He didn't so much *write* these lyrics as allow them to *pour forth* from his soul. Ten Clubber Jeff Wilder, of Sunrise, Florida, feels the song's power, too. He told us, "There's a long personal story associated with it that I choose not to go into. But it's one song that's always connected with me emotionally."

Not Bad, for a Team of Rookies

On the day they first entered the studio to record *Ten*, the band had only been together for five months and had only played about twenty live shows. But Stone and Jeff's extensive prior experience proved critical in creating a diverse album and knowing the path of least resistance to making that album a reality.

Sales of *Ten* were slow upon release, but by the second half of 1992 it had risen to the number two spot on *Billboard*, and it remained a constant presence on the charts for the next two years. Currently, it has been certified Platinum *thirteen* times, and all three of the official singles—"Alive," "Even Flow," and "Jeremy"— were big hits. On all levels, the game plan was executed to perfection. *Ten* remains an iconic record that captures the moment of a band just getting to know one another personally and professionally. The results were what Eddie would refer to in later years as "not so much 'garage rock' as it was groove rock," due primarily to the dual guitar techniques of Stone and Mike.

Support Tours

Pearl Jam would tour extensively in support of *Ten*, both at home and abroad, both as opening act and as headliner, all the while maintaining a grueling pace that would leave them, at times, exhausted.

North America

Officially, it all began north of the border at Harpo's in Victoria, Canada, on September 25, 1991, and ran smoothly for nearly three weeks. They hit Vancouver the following night and then headed south for Portland. The *Ten* Tour rolled into California on September 30, stopping in San Francisco, Los Angeles, and San Diego, before moving on to Phoenix, Arizona. Pearl Jam did the Texas *three*-step from October 9 through 11, playing gigs in Austin, Dallas, and Houston. Staying south, they hit Georgia and North Carolina. Then things took an interesting turn. They cancelled their October 15 gig, scheduled for Washington D.C.'s Nightclub 9:30, but they had a good reason.

I'm a Pepper, You're a Pepper, Who *Wouldn't* Want to Be a Pepper, Too?

Halfway through their opening tour to promote *Ten*, Pearl Jam cancelled as a headliner in order to serve as the opening act for the Red Hot Chili Peppers on their *Blood Sugar Sex Magik* Tour in the fall of 1991. It was a good move, engineered by founding Pepper Jack Irons, as it got the band some serious exposure in larger venues. Jack, of course, had been the man behind Pearl Jam's proverbial curtain since the beginning of the band's career, except for the brief time he was in front of it, drumming. Touring arenas with the Smashing Pumpkins and Nirvana, as well as the Peppers, was a major marketing coup for the benefit of all concerned.

The first of these opening slots found Pearl Jam supporting the Smashing Pumpkins and the Red Hot Chili Peppers at the Oscar Meyer Theater in Madison, Wisconsin. This was the first of forty-two shows that would find Pearl Jam opening for one, or both, of these bands until mid-December.

Pearl Jam managed to squeeze in a few of their own small club shows in between supporting the Peppers and Pumpkins. On November 4, they hit the Student Union Ballroom at UMASS Amherst, with the support of Jack Iron's band,

Eleven. Two days later, they played the Haunt, a club in Ithaca, New York. This was soon followed by a dream come true on the Bowery: Pearl Jam headlined the legendary CBGB on November 8. On November 21, they played the Blind Pig in Ann Arbor, with a little help from the opening act, Zoo Gods.

After a Salt Lake City gig on December 15 in support of the Smashing Pumpkins at Club DV8, the band enjoyed a holiday break until December 27, before returning to open for the Red Hot Chili Peppers in Los Angeles. This time around the Smashing Pumpkins were out of the second slot, replaced by the surging Nirvana. The Los Angeles gig was the first of five that would find this power trio of bands in California, Arizona, and Oregon. Pearl Jam finished this leg of the tour as its own headlining act at Seattle's RCKNDY and Moore Theatre, and finally at a Rock for Choice benefit in Los Angeles on January 24.

Europe

It was a new year, and Pearl Jam had new worlds to conquer. The band headed to Europe for the first time and had an impressive run of headlining shows, most of them at club-sized venues. Between February 3 at the Esplanade Club in England's Southend-on-Sea and March 13 at Nachtwerk in Munich, Pearl Jam crisscrossed the continent. They played England eight times, the Netherlands six times (the gig at Concertgebouw de Vereeniging on March 3 was cancelled, or it would have been seven), and Germany five times. In between, they played one-offs in Sweden, Norway, Denmark, France, Spain, Italy, Switzerland, and Scotland.

Lean on me. Jeff Ament, Pearl Jam's burly bassist, has been a shoulder for Eddie to lean on ever since the Pearl Jam front man first arrived in Seattle. The two share a life-long affinity for basketball, surfing, and—rumor has it—they are both quite keen on music. *Photofest*

North America: Leg Two

With barely two weeks' rest, Pearl Jam returned to North America on March 25 as a headlining act with a series of shows at small- to medium-sized venues, clubs, and colleges. The ambitious, two-month leg featured forty-one scheduled performances, though four cancellations reduced that total to thirty-seven—still an impressive number. All told, Pearl Jam had hit twenty states, thirty-six cities, and three countries. Momentum was beginning to build, and the band was gaining a reputation as a killer live act, which caused copies of *Ten* to move off shelves more quickly. But there was no time for reflection and assessment just yet; Europe was ready for another helping of Pearl Jam.

Europe: Second Leg

This leg of the tour kicked off smoothly enough in Nürburg, Germany, on June 5. It was festival season in Europe, and after an appearance at London's Finsbury Park Festival on June 6, Pearl Jam found itself giving a momentous performance at the Pinkpop Festival in Landgraaf, the Netherlands, on June 8. They followed Pinkpop with five straight shows in Germany before hitting Italy, Switzerland, Austria, France, and Sweden. And then things took a turn for the worse.

A Foreshadowing?

On June 26, 1992, Pearl Jam appeared at the Roskilde Festival in Roskilde, Denmark, for the first time. They had seven more shows scheduled for this leg of the tour after Roskilde, including at least three more festival appearances, but fate would intervene. They had no way of knowing it when they took the stage that day, but this would be the last gig of the *Ten* Tour.

The band was physically, mentally and emotionally exhausted by this point, and someone had broken into their dressing room in Sweden the night before, stealing a number of their personal effects. Among the stolen items was Eddie's suitcase, full of his precious journals and notebooks. When the band ran into a hassle with Roskilde security personnel that day, they decided that they had had enough. They cancelled the remaining seven dates of the tour and headed for home.

After ten grueling months on the road to promote *Ten*, what hadn't killed Pearl Jam had honed them into a well-oiled machine. There would be no turning back.

6

All Causes Great and Small

Pearl Jam's History of Sociopolitical Activism

T hough the roots of Pearl Jam's sociopolitical activism predate the existence of the band, the band's commercial success has enabled them to put their money where their mouths are in terms of supporting the causes they deem worthy. Here, in no particular order, are just a few of the charities that Pearl Jam has supported over the years.

The Vitalogy Foundation

Let us begin with the home team, Pearl Jam's very own official charity, the Vitalogy Foundation. Under the "Activism" tab on pearljam.com, you will find the following words:

> The Vitalogy Foundation is a public nonprofit organization founded in 2006 by Pearl Jam and their manager [Kelly Curtis]. The Foundation supports the efforts of nonprofit organizations doing commendable work in the fields of community health, the environment, arts & education and social change.

Each band member has three or four "Spotlight Non Profits." For Mike, these include Treehouse, KEXP, the Jennifer Jaff Center, and, of course, CCFA (the Crohn's and Colitis Foundation of America). For Jeff, it's the Poverello Center, Ravenwood, and the Bureau of Fearless Ideas. For Matt, it's the Children's Hospital, War Child, and the Creative Visions Foundation. For Eddie, it's the EB Research Partnership, STTR, and J/P HRO. Finally, for Stone, it's the Downtown Emergency Service Center, Conservation International, and Partners in Health. These efforts run the gamut from addressing children's issues, education, poverty, homelessness, chronic diseases, war, the environment, disaster relief, community outreach, public health, and, of course, access to music education.

Whether individually or as a band, the members of Pearl Jam have never shied away from getting political, and they have been tireless in their efforts to get young people registered to vote. Here, in a striking long-sleeve T-shirt crafted by Crashious Roadside, Pearl Jam and their colleagues lend their support to Vote for Change.   *Jeremy "Crash" Crowley*

No Vote Left Behind

No Vote Left Behind is a Seattle-based PAC (Political Action Committee). Just prior to the start of the Vote for Change Tour, Pearl Jam donated the proceeds from their September 24, 2004, show at the Showbox in Seattle toward the group's efforts. Those efforts focused, as others have before and since, on rallying the youth vote.

America Coming Together (ACT)

The signature charity of the fabled Vote for Change Tour was America Coming Together, or ACT. While the Vote for Change Tour supposedly netted upwards of $15 million for ACT's efforts at getting out the vote and raising awareness among the potential electorate, the final tally for 2004 was decidedly more modest. Perhaps more importantly, their implicit goal of defeating George W. Bush's re-election bid failed. Yet, something good *did* come out of that October run of shows. Read on.

The Wishlist Foundation

The Wishlist Foundation was the silver lining that emerged from the gray cloud of the Vote for Change Tour. On October 5, 2004, Pearl Jam was booked for a gig in St. Louis, Missouri. According to the story on the Wishlist Foundation's website, a small group of Pearl Jam fans, among them Brent Hinson and Laura Trafton, decided that it would be a nice gesture if everyone would bring a can of food to donate to the local St. Louis Food Bank. They spread the word, and their fellow fans responded. Hinson and Trafton "organized the fundraiser party at Humphrey's in St. Louis and the response was overwhelming. Over two hundred pounds of food and clothing were donated by fans, with little promotion."

Within two years, the Wishlist Foundation became an official 501(c)(3) non-profit, independent of the band, and supports the band's philanthropic efforts. To date, the nonprofit has raised more than half a million dollars in support of a variety of charitable causes, and it shows no sign of slowing down.

Too Many "Choices"?

For personal reasons he has never fully expounded upon, Eddie Vedder has always been a big supporter of abortion rights, as evidenced by his piece, "Reclamation," in the November 1992 issue of *Spin* magazine, and published just a month shy of his twenty-eighth birthday. Therein, the twenty-seven-year-old singer seems to suggest, albeit cryptically, that had it not been for a young girlfriend having an abortion ten years earlier, he would have become a father at seventeen. Pearl Jam would never have existed, and he would not be here, writing this article.

The following charities were organized by like-minded folks. Voters for Choice was legendary feminist activist Gloria Steinham's pro-choice political committee.

Neil Young has been running the annual Bridge School benefit concerts for longer than Pearl Jam has been a band, as evidenced by this 25th Anniversary Edition compilation album. Pearl Jam does not appear at the benefit annually, but they *do* pop by every few years to show support for this groundbreaking institution. This particular collection features the band performing "Better Man," a song with a fascinating backstory, as you will see.   *Author's collection*

Rock for Choice was a decade-long series of concerts, dating back to 1991. Fittingly, the concept originated with Pearl Jam's friends, the pioneering Los Angeles female punk quartet, L7. In addition to inspiring ten years of donations to pro-choice charities, L7 is often credited with inspiring the Riot Grrrl scene; a double-barreled shot of political and artistic feminist empowerment. Eventually, Rock for Choice became organized under the umbrella of the Feminist Majority, an actual 501(c)(3) nonprofit that capitalized on all that artistic talent by releasing a series of compilation albums, which gave the movement another reliable revenue stream.

Ralph Nader: It's Not Easy Being "Green"

Ralph Nader was an attorney whose 1965 book, *Unsafe at Any Speed*, inspired the 1966 National Traffic and Motor Vehicle Safety Act. His other consumer advocacy works inspired the 1967 Wholesome Meat Act. He went on to pen several more books about environmental and public safety issues.

For whatever reason, thirty-five years or so into his career, he began to fancy himself as a presidential candidate. While not a Pearl Jam cause per se, Green Party nominee Nader was certainly a *Vedder* cause during the 2000 campaign. Between September 2000 and August 2001, Eddie appeared at no fewer than four Nader rallies. You have to appreciate the delicious irony that Vedder worked so hard to get Nader elected, yet his efforts inadvertently contributed to George W. Bush's victory. That victory, in turn, provided Vedder with eight years' worth of material to work with.

Jon Tester for US Senate

Montana Senator Jon Tester (D) is a lifelong friend of Pearl Jam bassist, Jeff Ament; they grew up together in Big Sandy, Montana. Big Sandy is a small world. Jeff's father, George Ament, was the town barber who allegedly gave Tester his signature "flat top" hairstyle and then went on to serve as the town's mayor for fifteen years. Tester rose through the ranks, from the local school board to the Montana state senate in 1998 and then on to the US Senate in 2006. He won reelection in 2012. Should he decide to run for reelection when his term ends in 2018, it is a safe bet that the Aments, and Pearl Jam, will be in his corner.

The Bridge School

The Bridge School is a 501(c)(3) nonprofit organization. According to its website, the institution in Hillsborough, California, was designed to meet the educational needs of children suffering from "severe speech and physical impairments." They do so through the use of cutting edge assistive educational technologies designed to facilitate students' ease of communication. They also work to foster the direct involvement of the students' families and community.

Among the notable members of the Bridge School community are school cofounders Neil Young, and his (now) ex-wife, Pegi Young, who drew their inspiration from dealing with the health issues of their son, Ben, who suffers from cerebral palsy, and daughter Amber, who, like Neil himself, is an epileptic.

The Annual Bridge School Benefit Concerts, held at the Shoreline Amphitheater in Mountain View, California, began in 1986, and the funds raised from that first show helped to finance its construction. Pearl Jam first came on board for the 1992 show and have returned regularly ever since.

The Maryville Academy

The Maryville Academy is a Catholic educational institution located near Eddie Vedder's birthplace, in Chicago, Illinois. The vintage charity evolved out of an earlier incarnation, St. Mary's Training School for Boys, which dated back to 1883 and was a phoenix that arose from the ashes of the legendary Great Chicago Fire.

Eddie Vedder came to support Maryville Academy through Pete Townshend. In one of our favorite bits of Pearl Jam activism lore, the band actually played a benefit concert for the Maryville Academy at the House Of Blues on September 23, 2002, as an opening act for the Who, albeit *without* Stone, who was out playing a benefit show for Conservation International that same night.

Conservation International

Conservation International is based in Arlington, Virginia, but has a global vision. The group, founded in 1987, is focused on environmental issues, such as those impacting clean air, potable water, food security, and climate change. Its approach is to identify problem areas, research plausible solutions, and then partner with corporate entities to implement solutions. The group has gotten its fair share of criticism over the years, not only for partnering with certain large energy companies, but also for questionable allocation of funds.

YouthCare

YouthCare focuses its efforts on the needs of troubled and/or homeless adolescents from ages eleven through eighteen. It is a Seattle-based residential program that aims to recreate a comfortable home-like environment, all while addressing the youths' educational and psychological needs, including substance abuse and teen pregnancy issues. Pearl Jam received the Marleen Alhadeff Volunteer of the Year Award in 2006 for their efforts on behalf of the organization.

Louis Warschaw Prostate Cancer Center

The Louis Warschaw Prostate Cancer Center is a part of the Cedars-Sinai Medical Center's Samuel Oschin Comprehensive Cancer Institute. Pearl Jam is both emotionally and financially connected to the Center because of their idol and friend, Johnny Ramone, who died of the disease. Ramone not only raised the band's awareness of the disease, he encouraged them to devote some of their charitable resources toward the cause.

(CCFA) Crohn's and Colitis Foundation of America

Mike McCready has suffered from Crohn's disease for most of his life, making the disease a close-to-home issue for Pearl Jam. Crohn's—and ulcerative colitis—can be debilitating, and the symptoms embarrassing. McCready, though a recognizable public figure for many years, did not feel comfortable enough to speak openly about his ailment until 2002.

CCFA's programs address these issues. Their key focus is on finding a cure, and as it says on their website, "to improve the quality of life of children and adults affected by these diseases." Their annual Camp Oasis allows boys and girls to enjoy the experience of going to summer camp in a comfortable environment, among their fellow sufferers. McCready has been a godsend to the organization, and he arranges an annual CCFA benefit concert. Whether as a part of Pearl Jam, as a solo artist, or fronting one of his many side projects, he devotes a tremendous amount of his time, money, and efforts toward helping CCFA reach their goals.

Teenage Cancer Trust (and Teen Cancer America)

Pearl Jam became involved in supporting Teenage Cancer Trust through their connections to the Who. The group originated in the UK in 1989, when Myrna Whiteson was lobbying to establish a cardiac unit for children at Guy's Hospital in London. She and her colleagues met the mother of a thirteen-year-old boy cancer patient, and the issue arose of where best to treat him. They surmised that the boy would benefit from being treated in an environment that catered specifically to the needs of his demographic. Within a year that idea became a reality, as Teenage Cancer Trust opened their first oncology unit for teens at Middlesex Hospital on November 22, 1990.

Within a decade, the groups' efforts caught the attention of the Who's Roger Daltrey. He became a patron of Teenage Cancer Trust, and, beginning in 2000, the man behind the group's annual Royal Albert Hall concert fundraiser. In November of 2011, Daltrey enlisted the help of Pete Townshend to bring Teenage Cancer Trust's model to the United States, where they founded Teen Cancer America. Pearl Jam continues to be an enthusiastic supporter of the Who's efforts in this regard.

The West Memphis Three

The "three" refers to Damien Echols, Jessie Misskelley Jr., and Jason Baldwin. When West Memphis, Arkansas, eight-year-olds, Steven Edward Branch, Christopher Mark Byers, and James Michael Moore, were found murdered in 1993, these three teenagers were arrested, tried, and convicted of the crimes. Echols was sentenced to death, while Misskelley Jr. and Baldwin each received life in prison without parole.

New forensic evidence surfaced in 2007, which set into motion a new round of legal proceedings, resulting in a plea bargain, a new sentence of time served, and finally, release on August 19, 2011. To this day there are people who feel Echols, Misskelley Jr., and Baldwin are guilty, and there are also those who feel they were the wrongfully imprisoned victims of a witch-hunt.

Pearl Jam, particularly Eddie, was in the latter camp. Indeed, he devoted an enormous amount of time, energy, and money helping to free the three convicts over a fifteen-year period. As he told *Rolling Stone's* Patrick Doyle, it was his face-to-face meeting with Echols that convinced him of the trio's innocence once and for all: "He just said, 'No.' But the way he said it, I'm sure he followed up with a sentence but that was all—it was just, you know—you can tell. You can tell." Case closed?

The September 11th Fund

The September 11th Fund was the result of a joint effort by two existing charity organizations: the United Way of New York and the New York Community Trust. Between the aftermath of the terrorist attacks and December of 2004, the fund raised the staggering sum of $534 million for the victims of September 11, their families, and the first responders. Pearl Jam's contribution to the September 11th Fund came in the form of a song, "Long Road," which Eddie and Mike recorded and filmed for the *America: A Tribute to Heroes Benefit.*

The Silverlake Conservatory of Music

This California-based 501(c)(3) nonprofit is near and dear to the hearts of Pearl Jam and many of their colleagues. Their focus is on making music education accessible to all children, regardless of socioeconomic status. Pearl Jam is the very embodiment of this idea.

The Cascade Land Conservancy (now Fortera)

This 501(c)(3) is the largest of its kind in Washington State. To date, they have helped to permanently preserve and protect 238,000 acres of Washington's land. As mentioned in *PJ20*, Pearl Jam and Soundgarden pooled their resources for a $400,000 donation to the nonprofit during the summer of 1997.

The Coalition of Independent Music Stores

The Coalition of Independent Music Stores (CIMS) began in 1995 as a solution to a problem that did not exist when the members of Pearl Jam were growing up: the viability of local, independently owned record stores. By 1995, independent record stores had become an endangered species, and CIMS came along to organize some of the survivors into a nationwide collective. Pearl Jam has supported CIMS' efforts both financially and by raising awareness.

Artists for Peace and Justice

The brainchild of Canadian filmmaker Paul Haggis, Artists for Peace and Justice was founded in 2009. As stated on Pearl Jam's official website, the fundraising group "encourages peace and social justice and addresses issues of poverty and enfranchisement in communities around the world." In the wake of the devastating earthquake that struck Haiti in 2010, the island nation became a focal point for the group's humanitarian efforts, which have included food, clean water, and the construction of three schools.

National Campaign to Close Guantanamo

This effort was begun by a group of military veterans and politicians, including Bob Gard and John Johns, two retired generals; Jon Soltz, the chairman of VoteVets.org; and Tom Andrews, the group's Director and a former US Congressman.

Pearl Jam and a group of their fellow artists, including R.E.M., Nine Inch Nails, Billy Bragg, Steve Earle, Rage Against the Machine, and Roseanne Cash came on board when it was brought to their attention that their music may have been used as a means of torturing the prisoners at Guantanamo. Suffice it to say, the musicians took exception to their music being used in this fashion.

The Northwest School

This one is personal for Stone Gossard, alumnus, Class of 1984. Since the fancy private middle and high school had just been founded in 1980, Stone was a member of the very first class graduating from the high school. He continues to support his alma mater to this day.

The Surfrider Foundation

The Surfrider Foundation was launched in 1984 by surfers from Malibu, California. The organization has grown exponentially during its thirty-plus year history, and it now has eighty-four chapters, dozens of high school and college clubs, and more than a quarter of a million supporters spread out across the country. For surfers like Jeff and Eddie, the health of the coastal environment is of paramount importance, and the Foundation focuses its efforts in those areas. As we discuss in Chapter 25, Pearl Jam has contributed to a series of benefit albums in support of the Surfrider Foundation.

Greenpeace

What began in 1971 with a group of Canadian hippies commandeering an old fishing boat to spy on American nuclear testing sites in Alaska has evolved into a modern organization of staggering proportions. Greenpeace remains steadfastly anti-nuclear *everything*, but they are also concerned with the chemicals that are poisoning our lands, climate change, the integrity of Arctic ice, the health of the world's oceans, food security through sustainable agriculture, and the rainforests.

Musicians were a part of Greenpeace's efforts long before Pearl Jam came along. One of our favorite Pearl Jam stories concerns Eddie's ambivalence toward his old Bad Radio song, "Better Man." He very nearly gave the song away to Greenpeace for Chrissie Hynde to sing on a benefit record. Producer Brendan O'Brien knew "Better Man" would be a huge hit, and he was finally able to talk Eddie into embracing his songwriting past. Greenpeace may not have gotten "Better Man," but Pearl Jam is still on their side.

Habitat for Humanity

Though Habitat for Humanity is denominational in the sense that it is Christian in origin, the work that they do is all-inclusive. And that work is simple, straight-forward, and pragmatic. Founded in 1976 by Millard and Linda Fuller, the group builds affordable homes for those who need them—over a million and counting to date! Further, they dedicate some of their funds to subsidizing home loans/mortgages for those in need of financial assistance. Perhaps the most famous names associated with the group are those of former President Jimmy Carter and his wife, Rosalynn, who have been partnering with Habitat since 1984. Pearl Jam got involved in fundraising efforts after Hurricane Katrina.

Jazz Foundation of America

The Jazz Foundation of America is another charitable organization that Pearl Jam supported in the wake of Hurricane Katrina. Historically, traditional jazz and blues musicians have been among the least well compensated. The organization was founded in 1989, with a mission to relieve some of the financial burdens faced by these talented ambassadors of American music so that they were more freely able to practice their craft. Circumstances facing these musicians were greatly exacerbated in the wake of Hurricane Katrina, particularly in the area of New Orleans.

Home Alive

The Seattle-based Home Alive aims to cut down on the incidence of violence against women by schooling women in the arts of self-defense. The genesis of the organization was an incident that struck close to home: the murder of Mia Zapata, lead singer of the Gits. That was enough to gain the attention and garner the support of many artists within the Seattle music scene. As discussed in Chapter 25, Pearl Jam joined an impressive roster of their colleagues in contributing to a 1996 compilation album, *Home Alive: The Art of Self Defense.*

The Mount Graham Coalition

The Mount Graham Coalition is one of the more intriguing charities that Pearl Jam has supported. To quote the wonderful *Two Feet Thick* website's notes on the matter:

> Mount Graham is the most sacred mountain to the traditional San Carlos Apache people and home to many plants and animals that don't exist elsewhere. The Mount Graham Coalition is an international group (associated with Earth First) working to protect the mountain from development of an astronomical complex of observatories that was then under construction by the University of Arizona.

Apparently, the University of Arizona had partners in high places, because the Vatican was also interested in constructing observatories for the purpose of seeking out extraterrestrial life. However, the project ran straight into a competing notion of sacrality: the (nearly) 11,000 foot high Mount Graham itself was sacred to the local tribes. As we discuss in Chapter 25, Pearl Jam took the time to play a couple of benefit concerts in support of the coalition and even petitioned the Clinton White House by writing a letter of support.

The NFL Kick Hunger Challenge

As Seattle Seahawks fans, Pearl Jam is often involved in their local NFL team's charitable efforts. In the days and weeks leading up to Super Bowl XLIX, those efforts included the NFL's Kick Hunger Challenge, which pits fans from each NFL city against one another to see which one can raise the most funds. The beauty of the system is that the challenge stokes the competitive fires, but ultimately everyone wins. All of the money raised within each city stays in that city. As noted on their website, "During the 2014–15 NFL season, the Kick Hunger Challenge provided more than three million meals to people struggling with hunger throughout the United States" Pearl Jam did their part by offering a limited edition "Flag Needle Shirt" for sale and then donating a portion of the proceeds to the challenge. A great team effort.

7

(Bad) Television

The Band Confronts an Unfamiliar Medium

B y and large, you will find that most music people aren't natural born television people. Pearl Jam has proven no different in this regard, and Eddie Vedder in particular made his aversion to the camera well known early on in the band's career. But born, as they were, during the television era, on the cusp of the digital media revolution, Pearl Jam has had to endure its fair share of screen time, whether they liked it or not. Funny enough, their small screen debut took place on the other side of the proverbial pond.

Ladies and Gentlemen, Pearl Jam

Pearl Jam's first television appearance took place in the United Kingdom on BBC Two's *The Late Show*. They performed the first single from *Ten*, "Alive." The segment aired on February 4, 1992. Suffice it to say, there would be more TV appearances to follow.

Live, from New York, It's Saturday Night!

On April 11, 1992, Pearl Jam followed their erstwhile second drummer, Matt Chamberlain, to *Saturday Night Live* at NBC studios in New York City. Sharon Stone was the host of the show that evening, and Pearl Jam was making their first appearance as musical guests. In addition to playing "Alive" and "Porch" for an appreciative studio audience, the band appeared in a skit with Sharon Stone, lampooning her infamous leg-crossing crotch-flash from the hit film, *Basic Instinct*. Nice work if you can get it!

Almost exactly two years later, on April 16, 1994, Pearl Jam made their second appearance on *Saturday Night Live*, this time hosted by Emilio Estevez. The band was visibly still reeling from the tragic suicide of Kurt Cobain less than two weeks earlier, and, in the case of Mike McCready, reeling for *other* reasons, too. This time around, the band played a snarling version of "Not for You," followed by "Rearview Mirror," and "Daughter," which they tagged with a bit of Neil Young's "Hey Hey, My My." The "Hey Hey, My My" tag was a subtle homage to Cobain, who had quoted the song in his suicide note.

Late Show with David Letterman (CBS) Season 10. November 14 and 15, 2002. David Letterman was always a fan of Pearl Jam, and he featured the band on his iconic show on several occasions.

Photofest

While certainly a memorable experience for those in attendance, not to mention the wider television audience, the moment was evidently lost on Mike McCready. As he acknowledges in *PJ20*, the guitarist was so drunk that he later had no recollection that the band had even *played* "Daughter," in spite of the fact that he can be seen on film smiling and waving appreciatively to the crowd after the song ended. If nothing else, this apparent on-stage blackout revealed that the guitarist had a reliable autopilot setting.

At show's end, as the cast and guests gathered onstage for the traditional bows and goodbyes, Eddie opened his jacket to reveal a small "K," fashioned from electrician's tape, affixed near his heart; he placed his right hand there in yet another subtle salute to the fallen Cobain. Twelve long years passed before Pearl Jam returned to *SNL* on April 15, 2006, and Lindsay Lohan was the host. The tight, focused, and largely clean-cut band charged through "World Wide Suicide" and "Severed Hand."

Most recently as of this writing, Pearl Jam appeared on *SNL* for a fourth time, on March 13, 2010, to play "Just Breathe" and "Unthought Known." This time around they also managed to get in on the fun by appearing in a sketch with Jude Law, spoofing the classic episode of *The Twilight Zone*, "Nightmare at 20,000 Feet," where a lone and hysterical airline passenger keeps seeing "something" outside on the wing of the plane. In the *SNL* parody, that "something" included the members of Pearl Jam.

Attempting to channel the sheer ferocity and volcanic intensity of the young Pearl Jam through acoustic instruments was, in retrospect, an ingenious idea. The sense of barely restrained mayhem is palpable here, as the band, through no fault of its own, turns in a performance for the ages. After this, they were free to crank the amps back up to eleven, and Mike McCready rejoiced.

Author's collection

David Letterman

From one legendary New York City television show to another we go. David Letterman had always been a big music fan, and it didn't take long for Pearl Jam to appear on his radar. Eddie Vedder popped up in February of 1996, in response to a recent bit of comic shtick that Dave and Paul Schafer had been doing with the song, "Black." In what appeared to the audience to be a spontaneous moment, Ed strolled onto the stage to demonstrate how to properly sing the chorus of "Black," and then left just as quickly. By September 20 of the same year, Pearl Jam were the musical guests, performing "Hail Hail" and "Leaving Here," though the television audience only got a taste of the latter song, as the show cut to commercial.

Less than two years later, a revitalized Pearl Jam appeared on May 1, 1998, to introduce their old friend and new drummer, Matt Cameron, to the world on "Wishlist." Eddie himself returned at the end of the month to appear briefly in a *VH1 Behind the Music* parody skit about Letterman's legendary bandleader, Paul Schaeffer. The following July, Eddie joined his musical father figure, Pete Townshend on "Heart to Hang Onto." In April 2000, Pearl Jam filed a "Grievance" on the Ed Sullivan Theater stage, and thus began a pattern of appearing on the show every other year.

On November 14, 2002, they taped "I Am Mine" and "Save You," the latter of which aired on the following night's show. By the time of their September 30, 2004, appearance, the band was in full-on protest song mode, offering a cover of Bob Dylan's "Masters of War." They returned in May of 2006 to perform "Life Wasted" and then kind of disappeared for a few years.

Eddie popped up solo again on June 20, 2011, to promote his album, *Ukulele Songs*, and to perform "Without You." Alas, all good things must come to an end. On May 18, 2015, Eddie Vedder returned to appear on Letterman's show for the final time, and sent the legendary host off to retirement in fine style with a heartfelt rendition of "Better Man."

The Tonight Show

When *The Tonight Show with Conan O'Brien* debuted on June 1, 2009, it featured red-hot comic actor Will Ferrell as the inaugural guest and Pearl Jam as the first musical guests. Great choices. After an enthusiastic introduction by O'Brien, the band took to the stage and launched into a taut version of "Got Some," before an appreciative crowd. The band was in excellent form, and O'Brien could not have been a more gracious host.

MTV Pulls the Plug on Pearl Jam

When Pearl Jam was asked to film an episode of MTV's hit series, *MTV Unplugged*, they didn't flinch. Circumstances on their first European jaunt had already forced them to play a few impromptu acoustic sets, so the pump was primed. Been there, done that. Though looking back we admit it seemed like a bit of a paradox at the time. Here was a young band—raw, angry, powerful, and inclined to play loud and heavy—channeling all of its aggression through acoustic instruments while seated on stools. The band recorded their episode on March 16, 1992, at Kaufman Astoria Studios in Queens, New York. This remarkable performance is readily available on YouTube, and it has certainly stood the test of time.

A Dutch Treat

Pearl Jam's June 8 appearance at the 1992 Pinkpop Festival in Landgraaf, the Netherlands, really illustrates the raw power and ferocious energy of the band's early live performances. But the only reason we are able to say that with any degree of confidence is that someone had the presence of mind to film and broadcast the festival on Dutch television, thus preserving it for the enjoyment of future generations.

A little more than a week later, the band's June 17 show at Milan, Italy's City Square was broadcast on Italian television, giving Italy its first good look at Pearl Jam.

The 1992 *MTV Music Video Awards*

Given Pearl Jam's almost instantaneous commercial success and corresponding critical acclaim, it was inevitable that nominations, awards, and award show broadcasts would soon follow; not that the band was necessarily always happy about that.

On September 9, 1992, Pearl Jam found itself in a situation that would continue to prove awkward for them over the years: being nominated for an award and, adding insult to injury, having to *perform* at the award show. Given their disdain for terms like "grunge" and "alternative," we're quite sure that the title of the award they were nominated for—"Best Alternative Video" (for "Alive")—was a sore spot, too. And what an eventful show this proved to be. Dana Carvey hosted, while radio legend Howard Stern dropped in (quite literally) to regale the crowd with his "Fartman" character shtick.

Meanwhile, backstage, tensions were running high between Guns N' Roses and Nirvana, and who can ever forget the sight of poor Krist Novoselic braining himself with his own awkwardly tossed bass guitar during "Lithium"? Pearl Jam was not heartbroken to lose the award to Nirvana's "Smells Like Teen Spirit" that night, but they had their own share of drama surrounding the performance. The suits (both those at MTV and at their own record com-

Pearl Jam and Nirvana: Ships That Passed in the Night

While the two bands both caught the wave of the "Seattle Scene" explosion, the truth of the matter is that they did not really know one another very well at the time. Kurt Cobain caused something of a stir when he publicly responded to a reporter's question about Pearl Jam by saying, "I have always hated their band." Evidently, he was referring specifically to his dislike of the band's *music*, which he viewed as too much like classic rock and not "punk" enough, and not the band's members. Their paths did cross on occasion, but they barely knew one another socially at the time.

The mass media, however, loves controversy and gossip, and soon the quote was repeated in every newspaper and magazine, as they tried to portray the two powerhouse bands as rivals. This had echoes of the Beatles versus the Stones, another manufactured rivalry from decades past. As in the historically earlier example, the band members didn't really know what to make of the whole thing.

Mark Yarm relates the story behind Eddie and Kurt's backstage slow dance in his 2011 book, *Everybody Loves Our Town: An Oral History of Grunge*. While Eric Clapton was on stage playing "Tears in Heaven," Cobain's wife, Hole singer Courtney Love, decided to have some fun. She said, "I shoved Kurt into Eddie and I shoved Eddie into Kurt, and then I laughed, just chuckled, because it was genius. I loved it." The now famous footage, later unearthed by Cameron Crowe for *PJ20*, was filmed by Love's Hole bandmate, Eric Erlandson. It was a lighthearted moment, though Yarm says that, to the best of his knowledge, Cobain never publicly retracted the comments he made about Pearl Jam's music; though he did concede that Vedder was "a nice person" and that the two singers once shared a phone call.

pany) wanted them to perform "Jeremy," though Eddie had his punk rock heart set on covering the Dead Boys' "Sonic Reducer." The suits got their way, and Pearl Jam's awkward relationship with awards shows was off to an entertaining start. A lasting image from that evening's festivities had to be Eddie (clad in an Army helmet) and Kurt Cobain slow-dancing together and sharing a warm hug backstage while guitar god Eric Clapton performed his hit, "Tears in Heaven." You can thank

Cameron Crowe for his detective work in unearthing this footage and including it in the *PJ20* film.

Singled Out

Pardon our use of the outdated idiom, but have you ever had "one of *those* days"? Pearl Jam certainly did, when they were roped into playing the premiere party for Cameron Crowe's *Singles* the very next day after the 1992 *MTV Video Music Awards*. This event, dubbed *MTV's Singles Scene Party*, was held on September 10, at the Plaza Park Hotel Ballroom, and was scheduled to air the following week.

Unlike a typical concert, which is a fairly linear affair, these made-for-TV events tend to involve a *lot* of waiting around. And when you're a young rock and roll band, cranky to begin with at having to be there, bored out of your minds from all of the down time, and faced with the temptation of readily available libations, well . . . shenanigans tend to ensue. There's no better way to phrase this: the band got *smashed* and turned in a sloppy train wreck of a performance as a result. The fact that they were able to salvage anything at *all* for the broadcast the following week (September 18) is a testament to the skills of the video editors. And while watching the available video footage may be amusing for us today, it was clearly an embarrassing situation for the band members, and it led them toward a more isolationist approach regarding their future public appearances.

Say "Uncle"

Before you knew it, it was time for another round of the *MTV Video Music Awards* (September 3, 1993). The second time was the charm for Pearl Jam, as they took home an armful of the so-called "Moonman" trophies. For reasons that continue to perplex us to this day, "Jeremy" wasn't even *nominated* under the Best Alternative Video category, as "Alive" had been the previous year. That particular Moonman went to Nirvana for the second year in a row, this time for "In Bloom." But it was just as well, because the familiar Mark Pellington version of "Jeremy" won for Best Group Video, Best Metal/Hard Rock Video, Best Direction, and Video of the Year. So naturally, and in typical contrarian Pearl Jam style, winning all of these accolades and trophies compelled them to *stop* making videos altogether, lest they be so honored again.

Performance-wise, they managed to up the ante by playing "Animal," the aggressive second track from their forthcoming second album, *Vs.*, before being joined onstage by the legendary Neil Young, who brought the house down by leading Pearl Jam through an incendiary version of his "Rockin' in the Free World."

From Honolulu to London

While the band was performing the first of two gigs in Honolulu, Hawaii, on September 25, 1992, the BBC aired a twenty-minute interview with Eddie Vedder, who, for good or for ill, had swiftly become the undisputed spokesman for the band.

To Honor a Legend

On October 16, 1992, Mike McCready and Eddie Vedder joined a slate of industry giants at the "World's Most Famous Arena," NYC's Madison Square Garden, to honor the living legend Bob Dylan on the occasion of his thirtieth anniversary in the music business. Appropriately enough, the Dylan tune they performed was a haunting acoustic version of one of his signature protest songs, "Masters of War," with G. E. Smith, the omnipresent musician's musician, joining them on mandolin. While "steal the show" may be a bit of an exaggeration, particularly in that vaunted company, Eddie and Mike certainly acquitted themselves well and gained a lot of notice and respect that day.

Should Old Punk Rockers Be Forgot?

As the year drew to a close, Eddie very nearly accomplished his goal of honoring the Dead Boys live, on the air. At the very end of CBS' New Year's Eve broadcast on December 31, 1992, there was just a brief snippet of Pearl Jam performing "Sonic Reducer." And then, the inevitable happened: they cut to a commercial.

When One Door Closes

As discussed in greater detail in "Chapter 10: Pearl Jam and the Rock and Roll Hall of Fame," January 12, 1993, found Eddie breaking new ground at The Rock and Roll Hall of Fame induction ceremony, when he gave the induction speech for the Doors and then put his natural baritone voice to good use by joining the surviving Doors in performing a selection of the legendary band's songs. Watching that evening's performance, one got the impression that we would be seeing more of Eddie Vedder at future induction ceremonies.

The band would later appear at the 1995 Rock and Roll Hall of Fame induction ceremony, when Eddie gave the speech For Neil Young, again in 2002 when he inducted the Ramones, and finally in 2007, when he inducted R.E.M. For a more robust discussion of those ceremonies, check out chapter nine.

The 1993 American Music Awards

Barely two weeks later, on January 25, 1993, Pearl Jam was among the honorees at the twentieth annual American Music Awards. They beat out TLC and Arrested Development for the "Favorite Pop/Rock New Artist" award, and defeated such household names as Mr. Big and Ugly Kid Joe to take home the "Favorite Heavy Metal/Hard Rock New Artist" award. The floodgates were beginning to open.

Sour Grapes at the 1996 Grammy Awards

If we were not such huge fans of the band, we might have subtitled this section "Lack of Grace Under No Pressure Whatsoever." While reluctantly accepting the Grammy for "Spin the Black Circle," which won in the Best Hard Rock Performance category, Eddie displayed an unpleasant side of his personality by first questioning the meaning of the award and then appearing to make the moment all about *him*. After mentioning that the band was just there to relax, and that he just wanted to watch the show, he telegraphed the blow to come by saying "I hate to start off with a bang. I'm going to say something typically me, on behalf of all of us. I don't know what this means; I don't think it means anything."

With Stone grinning awkwardly, looking at his feet at one point, and the audience laughing nervously, Ed continued: "That's just the way I feel. There's too many bands and you've heard it all before." Then he upped the awkwardness ante by going off on a tangent about his late biological father before finishing with, "Thanks, I guess." Ouch.

This was certainly a tough act to follow, but Stone stepped gamely to the microphone and offered an awkward moment of his own, thanking former drummer Dave Abbruzzese (who had played on the track). Stone also got in a more traditional "thank you" for all of the band's family and friends. Mike (who reacted visibly and *audibly* at Stone's mention of the long-since-fired Abbruzzese), thanked his Mom and Dad, and then—ever the team player—sent out a thank you to "the other Seattle factions," mentioning Alice in Chains specifically. The others, perhaps sensing that the moment had passed, said nothing. Jeff just took his award and walked. Jack Irons wore dark sunglasses and appeared decidedly ill at ease the entire time. Can you blame him? This was not one of Eddie's finer moments, and in later years he expressed regret for the incident.

America: A Tribute to Heroes

On September 21, 2001, the fires beneath the rubble of the World Trade Center were still burning while Eddie and Mike joined Neil Young at a CBS studio on the other side of the country. They recorded the song "Long Road" as a contribution to the *America: A Tribute to Heroes* telethon, which aired on December 4.

With *Friends* Like These

This one is more of a fun factoid than an actual televised Pearl Jam appearance. And it just goes to show you that you never know how someone is going to react until you actually ask the question that has been on your mind. In this case, the makers of the hit TV series, *Friends*, wanted to use a Pearl Jam song in their series finale. They asked, and the band agreed. We were just as surprised as you. And so it came to pass, that on May 6, 2004, "Yellow Ledbetter" was featured during a pivotal scene in the final episode of *Friends*.

A Change You Can See—and Hear

The finale of the historic, if not entirely successful, Vote for Change Tour took place on October 11, 2004, and was aired on the Sundance Channel. The broadcast provided an opportunity for the home audience to see what they had been missing, as well as some welcome publicity for the signature charity, America Coming Together (ACT).

Pearl Jam Gets a "ReAction"

On September 10, 2005, a video of Pearl Jam's September 7 Saskatoon performance of "Given to Fly" aired on multiple networks as a part of *ReAct Now: Music & Relief,* a fundraiser for the victims of Hurricane Katrina. It was not a benefit concert per se, but a collection of performances by more than fifty artists spread out at venues across North America and cobbled together into a virtual benefit concert through the magic of television editing. The proceeds, which exceeded $30 million, went toward funding the relief efforts of established charities such as the American Red Cross, the Salvation Army, and America's Second Harvest.

Later with Jools Holland

On April 25, 2006, Pearl Jam taped three songs for an episode of *Later with Jools Holland,* which would air on BBC2 the following month, on May 5, 2006. The featured songs included "World Wide Suicide," "Severed Hand," and "Alive," which by this point had become the band's signature anthem.

VH1 Storytellers

May 31, 2006, found Pearl Jam performing and recording ten songs at the Avalon in New York City (formerly the Limelight, Peter Gatien's infamous nightclub, constructed within the shell of the deconsecrated Episcopal Church of the Holy Communion) for an episode of *VH1 Storytellers.*

After a somewhat rambling introduction, during which he managed to get in a few of his traditional zings at Dick Cheney and George W. Bush, Eddie got things started with a rousing version of "Better Man." By all accounts, it was a memorable evening of music, storytelling, and a Q&A session with the assembled faithful.

The final product—heavily edited, as all of these episodes by necessity must be—eliminated several of the songs recorded during the live performance on May 31. Among the songs that did not make the cut were "Unemployable," "Sleight of Hand," "Army Reserve," and "Insignificance."

The remaining six songs and stories deemed air-worthy included the aforementioned "Better Man," "World Wide Suicide," "Gone," "Alive," a cover version/revision of the late Phil Ochs's "Here's to the State of Mississippi," and "Life Wasted." Eddie, naturally, did most of the onstage storytelling, though Stone, Mike, Matt, and Jeff each managed to get in some airtime during the interview clips that were later edited into the mix.

Among the themes that arose that evening were relationships, both good and bad, the rising toll of automobile metaphors in Pearl Jam's songs, and, of course, the War on Terror and the many shortcomings of the Bush administration. Eddie made direct references to Bruce Springsteen, Lou Reed, and the legendary folksinger Phil Ochs. Indeed, Eddie's solo rendition of "Here's to the State of Mississippi" is the longest segment of the show. Perhaps the most revelatory moment was when Eddie offered his thoughts on how the band's fans gradually helped alter the meaning of his quasi-autobiographical song "Alive," which was a healing process of sorts that "lifted the curse" and provided him with a story that he recounts to this day.

VH1 Rock Honors: The Who

On July 12, 2008, Pearl Jam joined several other bands in paying tribute to their childhood heroes, the Who. *VH1 Rock Honors* even allowed long-time Pearl Jam producer Brendan O'Brien to dust off his keyboards and get in on the act. This expanded version of Pearl Jam, featuring a dapper O'Brien and augmented by strings and horns, performed "Love, Reign O'er Me" and "The Real Me" before an enthusiastic audience. This is a wonderful performance to behold, for it shows a band that is every bit as ecstatic as their audience, and it exudes a powerful sense of joy.

Pearl Jam on the Case

Cold Case, that is. The CBS police drama once aired during the coveted Sunday prime time hours and generally enjoyed a viewership of between 10 and 15 million. One of the show's calling cards was that they would often feature episodes with soundtracks by a single, noteworthy artist. For the two-part episode that closed out season six on May 3 and 10, 2009, that artist was Pearl Jam. This earned them the distinction of being the *only* band whose music was featured exclusively in two *Cold Case* episodes. As you might imagine, it takes quite a few songs to fill two one-hour-long episodes of a television drama, so sixteen Pearl Jam originals were featured over the course of the two-part finale.

Austin City Limits

On October 3 and 4, 2009, Pearl Jam made their debut at the fabled Austin City Limits. They recorded the performance on October 3 for PBS's *Austin City Limits* television program, which was scheduled to air on November 21. The iconic show had a watershed year in 2009, as it celebrated its thirty-fifth season on the air and was recognized by the Rock and Roll Hall of Fame as being the longest running televised music program in history. Two years later, Austin City Limits was honored with the prestigious Peabody Award.

Jimmy Fallon

Jimmy Fallon has always been a music lover, and so it stands to reason that music has always been an integral part of his shows. Pearl Jam appeared on *Late Night with Jimmy Fallon* on September 8 and 9 of 2011. On September 8, they played "Olé," while old friend Cameron Crowe appeared to plug *PJ20*. Eddie was even a good enough sport to help Fallon out early in the show on one of the host's goofy comic songs, "Balls in Your Mouth." On the ninth, they returned to play "All Night," with an assist from house band, the Roots. At the end of that same month, Pearl Jam returned during "Pink Floyd Week" via video, offering a taped version of their cover of Pink Floyd's "Mother" on September 30.

It is a special thing for a band to be asked to perform on a late night television program. But for a band to be honored on a late night television program for a week straight, well, that is something on another level entirely. Shortly after the release of *Lightning Bolt*, during the week of October 21 through the 25, 2013, *Late Night with Jimmy Fallon* declared it to be Pearl Jam Week. Among the week's musical festivities were appearances by Chris Cornell with the Avett Brothers, Seattle Sub Popper Robin Pecknold, and Mike McCready with country singer Dierks Bentley and *Late Night's* legendary house band, the Roots. The honorees themselves performed on the final two nights, offering "Sirens" on the 23, and "Lightning Bolt," the title track from the recently released *Lightning Bolt* album, on the 24.

As for Mr. Fallon, let us just say that he is perhaps the most gracious and enthusiastic late night television host of all time when it comes to music. And now that he has ascended to "the big chair," hosting the *Tonight Show* since February 17, 2014, we are anticipating that Pearl Jam will be returning at some point to grace that stage as well. And when they do, you can bet we will be watching.

A Real Lollapalooza: Perry Farrell in Lolla-Land

The origins of the traveling rock and roll circus turned destination event lie with Perry Farrell, lead singer of Jane's Addiction. Farrell's original concept was for the festival to serve as Jane's Addiction's Farewell Tour. If you take into consideration that Jane's Addiction lasted from 1985 through 1991, and that the initial run of Lollapalooza lasted from 1991 through 1997, the irony is that this "farewell" lasted as long as the band itself. Longer, in fact, for Lollapalooza returned in 2003, skipped 2004 due to logistical issues, and rebooted in 2005. That 2005 reboot, which reconceptualized Lollapalooza as a destination event rather than a traveling circus, was so successful that the festival remains an annual three-day event. An additional irony is that Jane's Addiction returned, briefly, in 1997, and then again from 2001 through 2004. After another hiatus, they regrouped in 2008 and, aside from a few lineup changes, have been going strong ever since. Talk about your long goodbyes.

8

A Real Lollapalooza

Pearl Jam Joins a Traveling Rock and Roll Circus

The Second Coming of Lollapalooza

The second coming of the Perry Farrell-conceived traveling rock and roll revue proved to be the most impactful and infamous of all the incarnations that have followed. Playing nightly with the likes of the Red Hot Chili Peppers, Soundgarden, and Ice Cube fired the competitive spirit of all the performers, especially Pearl Jam, who thrived amidst the tour's youthful camaraderie. The band's nightly set poured the rockin' solid foundation that a lifetime of epic concerts has been built upon. Word began to spread quickly: this band was a must-see.

A Regular Who's *Who*?

Looking at the main stage lineup for Lollapalooza 1992 from our vantage point in 2015, most people will have one of two reactions. Either they will say, "Oh, wow!" or they will ask, "Okay, *who?*" The bold face names, such as the Red Hot Chili Peppers, Soundgarden, and, of course, Pearl Jam, jump right out at most people, giving them a sense of how this music has endured over the ensuing decades. It bears mentioning that a cursory glance at the ever-changing lineup for the side stage that year could very well garner a similar reaction. Gracing the side stage at different times during that tour were, in no particular order: Rage Against the Machine, Jim Rose Circus, Sharkbait, Archie Bell, Porno for Pyros, Basehead, Cypress Hill, House of Pain, Sweaty Nipples, Arson Garden, Seaweed, Seam, Green Magnet School, Boo-Yaa T.R.I.B.E., the Look People, Stone Temple Pilots, the Vulgar Boatmen, Truly, Skrew, Tribe, the Authority, Samba Hell, Café Tacuba Groovement, Gary Heffern with Ivan Krall, Ice T and Body Count, Luscious Jackson, Shrunken Head, Sometime Sweet Susan, Temple of the Dog, Dalai Lama, and Sweet Lizard Illtet.

Do you see what we mean? Most likely, you either asked aloud, "Seaweed?" or yelled "Cypress Hill! Cool!" Ice T and Body Count, of course, were veterans of the main stage during the first Lollapalooza in 1991, but were relegated to the side stage this time around.

The band Ministry might evoke blank stares today, but back in 1992 they were riding a wave of popularity, fueled in large part by the medium of the music video and the strength of their hit song/video, "Jesus Built My Hotrod."

By the time of Lollapalooza 1992, Ice Cube had already been out of N.W.A. for three years and had embarked on an ambitious and increasingly successful solo career, releasing his solo debut, *AmeriKKKa's Most Wanted*, in 1990, and making his big-screen film debut as the ill-fated Doughboy in John Singleton's moving coming-of-age film, *Boyz n the Hood*. But there were still many places on the concert circuit in the American heartland where Ice Cube and many of his colleagues never appeared. Enter Perry Farrell and his Lollapalooza.

While Ice Cube was busily kicking his solo career into high gear, Perry Farrell was busy launching the first Lollapalooza in 1991. Farrell's decision to book Ice-T and his band, Body Count, for that first go-around proved to be a stroke of marketing genius. Farrell had the vision and the foresight to realize that there was an audience waiting for hardcore rap in America's heartland, kids who might not

The Red Hot Chili Peppers predate Pearl Jam by the better part of a decade and played a critical role in the younger band's origin story. Suffice it to say, without getting all "butterfly effect" here, that had the Red Hot Chili Peppers never existed, there would be no Pearl Jam today. But then again you *knew* that already, didn't you?
Photofest

otherwise attend a rap concert, but who would feel comfortable seeing rap acts within the context of a packet show like Lollapalooza. As it turned out, the rap acts felt the same way, and were enthusiastic about plying their craft in front of a largely new and receptive audience. Ice T and Body Count's enthusiastic reception from the audiences at Lollapalooza 1991 paved the way for Ice Cube's solo booking for Lollapalooza 1992.

Also in the "Who?" category, the Jesus and Mary Chain hailed from Scotland and formed back in 1983, influenced by punk pioneers such as the Ramones and the Sex Pistols. By the time of Lollapalooza 1992, they were nine years into their initial sixteen-year run and had released their fourth album, *Honey's Dead*, earlier that spring. The band had a reputation for violence, drug use, and short, amphetamine-fueled sets. That reputation was cultivated, to a certain extent, by its management talking the talk, but evidence suggests that they also earned part of their reputation the old-fashioned way, by walking the walk. Their appearance on the tour was part of an effort to popularize the band in the United States, but those efforts proved largely unsuccessful. And the band, stuck in one of the earlier timeslots, was apparently miserable throughout the tour.

Finally there was the British band, Lush, whose music had been saddled by the British press with the most unfortunate-sounding sub-genre label of all time, "Shoegazing." Lush's appearance at Lollapalooza was a bit of a "boss's choice." Perry Farrell personally selected the band for the 1992 tour, which is all the validation one needed in this case. At least the members of Lush seemed to have a better time at the festival than their Celtic counterparts. These so-called "shoegazers" were usually finished with their set by two o'clock in the afternoon and could then spend the remainder of their day stargazing at the rest of the Lollapalooza 1992 lineup.

The Red Hot Chili Peppers lineup that headlined Lollapalooza 1992 featured founding members Anthony Kiedis on lead vocals and Flea on bass, along with Arik Marshall on guitar and Chad Smith on the drums.

As for our old friends, Soundgarden, they reportedly were not too thrilled about what they saw as the corporate undertones of the festival. But they soldiered on, taking the stage right after Pearl Jam and just before the headlining Red Hot Chili Peppers. At the very least, they were among friends.

Given their relative newcomer status, Pearl Jam, slotted third-to-last, had a fairly prestigious spot in the batting order. In effect, they were opening for Soundgarden and the Red Hot Chili Peppers, which made perfect sense from their perspective at the time. They were just happy to be playing music and were thrilled to be able to spend time with their friends, making music and shooting hoops.

Lollapalooza 1992 on the Road

The 1992 festival kicked off with two dates at the Shoreline Amphitheater in Mountainview, California, on July 18 and 19. Since Pearl Jam had only one album of original material under their belts at the time, their tight, typically forty-five-minute sets during the tour featured only a fraction of the variety we see in their modern-era sets. In fact, the first night's set differed from the second night's only by virtue of their opening the tour with "State of Love and Trust," and then the song order, essentially the tracks from *Ten*, gets shuffled around a bit. But most sets, apart from some carefully selected cover songs, featured some combination or other of "Deep," "Even Flow," "Why Go," "Once," "Black," "Jeremy," "Alive," and "Porch," the latter of which quickly evolved into a must-see set-closer and featured Eddie climbing, swinging from scaffolding, crowd-surfing, and stage-diving himself into a mess of welts and bruises on a nightly basis.

By the second day of the tour, Eddie, the supposedly "shy" guy from San Diego, was already delighting in displaying his antiauthoritarian side, taunting the professional photographers who had the run of the stage at the beginning of each band's set.

The third day, July 21, found the musical cara-

As much fun as it is for regular folks like us to attend festivals like Lollapalooza 1992, we assure you that it is *much* more fun for the bands. Here we see Eddie in one of his typically feisty moods, wearing the iconic brown corduroy jacket that inexplicably launched a fashion revolution, much to the chagrin of thrift store patrons everywhere.   *Photofest*

van north of the border at Thunderbird stadium in Vancouver, British Columbia, before dipping back down to Washington State the following day. At the Bremerton, Washington gig on July 22, Eddie joined Soundgarden onstage during their set to sing backup vocals (something he had already done to some critical acclaim for Chris Cornell on *Temple of the Dog*). Lest we forget to mention, the other minor detail of that day was the debut of the classic Mark Pellington "Jeremy" video on MTV, one of the more significant and life-altering events of the band's history.

After a couple of travel days, the troops headed east to the Rockies, landing at Fiddler's Green in Denver, Colorado, on July 25. The band whipped out a post-"Porch" cover of "Rockin' in the Free World" for the high altitude audience. After another travel day, Lollapalooza rolled into the Riverfront Amphitheatre in Maryland Heights, Missouri, on the twenty-seventh. There, Ed's daredevil shenanigans during "Porch" so unnerved the venue's management (to say nothing of the frayed nerves of his own band members) that they banned Pearl Jam from the place for the foreseeable future. No matter, as Missouri was merely the first stop of a grueling three straight days of musical madness.

The next day, the twenty-eighth, found them in Ohio at the Riverbend Music Center in Cincinnati, and then, as one would expect, they hit Cleveland the following day, on the twenty-ninth. Late July is typically the hottest time of the summer, and there is always a chance of thunderstorms. The Cleveland gig evidently had a little of that old Woodstock style magic. It rained during Pearl Jam's set (though the more modern sound equipment allowed the show to continue without interruption). Afterward—just as at Bethel, New York, back in August of 1969—the fields were a muddy mess, and the assembled masses, including Eddie and Chris Cornell, reveled in diving, sliding, and frolicking in the mud, much to the delight of the crowd.

After another travel day, it was off to Clarkston, Michigan, for back-to-back shows at the Pine Knob Music Theatre, as July gave way to August. And thence they traveled to the World Music Amphitheatre in Tinley Park in Eddie's home state of Illinois on August second.

The next stop on the tour was a horse of an entirely different color, as Lollapalooza pulled into the Saratoga Performing Arts Center in Saratoga Springs, New York. This August 4 gig was a mixture of rain and mayhem. As thunderstorm activity turned the venue into a mud bath, audience members broke through barriers, and either lightning or the effects of a nearby tornado managed to knock out the stage lights. Once again, the improvements in amplification equipment in the post-Woodstock era allowed the show to continue, despite the nasty weather.

Since they were already that far north, the tour then turned west and crossed the Canadian border for a gig at Molson Park in Barrie, Ontario, the very next night, August 5. A day of rest then led into back-to-back gigs at the Great Woods Center in Boston, Massachusetts on August 7 and 8. On the second night in Beantown, Pearl Jam played for a full hour and honored Aerosmith, the "Bad Boys of Boston," with a rousing cover of their early hit, "Sweet Emotion."

The next night found the caravan headed south for the first of what was supposed to be two nights at Jones Beach Amphitheatre in Wantaugh (Long Island), New York. They played the show on the ninth, opening with "Summertime Rolls," and played for nearly an hour, but the show on the eleventh got cancelled due to *rain*, of all things. East coast fans were none too pleased that Lollapalooza 1992's first rainout had to happen in New York.

New Jersey was the next stop, at Waterloo Village in Stanhope on the twelfth, where Pearl Jam turned in the first of two somewhat brief, forty-minute sets, encoring with "Rockin' in the Free World," which was already becoming their favorite cover. From there Lollapalooza dipped down south to hit Lake Fairfax Park in Reston, Virginia, on the fourteenth.

The audience was in for a genuine treat this on this night, as Chris Cornell appeared, at first, to be filling in for a missing-in-action Eddie. As if that were not crazy enough, Eddie suddenly reappeared and Pearl Jam plowed through "Once," "Why Go," and "Jeremy," leading into a rare Temple of the Dog appearance, as

Chris and Matt Cameron join them on "Hunger Strike." Not wanting to be left out of the fun, Soundgarden's Ben Shepard joined Pearl Jam on "Alive," which got everybody really amped up, jumping around and smashing instruments as if it were an old Who concert. At just forty minutes, we'll call this one short and sweet.

The next stop on the tour found Pearl Jam on a stage at the bottom of a ski slope in Scranton, Pennsylvania, on the fifteenth, at a venue known as Montage Mountain Performing Arts Center. There were hints of a possible Temple of the Dog sighting on this night, with Chris Cornell in plain sight as Pearl Jam played their set, but it was not to be. This was the first of two back-to-back Pennsylvania shows, the next night's being in Pittsburgh. The Pittsburgh set on the sixteenth featured the Who's "Baba O'Reilly," which was already beginning to gain momentum as a frequent cover song.

After that, the trail led south, with a stop in Raleigh, North Carolina, on the eighteenth, and then Lakewood Amphitheatre in Atlanta, Georgia, on the twentieth, where they covered "Baba O'Reilly" again, albeit this time with a good reason. The fact that the Who was the first band to ever play at this venue was all the excuse Pearl Jam needed to give it another whirl, and it proved to be a crowd pleaser.

The next three shows, all in Florida, found Pearl Jam about as far south and east of their hometown as one can possible get and still remain within the continental United States of America. The festivities began in Miami on the twenty-second at the Bicentennial Park Grounds. During a robust fifty-minute set, Eddie once again turned his attention toward the professional photographers and voiced his displeasure at their close proximity. Evidently, he was feeling feisty that day, because he then admonished the venue staff to turn on some hoses and get water to the crowd, before turning political and making his feelings known about the upcoming presidential elections.

The next day found Pearl Jam and their Lollapalooza brethren in Orlando for the first of two scheduled shows at separate venues. They hit the Central Florida Fairgrounds on the twenty-third and were buffeted by the winds of the encroaching Hurricane Andrew. The following day, on August 24, Lollapalooza was scheduled to roll into a place called the Edge, also located in Orlando. Hurricane Andrew apparently confused a lot of things. In fact, Pearl Jam's official website has a place marker listed for this show under their "Tours" tab, with the words, "Not sure if this show actually happened." The preponderance of evidence suggests that it did not. Happily, the tour was back on track the following day.

August 25 found Lollapalooza rolling northward to the Blockbuster Pavilion in Charlotte, North Carolina. The surprise one-time-only cover song that day was "If I Can't Have You," a Bee Gee's composition originally sung by Yvonne Elliman and the fourth single released from the celebrated *Saturday Night Fever* soundtrack in February of 1978. For the members of Pearl Jam, this was a song that had filled the radio airwaves on the cusp of their teen years.

Following a double dose of travel days, Lollapalooza headed west to St. Paul, Minneapolis, and stopped at Harriet Island on August 28. This was apparently a lively forty-five minute set, complete with guitar smashing from Stone and Mike, along with cameos from Al Jourgensen on "Why Go" and from Chris Cornell on "Jeremy." Eddie, clearly feeling curmudgeonly, devoted a great deal of his stage banter to criticizing Minneapolis. Evidently, on the band's last go-around, the fact that a hotel cigarette machine was locked after midnight caused Eddie to think of the place like a totalitarian regime, infringing upon the freedoms of its citizens. From the stage that night, he actually offered to "rescue" some of the locals with the band's tour bus after the show (though we haven't been able to determine if there were any takers).

The last show of August took place on the twenty-ninth at Alpine Valley in East Troy, Wisconsin, where the band turned in a fairly standard fifty-minute set before going off to have some fun jamming with their peers at the second stage. As August gave way to September, Lollapalooza rolled on, dipping back down south to the Lakewood Amphitheater in Atlanta, Georgia, on the first, and then down to UNO Soccer Field in New Orleans, Louisiana, on the fourth.

Then it was on to Texas. First up was the Fort Bend County Fairgrounds in Houston on the fifth, followed by the Starplex Amphitheater in Dallas on the sixth. Though the claim is belied by Pearl Jam's official website, some Pearl Jam aficionados claim that this was the show where they debuted their cover of the Dead Boys' "Sonic Reducer." The official version holds that the song debuted on the next stop of the Lollapalooza Tour, at the Desert Sky Pavilion in Phoenix Arizona, on September 8.

The Phoenix show found Eddie singing on the side stage with Chris Cornell in the middle of the afternoon, doing "Hunger Strike" and other Temple of the Dog tunes while Ice Cube commanded the main stage. Pearl Jam opened their set that night with "Sonic Reducer." The official records list this as the first time they played it live.

From there, the caravan rolled back to California. Pearl Jam spent the next two nights engaged in non-Lollapalooza related activities. There was the *MTV Video Music Awards* on the ninth, and the infamous "MTV's *Singles* Scene" fiasco on the tenth. Both of those events are covered elsewhere in this narrative, so we mention them only in passing here. By the next day, it was back to the fun and games of Lollapalooza, with a back-to-back-to-back run of shows at Irvine Meadows on the eleventh through the thirteenth. The Irvine Meadows shows were somewhat bittersweet for the participants because this three-day stand was to be the grand finale of Lollapalooza 1992. That sense of an approaching end to the tour manifested itself in the band's performances. All three shows found the band turning in frenzied sets at a blistering pace. It had become abundantly clear by this point that they were really enjoying themselves on Lollapalooza, playing short sets, jamming with their friends, and shooting hoops during their downtime. They didn't want it to end, and that sentiment was clearly shared by many of the other acts on the tour. It is a rare thing indeed in the life of a touring rock band to be able to spend quality time plying your craft while in the company of your friends and peers. Lollapalooza was like a big, traveling summer camp for the artists, who ordinarily would be off touring on their own, playing full shows in relative isolation from their peers (opening acts notwithstanding!). As if to emphasize this tacit understanding, the final show on September 13 featured

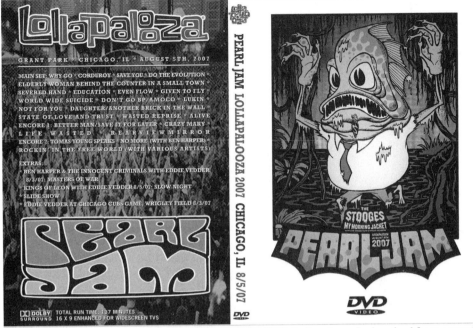

Fifteen years hence, return the conquering heroes. By 2007, Lollapalooza had evolved from a traveling rock and roll circus into a weekend-long destination event. Pearl Jam, the scrappy overachievers of 1992, returned to the Lollapalooza stage as a monumental, and well-respected, headlining act.
Author's collection

a full Temple of the Dog reunion, with all of the members of Pearl Jam and Soundgarden present and accounted for. They played "Hunger Strike" and "Reach Down" as a double-barreled encore, in front of an audience who were beginning to understand just what a big deal this was. It wouldn't happen again for another eleven years.

Lollapalooza 2007: Fifteen Years On, in "Sweet Home Chicago"

What a difference fifteen years makes. In 1992, Lollapalooza was the premiere traveling rock and roll circus, barnstorming west, east, south, north, and west again like a caravan of conquering warriors. Pearl Jam was a scrappy up-and-coming band on the cusp of international superstardom, and the world was rife with possibilities. With just two stages, a main stage and a side stage, Lollapalooza kept crowds entertained from morning through late evening, and then packed up and moved on through the night to do it all over again in another city.

Fast forward to 2007, and Lollapalooza is no longer a traveling circus. That model had fizzled out by 1997, and Lollapalooza went on hiatus for six long years, from 1998 through 2002. When Perry Farrell and his band, Jane's Addiction, tried to rekindle that old Lollapalooza magic for 2003, they were faced with the harsh reality that the nature of the music business had changed. Packet tours of this sort were no longer a viable model.

After cancelling the 2004 tour entirely, due to slow ticket sales, Lollapalooza reinvented itself for the summer of 2005 as a destination event, a la Woodstock and Watkins Glen. Instead of barnstorming across the country playing shows in different cities, Lollapalooza now pitches its tents in Chicago's Grant Park and waits for the people to come to it. Instead of the old two-stage model, there are now a plethora of corporate-sponsored stages, a development that surely would have stuck in the craws of the 1992 lineup.

The first new incarnation of Lollapalooza was held on July 23 and 24, 2005, across six stages, and featured different lineups each day. Evidently, the model proved to be successful, because for the following year, 2006, the festival grew by a third. Held on August 4–6, it was now three days long, and featured nine stages, all going at the same time. This same basic model remained in place for the following year, when Pearl Jam made their triumphant return to Lollapalooza in 2007. The festival was held over three consecutive days, August 3–5, at Grant Park in Chicago, Eddie Vedder's hometown. Nine corporate sponsored stages of activity, with eight out of the nine featuring music almost exclusively. The "main" stage in this new setup was the AT&T stage, and it was joined by the Bud Light Stage, the adidas stage, the MySpace stage (defunct since 2009, as one would imagine!), the Playstation Stage, the Citi Stage, the BMI Stage, the MOTO stage (featuring videogame competitions on Playstation), and the KIDZ stage, which ostensibly offered some entertainment for the next generation of Lollapalooza kids while their parents dusted off their flannels and got their mosh on.

Pearl Jam headlined the 2007 festival from the AT&T Stage on Sunday night, August 5. They were now the respected industry veterans they were destined to be, and already within planning distance for their upcoming twentieth anniversary. This would not be one of those blistering forty-five minute sets highlighted by Eddie leaping into the crowd from a camera boom, either. Those days were long gone by this point. This was a proper, full length Pearl Jam concert. Fast and furious had evolved into slow and steady. They played a seventeen song opening set, beginning with a blast-from-the-past, "Why Go," followed by a five-song encore and then a two-song second encore, for a total of twenty-four songs. Fittingly enough, the evening's festivities ended much as they often did in the old days, with a blistering rendition of Neil Young's "Rockin' in the Free World." It would be the last time Pearl Jam set foot on a concert stage in 2007. They wouldn't play together again for another ten months. Suffice it to say they made the most of it.

America, Chicago, and Then the Whole World

Lollapalooza has continued to enjoy a resurgence of popularity during the years since 2007, with Farrell and his partners bringing the festival and a cadre of A-list performers to Santiago, Chile; São Paulo, Brazil; and Buenos Aires, Argentina. Pearl Jam headlined the second incarnation of the São Paulo festival on March 31,

2013, and then went on to headline the festivities at the third Santiago incarnation of the festival a week later before a crowd of 70,000 on April 7, 2013.

And the Lollapalooza footprint continues to expand. As of September 12 and 13, 2015 (a month from the date of this writing), Lollapalooza will break new ground at Templehof Airport in Berlin, Germany. Lollapalooza, like Pearl Jam, continues to age gracefully.

9

Almost Famous

Eddie, Pearl Jam, and the Rock and Roll Hall of Fame

Cultural Touchstone or Mistake by the Lake?

Now well into its fourth decade of existence, the Rock and Roll Hall of Fame Foundation was the brainchild of Ahmet Ertegun, the late visionary musician, producer, and founder of Atlantic Records. Though the foundation was formed in 1983, it did not begin inducting musicians until three years later, and at this point the "Hall" remained merely a concept without a brick and mortar home. The debate over where to locate the physical plant was just the first in a series of controversies surrounding the hall that continue to this day.

As any Pearl Jam fan can tell you, music lovers are an opinionated bunch, and rarely easy to please. So when it came time to find a place to build the Rock and Roll Hall of Fame Museum, all of the usual suspects were considered: New York City, Detroit, and Memphis among them. So, why *Cleveland*, of all places, a city that even some locals half-jokingly refer to as "the mistake by the lake?" Fortunately, there is an answer to that question, and a definite method to the madness.

As it happens, the famed AM radio disc jockey, Alan Freed, hailed from Cleveland, and the city was the location for what is considered to be history's first rock and roll concert, the Moondog Coronation Ball. Freed, of course, is credited by many with coining the phrase "rock and roll," and he masterfully utilized the medium of radio to promote the spread of this new form of all-American music, not to mention providing a template for the role of rock and roll disc jockey. Freed's pioneering spirit, passion, and legacy eventually won out, and Cleveland was chosen.

It didn't hurt matters that Cleveland really needed a tourism-friendly project like this one and was willing to pony up a significant amount of money to see that it got done (we can just picture the citizens of Cooperstown, New York, nodding knowingly as people continue to flock to their Baseball Hall of Fame).

Ertegun's vision began to take shape ten years later, in June of 1993, when ground was broken on the construction site that, nearly two-and-a-half years later, became the beautiful Rock and Roll Hall of Fame that we see today, aging gracefully as it celebrates its twentieth anniversary.

Eddie Vedder, Toastmaster

So now that you know something about the Rock and Roll Hall of Fame background story, just how does a group of antiauthoritarian rockers like Pearl Jam fit into this picture? Primarily, they fit in through the person of mercurial lead singer Eddie Vedder, cast in the challenging role of public speaker, with decidedly mixed results over the years.

Rock and roll singers spend a good deal of their lives behind a microphone, staring out at an audience and conveying words and evoking emotions, but this does not automatically make them great public orators. There is a world of difference between singing a song for an appreciative audience and giving a credible speech in front of a room full of often skeptical industry bigwigs. Some singers, such as U2's Bono, are masterful public speakers, while other veterans, such as Billy Joel or Bruce Springsteen, have a natural ability to establish an easy rapport with an audience.

Pearl Jam has always been a literary-minded band, so it is fitting to see their image emblazoned here on a spiral notebook. Eddie Vedder is well known for his omnipresent notebooks, and he had one in his hands every time he strode to the podium to induct a band into the Rock and Roll Hall of Fame.

Ryan Byrne

The Doors

Eddie's induction speech for the Doors in 1993 was his first foray as toastmaster. When he approached the podium at Los Angeles' Plaza Hotel that January 12 evening—scratching his head, clad in a dark velvet jacket worn over a Cobain-esque, green, striped pullover—Vedder still had the bloom of youth upon him. With his long hair cascading past his shoulders and the residual elasticity of adolescence still informing the timbre of his speaking voice, he might have been any young rock and roll fan just discovering the brilliance of the Doors for the first time and not the lead singer of one of the world's biggest bands in his own right.

Eddie exuded an air of great humility throughout this brief speech, which, along with his "ums" and hesitant, affable stoner's delivery, seems to endear him to the assembled. With a nod to 1960s era excess, he opened with a one-liner about Ahmet (Ertegun) giving him "a couple of tabs of acid" to calm him down, which is all the proof one needed that Eddie was about as familiar with the effects of LSD as he was with the rhythms of stand-up comedy.

During the next segment of the speech, Eddie shared a series of humorous anecdotes about the creative ways in which each member of the Doors managed to avoid service in the armed forces—or, in Ray Manzarek's case, how he managed to get out of serving after he'd already enlisted—concluding that we ought to be grateful that they all remained free to create music.

88 Pearl Jam FAQ

The Doors, circa 1967. A trio of brilliant musicians often overshadowed by their iconic, mercurial lead singer. Where have we heard *that* one before? From left to right, drummer John Densmore, guitarist Robby Krieger, keyboardist Ray Manzarek, and the legendary "Lizard King" himself, Jim Morrison. *Photofest*

During the final segment of the speech, Eddie ran through the Doors' six studio albums, recorded between 1967 and 1971, and mentioned some of the standout tracks on each. While he wasn't able to fully articulate the brilliance of the Doors' music during this segment, he at least managed to convey his own sense of awe as a fan. We also love the fact that he employed the term "record" to describe the Doors' albums. These were, after all, vinyl releases originally, though many of Pearl Jam's generation no doubt first discovered the Doors on CD.

Eddie concluded in a similarly humble manner, saying that he was proud and honored to welcome and induct the Doors into the Rock and Roll Hall of Fame. Short, sweet, and to the point, the entire speech lasted under three minutes and was fairly well structured, although the delivery was a bit uneven at times. We'll give him a "B" for this first effort.

At the Helm

The performance aspect of the evening's festivities revealed that the surviving members of the Doors had hardly lost a step, musically. They were as tight and hypnotic sounding as ever and further augmented by the eclectic musician/producer Don Was on bass, adding a layer of depth to the sound. Was and Densmore provided a solid, rhythmic foundation, a worthy canvas for the artistry of Manzarek's vintage keyboards and Krieger's expressive guitar stylings. Eddie, with some fairly large shoes to fill, acquitted himself most admirably in the late Jim Morrison's stead.

The group ran through Doors' classics, "Roadhouse Blues," "Break on Through," and "Light My Fire," and all of the participants were in fine form. Even the Coltrane-ized snippets of "My Favorite Things" from *The Sound of Music*, so subtle on the album, are quite evident here during Krieger's "Light My Fire" guitar solo.

The song selection showcased the Doors at their heaviest ("Roadhouse") and most psychedelic ("Light My Fire"). Vedder, for his part, appeared to pour every ounce of his soul and energy into the vocal delivery, but only approached the front of the stage when it was actually time to sing. During the long, trippy instrumental breaks, he faded into the background, instinctively and respectfully allowing the veteran musicians their own well deserved moment in the spotlight.

Another Door Opens

In later years Vedder continued to display great humility about that night by suggesting that he was only chosen for the gig because his vocal range was very similar to Morrison's, but we suspect there was more to it than that. The remaining Doors were clearly impressed with Vedder's voice and talents, Jon Densmore in particular. In fact, the reunion that night may have planted some seeds and precipitated a tumultuous later chapter in the brilliant and tragic history of the Doors.

In fact, in *The Doors FAQ: All That's Left to Know About the Kings of Acid Rock*, author Rich Weidman cites a summer 2007 issue of *Classic Rock* magazine interview with Jon Densmore, in which the drummer says that the *only* way he would consider joining his fellow Doors' alumni on the road for a fortieth- anniversary celebration tour is if they could feature a lead singer of Vedder's caliber. Apparently, during the years following their 1993 Rock and Roll Hall of Fame induction, Ray Manzarek and Robbie Krieger got the itch to tour again and went out on the road in 2002 as the Doors of the 21st Century, with Ian Astbury of the Cult performing vocal duties. Densmore was not on board with this idea at *all*, and years of acrimony and lawsuits ensued. Densmore had clearly been struck by Vedder's singular talents, and Weidman quotes him from the *Classic Rock* piece as saying, "I'm not dissing Ian Astbury, but if you want to talk about greatness, then there's Eddie Vedder." Densmore knew greatness when he saw it; better than most. For the rest of the Doors' story, we leave you in the capable hands of Rich Weidman.

The Rock and Roll Hall of Fame Museum Rises

Two years to the day after he inducted the Doors into the Rock and Roll Hall of Fame, Eddie Vedder was once again tasked with delivering a speech at the 1995 Induction Ceremony. By this point in time we were just eight-and-a-half months away from the ribbon cutting ceremony at the Rock and Roll Hall Of Fame and Museum in Cleveland. The 1995 ceremony was also made special by the fact that it represents the twelfth anniversary of the Rock and Roll Hall of Fame Foundation and the tenth annual induction ceremony, which was held at the Waldorf Astoria in New York City. This was the year that MTV began taping the ceremonies for later broadcast rather than doing them live.

Neil Young

Eddie approached the podium like a man on a mission and raised a hand to the audience in greeting. He was wearing what appeared to be green slacks, a gray suit jacket over an orange collared shirt, and a black T-shirt.

Questionable sartorial choices aside, Eddie dove right into the speech with a Neil Young anecdote, a stoned-sounding "I can't get this thing out of my head" the only prologue. He then proceeded to tell a story about R.E.M.'s Peter Buck and Neil Young doing an interview (for which he did *not* provide the context), and the discussion was about how the recording industry had turned its back on vinyl records and analog sound in favor of the compact disc and digital sound. In the gospel of Neil, at least according to Ed, after lamenting the ascendency of digital sound, Neil went on to say that if the people who ran the Rock and Roll Hall of Fame were ever to induct him, he would "have a lot to say."

Clearly this is what Eddie was hoping for, as he continued, "So I hope Neil is feeling feisty tonight." At this point during the televised broadcast, the scene cut to a backstage shot of Neil, standing alongside Greg Allman and other honorees, watching Eddie's speech. The often-mercurial Young burst out laughing at the "feisty" remark.

Then, unexpectedly, rather than continue in his praise of the honoree, Eddie went off on a forty-second tangent about how some "smartass" had put Pearl Jam's table right next to Ticketmaster's table, and that there might be a food fight before the evening was over. A quick camera shot of his bandmates at the table revealed Jeff Ament wearing an embarrassed grin; either it was a trick of the light, or he was actually blushing.

Then Eddie turned his attention back to Neil, and the difficulties faced by Neil's assistant, Joel Bernstein, in cataloguing the artist's haphazardly labeled archival materials for possible inclusion in a boxed set. In lieu of reliably accurate dates and times, Bernstein chose to catalog the material by song title, at which point Eddie relates a humorous personal anecdote. He once accompanied Neil to those archives, but the sheer scope of the material unnerved the legend, a state of mind Eddie illustrated with a dead-on impersonation of Young freaking out, "I've gotta get out of here." The audience laughed appreciatively as Vedder noted, "I saw a man overwhelmed by his body of work."

At this point, Eddie delivers the most poignant part of his speech, relating Young's impact on Pearl Jam: "He's taught us a lot, as a band, about dignity, and commitment, and playing in the moment." Then, by way of analogy, Eddie mentions that when he hears the induction speeches for people like Frank Zappa and Janis Joplin, it makes him appreciate Young's continued presence: "I'm just really glad he's still here." And not only is Young still around, but his music remains every bit as vital as it has always been: "Some of his best songs were on his last record."

At this point, Vedder segued into his quick conclusion and maintained his sense of humor by welcoming Young as "a great songwriter, a great performer, a great Canadian." While Eddie's speech lacked in technical merits and structure, he more than made up for it with pathos; the audience could clearly sense that he was emotionally invested in his subject matter and reverential toward "Uncle Neil" Young. Young's music has had just as great an impact on us over the years as it has on Eddie, Stone, Jeff, Mike, and (at the time) Jack Irons, and it will endure long after we are gone. In that spirit, we award Eddie a B+ for the Neil Young speech.

Pearls Before Crazy Horse

After his own humble and heartfelt acceptance speech, an affable Neil Young took to the stage with Crazy Horse to perform "Act of Love." For the second number, he invited members of Pearl Jam to the stage, which precipitated an extended period of tuning up. Neil clearly wasn't comfortable engaging the audience in prolonged chatter during this process, but he certainly gave it his best shot.

In between Neil's comments, Eddie stepped up to the microphone and, ever the provocateur, asked the assembled Hall of Fame people, "Where's Pink Floyd?" (For those of you keeping score at home, Pink Floyd would not be inducted until the *following* year, in 1996. And Pearl Jam's old friend, Billy Corgan of the Smashing Pumpkins, would do the honors at the podium. We're not sure if Eddie's remarks provided the catalyst for Pink Floyd's induction or not, but at least he—along with the rest of us "Floydians"—got his wish).

While Young sorted out the moving pieces of this "Crazy Pearl Horse Jam," Eddie kicked back with his generously full wine glass, his foot resting on a drum monitor. Finally, the doubled up band (two bass guitars, three guitars, and Neil playing leads and sharing vocal duties with Eddie) launched into a spirited version of Young's "Fuckin' Up." As for Mike McCready and Jack Irons, they sat this one out. All in all, the performance was just over twenty minutes of noisy, chaotic, garage-rock fun, with the band and audience clearly enjoying the ride. And that, after all, is what it's all about.

The Ramones

Seven years and three months passed before Eddie once again ascended those steps and strode to the podium, this time to induct the Ramones into the 2002 class at the Rock and Roll Hall of Fame. The date was Monday, March 18, at the ritzy Waldorf-Astoria in New York City, a traditional New York "hangover day," coming, as it did, the day after the city's famed St. Patrick's Day Parade.

Eddie, for one, was in no danger of suffering from a hangover, as he strode purposefully toward the podium laden with an open bottle of red wine and a notebook. From the looks of things, he was going to be up there for some time. And, unfortunately, he *was*. This would not be one of his better speeches.

Eddie, with his hair shaved into a Mohawk, was clad in black pants, construction boots, a Ramones T-shirt and a black leather jacket. He looked like an ordinary punk rock fan, and not a famous rock star in his own right. We find it somewhat paradoxical that while inducting a band known for its blistering two-minute songs, Eddie decided to give his longest induction speech to date.

If you are thinking that this image looks hauntingly familiar, that's because it is. Rock and Roll Hall of Famers the Ramones once used this exact same motif on one of their own T-shirts. Imitation, it is said, is the sincerest form of flattery.   *Ryan Byrne*

Weighing in at a bloated sixteen minutes and fifty seconds, Vedder's halting and hesitant, often rambling, and frequently mumbled delivery was difficult to sit through—painful, really. He may not have been falling down drunk at the time, but the preponderance of auditory and visual evidence suggests that he was liberally buzzed and perhaps even a wee bit stoned. By about twelve minutes in, the Ramones themselves were standing up, clearly hoping to have their moment at the podium and get it over with. But Eddie was having none of it.

By turns he read from his notebook and spoke extemporaneously, but with little evidence that he had a clear structure in mind. On two occasions he paused for refreshment, swigging from the wine bottle at his feet. He regaled the audience with an anecdote about his first Ramones concert, told a strange anecdote about how he pays homage to Johnny Ramone by doing yard work at his house three times a week, accompanied by some of his fellow artists, and even half-jokingly cursed at the audience when some had the temerity to indicate that he was going on too long.

The highlight of the speech came when Eddie acknowledged the contributions of CJ Ramone, Dee-Dee's replacement, and the fact that the Hall overlooked CJ's tenure in the band, which lasted for more than 800 shows. He had CJ stand up at his table so that he could be acknowledged by the assembled, who applauded appreciatively. During the remaining minutes, Eddie took pains to single out Johnny Ramone for his friendship and mentorship. Eddie, as we have seen, always seemed to be seeking out father figures, and he was clearly in earnest about giving credit where he felt it was due. For his final anecdote, Eddie related a story he had heard from the Ramones' manager, Gary Kurfirst, about the late Joey Ramone slipping on an icy sidewalk and breaking his hip. While lying on the ground in obvious pain, Joey was extremely upset that no one stopped to help him, or even seemed to *recognize* him. For Eddie, this incident seemed to be a fitting analogy for the Ramones' career, during which they never enjoyed the respect and accolades they so richly deserved. That, he said, was part of what made this particular night so special.

And with that, finally, he welcomed the surviving Ramones up to the stage to collect their trophies and voice their thanks. Because of the inherent flaws in this speech, and with full acknowledgment of grade inflation, we give Eddie a "C" for his rhetorical efforts on this night.

The Ramones, circa 1992. From left to right, that's Dee-Dee's 1989 replacement, CJ, wrongfully overlooked by the Rock and Roll Hall of Fame; Eddie's dear friend and political polar opposite, Johnny; the one-and-only Joey, who would not live to enjoy the induction ceremony; and Marky, who replaced Tommy on the drums in 1978 and—apart from an alcohol-related hiatus from 1983 through 1987—remained with the band until they decided to call it a career in 1996.

Photofest

On Stage

Because Joey Ramone had passed away from cancer less than a year earlier on April 15, 2001, the surviving members declined to perform, but young punk rock acolytes Green Day took to the stage in their stead. Lead singer and guitarist Billy Joe Armstrong announced, simply, "We're Green Day, and we're gonna play Ramones songs." At that point, the lean, mean power trio proceeded to burn through a blistering set of Ramones classics: "Teenage Lobotomy," "Rockaway Beach," and "Blitzkrieg Bop." It was an all-out sonic assault that lasted for less than six minutes and clearly had the audience pumped up. Even legendary musician Steve "The Colonel" Cropper was standing beside his table, applauding and

smiling appreciatively. While many punk purists would dispute that this consti-
tuted a symbolic passing of the torch, it was inarguably a respectful, fitting tribute.

R.E.M.

Five years passed and, once again, Eddie Vedder was called upon to deliver an
induction speech at the 2007 Rock and Roll Hall of Fame Induction Ceremony
on March 12, his ponderous speech on behalf of the Ramones now but a distant
memory. Once again, the scene was New York City's beautiful Waldorf-Astoria,
and this time R.E.M. was the honored band.

Introduced to the throbbing strains of "Even Flow," Eddie Vedder bounded
purposefully up the stairs, a sheaf of papers in his hand. His assembled peers,
including a smiling Sammy Hagar, stood and applauded his arrival, while Eddie
gestured to the audience appreciatively in return. There was no evidence of the
omnipresent wine bottle tonight.

As the introductory music died down, Eddie began to address the crowd,
opening with a formal "Good evening." His voice, perhaps mellowed by age and
cigarettes, was deeply rich and resonant, with no remaining traces of adolescence.
The singer was wearing what appeared to be a heavy fleece shirt, over a two toned
peace sign T-shirt. He also appeared sharper and far more focused than he was at
this podium five years earlier. As if to illustrate that tonight's speech would have
some structure, Eddie started the audience off with a joke, saying that back when
he was in school, one of the greatest appeals of becoming a rock star was knowing
that you'd never have to write another paper or deliver another oral presentation.
He punctuated the line by holding aloft his sheaf of papers, much to the delight
of the crowd, many of whom laugh aloud.

Without missing a beat, Eddie said that he was "hugely honored" to be there
and then transitioned into the body of the speech. At first he celebrated R.E.M. as
a whole, likening them by way of analogy with painters before recounting their
origin story. According to the legend, vocalist Michael Stipe first met guitarist
Peter Buck at the Athens, Georgia record store where Buck was working, and the
two future bandmates enjoy a conversation about Patti Smith's early works.
R.E.M.'s rhythm section, drummer Bill Berry and multi-instrumentalist bass player
Mike Mills, enjoyed an even longer history together, attending the same school
and playing together in bands during high school, though they did not meet Stipe
and Buck until college.

Or, as Eddie put it that night in a genius stroke of elliptical editing, "The two
pairs of friends meet in college in Athens. Twenty-seven years later they're being
inducted into the Rock and Roll Hall of Fame." Then, perhaps in tacit acknowledgement of his self-indulgent Ramones speech, he asked the crowd, "You see how
I cut the middle out to make it move along?" The crowd, including the members of
R.E.M.—visible to the studio audience thanks to a backstage camera—laughed and
applauded appreciatively at the line, but Eddie still had about seven minutes left to
go. Fortunately for all concerned, it was a heartfelt and productive seven minutes.

The original R.E.M. lineup that long ago captured a young Eddie Vedder's imagination. From left to right: Mike Mills, Michael Stipe (*with* hair!), Peter Buck, and Bill Berry. The four were reunited onstage for this special night and performed for an appreciative audience.   *Photofest*

During this phase of the speech, Eddie extolled the virtues of the band members one at a time, beginning with his fellow vocalist, Michael Stipe. In perhaps his best line, delivered with a hand held to his heart for effect, Eddie said, "And I can say that, personally, there are things that I hold and feel very deeply about inside here that Michael Stipe put in there himself. This all happens without ever being able to understand a fucking thing he is saying."

The audience loved it and erupted with laughter. Backstage, the members of R.E.M. joined in. Eddie had the audience in the palm of his hand and went on to tell them about his first R.E.M. concert at a small place in Chicago during the summer of 1984. He told the audience that he went on to listen to R.E.M.'s album, *Murmur*, "twelve hundred and sixty times," listening incessantly because "I had to know what he was saying." He concluded the segment on Stipe with more poetic and effusive praise, concluding, "That's Michael; I love him."

Walking the Walk with Dewey Cox

Walk Hard: the Dewey Cox Story is a 2007 musical comedy film directed by Jake Kasdan, co-written by Judd Apatow, and starring the versatile John C. Reilly in the title role. The film is an unapologetic spoof of such biopics as 2005's *Walk the Line*, the Johnny Cash homage staring Joaquin Phoenix and Reese Witherspoon, and 2004's *Ray*, starring Jamie Foxx as the legendary piano man. Both of these films notched several prestigious nominations and awards, including several Oscars; *Walk Hard . . .* not so much.

Though Dewey's character is very Cash-like, the creators clearly delighted in throwing in character traits and story lines from the lives of a slew of other legendary music figures, too numerous to mention here. Besides, if you haven't seen it yet, why would we want to spoil the surprise?

The film was a box office disappointment, yet it garnered critical acclaim, including a Golden Globe nomination for lead actor John C. Reilly. It later made up some of its financial ground with the DVD release and has become something of a cult classic in the ensuing years.

For Pearl Jam fans, though, the star attraction is the scene where Eddie Vedder, in an extended cameo, inducts Dewey Cox into the "Lifetime Achievement Awards," an obvious parody of the Rock and Roll Hall of Fame. Eddie's induction of the mythical and fictional "Dewey Cox," a pure deadpan delivery, remains one of the most subtly hilarious moments in any rock and roll film. It also showcases a side of the Pearl Jam front man not often seen in public; the side with a sense of humor.

As for the band's guitarist, Eddie opined, "Peter Buck plays guitar like a guy who worked in a record store." The audience cheered the line, but Eddie felt the need to clarify his point further, lest it be misconstrued as a slight. Buck's playing is not "derivative" of all the music he picked up in the record store, but rather "fills in the holes" left behind by other guitar players before him, innovating and blazing a trail for alternative bands like Radiohead, Nirvana, and all who came after. Vedder rapped up Buck's tribute by saying, "From a record store in Athens to the Rock and Roll Hall of Fame is a tremendous journey."

Next, Eddie celebrated R.E.M.'s "secret weapon," Mike Mills, who was so much more than a bass player. Mills was a multi-instrumentalist who also played guitar, keyboards, piano, percussion, wrote songs, and sang a form of backup vocals that was more akin to a co-lead vocal and that added a haunting dimension of depth to R.E.M.'s music. As for Mills' visual presence, Eddie jokingly suggested that his penchant for wearing loud and wild suits may have precipitated drummer Bill Berry's near-fatal brain aneurysm, which he suffered on stage in Switzerland in the middle of a 1995 R.E.M. show. To make a long story short, Berry rejoined the band after he recovered and toughed it out until October of 1997, at which point he bought the farm. (No, really. He didn't *die*, he literally left R.E.M. to become a farmer, so Berry's presence at the induction ceremony that night was extra special, as it featured him playing music with his old friends for the first time in eight years).

Then Eddie turned serious and lauded the Swiss doctors who likely saved Berry's life following the aneurysm. He then praised Berry for urging his bandmates to continue R.E.M. without him, once he determined that his health and spirit would not allow him to continue. According to Ed, Berry told his band, "But I need to know that you will continue; I can't be the shmuck who broke up R.E.M."

Eddie, clearly a fan, suggested that even giving the band the honor of induction into the hall cannot hope to match what the band has given to the fans over the years. He then alluded to R.E.M.'s "social causes and activism," but did not go into detail. He concluded with great humility, "And by some strange power invested in me, right now, I hereby induct R.E.M. into the Rock and Roll Hall of Fame."

In qualitative terms, this 2007 speech marked a real comeback moment for Eddie, who redeemed himself admirably, half a decade removed from his Ramones debacle. His R.E.M. speech had structure, it had humor, and it was delivered, for the most part, quite skillfully. We'll award Eddie a well-deserved A-minus for this performance.

On Stage

In what was surely a treat for the audience, the four original members of R.E.M. took to the stage together for the first time in eight years, and began, as it were, with "Begin the Begin." The chemistry between the band members was still there, and musically speaking, it was as if the band had not lost a step. They went on to play "Gardening at Night," a song from their first recording, the 1982 EP, *Chronic Town*. For their third and final offering, "Man on the Moon," R.E.M. welcomed their inductor, Eddie Vedder, to the stage to share vocal duties with Michael, yet another in Vedder's apparently endless list of idols.

10

Vs.

An Album Title and a Harbinger

The Tale of the Tape

Recorded: Between March and May 1993 by Nick DiDia at Potatohead Studio in Seattle and at the Site in Nicasio, California

Produced By: Brendan O'Brien and Pearl Jam for Epic Records

Released: October 19, 1993

Singles: "Go," "Daughter," "Animal," and "Dissident"

Billboard: Debuted at number one on the *Billboard* 200 and stayed there for five weeks; a total of 950,378 copies sold that first week, sales to date: 6,010,000; certified seven times Platinum by the RIAA

Beating the "Sophomore Jinx"

The colossal commercial success of *Ten* and the accompanying cultural tidal wave of Seattle grunge chic presented Pearl Jam with a conundrum: what would they do for the proverbial encore? Would Pearl Jam, to paraphrase "Release," ride the wave where it took them, or would they veer off in a new musical direction altogether? They had already proven themselves to be worthy torchbearers for their musical idols from the 60s and 70s classic rock pantheon. Did they have another pitch in their repertoire, or would they stick primarily with their fastball? Growing increasingly uncomfortable with their meteoric rise to the status of rock idolatry, Pearl Jam would answer all of these questions with *Vs.*

Any whispers regarding Pearl Jam falling victim to a musical sophomore jinx were refuted by the release of *Vs.* in October of 1993. The album's debut at number one on the *Billboard* 200—with a record setting 950,378 copies sold in the U.S.—led to an industry-wide coronation of grunge and the coincidental "curse" of proclaiming Pearl Jam the biggest band in the world.

Their first (and only) appearance on the cover of *Time* magazine coincided with the first of their many appearances on the cover of *Rolling Stone*. The weight of their increasing popularity was just beginning to take its toll. It was simply too much, too soon, and certainly something the band had never anticipated or even imagined.

Eddie, let us not forget, began this adventure fully steeped in the whole punk rock ethos of independence. He had always envisioned himself driving around to

Fugazi: The DIY Guys

Let's start with that name, "Fugazi." Hardcore progressive rock fans know that the British band Marillion released an album and a song with that title back in 1984 but most likely came away thinking that "Fugazi" simply meant: "messed up." But "Fugazi" is etymologically an acronym dating back to Vietnam era American military slang. In that context, "Fugazi" stood for: "fucked up, got ambushed, zipped in," a succinct narrative describing the fate suffered by the fallen soldiers zipped into the piles of body bags awaiting transport home.

The macabre name aside, Pearl Jam, and Eddie Vedder in particular, held the band Fugazi in high regard because they were proactive, roll-up-your-sleeves guys who liked to handle as much of the band's business internally as they possibly could. In other words, they took a DIY, or "do it yourself," approach to the music business. The Washington, D.C.-based four piece formed in 1986 and began playing shows in 1987, which means that they predated Pearl Jam by roughly five years. The classic lineup consisted of Ian MacKaye on guitar and vocals; Guy Picciotto, also on guitar and vocals; Joe Lally on vocals and bass; and Brendan Canty on the drums. From 1990's *Repeater* through 2001's *The Argument*, Fugazi cranked out six albums in eleven years. Part of Pearl Jam's fascination with Fugazi was undoubtedly due to their own desire to be a small-scale punk band and knowing they could never go back there again. What Eddie wouldn't have given to be able to drive around in Fugazi's tour van for the rest of his career. But wistful longings for simpler times aside, Pearl Jam respected Fugazi for their ethical stances against overcharging fans for concert tickets—a theme which would resonate with Pearl Jam later on, during their fruitless war against Ticketmaster—and their disdain for violent slam dancing in "the pit." For these and a variety of other reasons, Pearl Jam looked to Fugazi as an ethically sound model for how a professional rock and roll band should conduct its business. While the enormous scale of Pearl Jam's operations prevented them from being able to follow in Fugazi's footsteps precisely, they did internalize many of the older band's lessons and applied them wherever it was feasible to do so. But sadly, all mentorships are finite in nature. Following the end of their 2002 UK fall tour, Fugazi went on what they termed an "indefinite hiatus." They have not returned since, though rumors of an impending reunion continue to abound.

gigs in a van, surfing during his downtime, and stapling his own Xeroxed promotional posters to telephone poles to alert the fans about upcoming gigs, like DIY pioneers, Fugazi.

That adolescent vision of the ideal rock and roll lifestyle bore little or no resemblance to the exploding international superstardom that enveloped Pearl Jam. By the time the band entered the studio to begin work on their follow-up to *Ten*, the storm outside was just beginning to gather strength. Quite understandably, the boys were finding it difficult to cope.

Into the Studio

Studio rehearsals for *Vs.* began on the proverbial home court—Potatohead Studios in Seattle, Washington—in February of 1993 and continued throughout the month. But that homestand would prove to be merely a warm-up session for a road trip south.

The first move to record the follow-up to *Ten* was to leave the madness of Seattle behind. In March of 1993 the band relocated to San Rafael, California, which was home of the Site, a state-of-the-art studio. This was the big time, for sure. The facility lacked for no amenities, offering the atmosphere of a luxury resort. The band members all seemed to embrace the relaxed environment of the Site, although there was one notable exception: its enigmatic lead singer.

Eddie Vedder was incapable of wrapping himself around the creative process at hand under these cushy conditions. He began to literally retreat from the scene by sleeping in his truck or a claustrophobic sauna room while frequently escaping to San Francisco some thirty miles away to talk to random people on the streets. Perhaps, on some level, Eddie sensed that his days of being able to do things of this nature were growing numbered. But despite the challenges the band members faced, all of the obstacles were eventually overcome. The process worked, thanks in part to the considerable influence of a new creative voice.

The Red Hot Chili Peppers had introduced Pearl Jam to producer Brendan O'Brien during the legendary Lollapalooza 1992 caravan, and now they were scheduled to work with him for the first time. O'Brien's work with the Black Crowes had particularly impressed both Jeff and Stone. O'Brien had been given a one-day "tryout" at his home studio in Atlanta, passed the test, and made the Pearl Jam team. O'Brien, in effect, became the band's musical coach, structuring the days along the lines of a team training camp, complete with meetings in the morning, softball games in the afternoon, and recording time later in the day/evening.

O'Brien favored the approach of developing each song as a separate entity. With Vedder feeling stifled by the luxurious surroundings, the system began to break down. Jeff talked about how, over a period of ten days, the band had as many as fifteen different song ideas, but Eddie was still working on lyrics for the fourth or fifth one. Eddie's creativity was suffering at the Site, and he felt the need to withdraw to places that better served his muse.

The final product was a clear reflection of the album's title. The band felt they were at war, versus the music industry and its star-maker machinery that had anointed Eddie a "voice of his generation," along with his doomed Seattle counterpart, Kurt Cobain of Nirvana. And soon enough it would be Pearl Jam versus Ticketmaster and its monopolistic control of the concert ticket business.

Now, with only six months of post-*Ten* experience to draw on for its sophomore effort, Pearl Jam produced a much more aggressive, raw-edged sounding album. The overall result is a less anthemic, more authentic live sound. Instead of a follow-up flop, *Vs.* became a record-setting album, selling an astounding 950,378 copies during its first week in October 1993 (more copies than the other nine records *combined* that followed it on the *Billboard* Top 10). The commercial success of the album resulted in Pearl Jam establishing a new policy of limited interviews, television appearances, and no videos on the heels of capturing four MTV Video Music Awards for "Jeremy" in 1993.

Now with Dave Abbruzzese on drums, the O'Brien system of creating one song at a time allowed the band to flex their collective, creative muscles. This approach suited the band much better and helped facilitate the recording process. The band

Sophomore jinx? *What* sophomore jinx? *Vs.*, Pearl Jam's eagerly awaited follow-up to *Ten*, proved to be one of the best-selling (and fastest-selling) albums of all time. The second single, "Daughter," remains a perennial favorite.   *Author's collection*

simply sounded more like a band, a byproduct of gaining cohesion in the time honored tradition of simply playing live. The road, though taxing, had been very good to Pearl Jam and helped them to establish their musical identity.

The Tunes

The first session week produced "Go," "Blood," "Rats," and "Leash" before the proceedings slowed down to a more modest pace. The final product spanned the rock and roll gambit: hard rock, punk rock, acoustic ballads, and a little funk thrown in for good measure.

"Go"

The first single, "Go"—Grammy nominated for Best Hard Rock Performance— surges forward, bolstered by Jeff's punk bass line. The piercing guitar riff by Stone, coupled with Mike's stinging solo—after which he reportedly hurled his guitar to the ground after the keeper take—provide the musical backdrop for a song that evolved from describing a stalled car to an abusive relationship: as was the case with "Once," "Go" opens the record in attack mode. The immediate impact of Abbruzzese is felt, not only regarding his staccato drumming, but also in his coming up with the lynchpin guitar riff. It was a welcome revelation to learn that the young Texan was a multi-instrumentalist.

"Animal"

"Animal" evolved from an instrumental demo that dated back to the 1990 originals that formed the core of *Ten*. The album's third single mentions the album's original proposed title, "Five Against One," which actually appeared on some cassettes that had been pressed early. Lyrically the tables are turned from the opener: the narrator going from the abuser to the victim.

"Daughter"

Pearl Jam then follows the propulsive musical combination punch that opens the album with an acoustic ballad. "Daughter" takes the listener inside yet another form of abuse, this time involving a parent and child.

With Jeff playing upright bass and Mike's haunting solo, Vedder depicts a tale of a learning disability and its distorted perception. The second single from the record, "Daughter" remains one the band's most recognizable, signature songs. When played live it is often "tagged" with an excerpt from another song. For example, Dead Moon's "It's Okay" is a personal and preferred Pearl Jam fan favorite "Daughter tag."

"Glorified G"

The origin of "Glorified G" was a conversation during the recording sessions between Ed and the new drummer, Dave Abbruzzese. Abbruzzese revealed that he had purchased guns (a revelation that many believe to be at the heart of a personality conflict between the two). Hailing from Texas, where the gun culture is very prominent, Abbruzzese assured his bandmates that what he owned were "glorified versions of pellet guns," not AK47's. Nevertheless, the song became a vehicle for Vedder to make a political statement regarding guns, enhanced musically by a funky Stone guitar riff and a jangly country strummed line from Mike. As for the dynamic between Ed and Dave, it remains a source of speculation to this day, and is a story for another time, in any case.

"Dissident"

"Dissident" takes on a different form of betrayal. A woman takes in a political fugitive, but in the end, she turns him in to the authorities. As a result of her betrayal, she is overwhelmed by feelings of guilt that consume her. Her life is now devoid of meaning. "Dissident" became the album's fourth single.

"W.M.A."

Racism is the subject of "W.M.A." which stands for "white male American." With a two-measure drum track looped throughout the song and a number of other percussion elements added to a rock steady Ament bass line, Ed provides a personal story of hanging outside the rehearsal studio with a black friend. Upon witnessing him being harassed by the police, an angered Vedder returned to the studio and recorded the vocal track. The liner notes of the album include a photograph of Malice Green, a Detroit man who died while in police custody—a scenario that remains all too familiar two decades later.

"Blood"

"Blood" provides a scathing indictment of the media (another topic that continues to resonate today) and its voracious, destructive excesses. Ed addresses the creation of his personal cult status in no uncertain terms, taking ownership of the situation with his lyrics. This is not the sarcastic, tongue-in-cheek query of the Rolling Stones' "It's Only Rock n' Roll (But I Like It)" two decades earlier, in which Mick Jagger wonders aloud whether his blood spilled all over the stage would be enough to satisfy the voracious appetites of the fans and media. By Pearl Jam's time, things had clearly changed, and in our current age of social media, the stakes, particularly for public figures, have been exponentially raised. Eddie is not so much concerned with the fans here, as he is with the relentless attention of the press. The lyrical imagery of needles stabbing down into the printed pages is vivid, and the fact that he refers to himself in the third person twice indicates his feeling that he is the focal point for all of the press' bloodletting. The press is a relentless, devouring circus, sucking the life out the reluctant icon bleeding for his craft.

"Rearviewmirror"

"Rearviewmirror" is an all-Ed effort, both musically and lyrically. One of the first songs he wrote on guitar, "RVM" is a cathartic song of escape that gains momentum amidst swirling guitars and an incendiary drum track. Again, the escape appears to be from physical abuse. The final song produced for the album was an indication of Vedder's desire to escape from the recording environment at the Site that had made him so uncomfortable. Evidently, he was not the only one. If you listen attentively, at the end of the track you can actually hear Abbruzzese throw his drumsticks against the wall. Under intense pressure from "Coach" O'Brien, he then reportedly punched a hole in his snare drum and hurled it off the side of a cliff outside the studio. Temper, temper, Dave.

"Rats"

A whimsical, yet ever biting Vedder offers that "Rats" may be "a lot more admirable" than humans in their socialization, and the much-maligned rodent provides him with an ideal vantage point from which to be critical of humanity. Musically, the song provides a nice, deep dose of funk, in the spirit of their patrons, the Red Hot Chili Peppers. Finally, in a clever bit of cross-generational intertextuality, the lyrics end with a winking nod to Michael Jackson's hit "Ben," the titular track from the corresponding movie soundtrack. There are some who will persist in considering "Rats" to be merely a "filler" song, but we maintain that there is a good deal of substance here.

"Elderly Woman Behind the Counter in a Small Town"

"Elderly Woman Behind the Counter in a Small Town" is another all-Ed effort, and it represents a dramatic departure from Pearl Jam's penchant for one-word song titles. Vedder wrote the song in a small room he occupied outside of the main house where the band lived during the recording of *Vs.* Falling together musically

The Surf Punk Meets the Godfather

There was never any doubt about Eddie's favorite band. Long before he became a rock icon, he was a passionate fan. Of all his influences, the Who stood alone atop his rock and roll Olympus. During interviews, Vedder often describes how Townshend's music touched him on a personal level. His oft-cited remark that he should have been sending Townshend Father's Day cards was an expression of raw emotion. As Pearl Jam's star ascended, it was only a matter of time before Eddie met his idol.

On August 3, 1993, while performing in support of his album, *Psychoderelict*, Townshend put the word out that he wanted to meet Vedder. Spotting Eddie in the crowd, Pete paused in the middle of "Rough Boys" to acknowledge him. Backstage, Ed confided his trepidation concerning his sudden celebrity to the man he once described as the "most important person to me musically, and probably in other ways, too." Pete assured Ed that fame had chosen him, and not the other way around. Those words—coming from a source that Vedder implicitly trusted—must have resonated, because Vedder didn't "run off to Hawaii and become a bum on the beach" as Townshend speculated he might!

Ed played with Pete for the first time on August 16, 1998, at the Maryville Academy benefit at the House of Blues in Chicago. They performed Townshend and Ronnie Lane's, "Heart to Hang Onto," along with the Who's "Magic Bus" and "Tattoo." Thus began a long association that often coincides with the Teenage Cancer Trust Benefit at the Royal Albert Hall in London. During the 2010 benefit, Ed, the "surf punk," got to play "the godfather" during the Who's full-blown performance of *Quadrophenia*, an album that Vedder considered to be a reference point for his life.

Kindred spirits a generation apart, Ed's approach to music aspires to Townshend's. As Vedder noted in an essay for *Rolling Stone*'s 100 Greatest Artists, Townshend "demanded that there be spiritual value in music" and that he "happened to be on a quest for reason and harmony in his life." During a 2009 interview with *Uncut* magazine, Vedder reflected:

If it weren't for people like Pete, rock musicians might not write music that's as forthcoming as it is. Pete was one of the first rock song writers who realized that pain can sometimes be the best art—when you as a listener share in that pain you realize that you're not the only one.

It would be impossible to overemphasize the importance of the Who, and Pete Townshend in particular, for the development of Eddie Vedder as a songwriter. The Who's 1973 album, *Quadrophenia*, must be considered one of the founding texts in Pearl Jam's own creation myth. From left to right: Roger Daltrey, Keith Moon, Pete Townshend, and John Entwistle.   *Photofest*

in about "twenty minutes," according to Ed, the acoustic song took on a waltzing melody. The song tells a story of an aging woman who recognizes an old flame who had moved on, became successful, and then returned to the small town. She is too self-conscious to acknowledge her long lost lover, embarrassed, perhaps, that she remained behind in their hometown and never really achieved anything. She doesn't say anything, and the opportunity to reconnect with him passes her by. The song, arguably one of Pearl Jam's most beautiful, has long been a concert favorite, and the Pearl Jam crowd often takes over the vocals in a sing-along, much to Vedder's delight.

"Leash"

"Leash" is a song that disappeared from the Pearl Jam concert set lists for some twelve years and remains a live rarity. The song is yet another commentary on Eddie's resistance to becoming a role model or leader, much like Dylan before him, who kept the folk music community that had nurtured him firmly at arms' length, alienating many people in the process. The song rocks hard in an attempt to offer a sense of unity or equality between the band and its fans. No, I'm not some media-created "Voice of a Generation," Ed seems to be saying; I'm not bought, sold, or enslaved. Wishful thinking on his part, you say? Perhaps. But his lyrics and his actions from this period reveal a young man who is clearly very uncomfortable with any suggestion that he is somehow a role model.

"Indifference"

The album closes with the stripped down, smoldering "Indifference." The contrast between the lyrical push and the musical pull encapsulates the band's state of turmoil at the time with their resolve firmly in place.

Support Tours

Pearl Jam's fall tour of the United States in support of *Vs.* concentrated on the West Coast. In a foreshadowing of the coming war with Ticketmaster, the band insisted that there be an $18 cap on ticket prices during this tour. As ever, the goal was twofold: to thwart the efforts of scalpers to get ahold of all the really good seats, and, of course, to allow the fans greater access to the band's performances. Unfortunately, if history teaches us anything, it is that you cannot stop ticket scalping. Perhaps in the future, emerging technologies will help to solve the problem, but back the early 1990s it was just a fact of life, and Pearl Jam was attempting to deal with it in the best way they knew how. Whatever their motivation may have been, Pearl Jam's insistence on an $18 price cap annoyed the hell out of concert promoters, venues, and Ticketmaster, who knew the band could easily command three times that price and still sell out all of their shows. By that mathematical reckoning, the two legs of the *Vs.* Tour earned about $2 million less than they could have. But Pearl Jam persisted in their belief that the fans' economic interests trumped those of everyone else, despite the protestations of all the other factions in the concert promotion world.

Fall 1993: West Coast

They kicked off the tour with a pair of warm-up gigs: one on the home court at The Showbox in Seattle on October 25, followed by a gig at the Catalyst in Santa Cruz on the twenty-seventh. The "official" first leg of the tour began at the Warfield Theatre in San Francisco on the twenty-eighth and led the band through a total of twenty-seven shows. Among the highlights of this run were a Halloween show at the Greek Theatre in Los Angeles and a November 4 stop at the fabled Whisky a Go Go in West Hollywood. The tour culminated in a three-day blowout at the

Seattle Center on December 7–9. It would be three months before the band hit the stage again.

Spring 1994: East Coast

There were no "warm-up" gigs this time around. The band jumped right back in with a double dose at Denver, Colorado's Paramount Theatre on March 6 and 7, before diving down to the shores of the Gulf of Mexico in Pensacola, Florida. All told, this leg of the tour would consist of twenty-five shows in nineteen cities, and Pearl Jam was logging a lot of air miles along the way. For reasons that are not entirely clear, New York City got the short end of the stick on this leg of the door. There was only one show, at the Paramount Theater on April 17. As rock fans and locals know, the Paramount used to be called the Felt Forum and is now called the WaMu Theater at Madison Square Garden. But the name isn't the issue. The issue is that it seats fewer people than Radio City Music Hall.

Summer 1994: Cancelled!

That's right, cancelled. There was supposed to be a summer 1994 leg of the continuing tour to support *Vs.*, but while the aforementioned Spring leg of the tour was taking place, a lot of things in Pearl Jam's world changed, and not for the better. In March, in Chicago of all places, the band first discovered that Ticketmaster was tacking "Service Charges" onto their base ticket prices. This discovery kicked off a series of events (chronicled in the next chapter) that would alter the course of the band's history forever. Also, as we will explore later, a lot of the studio sessions for the next album, *Vitalogy*, were taking place in between shows on the *Vs.* Tour, and it was becoming increasingly clear to the band, particularly Eddie and Jeff, that the drummer situation with Dave Abbruzzese had become unsustainable; a change would have to be made. But the real catalyst for change, the event that really knocked Pearl Jam for a loop, was the death by suicide of Kurt Cobain, on or around April 5. From the band's perspective, it was starting to feel like it really was Pearl Jam vs. the world, and the war on several fronts was just beginning.

Not for You

The Ticketmaster War

A Drop in the Bucket at a Drop in the Park

Unbeknownst to most fans, the opening salvos of what would become an all-out war with Ticketmaster were fired early on in the band's career, during their preparations for the "free" Seattle concert known as A Drop in the Park. As discussed elsewhere in this narrative, the city of Seattle had given the band a hard time with their plans to put on this free concert, denying them permits and even forcing the cancellation of an earlier incarnation of the show scheduled for the Gas Works Park in May 1992.

Though noble and civic-minded, in the spirit of the Grateful Dead's frequent and clandestine free shows in San Francisco's Golden Gate Park decades earlier, Pearl Jam's efforts were more organized and driven by more than one motivation. They wanted to reward the hometown fans for their support by putting on a free show with a roster of like-minded bands, but they also wanted to register people to vote in the hopes that they would do so during the upcoming election cycle (and preferably *against* George W. Bush).

Finally, after all of the proverbial hoops had been jumped through, the city of Seattle awarded them permits to stage the show at Warren G. Magnuson Park on September 20, 1992. Pearl Jam was to foot the bill for the show, estimated at about $125,000 (which was already close to the *entire* payroll for all of the acts who performed at Woodstock). But, because of security concerns, the show could not be a "come-all-ye" type of affair. The city insisted that attendance be limited to 30,000 fans and that tickets be distributed for the event.

Pearl Jam approached Ticketmaster to distribute the tickets. When Ticketmaster informed the band that they expected a service charge of $1.50 per ticket for their efforts, adding $45,000 to Pearl Jam's expenses, the band balked. In all fairness, if the band, in their naiveté, were somehow expecting Ticketmaster to offer their services free of charge, that would have been an act of purest optimism on their part. Such altruism is rare among large corporations. There is no such thing as a "free" concert; somebody always has to pay the bills, and in this case it was Pearl Jam, local heroes and would-be electoral kingmakers. The band maintains that they expected Ticketmaster to be compensated for their work, but they disagreed with the notion that said compensation should amount to $1.50 per ticket.

It does beg the question of where Pearl Jam gained their notions about the economics and logistics of ticket printing and distribution, and that question will remain relevant throughout this discussion. Eventually, they worked out a deal with Seattle city officials to distribute the tickets and used the local radio stations to help spread the word on where fans could find them, but the incident with Ticketmaster had left a bad taste in their mouths. As it turned out, this was merely the first of several scenarios wherein Pearl Jam and Ticketmaster failed to see things eye to eye.

The Bucks Stop Here

Before we delve deeper into the specifics of the following case, it is important for us to remember that during the planning stages of the *Vs.* Tour, Pearl Jam insisted, much to the chagrin of everyone in the concert promoting world, that their base ticket prices be capped at $18, a rate that was well below the market average at that time, particularly for a band as hot as Pearl Jam was during the early 1990s. Though their hearts may have been in the right place when they set this price cap, the fact that they leveraged their popularity in this manner had ramifications that would come back to haunt them down the road. For a time, it would drive them off the road entirely.

Business and Scholarships Don't Mix

During the first leg of the *Vs.* Tour, the one that concentrated most of the band's efforts on the western half of the country, Pearl Jam planned to wrap up the festivities with a three-day run at the Seattle Center Arena on December 7–9, 1993, with part of the proceeds from ticket sales going to benefit the Seattle Academy of Arts and Sciences.

Their idea was for the Academy to use those funds for merit-based scholarships that would cover the cost of tuition for two lucky students to attend the prestigious Northwest School (of which Stone Gossard was an alumnus). Pearl Jam would put up $20,000 from their take, and, at least according to their manager, Kelly Curtis, Ticketmaster's local representative agreed to provide matching

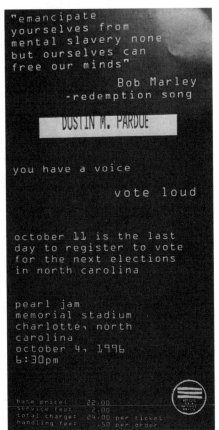

Operating for several years outside the realm of Ticketmaster, Pearl Jam added a personal touch to its own concert tickets. This one, printed expressly for the use of professional rock and roll photographer and author Dustin Pardue, features a familiar Bob Marley quote and a friendly reminder about voter registration, and, as you can see, all of the charges are clearly itemized.   *Dustin Pardue*

funds in the same amount, taken from their $3.50 per ticket service charge (or roughly $1.00 per ticket), or however Ticketmaster saw fit to package the $20,000. Evidently, someone hadn't gotten the memo.

Just before the tickets were scheduled to go on sale, Kelly Curtis got a phone call from none other than Fred Rosen, the CEO of Ticketmaster, who had a slightly different perspective on the arrangement Curtis had made with his company's local representative. So different, in fact, that Rosen was now calling to put the kibosh on the entire deal. It turned out that the local representative had never received official clearance to offer Pearl Jam those matching funds, so Rosen called to renegotiate the deal in the eleventh hour. He initially insisted that the service charge be jacked up to $4.50 per ticket, in order to cover the cost of the "charitable donation."

Predictably, when the band heard the news, they were, for lack of a better term, pissed off. So much so, in fact, that their initial gut reaction was to have Curtis pull the plug and tell Rosen to cancel the shows altogether. But cooler heads prevailed . . . somewhat. Curtis and Rosen got on the phone, and over the course of an hour they hashed out a Plan B, in which Ticketmaster agreed to pony up $14,000 for the charity, and lower their service charge to $3.25 from the original $3.50.

The tickets went on sale, and the shows went on as planned, but the charity only received $34,000, instead of the original target amount of $40,000. Evidently Fred Rosen drives a hard bargain. No word on whether the local Ticketmaster rep was fired for overstepping his bounds, but we can bet he was at least called on the carpet by Rosen. Apparently, even Kelly Curtis was taken aback by the ruthlessness of Rosen's negotiations. Like the band he represented, Curtis was beginning to learn that big corporations like Ticketmaster are not in the charity business. The experience was an eye-opener for band and manager alike, but more drama lay ahead for the second leg of the tour, during the spring of 1994.

More Hot Air Blowing in the Windy City

After three months off the road, the *Vs.* Tour reconvened for the Spring, 1994 leg of the tour. This time, they kicked things off on March 6 with a pair of shows in Denver, Colorado, perhaps to make up for the November 28 show that was cancelled in Boulder during the last leg. After a quick stop in Pensacola, Florida, Pearl Jam headed to Eddie's hometown in Chicago, Illinois, for two shows.

One show was scheduled for the general public on March 10 at Chicago Stadium, which was in the midst of its final season as the home of the NBA's Chicago Bulls and the NHL's Chicago Blackhawks. The other show was scheduled for March 13 at the New Regal Theater, a small venue with a seating capacity of only 2,250. This show was booked exclusively for members of Pearl Jam's loyal fan club, the Ten Club.

This time around, the band's issue with Ticketmaster had to do with their imposing a $3.75 service charge on top of Pearl Jam's base price of $18. You will note that the price of the service charge was now a quarter higher than it had originally been during the Seattle showdown back in December. One does have to wonder if this price hike was Ticketmaster's way of recouping the revenue they lost after they lowered their service charge to $3.25 for the Seattle shows, or just a not-so subtle "F U" to the band.

At the band members' behest, Curtis got ahold of Ticketmaster's general manager in Chicago and negotiated a deal wherein Ticketmaster agreed to clearly identify, on the printed tickets, their service charges as being a separate fee from the base price of the tickets. The general manager agreed to those terms, but then reneged on the deal just before the tickets were scheduled to go on sale. This precipitated yet another round of posturing, with Pearl Jam threatening to cancel the show and take their business elsewhere. Finally, albeit begrudgingly, Ticketmaster agreed to print the itemized tickets the way Pearl Jam had asked them to, but thereafter they drew a line in the sand. This was a one-time favor, as far as Ticketmaster was concerned, and Pearl Jam should not expect such a concession for future bookings.

Dirty Business in the Motor City

Pearl Jam decided to get cute with their March 19 show, scheduled for Detroit's Masonic Theater. They decided they would hold a ticket lottery, and then distribute their own tickets through their fan club (another play taken directly from the Grateful Dead's playbook). In this manner, they would bypass Ticketmaster altogether, and everyone would be happy, right? Wrong.

Their actions resulted in Ticketmaster sending a cease and desist letter to the concert promoter. They threatened the promoter with legal action for violating what they saw as their exclusive agreement to sell tickets for the venue. Straining credulity, but according to Pearl Jam's prepared statement for Congress, Ticketmaster somehow hacked into the promoter's ticket machine, disabling it, and effectively shut down his whole operation.

A Small Venue in the Big Apple

A month later, Pearl Jam figured they'd try their luck with another attempt at an end-run around Ticketmaster, with predictable results. A show was scheduled for April 17 at the Paramount Theater, which, as locals and concert aficionados can tell you, is a smaller venue located directly below the main venue at Madison Square Garden in the same building (if you've ever wondered why you needed to take an endless series of escalators up to your seating level at MSG, even when you had "good seats," now you know why). It was also the last scheduled stop on the spring 1994 leg of the *Vs.* Tour, so they figured they had nothing to lose by trying. Pearl Jam arranged for tickets to be sold through the Paramount Theater box office, and then proceeded to publicize this fact through promotions on the local radio stations.

Here again, just as with the Detroit case, Ticketmaster saw these actions as being in violation of their exclusive agreement with the venue, and they threatened the Paramount Theater with legal action. Pearl Jam, for their part, considered

LONG ROAD
CORDUROY
GRIEVANCE
GOD'S DICE
HAIL   HAIL
NUTHING AS IT SEEMS
    GIVEN TO FLY
    EVEN FLOW
        MFC
    WISHLIST
OFF HE GOES
DAUGHTER/ IT'S OK
    BETTER MAN
    (THIN AIR)
INSIGNIFICANCE
    RVM
    BLACK
    PORCH
    ?   ?

Speaking of the personal touch, hand-written set lists have long been a staple of Pearl Jam's live performances, and they've become a coveted collectible among fans. This one, from the personal collection of frequent Pearl Jam photographer Dustin Pardue, features question marks after "Porch," leaving the encore open to a world of possibilities.   *Dustin Pardue*

their own actions to be merely a means of "experimenting with these alternative distribution arrangements," as they later pointed out in their statement to Congress.

Now Is the Summer of Our Discontent

In the wake of the first two legs of the *Vs.* Tour, Pearl Jam was not happy with what they perceived to be manipulative and threatening practices by Ticketmaster. Whenever they tried to make one of their "end runs" around them, Ticketmaster would respond by going after their booking agent or by threatening the venues and promoters with legal action. Basically, the impression Pearl Jam got was that Ticketmaster was a bully, threatening to run everyone out of the business who didn't play by its rules.

So, predictably, while planning for that coming summer's coast-to-coast American tour, Pearl Jam decided that instead of backing down and playing things Ticketmaster's way, they would instead up the ante and make the negotiations even *more* difficult. Pearl Jam, still insistent upon maintaining their $18 per ticket cap price, further insisted that any service charges levied by Ticketmaster be capped at 10 percent of the base price, effectively keeping their ticket prices at under twenty dollars (not counting taxes, of course!).

Ticketmaster flat out refused to do business on those terms, and went after Pearl Jam at the concert promoter level, telling promoters that Pearl Jam's moves were a detriment to the business for all parties concerned, and that they shouldn't have dealings with them. Later on, in their congressional testimony, Pearl Jam cited a memo from Ben Liss, then head of the North American Concert Promoters Association, telling his members that Ticketmaster meant business:

> Ticketmaster has indicated to me that they will aggressively enforce their contracts with promoters and facilities. Ticketmaster's stance is that they have been loyal to their partners in this business and they hope and expect their partners will reciprocate.

Nothing subtle about the meaning behind that message, is there? But, wait, there's more. The following day, the membership received an updated memo from Liss, this time citing Ticketmaster CEO Fred Rosen and his views on the Pearl Jam situation explicitly. The bottom line was that Ticketmaster wasn't going to be content with a mere slice of the pie. They weren't going to do the legwork to sell a portion of the tickets for a given venue while Pearl Jam distributed the rest any way it saw fit. This was an all-or-nothing proposition. The concerned parties had clearly reached an impasse. Pearl Jam was faced with two choices: either go along with the Ticketmaster program, or don't tour at all. They chose the latter. There would be no summer tour in 1994. Instead of working on an itinerary of concert venues, they would put their efforts into a lawsuit instead.

We would like to make it clear that the Department of Justice had already been conducting an investigation of Ticketmaster's practices during this time and that they had invited and even encouraged the Pearl Jam camp to file a memorandum. Ever since Ticketmaster's 1991 acquisition of its largest competitor, Ticketron, they had been concerned about an apparent monopoly. Pearl Jam's issues with the company provided the perfect opportunity to put those ideas to the test. Much that has been written about this incident tends to sublimate the fact that it was the Department of Justice who first reached out to Pearl Jam and encouraged them to file the memorandum. This wasn't simply a case of a disgruntled band suing Ticketmaster. In essence, this would be a test case. Think of it as the music business equivalent of the 1925 Scopes Monkey Trial, only this was a hearing and not a trial.

Toward that end, and in accordance with the testimony they later gave before Congress, Pearl Jam's "attorneys at Sullivan & Cromwell filed a memorandum with the Antitrust Division of the Department of Justice." In that memorandum, the band laid out for the DOJ the actions that Ticketmaster had been taking to interfere with Pearl Jam's rights to dictate ticket prices and terms. Implicit in the language of their memorandum was Pearl Jam's firm belief that they and they *alone* maintained exclusive rights in determining the prices and terms for tickets sold to their concerts. But was this really the case?

Jeff and Stone Address Congress

Eventually, the publicity surrounding Pearl Jam's battle with Ticketmaster led to the halls of Congress, and on June 30, 1994, Jeff and Stone were summoned to testify before the Information, Justice, Transportation, and Agriculture Subcommittee of the House Committee on Government Operations, concerning their experiences dealing with Ticketmaster. This was a golden opportunity to have their voices heard in an entirely new context. Or was it?

Between reading the band's prepared written statement and studying the audio and video records of their oral testimony during the proceedings, one gets the impression that Stone and Jeff were there in earnest, that they had done their due diligence in preparing for this moment, and that they were taking this matter very seriously.

The same, however, cannot be said for certain members of the Information, Justice, Transportation, and Agriculture Subcommittee of the House Committee on Government Operations. Faced with the novelty of hearing testimony from members of a famous rock and roll band, many of them behaved in an unusual manner and did not seem to take Stone and Jeff all that seriously. Perhaps the most condescending remark came from congresswoman Lynn Woolsey, who famously blurted out, "You're just darling guys." Predictably, some members asked them what the band's name meant, and others wanted to discuss the band's music; one even said he'd been practicing Pearl Jam songs on his guitar! Stone and Jeff found the whole experience quite exasperating, and Kelly Curtis agreed.

Dressed to Grill

As for Stone and Jeff's questionable sartorial choices while appearing before Congress that day, what can we say? They were, and remain, rock stars; they were young at the time and wanted to look the part. Stone at least made a half-hearted

attempt to appear professional. He wore a collared shirt, with the top button fastened, and his hair was cropped short. But the shirt was baggy, peach colored, untucked, and he wore no tie. Jeff, however, opted for an Army green windbreaker, worn half-zipped over a white T-shirt. He rarely appeared in public hatless in those days, and this day was no exception. He wore his Seattle Supersonics cap backwards over a blue bandana. Please understand that we have no intention of playing fashion police here, but one cannot help but wonder if they would have garnered more respect during that hearing had they broken out the tailored suits.

Not just any old Mr. "Sew and Sew," Jeremy "Crash" Crowley, of Crashious Roadside fame, has been commissioned to design and handcraft many beautiful Pearl Jam-themed articles of clothing over the years. In addition to Pearl Jam, he has worked for Soundgarden, the Police, Iggy & the Stooges, "Uncle Neil," and even the Rolling Stones. If you've ever wondered where your concert merchandise comes from, check out this guy; he'll be hard at work on yet another design.

Jeremy "Crash" Crowley

If You Thought the *Last* Tour Was Tough

The cancellation of the summer 1994 leg of the *Vs.* Tour effectively meant that the tour had officially ended, with a whimper instead of a bang, at New York's undersized Paramount Theater on April 17. As it turned out, this was also the last time that drummer Dave Abbruzzese would ever perform live with the band. Their testimony before Congress that summer, followed by their continuing impasse with Ticketmaster, also meant that Pearl Jam would not set foot on a stage anywhere in the world for another ten months.

When they did finally return, it was in support of their November 1994 album, *Vitalogy*. They had already appeared in public a few weeks prior to the start of the *Vitalogy* Tour, of course. As we discuss in the Rock and Roll Hall of Fame chapter, the band members sat cringing at their table as Eddie (who had *not* testified at the congressional hearing) went off on an anti-Ticketmaster tangent in the midst of his induction speech for Neil Young. That was on January 12, 1995, and they were scheduled to hit the road on February 5, with Jack Irons now manning the skins.

As we learn in the *Vitalogy* chapter, the band began that tour on safe and familiar ground, with two warm-up shows at Seattle's Moore Theatre, followed by a college gig in Jeff's hometown of Missoula. After that it was off to Asia and Oceania for two straight months of gigs far outside the sphere of Ticketmaster's influence. But they couldn't avoid the United States forever, not if they wanted to remain viable in the music business.

They returned stateside in June and July of 1995 with disastrous results. They were now using a small ticketing company, ETM, as their ticket broker. Six of their fifteen scheduled shows, including the five following Eddie's infamous Golden Gate Park "food poisoning" fiasco, were cancelled; not a good ratio by any standard.

Your Tax Dollars at Work: The Wheels of Justice Turn . . . *Slowly*

In spite of the circus-like atmosphere that prevailed during that 1994 hearing, and all of the excitement that stemmed from having two members of one of the biggest bands in the world appear before Congress, concrete action was taken. In the aftermath of Stone and Jeff's testimony, Congressman John Dingell, a Democrat from Michigan, wrote a bill called the Ticket Fee Disclosure Act of 1995, which would require Ticketmaster to fully disclose and identify their service charges on their tickets. Kelly Curtis was encouraged that the issue finally seemed to be getting the national attention it deserved. The news may have been heartening, but the bill went nowhere.

On July 5, 1995, the Department of Justice announced that it was closing its antitrust investigation into Ticketmaster's contracting practices. Ticketmaster had launched a *huge* counterpropaganda campaign and hired the best lobbyists and public relations experts in the business to help sway the investigation in their favor and to combat the negative publicity brought upon them by Pearl Jam's efforts. They spent untold millions of dollars to influence the public's perception, and there was no way for Pearl Jam to compete at that level. Ironically, Pearl Jam's decision to use ETM to process tickets for their non-Ticketmaster tour in 1995 may have helped to prove Ticketmaster's point that they were not, in fact, a monopoly. And, of course, it did not help Pearl Jam's cause that they were the *only* band on this doomed crusade.

On July 6, 1995, Pearl Jam issued a statement expressing their disappointment with the Department of Justice's decision, and lamented that the fans, those "consumers of live music," would be the ones who suffered as a result. Then with nary a hint of irony, they (inadvertently, of course) ensured that their fans would continue to suffer when they resolved to continue their boycott of the ticketing giant. Ticketmaster, of course, crowed at the news, and issued a statement trumpeting their vindication.

Later on, when the Republicans became the congressional majority during the fall elections, any plans the Department of Justice may have had for a second hearing were shelved indefinitely. And Dingell's bill was essentially dead on arrival.

Back to Work

In the wake of the disappointing news, Pearl Jam wrapped up the summer leg of the *Vitalogy* Tour with two shows in Milwaukee on July 8 and 9, and one at Soldier Field in Chicago on July 11. Then, for most of the band, it was off to Europe during August to support Neil Young on the eleven-date *Mirror Ball* Tour, which gave Eddie a break and gave producer Brendan O'Brien the opportunity to take the stage as a keyboard player. But the band's touring problems on the home front would still be waiting for them when they got back home.

When the band finally regrouped for the fall leg of the *Vitalogy* Tour, there were just four shows scheduled for September, none in October, and five in November, and most of those were makeup dates for the shows that had been cancelled during June and July.

The Ticketmaster war was forcing Pearl Jam off the beaten path, where they would play at random, barely accessible, and, in many cases, inadequate concert venues, which led to widespread problems with ticket forgery, delays, and even cancellations. It's not so easy going it alone.

No Code, and *Still* No Ticketmaster

Pearl Jam's ethical resolve continued throughout the *No Code* Tour, and by this point one had to wonder if anyone was even paying attention to the issue anymore. After two or three years of this, people were just growing accustomed to the fact that Pearl Jam concerts were now a rare occurrence in the United States. This trend continued throughout the *No Code* Tour into the autumn of 1996. Not counting the obligatory warm-up gig at Seattle's Showbox—where there were no Ticketmaster implications, anyway—the official tour consisted of just fourteen stateside gigs, the final two of which were short, Bridge School Benefit sets; so just twelve proper, full-length concerts. Once again, our loss was the rest of the world's gain, as Europe got a solid twenty shows during the end of October and on through November.

We *Yield*!

Pearl Jam hit the touring band's equivalent of rock bottom during 1997, when they played only five times in their native country. During one of these shows, at the Catalyst, a club in Santa Cruz, California, they appeared under an alias, "the Honking Seals." The other four dates—November 14, 15, 18, and 19—found the band in the role of opening act for the legendary Rolling Stones. So, in essence, the only show they headlined stateside during all of 1997 was a club date where they appeared under an assumed name. Clearly, things needed to change, and change they did.

Pearl Jam released their fifth studio album, *Yield*, in February of 1998. When they announced the schedule for their *Yield* support tours, it quickly became obvious that the war had ended. Ticketmaster was once again handling Pearl Jam's ticket sales. After four long years the war was finally over, and it was back to the business of rock and roll.

Aftermath

The irony here is that the band's Herculean efforts to protect their fans from the evils of Ticketmaster only served to annoy and alienate many of them along the way. Four years is an eternity in the lifetime of a music fan, and for teenagers in particular. Times and tastes change, new bands come along, and some fans move on. Of course, Pearl Jam always wanted to downsize their operations a bit, so this contraction of the fan base was perfectly fine by them. It was now all about quality, not quantity.

Ultimately the band had been doomed from the start to lose this war with Ticketmaster, but the valiant effort served to deepen their bond with the most ardent, core members of their fan base, the true believers. The overall experiences of these years also served to formulate many of the fan-friendly, ticket-related policies that exist today for Ten Club members, who are assured a first shot at tickets (thereby usually getting the best seats in the house). Pearl Jam's Ticketmaster war also helped to raise awareness among the general public about exactly what went into ticket pricing, so it wasn't a total loss, by any means. Those years seemed interminable at the time, but given all that has happened in the world of Pearl Jam since, they are now but a distant memory.

12

Vitalogy

Is *This* a Healthy Band?

The Tale of the Tape

Recorded: New Orleans, Louisiana, November 1993, during the *Vs.* Tour ("Tremor Christ" and "Nothingman"). Subsequent sessions were held during 1994 in Seattle, Washington, and Atlanta, Georgia, culminating in October 1994 at Seattle's Bad Animals Studio.

Produced By: Brendan O'Brien and Pearl Jam

Released: November 22, 1994 (vinyl); December 6, 1994 (CD and cassette)

Singles: "Spin the Black Circle" (11/8/1994); "Not for You" (3/21/1995); and "Immortality" (6/6/1995)

Billboard: The vinyl version moved 34,000 copies during its first week of release (a record for vinyl during the CD era that would stand until it was broken by Jack White's 2014 release, *Lazaretto*). Two weeks later, the CD version moved 877,000 copies during its first week of release, making *Vitalogy* the second fastest selling album in history (second, that is, to Pearl Jam's previous release, *Vs.*) Talk about competing with yourself. The RIAA has since certified *Vitalogy* Platinum five times over. As of July 2013, *Vitalogy* had moved 4.77 million copies.

How to Succeed in the Music Business Without Really Trying

Despite lost tour dates, a disdain for interviews, and a moratorium on producing music videos, Pearl Jam's third album, *Vitalogy*, hit stores—on *vinyl*, no less—on November 22, 1994, almost one year to the day after *Vs.* The CD and cassette versions followed two weeks later, hitting store shelves on December 6. Through no fault of their own, and, some would argue, in spite of their best efforts to the *contrary*, the band once again found itself with a number one *Billboard* debut. Pearl Jam's apparent career mantra, "how to succeed in the music business without really trying," seemed to be working to perverse perfection. We have to admit, this wasn't bad for a bunch of guys who weren't really communicating with one another during the recording of the album. Can you imagine if everyone had actually been on the same page? (Cue Pink Floyd's "Have a Cigar.")

Whereas *Vs.* established the band's versatility as a rock and roll entity, *Vitalogy* seemed to highlight the band's idiosyncrasies, with a more experimental approach on many tracks. The formula translated into huge record sales, a burgeoning following, and an increasing uneasiness on the part of the band members in response to it all.

Into the Studio

The bulk of *Vitalogy* was written and recorded while Pearl Jam was touring in support of *Vs.* The band took advantage of breaks in their touring schedule to work at studios in New Orleans, Seattle, and Atlanta. Once the *Vs.* Tour ended in early 1994, they finished recording *Vitalogy* at Bad Animals Studio in Seattle. The album's release date was either held back by Epic Records or was delayed because of the band's ongoing war with Ticketmaster, according to conflicting sources. In our experience, record companies carefully select their album release dates to maximize potential sales. It is a marketing strategy, nothing more. As for the band's ongoing feud with Ticketmaster, the old show business adage applies: there is no such thing as "bad publicity."

Perhaps the only thing that was not in conflict at the time was the tacit understanding that the *band* was in conflict; or, as it might be phrased in classic *VH1 Behind the Music* parlance (cue the overdramatic voiceover), "Off stage, things were falling apart." Suffice it to say, the boys were not playing well with one another.

With the clarity afforded us in hindsight, it is all too easy to point out that group conflicts of this nature are usually the result of the group members employing ineffective communication strategies. Everybody seemed to know something was wrong at the time, but nobody seemed to be doing much about it. Producer Brendan O'Brien diagnosed the band's ailment as an implosion and correctly surmised that the problems were arising from within the ranks. Bassist Jeff Ament, an amiable guy if ever there was one, realized that communication among his bandmates was at an all time low. Soon to be ex-Pearl Jam drummer Dave Abbruzzese focused on the fact that Stone Gossard was no longer the mediating presence in the band. While all of their observations may have been accurate, they weren't necessarily helpful in terms of healing the band's wounds.

The silent coup was now complete. Eddie, for the first time on *Vitalogy*, was making all of the final decisions. For Stone, the overall situation deteriorated to the point where he contemplated quitting the band altogether. The strong collaborative effort the band had forged on *Vs.* was somehow lost, and Gossard resented the fact that the overwhelming majority of the songs were written just minutes before they were recorded. When you look at the situation from Stone's perspective, you cannot help but sympathize. This was *his* band; the band he had created with Mike, and then his old friend Jeff, in the hopes that their third time would be the charm. From the disappointing end of Green River through the tragic ending of Mother Love Bone, Pearl Jam represented their third trip down the proverbial aisle, and the wedding reception was now in full swing. Then suddenly the shy San Diego surfer they hired as a lead singer had revealed himself to be a once-in-a-generation genius, and he slowly but surely overshadowed everyone and everything in his path. For Stone and Jeff to be shunted aside like that at the

Mike McCready Comes Clean

Like a lot of young rock and rollers, Mike McCready enjoyed the party lifestyle early on in his career. Overwhelmed by Pearl Jam's rapid ascent to superstardom and still lacking full confidence in his remarkable musical abilities, he began drinking heavily to cope with the stress. It soon became apparent to everyone around him that Mike was vulnerable to addiction, and his drinking and fondness for cocaine led him into some crazy shenanigans: running around naked, blacking out on stage, and feeling sick a lot of the time. As the rest of the world would learn later on, he was also suffering from Crohn's disease, but he wasn't ready to talk about this condition just yet. All the added drinking could not have been kind to his already compromised digestive system, and the normally slender guitarist grew painfully thin.

Fortunately, he also had the support of his bandmates. The rest of the band began getting on his case for getting drunk all the time but made no moves to fire him or do anything so drastic. Fortunately, during the production phase for *Vitalogy*, Mike had the presence of mind to check himself into Hazelden Rehabilitation in Minnesota to dry out and get himself clean. He had witnessed firsthand the horrors wrought by unchecked addiction and realized he wanted no part of that. Hazelden proved good for Mike, both in terms of his health and his vocation. He met other musicians there, such as Chicago bluesman John "Baker" Saunders, who would become his bandmate in Mad Season. Mike's sobriety remained intact until the *Binaural* era in 2000, when a bout with prescription pain medication addiction led him back to rehab for a tune-up. Otherwise, he has kept himself on the straight and narrow ever since Hazelden.

moment they were beginning to enjoy both critical acclaim and commercial success must have been galling on some level.

One cannot help but be reminded of the Rolling Stones' founder, Brian Jones, who would have happily plugged away his entire career playing American blues standards in small clubs, oblivious to the need to write original music. But then suddenly their manager, Andrew Loog Oldham, had different ideas, and now Mick and Keith were running the show, writing the songs, and getting all of the media attention. Different circumstances, of course, but still difficult for the person being left behind. When you factor in guitarist Mike McCready's trip to rehab for alcohol and cocaine abuse, and the firing of Abbruzzese in August due to unresolved philosophical and personality issues with Ed and Jeff, this was clearly a band on the brink.

Just when the band's growing pains were becoming unbearable, a familiar name, dating back to the fateful delivery of the original demo tape, returned to the scene. Re-enter Jack Irons, who was a calming, rock steady influence both on and off the stage. The original drummer for the Red Hot Chili Peppers, Irons made his Pearl Jam recording debut on the sonically challenging "Hey Foxymophandlemama, That's Me" (aka "Stupid Mop").

The Tunes

The emergence of Vedder as a guitarist also became more of a factor in the overall creative process. Eddie's style led to a more stripped down, punkish finished product on several of the new songs. Ed's rhythm guitar playing led to a more rhythmically oriented album that Mike described as much less conducive to lead guitar solos. Here is a rundown of the fourteen enigmatic tracks.

"Last Exit"

Continuing in the form of the first two albums, "Last Exit" rocks hard and is a pounding opening salvo to a mixed bag of an album. Musically, the song begins with what sounds like a pre-show tuning session, when all of a sudden the music morphs into an "Oh, Pretty Woman" drum intro before all hell breaks loose. Lyrically, as is often the case, the song is open to interpretation. We feel that the tension among the band members at the time inheres in the lyrics, which seem to be setting the stage for, well, an "exit" of some kind.

"Spin the Black Circle"

"Spin the Black Circle" was the album's first single. The song is an unabashed love letter to vinyl records, which were then in a rapid state of decline in the industry, as the compact disc became the medium of choice for disseminating commercial music. Vedder took one of Stone's slower guitar riffs and sped it up exponentially, creating a hardcore punk, all-out assault. Mike, as some have suggested, seemed to be channeling the New York Dolls punk icon Johnny Thunders with his leads, while Eddie belted out his vocals amidst the cacophony. For all of its lack of subtlety, "Spin The Black Circle" earned Pearl Jam its only Grammy Award of 1996, for Best Hard Rock Performance.

"Not for You"

"Not for You" delivers a ringing volley across the bow of both the music industry and Ticketmaster. What better way to discuss the preservation of the sanctity of youth and the salvation of rock and roll than with a good old-fashioned, three-chord, riff-heavy rocker that gave Mike a chance to showcase the gift he received from Tom Petty, a vintage twelve-string Rickenbacker guitar? An angry song, to put it mildly, "Not for You" stands as Pearl Jam's strongest statement against the music business and all of its machinations. To Pearl Jam, the music belonged to the artist and the audience, not to the middlemen. Implicitly, the song may also have been Eddie's way of raging against the dying light of his own fading youth and entering adulthood kicking and screaming.

"Tremor Christ"

"Tremor Christ" is a little slice of psychedelia in the spirit and tradition of *Sgt. Pepper's Lonely Hearts Club Band*. They recorded this unusual, Beatles-like marching tune at the New Orleans studio, and Mike, in particular, was impressed at how quickly it came together.

"Nothingman"

"Nothingman," a gorgeous Jeff Ament ballad, also emerged from the New Orleans sessions. This song was another example of a tune that came together very quickly. Musically, "Nothing Man" reveals a band that finally seems comfortable in its own skin performing ballads. From a lyrical perspective, it would be difficult to argue

Like the members of Pearl Jam, we are nostalgic for the 45-rpm vinyl singles of our youth. The band has made every effort over the years to preserve this time-honored musical medium. Here, appropriately enough, is "Spin the Black Circle," a song which celebrates the tactile and auditory joys of vinyl records.   *Author's collection*

that this is not a depressing song. The words seem to suggest a once-strong relationship gone sour, perhaps due to broken trust. The feelings of loss, loneliness, and regret are palpable here, even if the overall sound of the song has a soothing quality to it.

"Whipping"

"Whipping" returns to the band's punk persona with a snarling, straightforward charge. Inside the album packaging, the song's lyrics are written on a copy of a petition addressed to then President Clinton and condemn the killings of abortion doctors by "pro-life" advocates. Whether that pairing is coincidental or an overtly political act remains open for interpretation.

"Pry, To"

"Pry, To" references the downside of rock idolatry, as Vedder repeatedly intones the letters that spell the word "privacy" as if to emphasize how important his privacy is to him. A page in the album packaging for "Pry, To" features the medical definition of the word "nightmare"—Ed's perspective on fame articulated. It had become abundantly clear by this point that Eddie had a difficult time dealing with success. We guess he just felt like he had to spell it out for us. At just over a minute in length, "Pry, To" can scarcely even be considered a song. It is more of an emphatic statement.

"Corduroy"

"Corduroy" continues to address the theme of fame, with all of its inherent ironies. The song title refers to a moment when Eddie noticed a brown corduroy jacket— very similar to the one he recollected paying twelve dollars for—selling for about $650. The implication, of course, is that the price had been artificially inflated because of the fact that *Eddie* had worn a similar jacket; it was now a hip piece of "grunge" culture and thus worthy of the hefty price tag. High fashion was now officially exploiting the sartorial instincts of a group of guys who cared so little about their appearance that they generally filled out their wardrobes at the local thrift shops. It probably didn't help matters that the popular soap opera *General Hospital* had hired Latin music heartthrob Ricky Martin to portray a character who dressed just like Eddie. These were the sorts of things that drove Eddie crazy and made him cynical about fame.

Musically, "Corduroy" begins with a foreboding guitar riff that leads into a muscular power chord, which propels the song toward the vocal opening. Lyrically, Vedder expresses his personal frustration at the media mythmaking surrounding his image. The message is more covert than overt, however. You have to read between the antiauthoritarian, contrarian lines to decipher what exactly is bothering him. At times, Eddie seems to be channeling an old expression we often heard growing up, one of indeterminate origin (some claim it has Native American roots): never judge a man until you've walked a mile in their shoes/ moccasins. Likewise, Eddie seems to suggest that people could buy his clothes all they want, but they would never be able to wear them. In other words, no matter the affectations they adopted, they would never be able to understand what it was really like to *be* him. The end result is that "Corduroy" is classic Pearl Jam, with all of the participants at the top of their game.

"Bugs"

"Bugs" is the first of a cluster of quirky, pseudo jams that dominate *Vitalogy*'s second side. Armed with an accordion, Ed referenced a bad case of poison oak as the song's itchy inspiration, although a case could certainly be made for "Bugs" representing the people in his life, whether friend, foe, or fan. The sense of paranoia in the song could very well be another manifestation of Eddie's sense that he was being walled in and crushed by his fame.

"Satan's Bed"

"Satan's Bed" chugs along to a steady beat and, metaphorically speaking, is another example of a place Eddie doesn't want to be and will never be found. The imaginative imagery portrays his never-ending battle to somehow maintain perspective amidst the ever-growing distractions and corruption surrounding them. We interpret the song to be Eddie's poetic way of reminding people that he never sold out or compromised his sense of ethics.

Driven by some sinister guitar riffs, as befits the title, the song has been infrequently included in the band's live set lists.

"Better Man"

The story behind the music of the Pearl Jam classic "Better Man" remains compelling. Originally written by a teenage Vedder and recorded on a four track at his old apartment in San Diego, the song was first performed by Ed and his band, Bad Radio, in Southern California. The melody and chord progression of the composition are reminiscent of "Save It for Later" by the English Beat.

Brendan O'Brien first heard the band play "Better Man" during the sessions for *Vs.*, and he was blown away. Reportedly, he blurted out that he thought the song was a "hit," and he could not contain his enthusiasm. But O'Brien immediately realized from the band's collective reaction that he had committed an egregious error; these guys weren't looking to produce "hits" per se. They just wanted to concentrate on putting out high quality music.

We have to remember that the term "hit" was conceptually removed from the band's game plan at the time. Moreover, Eddie claimed that the song's subject matter was too personal and hit too close to home; this from the guy who wrote "Alive" and "Release." You will pardon us if we seem skeptical.

O'Brien wasn't giving up on "Better Man," however. He persuaded the band to play it again in the recording studio, and they rewarded him with a tentative, half-hearted attempt. Afterward, Eddie announced that he was giving the song to Chrissie Hynde of the Pretenders for a Greenpeace benefit album. O'Brien was in disbelief. How could the band give away what he perceived to be a smash hit?

A session was scheduled for Hynde to record the song, but as fate would have it, she never showed up. The original studio recording was not ready for prime time, and O'Brien reluctantly came to terms with the fact that it would not be included on *Vs.* His only consolation was that Greenpeace didn't have it either: save the whales, save the song.

"Better Man" finally appeared on *Vitalogy*. The song recounts the story of the abusive relationship between Eddie's mother and stepfather. The lyrically stark narrative directly addressed the dysfunctional family dynamics of the Mueller home: Eddie's mother trapped by the reoccurrence of her depression and trumped by the resignation that she couldn't find a better man. But O'Brien was right about one thing. "Better Man" is an incredible pop song.

One night, while introducing "Better Man" at a gig in Atlanta, Vedder made the following dedication to his stepfather, Peter Mueller, a California attorney: "It's dedicated to the bastard that married my momma." So, at the very least, recording and playing "Better Man" afforded Eddie with some opportunities to rail against the injustices of his childhood.

The song became a part of the band's hermetically unrelated "Man Trilogy" ("Better Man"/"Nothingman"/"Leatherman"), which has, at times, been played in concert. "Better Man," along with "Alive" and "Daughter," is more commonly thought of as one of the three cathartic crowd sing-along songs that define the Pearl Jam concert experience.

In the end, Brendan O'Brien was vindicated. "Better Man" spent eight weeks at the top of the *Billboard* Mainstream Rock Chart despite not being released as a commercial single. The *Billboard* Mainstream Rock Chart tracks radio plays, rather than sales. Yes, Brendan, "Better Man" was indeed a hit.

"Aye Davanita"

"Aye Davanita" was another glorified studio jam that seemed to foreshadow some of the less accessible material on *No Code*. Here, sandwiched between "Better Man" and "Immortality," it functions more like an intermission than it does a song in its own right.

"Immortality"

The ethereal "Immortality" is a Neil Young-like composition that came to be associated, in some people's minds, with Kurt Cobain's suicide, in spite of the fact that Eddie is on record denying any connection between the song and Cobain. "Immortality" was first performed on April 11, 1994, at Boston Garden, just three days after Cobain's body was discovered, but it was written while Kurt was still alive (if not altogether *well*) and Pearl Jam was on tour in Atlanta in support of *Vs.* In addition, Eddie was loath to even *say* anything about Kurt to interviewers after his suicide, lest his words be misconstrued as being exploitative. So the notion that Eddie would eulogize Kurt in song so soon after his untimely demise seems spurious at best. Nevertheless, and in spite of Eddie's protestations to the contrary, there are some people who will forever persist in linking the song to Cobain's suicide.

Musically, the song begins with a distorted acoustic guitar intro, reminiscent of Metallica's "Unforgiven." Eddie's vocal delivery is soft and wistful, with him nearly whispering the song's title. The lyrics are so poetic and indirect that they could be interpreted to mean just about anything the listener desires. For us, they do convey a sense of unease and restlessness, as if the protagonist will only find comfort in the afterlife and thereby achieve the state of being indicated in the song's title.

"Hey Foxymophandlemama, That's Me" (aka "Stupid Mop")

As noted on pearljam.com, the final track was recorded and mixed by Brett Eliason and is the first Pearl Jam recording to feature Jack Irons on the drums.

The "song," if you can call it that, includes actual audio recordings of mental patients rambling on, which, quite frankly, makes it unnerving to listen to. Pink Floyd fans will of course recognize that Pink Floyd pioneered this technique on 1973's *Dark Side of the Moon*, when they spliced in spoken-word audio clips from assorted characters working in and around the studio. In this case, the music, such as it is, seems to serve merely as a backdrop for the repeated ramblings of the recorded voices.

That's Some Package

The original album title was supposed to be *Life*. A reference to this original title actually appears on the back cover of the album's first single, "Spin the Black Circle." *Vitalogy*, which means "the study of life," is the title of a 1927 medical book that Ed found at a garage sale. Copies of this vintage book have become a collector's item among Pearl Jam fans.

Pearl Jam's desire to package the album to resemble the book that inspired it cost them an extra fifty cents per CD. The fact that the book itself was still subject to copyright laws further complicated the release and led to more personal material from the band and less of the archaic health references of the original written work appearing on the album cover and inside the thick, artsy booklet that

The title, cover art, and packaging of Pearl Jam's third album, *Vitalogy*, was taken from a 1927 book, *Vitalogy Encyclopedia of Health and Home*, that Eddie chanced upon at a garage sale. The elaborate packaging cost the band an extra fifty cents per unit sold, but art has always trumped profits in Pearl Jam's worldview.
Author's collection

accompanies it. The final packaged product looks very impressive but does not fit well on a standard size CD shelf.

Support Tours

It is important to bear in mind that when it came time to tour in support of *Vitalogy*, Pearl Jam was in the midst of its war with Ticketmaster, which made things interesting, to say the least. We devote an entire chapter to the Ticketmaster saga, and there you will find more details about the conflict. In this context, it bears pointing out that the band's issues with Ticketmaster and insistence on going it alone had a detrimental impact on their efforts to tour in support of *Vitalogy*. At the very least, the stalemate contributed to the tour's comparative brevity. The proceedings kicked off with three warm-up shows on familiar ground—two in Seattle, followed by one in Jeff's hometown of Missoula.

Asia

Then it was off to Japan for shows at venues in four different cities, including the fabled "Budokan" in Tokyo. Unfortunately, the gig in Kobe was cancelled. From there, Pearl Jam hit Taiwan, the Philippines, Thailand, and Singapore.

Oceania

After Asia, it was off to Australia for ten shows in six different cities, followed by the obligatory side trip to New Zealand for another pair of shows. After the New Zealand gigs, it was time for a break. The break lasted nearly three months.

United States: Midwest/West Coast

Finally, the band seemed to work out their itinerary for a United States tour and kicked off in Casper, Wyoming, of all places. Among the few highlights of this leg were back-to-back shows at Red Rocks on June 19 and 20, but this tour will be forever remembered for the June 24 show at Golden Gate Park. Eddie had been hospitalized prior to this show for food poisoning, but he left the hospital in a valiant effort to honor the old showbiz maxim that the show must go on. He dragged himself out on stage and managed to get through seven songs before he had to pull the plug. Looking back on it now, you can almost picture one of Eddie's bandmates yelling out from the stage, "Is there a rock star in the house?" Fortunately for all concerned (one never knows how a disappointed audience will react in situations like this), there was. Neil Young strapped on his guitar and calmly strode onto the stage to pinch-hit for the stricken Vedder. He led the band through fourteen songs and managed to coax some long jams out of them, in accordance with his traditional approach.

In the aftermath of the Golden Gate Park show, the next week's worth of shows were cancelled, up to and including the Fourth of July show that had been scheduled for New Orleans. The band did manage to squeeze in two gigs in Milwaukee and one in Eddie's hometown of Chicago on July 11 before beating a retreat to lick their wounds.

By September, Pearl Jam was ready to give it another go, but the nine dates on this truncated leg of the tour were all makeup dates for the seven shows that had been cancelled during the summer run. They weren't covering any new ground at this point. The road had never been so rough.

13

The *Mirror Ball* and "Uncle Neil"

A "Crazy Horse" of a Different Color

The Tale of the Tape

Recorded: January 26–February 10 at Bad Animals Studio in Seattle
Produced By: Brendan O'Brien for Reprise Records/Epic
Released: June 27, 1995, on Reprise Records
Singles: "Downtown," "Peace and Love"
Billboard: Hit number five on the *Billboard* 200; certified Gold by the RIAA

Of Neil and "Jam"

In 1995, Pearl Jam took its Neil Young idolatry to a whole new level. The record and tour supporting *Mirror Ball* created a cross-generational musical phenomenon that would inject an energizing shot of creative adrenaline into both teacher and students. The exhilarating experience of collaborating with their mentor seemed to offset the turmoil brought on by the band's "alternative touring" hardships. This was a good opportunity for Pearl Jam to get away from the difficulties inherent in using the do-it-yourself approach to stage a major rock tour. Meanwhile, Eddie was back home dealing with a stalker issue on the home front. Mainly, he was "dealing" with it by hanging out at Matt Lukin's house, which, as we will see later in this narrative, led him to write a great song. On the positive side of things, Mike was out of rehab and doing well, and they finally had Jack Irons for a bandmate, which is something Stone and Jeff had hoped for long before they had even heard Eddie's name. The roots for the *Mirror Ball/Merkin Ball* project can be traced back to the very naming of the band.

As Jeff Ament relates the oft-told tale in the book *Pearl Jam Twenty*, it was a particularly jam-heavy Neil Young performance at Nassau Coliseum on February 22, 1991, that had a profound effect on him, Stone, and Ed, the three future Pearl Jammers in attendance. "We were kind of panicked trying to figure out a band name, and he was having these long jams, and we just threw *Jam* at the end of *Pearl*." The result: the "death" of Mookie Blaylock. On March 9, 1992, Pearl Jam played

Heading into the studio to record *Mirror Ball* with respected veteran "Uncle Neil" Young was exactly what the band needed at this point in its career. The name "Pearl Jam" may not appear on the album cover, for contractual reasons, but the band's presence is clearly evident on every track. Besides, how many people can say that they have an "uncle" in the Rock and Roll Hall of Fame?

Author's collection

Young's "Rockin' in the Free World" for the first time at the Loft, in Berlin, Germany. The song today remains a crowd favorite and frequent encore closer. Later that year, on November 1, the band made its first appearance at Neil's annual Bridge School Benefit concert in Mountain View, California. The success of that appearance led to Neil, who was then backed up by the legendary Booker T. and the MG's, to invite the band, sans Ed, to open for him during an upcoming European tour. Pearl Jam worked the Young gigs, in between some headlining gigs of their own, and some additional openings for U2 in Italy during the early summer of 1993. Another karmic moment between the two generations of artists occurred when Pearl Jam staff member Eric Johnson noticed Neil driving his vintage black Cadillac. The license plate on Neil's Cadillac read "Pearl 10."

Their roads would converge again at the 1993 *MTV Video Music Awards* on "Rockin' in the Free World." Eddie gave the 1995 Rock and Roll Hall of Fame induction speech for Young, an event that was followed days later by two Voters for

Choice benefit shows in Washington, D.C. All of these events served to validate the inevitable: Neil was primed to make a record with the young band from Seattle. It would prove to be a valuable experience for everyone concerned.

Into the Studio

The timing for Young to do something different was perfect. For the ever-enigmatic Neil Young, the planted seed of an idea was now ready for harvest: record an album with Pearl Jam and do it their way on their turf with their man Brendan O'Brien in the central room producing. The result was a musical achievement that, some two decades later, is considered among the career highlights for both the teacher and the students. Over a four-day period beginning on January 26, 1995, the artists convened at Bad Animals Studio in Seattle with Brendan O'Brien (of *Vs.* and *Vitalogy* fame) to record *Mirror Ball*, Neil Young's twenty-second studio album.

It would prove to be a short but productive stay. They booked the studio for January 26 through February 10, but the actual recording time for the album totaled only four days, January 26 and 27, and then February 7 and 10. The rest of the time was spent writing songs, working them out by jamming on them, and then tweaking them until they got them just right.

The musical simpatico between Young and Pearl Jam (minus Ed, with the exception of just one of the record's eleven songs) was amazing to behold. The result was a loose vibe that accentuated the raw power and spontaneity of a live show. Somewhere between the "crank-it-up-to-eleven" bombast of a Crazy Horse record and Pearl Jam at their manic, punk rock best, the two generations of musical forces forged a mighty sonic alliance, breathing new life into both acts. Their common leftwing sociopolitical beliefs are shared and celebrated in the album's overall thematic/lyrical tone. The man who established The Bridge School with his wife, Pegi, had become a bridge for the next generation of classic rock.

The Tunes

The *Mirror Ball* sessions yielded thirteen songs, eleven of which made the final cut for the album. But as we will see, the remaining two "leftover" tunes would be put to good use also. Here, then, are the fruits of this legendary collaboration.

"Song X"

The pro-choice issue came to the forefront on the first two songs of the album. The opener, "Song X," features a to and fro musical sway, a sing-along chorus, and some Young riding the "Horse" guitar work, complete with a controlled feedback fight to the finish.

"Act of Love"

"Act of Love" was the one new song that Young played with Crazy Horse at both his Rock and Roll Hall of Fame induction and at the subsequent D.C. benefit shows, and it takes on a whole different feel when he is backed by Pearl Jam. The contrast between the melodic density of the Crazy Horse version and the rhythmic flavor of the Pearl Jam alternative serves as a stark reminder of why this collaboration was good for both sides. It also illustrated how the triple guitar interplay of Young, Gossard, and McCready could be effective. Young had previously opined that the Buffalo Springfield was the only band to ever effectively employ three guitars. This lineup seemed to have the potential to make that configuration work, too. The song's conclusion is a haunting, vaguely psychedelic sequence of distortion and feedback, giving a sense of the barely restrained power of those electric guitars—controlled chaos that slowly fades into nothingness.

"I'm the Ocean"

On "I'm the Ocean," Young provides a dose of autobiographical musical insight. The pace picks up, danger is looming, but the old man isn't backing down. The rhythm section of Ament and drummer Jack Irons (who was initially starstruck at the opportunity to play with Young) belie the fact that the subject is not going gentle into that good night. The title and imagery could easily be attributed to Vedder or Townshend, kindred spirits all, no doubt. There is a true camaraderie in this 7:26 opus.

"Big Green Country"

Young explores more familiar territory on "Big Green Country." In this "cowboys and Indians" tale, the Indians win the battle but certainly not the war. There is no room for John Wayne in Young's movie. Again the guitar interplay and vocal harmonies raise the stakes.

"Truth Be Known"

The proceedings slow down a bit on the doleful "Truth Be Known." Here the truth is not setting *anyone* free. It is instead a dose of hard reality. The instrumental break, though, does allow for more of the guitar interplay to come to the forefront, a truth that brings sensory satisfaction to the listener.

"Downtown"

A loving homage to the past, in this case where Neil came from and where Pearl Jam could only dream of, takes over on "Downtown." One of two singles released from the album, the three-chord groovin' tune received a 1996 Grammy nomination for Best Rock Song. A great, distortion-driven Young riff takes the listener on a retro journey back to the swinging sixties, with both Jimi Hendrix and Led Zeppelin in the house. The lyrical imagery is tongue-in-cheek and humorous, with old hippies reliving their past in a timeless room where people dance the Charleston beneath the mirror ball hanging from the ceiling. Young can even be heard on the record, commenting, "We know that one. That's funky." His downtown is a cool place where everybody wants to be seen.

"What Happened Yesterday"

There is an old adage that holds that if you can remember the sixties, you weren't there. Well, Neil Young was unquestionably there, and few would argue that he was an integral part of what made that often-mythologized decade so memorable. This brief, haunting tune starts off sounding like the introduction to a trippy Pink Floyd song, but then Young's voice kicks in, and it becomes clear that he remembers . . . *something*. He seems to be explaining to his listeners that, on some level, he will always channel that fertile musical past.

"Peace and Love"

After the brief prelude of "What Happened Yesterday," the generation gap is triumphantly closed on "Peace and Love." The only song on the album to include Eddie Vedder creates a compelling contrast. In one corner, representing his time—the 1960s—is Young, with his idealized, idyllic vision. In the opposite corner stands Vedder, a man of the 1990s, born of cynicism and pragmatism. As they trade vocals, their realization points to the same end result . . . John Lennon. The Lennon of "Give Peace a Chance" and "All You Need Is Love" is all you need to be reminded of: it's worth the trip no matter how difficult the journey. The song received a 1996 Grammy Award nomination for Best Male Rock Vocal Performance, but it lost to kindred spirit Tom Petty's "You Don't Know How It Feels."

"Throw Your Hatred Down"

The hard rocking "Throw Your Hatred Down" offers an insistent, plaintive plea. The anti-violence lyrical sentiments are set off by a snarling guitar assault. The atmosphere of the song evokes fond memories of Young's *Rust Never Sleeps* era and features a galloping, virtuoso performance by Jack Irons on the drum kit.

"Scenery"

The subject of fame, fortune, and their inevitable vagaries is inherent in "Scenery." The graveside imagery poses the eternal question: ultimately how much land *does* a man need? It is a fine point to ponder, along with the search for the true meaning of the words "bravery" and "heroism."

"Fallen Angel"

"Fallen Angel," the final song, offers a short coda to an album thematically populated by a number of songs that would have easily fit on a Pearl Jam album.

Looking Into the Mirror (Ball)

By all accounts the musical marriage was a rousing success. The timing for both was perfect. The fact that Eddie in effect stepped back and allowed Neil to front "his" band bolstered the band's overall confidence. To paraphrase a joke of Stone's: only Neil could be a Pearl Jam fan and then get rid of Eddie!

Their collaboration with Young also afforded the band an opportunity to delve into the three-guitar dynamic that they would later explore further with Ed's increasing contributions on rhythm guitar, both in the studio and in concert. Young's counsel, with regard to keeping the focus on the music, was a valuable lesson for the band as a whole and for, in particular, its often embattled and conflicted lead singer. There could be no denying that the whole project was a win-win for all concerned.

Because of contractual restrictions, there was no mention of "Pearl Jam" on *Mirror Ball*; there were only individual credits for the band members in the album's liner notes. They had gotten their act together in the studio, and fortunately there were no constraints about taking this show on the road.

Ed's "Got Id" on the "Long Road" to *Merkin Ball*

Originally slated for *Mirror Ball*, the Vedder composition "I Got Id," along with the haunting "Long Road," wound up becoming the Pearl Jam EP *Merkin Ball*. Written, by Eddie's own admission, in under half an hour, the confessional "I Get Id" (originally "I Got Shit") is more than a Freudian slip musically. Although credited to Pearl Jam, a makeshift configuration of Vedder, Young on lead guitar, Brendan O'Brien on bass, and drummer Jack Irons actually recorded it. A single that peaked at number seven on the *Billboard*'s Hot 10, "Id" is highlighted by some absolutely incendiary Young lead salvos backing one of Vedder's most far-reaching, tortured vocal turns.

With a hint of "Cinnamon Girl" in the chorus and with Neil shifting to pump organ, "Long Road" stands as one of Pearl Jam's most stripped down, emotive moments. Inspired by the death of his high school drama teacher, Clayton Liggett, Vedder picked up his guitar in the studio and began strumming a D chord for an extended period as the rest of the band joined him. What resulted was something simple yet majestic. In post-9/11 America, it took on a different meaning when Ed, Young, and Mike McCready offered it for the *America: A Tribute to Heroes* telethon. It's our favorite Pearl Jam concert opener. The two-song EP—a single for all intents and purposes—was released on December 5, 1995, and was well received. It has been certified Gold by the RIAA.

Support Tour

"Neil Jam," the popular nickname for the collaboration at the time, hit the road in August 1995 for eleven shows in Europe. Eddie sat this one out, but Brendan O'Brien came out of his producer's booth to join the band on keyboards, a role he loves to play. The live configuration featured Neil Young, in effect, fronting Pearl Jam. "Crazy Colts" instead of Crazy Horse, anyone? Whichever clever nickname you prefer for the hybrid band, all of the assembled musicians seemed delighted to be participating.

Neil and his Seattle-based colleagues got things started on August 12 at Sjöhistoriska Museet in Stockholm, Sweden. And they maintained a fairly grueling pace throughout the brief jaunt. The following night, August 13, found them at Heyday 2 in Roskilde in Copenhagen, Denmark. The tour continued unabated the very next night, as they rolled into the Waldbuehne at Berlin, Germany, where Heather Nova served as an opening act.

Following a day off, Neal Jam hit the Czechoslavakia Sports Palace in Prague, Czech Republic, on August 16, with the Levellers in the opening slot. The next day was a travel day. On August 18, they hit Residenzplatz in Salzburg, Austria, with the Levellers joining them for the second and final time. The following night found them at Festival in Switzerland.

Two days off followed, as Neil led the band to the Holy Land for two shows in Israel. The first was at Sultan's Pool in Jerusalem on August 22, followed by the Royal Amphitheater in Ceasaria the following evening. This was a relatively small crowd of 3,000 appreciative fans (they don't often get many top-shelf rock and roll acts in that part of the world, so this was definitely a treat for music fans and artists alike).

August 24 was another travel day leading up to an event that must have seemed like Old Home Week by comparison. This was the Pucklepop Festival in Hasselt, Belgium, on August 25, where Neil Jam was joined by Dave Grohl's up-and-coming post-Nirvana project, the Foo Fighters, old Seattle friends Mudhoney, and the enigmatic Rob Zombie, who was in town with his theatrical heavy metal band, White Zombie.

The following two evenings would find the collaborators in more music-friendly environs. They rolled into the Royal Dublin Showgrounds in Dublin, Ireland, on August 26, and then wrapped the tour up with a neat little bow at the Reading Festival in Reading, England. Reading was another "old home week" scenario, as "Neil Jam" once more found itself surrounded by familiar, friendly faces. Also appearing at Reading were such old friends as L7, Mudhoney, the Foo Fighters, and honorary big bro Chris Cornell, who was in town with Soundgarden.

In many ways, each of these eleven nights was much more predictable than the average Pearl Jam concert because Neil Young had them stick pretty closely to a

Neil Young is one of several older, established artists who have acted as mentors and de facto father figures for Pearl Jam. Young's impact on the band has been nothing short of profound, and the artists remain loyal to and supportive of one another to this day.   *Geffen/Photofest*

Upon further reflection, the *Mirror Ball* sessions yielded more material than could fit on the album, so Pearl Jam were able to get an EP called *Merkin Ball* out of the deal. Size-wise, it was really more of a single than a true EP, but *Merkin Ball*'s two songs "I Got Id," and "Long Road" have made quite a name for themselves in the years since.   *Author's collection*

regular set list. Pearl Jam's own set lists, even as early as the mid-1990s, were already becoming unpredictable, and they only grew less predictable with each passing album and as the band's working repertoire ballooned to hundreds of songs.

They opened *all* eleven shows with the *Mirror Ball* track "Big Green Country." Likewise, *all* eleven shows featured Neil's haunting solo classic "The Needle and the Damage Done"; the old Buffalo Springfield hit "Mr. Soul"; *Mirror Ball* tracks "Scenery," "Throw Your Hatred Down," and "Act of Love"; and the Neil Young and Crazy Horse classic "Cortez the Killer." How's that for consistency?

Ten of the eleven shows featured "Downtown," the closest thing to a "hit" on *Mirror Ball* (it reached number six on *Billboard*'s Mainstream Rock charts), and "Song X," the opening track from *Mirror Ball*. Eight of the eleven shows featured Neil Young and Crazy Horse's raucous crowd pleaser "Powderfinger," as well as Pearl Jam's personal favorite Neil Young song, "Rockin' in the Free World." Six shows featured Neil Young and Crazy Horse's "Mother Earth (Natural Anthem)."

Five shows featured Neil's solo classics "Comes a Time" and "After the Gold Rush," and the *Mirror Ball* cut "I'm the Ocean." Four shows featured the Neil Young and Crazy Horse anthem "My My, Hey Hey (Out of the Blue)," along with the Neil Young solo gems "Like a Hurricane" and "Don't Let It Bring You Down." Three shows featured "Hey Hey, My My (Into the Black)," the Neil Young and Crazy Horse companion piece to "My My, Hey Hey (Out of the Blue)." On two occasions, they broke out "Peace and Love," the soon-to-be Grammy nominated eighth track from *Mirror Ball*.

As for one-offs, the rarest of the rare on this tour, they played the Neil Young and Crazy Horse favorite "Down By the River," the ancient and trippy Buffalo Springfield gem "Broken Arrow," and, last but not least, another one of Pearl Jam's favorite Neil Young and Crazy Horse songs to cover, "Fuckin' Up."

As for *Mirror Ball* songs that never graced the stage, at least not during these eleven dates, we have "Truth Be Known," "What Happened Yesterday," and "Fallen Angel."

Upon Further Reflections

Pearl Jam, sans Eddie, had backed Neil Young on a European tour, a tour that also took the cross-generational group to Israel. This was a tour that Young's long-time manager, Elliott Roberts, referred to as "one of the greatest tours" in Young's bio *Shakey*. Playing both *Mirror Ball* material and Young's classics was a rock and roll fantasy made reality for the Pearl Jam band members. As Stone Gossard told *Spin* magazine in 2001, the visit from Uncle Neil "came at a time when we needed it . . . our band seemed too serious." In retrospect, Young gave the band a fresh perspective from a wizened voice. Stone went on to credit Neil as "instrumental in why we're still a band."

Though, to date, Pearl Jam has never again served as Neil Young's touring band, the bond between the band and the living legend remains intact and stronger than ever. Pearl Jam continues to support the Bridge School and can be counted on to appear at the benefit every few years.

The final word of this chapter should go to our fellow FAQ Series author, Glen Boyd (*Neil Young FAQ: Everything Left to Know About the Iconic and Mercurial Rocker*), who summed up the Neil Young/Pearl Jam musical marriage on *Mirror Ball* thusly:

> . . . arguably the best pure hard-rock record of Young's entire career—a sonic blast of musical Dexedrine combining the punk rock energy of the Ramones with the tight musical chops you'd more likely associate with a group of seasoned pros like Booker T. and the MG's.

14

No Code

Off They Go!

The Tale of the Tape

Recorded: At the Chicago Recording Company in Chicago, Illinois, Kingsway Studio in New Orleans, Louisiana, by Nick DiDia, and at (Stone Gossard's own) Studio Litho in Seattle, Washington, between July 12, 1995, and May 1996

Produced By: Brendan O'Brien and Pearl Jam for Epic

Released: August 27, 1996

Singles: "Who You Are" (July 30, 1996); "Hail, Hail" (1996); and "Off He Goes" (1996)

Billboard: Debuted at number one on the *Billboard* 200, selling 366,500 copies that first week; *No Code* "only" achieved single Platinum certification by the RIAA.

Do Not Resuscitate

No Code seemed to be a fitting title for Pearl Jam's 1996 album since the band was committed to lowering their profile. The title resonated with their policy of no interviews, no videos, and, for all intents and purposes, no promotion of *any* kind. With the fallout from their losing war with Ticketmaster continuing, you can add virtually no *touring* to the list, at least not much in the continental United States. There was still a lot of stress within the band at this time: stress with one another, and stress collectively in relation to the outside world. For the first time in the band's brief history, you could argue that the stress rose to the level of an existential threat. At times their future seemed to be in doubt.

Fittingly, perhaps, the album debuted at number one on the *Billboard* charts but then took a precipitous dive in sales. This was a band clearly at a crossroads. As a byproduct of their introspection, *No Code* stands as a significant departure from the band's sound on a number of tracks. A wider range of instrumentation, emotions, and overall jamming quality supports the album's title emphatically. If ever there was a band that played hard to get with their musical public, it was Pearl Jam circa *No Code*. The longer form and improvisational quality of the record can be summed up by Vedder's comment on the state of the band at the time: "The more you think, the more you stink."

Into the Studio

The creation of Pearl Jam's fourth album began at the Chicago Recording Company in Chicago, Illinois, the day after their nearly three-hour, thirty-one song, epic live performance at Soldier Field. Pearl Jam played on the very same stage where Jerry Garcia had played what would prove to be his final Grateful Dead show just days before.

The weeklong series of studio sessions took place during a Windy City heat wave that was responsible for the deaths of some 600 people, but it proved to be a fruitful week for the band, despite the palpable internal strife among the members. After another week in a New Orleans studio and a final round of sessions at Stone Gossard's Litho Studios in Seattle, the result was the final product, the aptly titled *No Code*.

The album turned out to be a combination of eclectic ballads, psychedelia, world beat, and good old-time garage rockin'. *No Code* broadened Pearl Jam's base of musical styles, while at the same time narrowing the band's *fan* base for the first time. Their third collaboration with producer Brendan O'Brien, *No Code* was the group's first effort that did not achieve Multi-Platinum status, at least not in the United States. It went double platinum in Canada and also charted well in Europe and Oceania. It was also the first full album to feature drummer Jack Irons, the ex-Chili Pepper and Pearl Jam matchmaker, who played an important part in the album's formation. Musically, his looser, funkier, groove-oriented approach contrasted sharply with the harder hitting Dave Abbruzzese. Music aside, his calming presence played a significant role in improving team morale, a dynamic that is akin to a veteran ballplayer joining a team that is already contending for a pennant.

The Tunes

As for the songs themselves, many of them originated from studio jam sessions, as opposed to band members bringing in tunes in a more complete form. Two exceptions were "Habit," and "Lukin." Both were frenetic, punk-paced, and brought in by Eddie. Overall, *No Code* clearly distanced the band further from the more anthemic, stadium sound of *Ten*.

"Sometimes"

The theme takes hold right from the drop of the needle with the opening cut, "Sometimes." The narrator of the song seems to be seeking egalitarianism, a place where he can blend in with the crowd. We particularly like the metaphor suggesting that a book blends in best on a shelf filled with other books. Thematically, the song certainly seems to capture the ethos of the band at the time. Sonically speaking, "Sometimes" is merely the calm before the storm.

The spirit of Pearl Jam drummer emeritus Jack Irons looms large
over "Who You Are," the single he composed with Stone Gossard,
which features lyrics by Eddie Vedder. With its mesmerizing
polyrhythms and Eddie on electric sitar, the song evokes fond
memories of George Harrison's late era work with the Beatles.

Author's collection

"Hail Hail"

Let the power chords fly! The primal punch of "Hail, Hail" is striking, as the entire
band seems to come in simultaneously, and at full volume. Lyrically, the song is
a description of two people attempting to survive a troubled relationship, and it
follows up with a nod to the lucky ones that seem to have attained happiness. In
other words, the title is a tip of the cap to those who have managed to work things
out in love.

"Who You Are"

Irons' polyrhythmic drumming pattern becomes the foundation for the next song,
"Who You Are." With Ed playing electric sitar—a homage to the Rolling Stones'
"Paint It Black" and several of the Beatles' offerings—the band made the curious
decision to release the very non-commercial sounding song as the album's first
single. "Who You Are" has a tribal, mildly raga feel to it, which provides an almost
hypnotic effect. This just may be our favorite track on the entire album.

"In My Tree"

It remains Irons' show on "In My Tree" as his rapid, rat-a-tat tribal drumming,
accompanied by Jeff's pulsating bass lines, propels the song forward with Ed

lyrically weaving some clever homophones together. The prevailing theme, once again, is the desire for sanctuary from the trappings of celebrity. Texas Ten Clubber Terri McNelly tells us, "As I've aged I've become more in tune with this song. To me it mirrors my feelings around keeping your life simple and only including those things and people that add positive value to your life; get rid of the noise."

"Smile"

The only Jeff Ament composition to make the *No Code* cut, "Smile" would be right at home on a Neil Young record. Ed composed the lyrics while he was onstage, inspired by a note he found scribbled into his notebook by the Frog's Dennis Flemion, which read: "I miss you already; I miss you always." For the most part, though, the meaning of the lyrics remains unclear—perhaps deliberately so. Though dominated by Crazy Horse-style distortion and power chords, Vedder's harmonica breaks help to keep the mood lighthearted.

"Off He Goes"

"Off He Goes" becomes Vedder's self-portrait. The narrator describes a friend's now-you-see-him, now-you-don't nature and its effect on him. The subtle acoustic ballad, featuring Jeff on upright bass, is an acknowledged Pearl Jam classic and another song that demonstrates the influence of working with Young. Producer Brendan O'Brien has referred to it as one of Pearl Jam's "most meaningful songs" and alluded to its haunting quality. To Vedder it became a musical mea culpa for his being, by his own admission, a poor friend, the type who can be perfectly fine and enjoying himself one moment, and then walk out the door without saying "goodbye" the next.

Sonically, the acoustic guitar intro of the song is reminiscent of the Beatles' "And I Love Her," and then soon thereafter calls to mind Neil Young's "Winterlong," with the wisdom, wistfulness, and poetry of Paul Simon's best. Without question, this is one of the most mellow, easygoing songs Pearl Jam has ever recorded, and it certainly merits mentioning in that vaunted company of legends.

"Habit"

"Habit" is an impassioned plea to a friend who is addicted to drugs. Many Pearl Jam fans interpret the song as being something Eddie wrote for Mike McCready, who certainly suffered some consequences on account of his alcohol and cocaine habits. On the other hand, let us not forget the history of the man behind the drum kit. Eddie knew Jack Irons very well, and he was certainly familiar with the tragic tale of Hillel Slovak, Jack's fellow founding Red Hot Chili Pepper. Unfortunately, trips to rehab did nothing to alleviate Slovak's heroin habit, and he soon succumbed to the opiate's insidious power. But the truth of the matter is that the song is applicable to the lives of anyone suffering from bad habits and addictions. Lyrically, it remains universal.

Musically, the dark subject matter of the song finds the band back in full hard rocking glory, with Eddie howling and snarling his way through the vocals. There's even a bit of the old Kiss influence evident in the mix for the sharp-eared listener.

"Red Mosquito"

"Red Mosquito" features Mike McCready front and center, playing slide guitar (using a Zippo lighter as a slide, no less), which gives the song a vintage 1970s hard rock feel. Sure, for the pure "coolness" factor, it's tough to beat Jimmy Page playing the Les Paul with the violin bow, but McCready's Zippo slide was in the ballpark. "Red Mosquito" recounts the awful day that Ed spent dealing with food poisoning in his San Francisco hotel room and during the band's show at Golden Gate Park.

If you are thinking that the song title doesn't quite seem applicable to a case of food poisoning, you are not alone. The nearest pop cultural referent we could find for the expression "red mosquito" comes from an episode of Fox's hit sitcom *Married with Children*, in which Al Bundy dreams of his wife, Peggy, as a giant "red mosquito," sucking money out of his wallet. Perhaps Eddie ought to have titled the song "Tuna Salad Sandwich Surprise" instead; at least that would have been closer to the truth.

As discussed earlier, that infamous concert, held at Golden Gate Park in front of a crowd of 50,000 fans, ended after only seven songs for Vedder, as his symptoms became unbearable. As luck would have it, Neil Young was in attendance that day, and he stepped up to the plate to finish the show. Needless to say, there were some in the crowd who remained unhappy, despite Neil Young's valiant efforts in lending a hand.

Lyrically, "Red Mosquito" is just as opaque as the title. It doesn't mention any of the aforementioned specifics at all. It presents one of those situations where you really need to read between the lines. In the process, Eddie managed to pen a song that reminds the listener that one ought to be mindful of one's own mortality. Disaster is often just a footstep behind, and things can go south pretty quickly if we're not careful.

"Lukin"

The title of "Lukin" refers to the name of a ubiquitous Seattle musician, the former Mudhoney and Melvins' bassist, Matt Lukin. Thematically, the song recounts a period of time in which Eddie was being harassed by a stalker, a woman who may or may not have been armed with a gun and who claimed Eddie raped her and that, as a result, he was the father of her son. While all of this madness was going on, Eddie and his wife would often avoid their own house and come by and use Lukin's kitchen as a place to hang out, chat, and have a few drinks. As for the ferocity and terseness of the song—which weighs in at a snarling one minute and thirteen seconds—that, too, may have been attributable to Lukin's influence. The story goes that he was always busting Eddie's chops about Pearl Jam's songs being too long. Naturally, Eddie responded with an offering that was even shorter and faster than most Ramones songs.

"Present Tense"

The simpler-is-better concept of *No Code* comes into focus on "Present Tense." Ed drives this point home over a musical backdrop that changes speed and direction throughout. At one point, Jeff's growling bass even functions as the lead instrument. Lyrically, it is one of the band's more introspective and philosophical songs. In the end it's not about the past or the future, only about the here and now. For those who think this sounds like the boys regurgitating the Jedi wisdom of beloved *Star Wars* character, Yoda, philosophers have been debating the value of present-mindedness for millennia. "Present Tense" can be considered Pearl Jam's own contribution to this great conversation. Moreover, the reflective angle of the lyrics in correlation to the band's whirlwind history up until then is inescapable.

"Mankind"

"Mankind" was Stone's Keith Richards moment, as he wrote the lyrics and sang lead vocals. "Mankind" is noteworthy for being the first Pearl Jam song *not* featuring Eddie's lyrics and lead vocal (unless, of course, you count "Hey Foxymophandlemama, That's Me" [aka "Stupid Mop"]). The notion of Stone taking the lead here reminds us of an old Keith Richards anecdote. While expressing admiration for his song,"Happy," someone once asked Keith why he didn't sing more often. Keith, who to this day delights in needling his fellow "Glimmer Twin" Mick Jagger, responded with the question, "What would Mick do?" He was being facetious, of course, since Mick has been known to strum a rhythm guitar and blow a mean harmonica.

In his singing debut, Stone submits a scathing observation of grunge poseurs. But rather than pointing his finger at anyone in particular, Stone seems to acknowledge the ubiquitous nature of such imitation as being simply a part of human nature. There is a sort of cross-pollination that occurs with the creative process, in which every artist, whether deliberately or not, has a degree of influence on every other artist. As for his vocals, we nod our heads in approval. We think he acquitted himself quite admirably.

"I'm Open"

Dating back to San Diego and Eddie's humble pre-Pearl Jam days, "I'm Open" once functioned as a mantra of sorts for the singer, who was opening himself up and listening for any message the universe might have for him concerning his future, his destiny. The most important message Eddie received, from where we are standing, was the one that eventually arrived courtesy of Jack Irons, who was holding Stone Gossard's fabled demo tape.

In this incarnation, the spoken word beginning of "I'm Open" is evocative of the Doors' *American Prayer* album, released posthumously, in Jim Morrison's case, and featuring the fated singer reading poetry aloud while the surviving members of the Doors provided the background music. It adds a little air of mystery to the band, and it also helps to expand the boundaries of their sound.

"Around the Bend"

"Around the Bend" concludes the proceedings. A lilting lullaby to Irons' son, the song begins with a gentle drum pattern and cocktail piano melody, as Eddie sings the soothing lyrics. Piano and drums are soon joined by acoustic guitar pickings and subtle bass murmurings. While not quite the poetic masterpiece of Bob Dylan's "Forever Young," "Around the Bend" is certainly in the tradition of rock star fathers' lullabies, and it also calls to mind John Lennon's "Beautiful Boy," written for Sean, his son with Yoko Ono. In Irons' song, the father seems resolved not to miss any more of these precious moments. Lyrically, the song also embraces the cyclical nature of the passage of time; indeed, it is the sun itself that lies around the proverbial bend.

Another Weird Package Deal

The album packaging included 144 Polaroids, forming a square. Among the eclectic mix of images: NBA bad boy Dennis Rodman's eyeball and Vedder's foot after being stung by a stingray.

Up to Code

The music critics' reactions were mixed. Some reviewers admired the band's courage in setting out to break their musical mold, while others bemoaned the overall lack of continuity.

For Pearl Jam the record clearly achieved the desired effect: it scaled back their celebrity. The result was the beginning of their diehard fans closing ranks. It was the death and the birth of Pearl Jam Nation at the same moment in time. The country had closed its borders and thus reduced the population within.

As for the title, Vedder has suggested that it was a metaphor for the album (or perhaps even the band itself). In medical jargon, the term "no code" refers to a "DNR, or "do not resuscitate" order, the withholding of CPR in accordance with a patient's wishes. From a musical perspective, the medical metaphor was evident. Eddie reasoned that if the record turned out to be a complete failure, the title would stand as evidence that the band had already owned up to that fact in its own subliminal way. *No Code* was a statement by a band that was in transition from being rock superstars to working musicians. For Pearl Jam, the code had been broken, and they didn't seem to care who or how many had deciphered it by this point in their career.

Pearl Jam's avant-garde aesthetic sensibilities were on full display once more in the cover art and packaging on 1996's *No Code*. The view here is of the back cover featuring the track listings, but when you open it out fully, you get four quadrants featuring a total of 156 Polaroid images.   *Author's collection*

Support Tours

The abbreviated *No Code* US Tour was highlighted by the Randall's Island, New York show (FYI: this was co-author and Ten Club Member Bernie Corbett's *first* Pearl Jam concert; the first of many, as it turns out). This was a 32-song, 168-minute marathon of a show—the band's longest gig to date at the time.

North America: East Coast

The East Coast missed out on Pearl Jam entirely during 1995s *Vitalogy* Tour, which concentrated on venues in the Midwest and on the West Coast. But now, in 1996, the East Coast was poised for some Pearl Jam action on the *No Code* Tour. Unfortunately, the war with Ticketmaster was still in full swing, and many of the logistical problems that plagued the truncated *Vitalogy* Tour would remain problematic during the abbreviated *No Code* Tour.

As was their custom by this time, Pearl Jam got things started with a warm-up gig on September 14 at the Showbox in Seattle, because nothing prepares a band for a road trip better than getting a rousing sendoff from the hometown crowd. The first "official" gig of the tour also took place in Seattle, at KeyArena, home of the Seattle Supersonics, two days later.

From there, after a four-day break, it was up and over to Toronto to perform for our Canadian neighbors at Maple Leaf Gardens. Sadly for Canada, this was a one-shot deal, but the East Coast of the United States didn't fare much better. Only a dozen more shows remained on the calendar, including the two Bridge School Benefit shows at the Shoreline Amphitheatre in Mountain View, California, on October 19 and 20.

Among the highlights of this brief run was a "Worm" sighting at the Augusta, Maine show. The Chicago Bulls' infamous bad boy and Pearl Jam celebrity fan, Dennis Rodman, made a memorable appearance, not only at the show, but also on the stage. He strode onto the stage at one point and offered Eddie a bottle of wine, and he later gave the diminutive singer a piggyback ride across the stage while the band played "Alive." Many in the Pearl Jam community grumbled at Rodman's antics, but the NBA legend still considers that night to be one of the highlights of his crazy, well-publicized life.

The overall consensus of Pearl Jam's US fans was one of dissatisfaction; not with the band or their music, but with the logistics. The non-Ticketmaster venues were hard to get to, off the beaten path, and often in poor condition. Moreover, it was difficult to get tickets to the shows in the first place.

Europe

Pearl Jam fans on the other side of the pond had an easier time getting to see their favorite band and a better overall experience. This nineteen-show excursion led Pearl Jam through Ireland, England, Poland, the Czech Republic, Italy, Germany, Switzerland, the Netherlands, Hungary, Turkey, Spain, and Portugal. One notable highlight was the November 3 gig in Berlin, which was broadcast over the radio for the benefit of those fans who couldn't get tickets. They ended this European leg with back-to-back shows at the Dramatico in Cascais, Portugal, and that was all she wrote, as far as a *No Code* Tour was concerned. This would be their last time on stage during 1996. When all was said and done, the *No Code* Tour was only thirty-four shows, including the warm-up club date at The Showbox. Clearly, something needed to change.

Decoded

We are fairly certain that it wasn't just the album that was responsible for the apparent contraction in the band's popularity at the time. All artists go through ebbs and flows in their popularity at different points in their careers. That is only natural. As these words are being written, it was fifty years ago to the day that the Beatles played Shea Stadium and ushered in the era of stadium-scale rock and roll performances. The Beatles could scarcely poke their heads out of a window for fear of being overwhelmed by swarms of crazed, screaming teenage girls. Fast forward half a century, and the two surviving Beatles, Paul McCartney and Ringo Starr, remain hugely popular, but they can go out for dinner or to a theater without fear of inciting a riot.

The collateral damage of the band's war with Ticketmaster was unquestionably taking its toll, not only on the band, but on their fans, as well. The DIY touring approach that Pearl Jam attempted to implement only led to greater stress and overall tension within the band. DIY is fine if you're Fugazi, but the Pearl Jam economy of scale was simply too large to be successful while taking this approach to touring. And by this point, they had tried it during 1995 with *Vitalogy*, with disastrous results, and again in 1996 with *No Code*, on a tour that was only slightly better (at least there were no cancellations this time around). But let's be honest, when you're among the biggest bands on the planet and you're only giving your American audiences a dozen shows per year, your fans are going to be disappointed. This approach to touring was clearly unsustainable.

A *No Code* Coda

On October 17, 2014, almost two decades after *No Code*'s release, Pearl Jam played the album in its entirety in Moline, Illinois. The show became an instant classic for the hardcore disciples, who were rewarded for matching the band's perseverance. The result was a night of overwhelming camaraderie, code not withstanding.

15

Yield

The Tale of the Tape

Recorded: February–September 1997 by Nick DiDia, at Studio Litho and Studio X, in Seattle, Washington

Produced By: Brendan O'Brien and Pearl Jam

Released: February 3, 1998, by Epic

Singles: "Given to Fly" (January 6, 1998); "Wishlist" (May 5, 1998); "Do the Evolution" (August 24, 1998)

Billboard: Number two on the *Billboard* 200: 358,000 first-week copies sold; RIAA-certified Platinum. *Yield* never hit the number one spot, ending the band's streak at four albums in a row.

So, Pearl Jam *Yields?*

What seemed to be an inevitable withdrawal from even a glimmer of the spotlight followed Pearl Jam into 1997. The band regrouped with producer Brendan O'Brien and channeled its energy toward the *No Code* follow-up, *Yield*. A band closely associated with the prowess of their live performances and accompanying persona would not perform in public until November, playing a club date under an assumed name, and then opening four shows on the Rolling Stones' *Bridges to Babylon* Tour at Oakland's Alamada County Coliseum.

Into the Studio

As Pearl Jam headed back into their twin hometown studios, X and Litho, to record their fifth album, the strong sense of survival was palpable. Of the four most influential bands to emerge from the Seattle music scene—labeled and mislabeled the Grunge Era—of the late 80s and early 90s, only Pearl Jam remained standing, recording and touring. Who would have picked them in a survival pool? Soundgarden had apparently disbanded, while both Nirvana and Alice in Chains suffered the tragic loss of their respective front men, guitarist Kurt Cobain and lead singer, Layne Stayley. Thus it was left to Pearl Jam to carry the banner for the Great Northwest rock revival that had given them birth.

The result was an album that once again had a title that articulated a deeper meaning. Yes, *Yield* was the title, but it was also exactly what Pearl Jam had to do to be in their survivalist position. The band conflicts, far more creative and artistic than anything personal, were resolved. The result: a record that all the participants felt was a bona fide team effort. Everybody got to have their say, and they were now operating like a band ought to. In retrospect, *Yield* blazed the trail that the band has essentially remained on to this day.

The meaning of the title can be extended to the unsuccessful end of Pearl Jam's war with Ticketmaster. Standing alone, the band eventually capitulated to the monopolistic corporate ticket purveyor. The "surrounding bullshit," to borrow a phrase from "Off He Goes," simply proved too insurmountable for Pearl Jam to tour. The logistical obstacles in their path made it untenable. By "yielding" to Ticketmaster, Pearl Jam had earned the undying admiration of its fans, fans they could now reach in a conventional concert setting once again. The war was lost but the battle had been won.

The new creative product was unquestionably more accessible. A more straight-forward overall approach yielded an album that successfully explored softer acoustic tunes, alongside the alternative and garage rock that the band had a history of doing well. Lyrically, the album bore more than a passing resemblance to *No Code*. Overall, Pearl Jam's members were clearly more comfortable with each other and their band dynamic, but they remained far from complacent in their demeanor.

Yield would also be the fourth consecutive—and last for a decade—production collaboration with Brendan O'Brien. Ironically, his impact on the record was perhaps at its most prominent. Ever an advocate of Pearl Jam being more accessible, O'Brien's keen musical sensibilities were in evidence throughout. The accompanying praise from band members makes his departure all the more curious. In sports parlance, it was the equivalent of a coach leaving after an outstanding season.

In order to move forward creatively, Pearl Jam needed to bridge the gap between the conflicting methodologies of their previous records. The overriding question of developing music from riffs and fragments, as opposed to band members coming in with completed songs, was

A *Yield* sign display—one which would look right at home in any record store—from the voluminous collection of Ten Clubber and noted Pearl Jam merchandise collector Ryan Byrne. With an uncanny knack for choosing album titles that capture the essence of the moment, Pearl Jam releases *Yield* just as it ends the Ticketmaster war and returns to a more conventional touring cycle. *Ryan Byrne*

once again at the core of the creative discussions. O'Brien was pleased to see that most of the songs arrived at the studio in a completed form. As a result, Eddie felt less pressure to lyrically finish the songs that other band members submitted. He also relinquished his de facto song selection authority, after essentially making all of the final track decisions on the band's previous two records. This fundamentally changed the band's political system from a dictatorship to a democracy. A more relaxed Vedder now had a greater opportunity to work with his fellow band members in the development of their own songs.

An additional irony, concerning *Yield*, was the final Pearl Jam album appearance by Vedder's close friend, drummer Jack Irons. Irons' battle with bipolar disorder took its toll on him physically, as well as mentally, especially when the rigors of touring were factored into the equation. Alas, just as Irons truly felt like a member of the band during the *Yield* sessions, the looming support tour compelled him to step aside. The loss of the affable Irons was perhaps the unkindest yield of all at the time.

The Tunes

Pearl Jam recorded at least seventeen songs during the studio sessions, and thirteen of those tracks made the final cut for *Yield*. Collectively, the thirteen tracks— or *fourteen*, technically, if you count the "hidden track," "Hummus," which appears in the midst of "All Those Yesterdays"—weigh in at a fairly lean 48:37. Here is the diverse lineup of songs.

"Brain of J."

The album opener connects back to the first three albums, which each began with a heavy dose of hard rock. "Brain of J." is political commentary at a punk rock pace. In the opening line, Vedder wonders aloud about who might have the brain of our former president, John Fitzgerald Kennedy. For more than a half a century, a legion of conspiracy theorists have been asking that same question regarding the events of November 22, 1963. The Pearl Jam theory articulated in the song's lyrics refers to a government plan of secrecy designed to mollify the public; the missing brain being at the center of the truth regarding what happened on that fateful assassination day.

"Faithfull"

Another Pearl Jam moment of irony is exhibited in the next selection, "Faithfull," with music written by Mike McCready and lyrics by Eddie Vedder. The intentional misspelling of the title targets the real message: the intentionally fraudulent nature of organized religion. When Eddie sings of the universal nature of religious belief, it is a reference to Marx's "opiate of the masses" myth, not the actual faith endorsed by church dogma. No matter what your religious beliefs, or lack thereof, the song succeeds sonically, fueled by the guitar tandem of Mike and Stone.

"No Way"

Stone Gossard factors prominently in "No Way." A direct statement of resistance to the band's "rock god" status, the lyrics find the band in a position of resignation and establish a passive stance, in sharp contrast to "Indifference," the final track on *Vs.* The irony that no band has done more to make a difference in their charitable work resonates to an even greater degree seventeen years after the song's release. It is the ultimate message, to just *live*.

"Given to Fly"

The album's first and most popular single, "Given to Fly" deserves its place in the Pearl Jam pantheon. With music written by Mike McCready while he was stuck in his condo on a rare Seattle snow day, "Given to Fly" is a majestic rock and roll moment. The slowly building main guitar riff mimics the action of ocean waves crashing and receding at the shoreline.

McCready, a huge Led Zeppelin fan, readily acknowledges the influence of the band on the song. He has also endured good-natured ribbing from Led Zeppelin front man, Robert Plant, who once referred to the song as "Given to California," based on its similarity to the *Led Zeppelin IV* track, "Going to California." Nevertheless, from Jack Irons' deft use of the tom toms to one of Vedder's most impassioned vocals, the song succeeds on a grandiose, anthemic level. It has become a fan favorite live and always gets a rousing emotional reception from the faithful.

"Wishlist"

The versatility of the band shines through on "Wishlist," an all-Ed offering. The song features an Eddie Vedder guitar solo, performed with an *Ebow*, no less (Hendrix is surely watching, wherever he is). Built around thirteen wishes— which puts Eddie about ten wishes *ahead* of your average genie—the tune contains just two very basic chord changes. With an original "stream of consciousness" running time of eight minutes, Ed picked out the better wishes for the finished product, which clocks in at 3:26. The song rolls along at a bouncy tempo with the narrator coming to an epiphany about how fortunate he is—a testament, perhaps, to the fact that Ed and his bandmates had reached at least *some* semblance of contentment.

"Pilate"

The next cut, "Pilate," is one of two Jeff Ament compositions that appear on *Yield*, and the first of several on the record that contain a strong literary connection, in this case Mikhail Bulgakov's *The Master and Margarita*, written between 1928 and 1930 but unpublished until 1967. In this satire, the song's protagonist relates to Pontius Pilate as a fellow dog owner. The inspiration took root in a recurring dream that Ament had, which found him sitting on a porch as an old man with his dog.

The delicious irony of coming across a *Yield* sign in the middle of nowhere on a road near Billings, Montana, where there is clearly nothing to yield *to*, appealed to Jeff Ament's artistic sensibility, and thus was the visual motif for the album born. The serene tableau of the album cover also effectively captures the maturation and growing sense of acceptance in the band members' worldviews.

Author's collection

"Do the Evolution"

A second direct literary reference can be found on "Do the Evolution." Author Daniel Quinn's book, *Ishmael*, was on Ed's reading list at the time, and it profoundly influenced the track's message. Subtitled "An Adventure of the Mind and Spirit," Quinn's work raises questions about modern day technology and control. The accepted tenet that human beings reside at the top of the evolutionary chain is sarcastically called into question. This from the same band that previously pondered whether rats should perhaps rank higher. A rumbling riff, credited to Stone Gossard, provides the engine to propel the evolutionary tale forward with a nod to Iggy Pop's Stooges. Vedder's personal favorite offering on the album, he has described it lyrically as "a conversation with a man and an ape," with the most remarkable observation being how close they really are despite the sum total of man's time on Earth. No matter your Darwinian perception, keep on rockin' because, after all, it *is* evolution . . . baby.

"Untitled" (aka "The Color Red," "Red Bar," or "Red Dot")

The brief (1:06) instrumental "Untitled" is also referred to as "The Color Red," "The Red Bar," or "Red Dot," since a single red dot adorns the back cover of the *Yield* album.

"MFC"

The fleeting interlude after "Untitled" leads directly into "MFC." Although still ranking well behind the man he saw live at the very first concert he attended, Bruce Springsteen, Eddie Vedder has written a few car songs, and "MFC" is one of them. Indeed, the letters stand for "Mini Fast Car." Similar to "Rearviewmirror," the protagonist is in a car looking to escape, driving for the purpose of, as Eddie so eloquently described it, "getting the fuck out of a problem."

"Low Light"

The second Jeff Ament penned tune "Low Light" is a serene ballad that answers the question posed by his recurring dream of the future in "Pilate." For Jeff, the answer will be found in his "gratefulness at finding a place of calm and peace at my center." He will be fine with the porch, the dog, the wisdom and the simple good fortune of longevity. Ament poignantly expressed the band's overall cooperative approach to the creative process when he observed that having Vedder put his "heart into singing lyrics that I wrote, can't be put into words."

"In Hiding"

A third literary reference on the album is the song "In Hiding." Taking root in a Stone Gossard guitar riff originally recorded on a microcassette, the song developed into perhaps the strongest collaborative effort on the album. Jack Irons proudly referred to it as a bona fide "band track." The musical dichotomy of the soft verses building to epic, revelatory choruses works to perfection. Vedder's lyrical literary inspiration was Los Angeles skid row author, Charles Bukowski, the subject of the movie *Barfly*. Ed learned from his friend, film director and actor Sean Penn, that Bukowski had a regimen of periodically removing himself from day-to-day life for a few days in order to, as he put it, renew his "will to live once again." The aftereffect of such solitude is described in the album's liner notes by Bukowski himself, who writes, "The first human face you see will knock you back fifty percent." In summation, credit Stone's microcassette and Bukowski's unusual socialization for creating a Pearl Jam classic with all participants at their collaborative best.

"Push Me, Pull Me"

The next track opens with a brief sampling of the Jack Irons' composition, "Happy When I'm Crying." It serves as the lead-in to the plodding tempo of "Push Me, Pull

Me."Another testament to the manipulation of the band collectively, and Vedder specifically, brings him to an extremely fatalistic conclusion.

"All Those Yesterdays" (with hidden track "Hummus")

The record wraps by extending the theme of the preceding song. "All Those Yesterdays" directly espouses one's ability to shed the emotional baggage of the past as an imperative in the search for some semblance of inner happiness. To a lilting musical backdrop, reminiscent of the Beatles' later days, Vedder explores the possibility and its liberating effect. To escape the present, go "In Hiding." To erase the past, focus on "All Those Yesterdays." Keep the focus in the moment. The present is all that really matters.

The Verdict

The album *Yield* remains a favorite among Pearl Jam fans to this day. During their most recent run across the Midwest—in Milwaukee on October 20, 2014—the band treated the fans to a mid-first-set performance of the album in its *entirety*, taking a play directly out of the Pink Floyd and Roger Waters playbooks. The presence of "Given to Fly," "Wishlist," "Do the Evolution," and "In Hiding" alone makes the album a very enduring moment in Pearl Jam's career and, relative to the process, an honestly collective one.

The release of *Yield*, on February 3, 1998, garnered a number two *Billboard* ranking right out of the gate, with 358,000 copies sold. And then, similar to *No Code*, the album made a quick descent. The first single, "Given to Fly," charted and appeared to be an infinitely better choice than "Who You Are," the ethereal, sinewy debut single from *No Code*. Overall, the band appeared to have gotten past many of the stressful issues that had held them back personally and artistically. Not surprisingly, *Yield* evolved into a more accessible record. The team concept in the creative process was clearly on display. A band weary from the fight, and a fan base leery from their non-Ticketmaster concert experiences, brought Pearl Jam back to the conventional touring track. As Ten Clubber Jeff Wilder said of *Yield*: "It shows off all sides of them." Matt Spitz, guitarist for the Lost Dogs: A Tribute to Pearl Jam, said, "*Yield* was the first album I got into, and it'll always be my favorite."

Rolling with the Stones

Like they say, there's always a bigger fish. Pearl Jam, as huge of an international success as they were, had no qualms about opening for the living legends the Rolling Stones. The Stones' *Bridges to Babylon* Tour found the boys supporting the World's Greatest Rock and Roll Band for four fun-filled nights at the Oakland Alameda County Coliseum in Oakland, California, on November 14, 15, 18, and 19, 1997. Other than the gig they played at The Catalyst in Santa Cruz on the twelfth, appearing under the alias "the Honking Seals," these Rolling Stones

"Do the Evolution": Back to MTV, Baby!

Pearl Jam returned to the world of MTV with a bang. Their first video offering in seven years (since "Oceans") was rather ambitious. The goal: a depiction of the entire prehistory and history of humanity in under four minutes flat!

The animated production that accompanied Pearl Jam's "Do the Evolution" required sixteen weeks and the work of a hundred artists. In no particular order, the Crusades, the French Revolution, the KKK, World War I, the Nazis and the Holocaust, the "troubles" of Northern Ireland, the Wall Street Crash of '29, Slavery, Whaling, Manifest Destiny, Vietnam, the collateral damage of civilians in modern warfare, rape, rampant urbanization, capital punishment, vivisection, pollution, genetic modification, techno-progressivism *all* play out in front of a crazed, black haired woman; a dancing and laughing "Miss Death."

After identifying the lengthy list of human tragedies, justice is meted out. An array of authority figures are skewered, including a judge, religious leaders, dictators, and finally an American presidential candidate in puppet form, no less.

The final segment offers a glance toward a future that appears to be hopelessly bleak. An obliteration of a futuristic city inhabited by clones, the subtle takeover of the human mind by technology, and finally, predictably, the "big one," a nuclear explosion and its aftermath, resulting in a planet damaged beyond recognition. A modicum of hope is offered by an image of Earth as ovum: the possibility of rebirth perhaps? Only if you haven't been paying attention. No, all that's left alive is a chirping cricket. There are no human survivors (not even Keith Richards). The final image is a damaged yield sign, alluding to the album's title.

The video, co-directed by Kevin Altieri and Todd McFarlane, was nominated for Best Music Video Short Form at the 1999 Grammy Awards. A compelling return to the medium for Pearl Jam.

---

opening slots were the only opportunity Pearl Jam fans would have to see their idols during 1997. But there was light at the end of the tunnel.

Support Tours

Having "yielded" to the idea of doing business with Ticketmaster, Pearl Jam was now in a position to take their show back on the road and play at places they had not played in several years. The months ahead would take them all around the globe, but first up was a show in the fiftieth state.

Aloha, Pearl Jam, and Mahalo

Up until this point, Pearl Jam had been in the habit of prefacing their tours with warm-up gigs at local Seattle clubs like the Showbox. This time around, in later February of 1998, they opted for the warmer climes of Maui, Hawaii, where they played two shows at the Alexander M. Baldwin Amphitheatre, bringing Mudhoney along for the ride as openers.

Oceania and Jack Iron's Final Show

But rather than heading northeast to California and beginning a tour of the continental United States, Pearl Jam instead boarded planes and flew in the opposite direction, to New Zealand, where they wrapped up the shortest month on the calendar by playing gigs at the Queen's Wharf Event Centre in Wellington, and Ericsson Stadium in Auckland.

Then it was off to Australia for the month of March. Melbourne was the first stop, where they played a series of three shows at Melbourne Park on the second, third, and fifth. The Melbourne run was followed by a show in South Australia's capital city, Adelaide. Sydney was up next, and the locals there were treated to three Pearl Jam shows at the Sydney Entertainment Centre on the ninth, eleventh, and twelfth. A deuce at the Brisbane Entertainment Centre was then followed by another deuce at the Perth Entertainment Centre. The second of the Perth gigs marked a bittersweet moment in Pearl Jam history, for it would prove to be drummer and erstwhile band matchmaker Jack Irons' final show as Pearl Jam's drummer. It was the end of an era.

Due to the band's unusual set of circumstances with the Ticketmaster situation, Irons had enjoyed a fairly light touring schedule during his tenure with the band up until this point, which suited him fine. But with the release of *Yield*, and Pearl Jam's return to a more typical touring schedule, Irons' struggles with bipolar disorder began to exact a physical, spiritual, and emotional toll on him. Faced with the looming prospect of a monster North American tour, he came to the realization that he could no longer maintain that grueling pace of touring, and unfortunately, he was forced to quit the band in April 1998.

A Welcome Matt: We Know What You're Doing Next Summer

The band's sadness at losing the well-respected Irons was tempered somewhat by another unexpected, albeit bittersweet, turn of events. Because Soundgarden had apparently broken up, another drummer that the members of Pearl Jam had long coveted became available. The timing for Matt Cameron to join the team as a "free agent" was absolutely perfect, at least from Pearl Jam's perspective! From Cameron's end, the timing was a little tight. The story goes that Ed, Stone, and Kelly Curtis all got on the phone and called him out of the blue, on short notice, wondering what his summer plans were. The schedule required him to learn about eighty songs over a two-week period, but he put the time in and got them down. As with his predecessor, Irons, Cameron began his tenure with Pearl Jam on a temporary basis, but somewhere in the middle of the tour, Pearl Jam made it official, and Matt Cameron became their man, and he continues to man the skins to this day.

When a drummer can afford to have his name printed on his drumsticks, we suppose it is safe to assume that he has arrived. Here, from the personal collection of Dustin Pardue, is a pair from the mighty Matt Cameron, of Pearl Jam *and* Soundgarden fame.

Dustin Pardue

North America

The *Yield* North American Tour became hugely successful. A DVD documentary on the making of the album, *Single Video Theory*, and their first live album, *Live on Two Legs*, complemented the tour. Pearl Jam was back in the game, and winning. They had yielded to both inner pressures and outside forces, and emerged stronger for the experience. And the fans were appreciative.

West Coast

The first leg of the first proper North American Pearl Jam tour since *Vs.* kicked off in Jeff's hometown of Missoula on June 2. Between then and July 22, the band performed a total of twenty-two shows, wrapping up the first leg of the tour in triumphant style, at home in Seattle at Memorial Stadium.

East Coast

They would not rest on their laurels for long. Barely four weeks later, they kicked off the second leg of the tour at the Deer Creek Music Center in Noblesville, Indiana, and the Breslin Student Events Center in East Lansing, Michigan. Yes, they gave Detroit a miss this time around, for reasons that were never made clear. All told, this second North American leg of the tour would feature twenty-five shows, two of them in Canada, the rest in the continental United States, highlighted by back-to-back shows at Madison Square Garden on September 10 and 11.

This leg of the tour wrapped up in Mike McCready's home state of Florida, when the band performed two nights in a row at the Coral Sky Amphitheatre in West Palm Beach on September 22 and 23. Not counting the baker's dozen with Jack Irons back in the winter and spring, the next two legs of the tour consisted of forty-nine shows. As we will see in the next chapter, these shows would provide the source material for Pearl Jam's first official live album. Whether they had "yielded" or not was ultimately irrelevant to the fans. All that mattered was that Pearl Jam was now, officially, back in business.

16

Live on a Dozen Legs

Pearl Jam Throws the Fans a Bone

LIVE ON TWO LEGS

The Tale of the Tape

Recorded: By Brett Eliason, during the band's 1998 North American Tour in support of *Yield*, at venues from coast to coast, June 24 through September 23

Released: November 24, 1998, by Epic

Billboard: RIAA-certified Platinum album. It debuted at number 15 on the *Billboard* 200.

The Source Material

When one stops and ponders all of the hassles Pearl Jam had been through in the years leading up to *Yield*, it really was a feel-good moment for fans to see them finally get back to a more robust and normal touring schedule. With the end of the Jack Irons era and the beginning of the Matt Cameron era, the band, although they had no way of knowing it at the time, was entering an unprecedented period of stability. The time seemed right for them to record their first live album. All of the tracks included on *Live on Two Legs* were recorded during the summer 1998 leg of the band's *Yield* Tour. In that sense, the finished product can be thought of as a souvenir, a gift from the band to their long suffering fans who had stood by them during that four year period of turbulence. And what a gift it was.

All told, the sixteen tracks recorded for *Live on Two Legs* add up to just over an hour and ten minutes of live music. That, of course, is a much shorter span of time than one would experience at an actual Pearl Jam concert. However, because of the manner in which the recordings were curated, the live album provides the listener with a high-quality sampling of the concert experience, the sonic equivalent of the previews one sits through in a movie theater. In fact, one can say that it serves a dual purpose. Not only is it a souvenir of the summer 1998 leg of the *Yield* Tour, it is also a teaser for Pearl Jam concerts to come.

"Corduroy"

"Corduroy," that ode to the absurd price gouging for replicas of Eddie's thrift store wardrobe, was recorded on the lead singer's home court, at the United Center in sweet home Chicago on June 29.

"Given to Fly"

The most popular single from *Yield*, "Given to Fly" was also a concert favorite. This version was recorded at the Forum in Inglewood, California, on July 14.

"Hail Hail"

Recorded two days after "Given to Fly," "Hail Hail," one of the harder rocking tunes from *No Code*, was captured on tape at another west coast gig, at the ARCO Arena in Sacramento, California, on July 16.

"Daughter" "Daughter/"Rockin' in the Free World"/"W.M.A."

This brilliant Pearl Jam concert moment is from the later East Coast leg of the *Yield* Tour. It was captured at Constitution Hall in Washington, D.C. on September 19. This track provides a perfect example of what hardcore Pearl Jam fans are talking about when they use the term "Daughter tag." While "Daughter" remains the musical structure of the entire piece, the extended jam format provides lead vocalist Eddie with the opportunity to engage the audience by working in lyrics from other songs, be they covers, originals, or, in this case, both.

"Elderly Woman Behind the Counter in a Small Town"

Given the reputation of Florida as *the* destination spot for elderly retirees, this song seems like the perfect selection for a West Palm Beach show. "Elderly Woman Behind the Counter in a Small Town" was captured at the Coral Sky Amphitheatre on September 23, making this the last song recorded during the tour that would make the final track listing for *Live on Two Legs*.

"Untitled"

Just when the track listing seemed to be following chronological order, "Untitled" was taken from the Merriweather Post Pavilion gig in Columbia, Maryland, a week earlier on September 18.

"M.F.C."

Casting chronology completely aside, "MFC" dates from June 27 at the Alpine Valley Music Theatre in East Troy, Wisconsin, the second show of the first back-to-back on the earlier, Midwest/West Coast leg of the tour.

"Go"

More East Coast action, with the raucous, Grammy-winning barnburner, "Go." This blistering version was preserved for posterity on September 8 at Continental Airlines Arena in East Rutherford, New Jersey, an arena that will forever be known simply as "the Meadowlands" to New Yorkers. Perhaps the Matt Cameron factor plays a role, but for our money, this version far outstrips that on 1993's *Vs.*

"Red Mosquito"

This one is from an earlier New Jersey gig on August 29 at Blockbuster Music Entertainment Centre in Camden, New Jersey. Rising to the challenges of their gritty environs, Pearl Jam nails it here, coming across with all of the power and swagger of a heavy metal Lynyrd Skynyrd.

"Even Flow"

Thanks to the magic of musical production technology, this version of "Even Flow" (by this time a bona fide Pearl Jam *classic*) is a hybrid mixed from two separate

From the breadth of *Live on Two Legs* to the depth of *Live at the Gorge 05/06*, Pearl Jam was clearly experimenting with different ways to recreate the live experience outside the context of the concert venue. This seven-disc collection cobbles together three shows at the Gorge Amphitheatre into a cohesive whole. Pictured here is one of the three discs from the September 1, 2005, show. *Author's collection*

Official Bootleg: A Jammer's Favorite Oxymoron

As time kept on slippin' into the future, Pearl Jam found a new way to accommodate those fans who wished to own a recording of their favorite concert. They decided to record *all* of their shows and release them as "official bootlegs." This most noble of experiments began during the *Binaural* Tour, when Pearl Jam released all seventy-two shows—in three separate waves—as double CDs in simple cardboard packaging. The tour's grand finale, at Seattle's KeyArena, was the lone exception; it was released as a *three*-disc set and actually hit ninety-eight on the *Billboard* 200. Because of the success of the experiment, Pearl Jam found itself setting a record for most albums debuting on the *Billboard* 200 simultaneously. Of those initial seventy-two, the band members declared eighteen of them to be "Ape/Man" shows, which is Pearl Jam jargon for "damn good shows."

The band repeated the experiment for the 2003 tour, with a few tweaks. Once again, all seventy-three of the shows would be released, but not automatically. The majority of the shows had to be pre-ordered through pearljam.com and delivered by mail. Six of the shows, thought to be exemplary, were automatically released to stores, with a seventh released only in Mexico.

By the Fall 2005 tour, the CD releases had evolved into MP3-only, and by Spring 2006, MP3-only had evolved into "Free Lossless Audio Codec," or FLAC format. To wit, there were thirty-two MP3-only bootleg releases during 2005, and another seventy-one new-and-improved FLAC releases during 2006. Pearl Jam bootlegs were now not only official, but they were also being made using cutting edge technology.

For reasons that remain unclear, there were no official bootlegs released during the Summer 2007 European tour, but the coveted collectibles were back on the menu for 2008, with a buyer's choice of MP3, FLAC, or good old CDs, which were already beginning to seem quaint by this point. There were thirteen released in 2008, thirty-two in 2009, twenty-four in 2010, nineteen in 2011, sixteen in 2012, twenty-eight in 2013, and eighteen in 2014. At press time, there were ten shows on the schedule for 2015, and all indications are that the "official bootleg" program will continue to grow. With 398 official bootlegs released to date, and 3.5 million total copies sold, there is no end in sight.

performances: August 25 at Star Lake Amphitheatre in Burggettstown, Pennsylvania, and August 31 at Hardee's Walnut Creek Amphitheatre in Raleigh, North Carolina. If you love the way this sounds, be sure to give proper credit to Brett Eliason and all the hardworking studio staff.

"Off He Goes"

Back to the earlier West Coast leg of the tour for another gem from the July 14 gig at the Forum in Inglewood, California. The July 14 gig is the only show featured on more than one track. "Off He Goes" provides a glimpse of Pearl Jam's mellower side.

"Nothingman"

Fourth of July Eve, as in July 3, found the boys at the Sandstone Amphitheater in Bonner Springs, Kansas. A proper ballad, the immediacy of this live version of "Nothingman" packs an emotional wallop. Very sweet.

By the time *Live on Two Legs* was released, right around Thanksgiving of 1998, Pearl Jam was already long established as one of the premier live acts in rock and roll. This long-awaited gem provided fans with an aural snapshot of the past summer's tour and made for one heck of a holiday stocking stuffer. Little did we know it at the time, but it also heralded an unprecedented torrent of live releases to come.
Author's collection

"Do the Evolution"

Recorded at the Forum in Inglewood, California, on July 13. You will recall that early on during the band's career, Jeff Ament was concerned about making music videos. Eddie didn't seem to care much for it, either. All of the band members wanted people to remember Pearl Jam's songs on the songs' own merits, rather than on the imagery of the videos. When we think about that phase, our minds always turn to this song, and, of course, the Grammy-nominated Kevin Altieri video. In this case, we think Ament was half right. The animated video is stunning, and deserving of all the accolades it received, but the song still stands strong on its own merits, particularly in a live concert setting. Eddie delights in the throat-shredding vocals as the band powers through the song at breakneck pace.

"Better Man"

The award for "Earliest Recorded Song" on *Live on Two Legs* goes to Vedder's Bad Radio holdover tune, "Better Man," taped on June 24 at the Rushmore Civic Center Arena in Rapid City, South Dakota. This was not only the fourth show of this leg of the tour, but the fourth official tour date of Matt Cameron's Pearl Jam tenure. The joyful sound of the audience singing along is one of the more enjoyable features of the album.

"Black"

Another classic from *Ten*, this version of "Black" comes from the September 7 gig at GTE Virginia Beach Amphitheater, located (where else?) in Virginia Beach, Virginia. The enthusiastic audience adds a sixth horizon to the seminal tale of heartbreak and loss, and Mike *really* lets it rip on the solo. This version packs a punch, for sure.

"Fuckin' Up"

Last but not least, *Live on Two Legs* ends with a nod and a dedication—"This is for Neil" (to Neil Young)—as the band cranks out "Fuckin' Up" on September 15 at Great Woods in Mansfield, Massachusetts. In the context of the album, it is a fitting finale, and it seems like the band have left the stage for good. Indeed, Eddie walks off, saying "See you tomorrow." At the actual show, they would return to play "Yellow Ledbetter" as a second encore.

Between the Legs

In the time between the fraternal twin bookends of the two live "Legs" compilations, Pearl Jam also managed to release three other official live albums. In direct contrast to the "Legs" releases, which both feature tracks cobbled together from different concerts in different places, the intermediary releases either chronicled tracks from a particular show, or from a particular venue.

Pearl Jam Cares, at Benaroya Hall

The first of these releases was titled *Live at Benaroya Hall*. It was recorded, as one would expect, live at Benaroya Hall in Seattle, Washington, on October 22, 2003. Why release this particular show? The hometown concert was a latter day "Pearl Jam Unplugged," an all-acoustic concert held as a benefit fundraiser for YouthCare. Because the recording features a complete show, the package released on July 27, 2004, was significantly larger than the "Legs" compilations. The twenty-six song *Live at Benaroya Hall* was released as a two-CD set and as a limited edition four-record vinyl set for Ten Clubbers only. Predictably, the hardcore Jammers snapped up those 2,000 copies in the blink of an eye. In general, expensive double live CDs are a tough sell, even for a veteran band like Pearl Jam. *Live at Benaroya Hall* sold a modest 52,000 copies during its first week of release, which was good enough to earn it the number eighteen spot on *Billboard*. But commercial success was never the driving force. Remember that this is *Pearl Jam* we are talking about here; raising funds for YouthCare was all that mattered in this case.

Pearl Jam (If Not Record Store Owners) on Easy Street

About a year and a half later, Pearl Jam got the itch again. This time around, the goal was a stimulus package, of sorts, for the band's favorite local record store—Easy Street Records in Seattle, Washington—and, by extension, *all* of the independent record stores who were members in good standing of the Coalition of Independent Music Stores. Like they say, charity begins at home.

They decided to perform a live set at Easy Street Records on April 29, 2005, record it, whittle it down to an EP-sized collection, and then distribute it exclusively to the aforementioned Coalition of Independent Music Store sites. Why not simply release the *entire* show as a full live album, you ask? The band's reasoning was sound enough. People would be more apt to shell out a few bucks for a novel live Pearl Jam EP out of sheer curiosity than they would be to invest fifteen, twenty bucks on a full-sized live LP.

Pearl Jam Gorges Itself

Barely four months later, Pearl Jam's pendulum began to swing from minimalist humanitarianism to wretched excess. On September 1, 2005, they performed the first of three shows at the Gorge Amphitheatre in the Columbia River town of George, Washington. Shows two and three wouldn't take place for nearly another eleven months, a back-to-back at the Gorge Amphitheatre on July 22 and 23, 2006.

This time around, rather than compiling live recordings from a variety of venues during a single tour, or from a variety of venues over a *series* of tours, Pearl Jam was confining its efforts to three shows from a single venue over a span of eleven months. This project wasn't intended to produce a charity EP or a double live CD of a single show. This time around the band was thinking big, as in *boxed set* big. The result, finally released on June 26, 2007, was a one hundred-song, seven-disc boxed set titled *Live at the Gorge 05/06*. The voluminous collection featured nearly eight hours of live Pearl Jam—a Jammer's dream come true, provided one had the funds. The paradox, of course, is that the bigger the box, the slower the sales. *Live at the Gorge 05/06* barely made a blip on the *Billboard* charts, debuting at number thirty-six with 19,000 units sold during the first week, and barely 30,000 during the first year. Ten Club members had to be content with their annual members-only holiday singles because *Live at the Gorge 05/06* was clearly only a holiday "stocking stuffer" for a lucky few!

A DOZEN YEARS AND TWO MONTHS LATER: *LIVE ON TEN LEGS*

By the time Pearl Jam was ready to release *Live on Ten Legs* in 2011, live albums of this nature had become something of an anachronism. They had long since been replaced in the hearts and minds of music fans by the increased availability of things like Pearl Jam's aforementioned "official bootlegs." But Pearl Jam is a band that honors tradition, and they can afford to continue honoring the tradition of the live album.

A Tale of the Tape

Recorded: Between 2005 and 2010 by John Burton

Released: January 17, 2011

Billboard: Number 21 on the US *Billboard* 200

The Source Material

All of the songs featured on *Live on Ten Legs* were originally recorded at Pearl Jam concerts between 2005 and 2010, a period of activity that spans roughly five years. It is often described as having been recorded between 2003 and 2010, but we could find no evidence that any of the tracks on the album were recorded prior to September 12, 2005, when the killer version of "Jeremy" that appears here was captured at the John Labatt Centre in London, Ontario, Canada.

Its spiritual predecessor, *Live on Two Legs*, was comprised solely of songs recorded over a period of three months during the *Yield* Tour in the summer of 1998, which gives the earlier collection of live tracks a sense of wholeness. Not so on the later collection, which feels cobbled together. That sense of discontinuity is noticeable when you listen to it, too. Rather than providing a snapshot of a moment in time, as the best live albums in rock history do, *Live on Ten Legs* is more akin to a box of old family photographs strewn about in a drawer, with very little sense of space or time.

It is worth noting that in the era of the compact disc, and moving forward into the era of purely digitized music, there has been less emphasis on the notion of an album as a single, cohesive narrative. That being said, the span of time covered here on *Live on Ten Legs* was deliberate, for the album was conceived as a celebratory way to kick off the band's twentieth anniversary year, which was the first of many such celebrations in 2011, as it turned out. In that spirit, and without further adieu, let us take a listen as we delve back into Pearl Jam history.

"Arms Aloft"

The album kicks off with a cover of Joe Strummer and the Mescaleros' "Arms Aloft," recorded at the Werchter Festival in Werchter, Belgium, on the Fourth of July 2010. The cover song came during the first set, immediately following the Pearl Jam classic, "Even Flow." As is the case with all of the tracks on *Live on Ten Legs*, this entire show is also available as one of Pearl Jam's official bootlegs. "Arms Aloft" is a loving tribute to the memory of Joe Strummer, an early hero and patron of Eddie's, who passed away unexpectedly three days before Christmas 2002.

"World Wide Suicide"

"World Wide Suicide" was recorded on September 22, 2006, in Prague, Czech Republic at the Sazka Arena, where it was the sixth song in Pearl Jam's first set. An official bootleg exists for this show. The track sounds fine, but were it not for the audience sounds kicking in during the last thirteen seconds, you could easily be forgiven for thinking you were listening to a studio track.

"Animal"

Recorded on September 13, 2006, at the Bern Arena, a venue named for after its town of Bern, Switzerland. This version of "Animal" was the second of seventeen songs played during the first set that evening. And yes, there is an official bootleg. "Animal" comes across as more organic here. The audience is present in the mix, and the feeling is palpable that they, and the band, are just getting warmed up.

"Got Some"

Recorded in Eddie's old stomping grounds of San Diego, California, on October 9, 2009, at the Viejas Arena, "Got Some" was the fifteenth song played in a seventeen-song first set. Eddie addresses the crowd in Spanish at the outset before the band launches into the song. Given the song's position in the set list, the band sounds remarkably fresh, with Matt Cameron's drums galloping along to the delight of an energized audience.

"State of Love and Trust"

"State of Love and Trust" was recorded outdoors in historic Hyde Park in London, England, on June 25, 2010. It was the sixteenth song played that evening during a robust, twenty-song first set. The song is rendered here at a breakneck pace, with a perfect balance in the mix between instruments, vocals, and audience. You can hear the vastness of Hyde Park in the mix.

"I Am Mine"

Recorded on November 10, 2006, at the Brisbane Entertainment Centre in Brisbane, Australia, "I Am Mine" was the twelfth song played that evening in the midst of a seventeen-song first set, but the energy level is still high.

"Unthought Known"

Wuhlheide—a venue in Berlin, Germany, in which the band played on June 30, 2010—was the setting for this version of "Unthought Known." Finally, here, we break the pattern of first set songs with the song that kicked off that evening's second encore set. The Berlin audience is on their feet, clapping in time, and clearly ready for more. The versatile Matt Cameron is audible and strong on backing vocals here, as the Wuhlheide audience bounced up and down with joy.

"Rearviewmirror"

"Rearviewmirror" was captured live at the Subiaco Oval in Perth, Australia, on November 25, 2006. On this particular evening, the song had the distinction of being the closing number of the marathon, twenty-song first set. The middle jam features all of the musicians firing on all cylinders, as sharp and as tight as if it were the first song. "Rearviewmirror" builds here to a powerful crescendo, much to the delight of the screaming crowd. Talk about going out with a bang!

"The Fixer"

"The Fixer" was recorded in Boston, Massachusetts, on May 17, 2010, at the beautiful TD Garden, named for its corporate sponsor, TD Bank. The modern venue is the home of the NHL's Boston Bruins and the frequent NBA champions, the Boston Celtics. On this night, it was Pearl Jam's home, and they did not disappoint. "The Fixer" was the third song played near the beginning of what would become a twenty song first set. You can hear the band members getting in touch with their inner Kiss fans on this poppy number, and everyone, band and audience alike, seems to be having a wonderful time.

"Nothing as It Seems"

Everything *was* as it seemed on November 22, 2006, at the Adelaide Entertainment Centre, in Adelaide, Australia; it seemed like Pearl Jam was in town, and they were. They broke out "Nothing as It Seems" six songs into an eighteen song first set, and for our money, they managed to one-up the version on *Binaural*. The audience clapping along to the strums of the acoustic guitar lends the song a feeling of communal spirit. The pace of "Nothing as It Seems" allows all of the musicians an opportunity to shine, but McCready is a standout here, wringing some gorgeous note from his guitar.

"In Hiding"

There was nowhere to hide when Pearl Jam performed "In Hiding" at the Bill Graham Civic Auditorium in San Francisco, California, on July 18, 2006. "In Hiding" came out of hiding late during the first set, the fifteenth of eighteen songs, and Eddie was anticipating an audience sing-along . . . and he got one. The San Francisco crowd was really into it.

"Just Breathe"

"Just Breathe" was recorded live at the "World's Most Famous Arena," Madison Square Garden, on *both* May 20 and 21, 2010, so it should come as no surprise that there seems to be some confusion as to which version made the cut for *Live On Ten Legs*. At the first show, "Just Breathe" appeared as the third song during the first encore. During the second show, Pearl Jam took a second breath, with "Just Breathe" making an appearance as the second song of the first encore. The evidence we've examined leans in favor of the version from the second show, on May 21, as being the one to make the cut here. *Both* nights were great, of course, as evidenced by their respective official bootlegs. Ed's acoustic guitar hearkens back to the mighty Led Zeppelin, who also did some of their most beautiful work with wooden instruments. This is a gem.

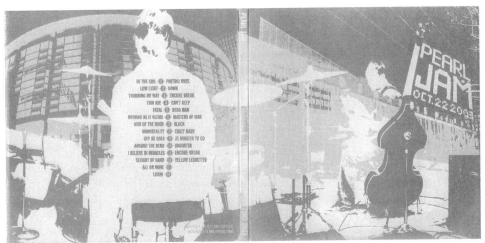

OF THE GIRL ·1· PARTING WAYS
LOW LIGHT ·2· DOWN
THUMBING MY WAY ·3· ENCORE BREAK
THIN AIR ·4· CAN'T KEEP
FATAL ·5· DEAD MAN
NOTHING AS IT SEEMS ·6· MASTERS OF WAR
MAN OF THE HOUR ·7· BLACK
IMMORTALITY ·8· CRAZY MARY
OFF HE GOES ·9· 25 MINUTES TO GO
AROUND THE BEND ·10· DAUGHTER
I BELIEVE IN MIRACLES ·11· ENCORE BREAK
SLEIGHT OF HAND ·12· YELLOW LEDBETTER
ALL OR NONE ·13·
LUKIN ·14·

The rationale for releasing this October 22, 2003, Seattle concert as a live album was two-fold: it was an all-acoustic show, and it was for the benefit of one of the band's favorite charities, YouthCare. More than enough reason to "pull the plug" again and show off their evolving acoustic chops.

Author's collection

"Jeremy"

Nearly fifteen years after its suicidal teen protagonist's untimely demise, "Jeremy" put in an appearance at the John Labatt Centre in London, Ontario, Canada, on September 12, 2005. In what was perhaps a subtle nod to the misfortune inherent in the tragic tale, "Jeremy" arrived in the thirteenth slot of a seventeen-song first set. Eddie sounds a bit winded at first, frankly. It is hard not to smile at the audience's enthusiastic participation when it came time to drop the proverbial "F-Bomb"! With the passage of time, a different drummer, and the addition of Boom Gaspar, "Jeremy" has evolved into almost a different song. It has lost none of its power but now boasts additional layers of sound.

"Public Image"

Pearl Jam played "Public Image" as the fourth song of their six-song second encore at the Heineken Jammin' Festival in Venice, Italy, on July 6, 2010. Something's "rotten" in Italy, as Pearl Jam covers John Lydon (aka Johnny Rotten)'s post-Sex Pistols band, Public Image Ltd., and the signature song from their 1978 debut album, *Public Image: First Issue*. Pearl Jam always rises to the occasion whenever they cover punk rock royalty, and "Public Image" is no exception.

"Spin the Black Circle"

Pearl unleashed "Spin the Black Circle," their heartfelt ode to vinyl records, as the third song of their first set at Copps Coliseum in Hamilton, Ontario, Canada, on September 13, 2005. And if you thought this one was a barnburner in the studio, the live version here will knock you right off your feet.

"Porch"

When Pearl Jam went into "Porch" as the last song of the first encore at Ferrocarril Oeste Stadium in Buenos Aires, Argentina, on November 26, 2005, nobody had to stand back. Eva "Evita" Peron herself would have been impressed. Had this been twelve or thirteen years earlier, Eddie would no doubt have been climbing up onto the rafters and leaping into the audience with reckless abandon. But the wild child surf punk had long since evolved into a wizened poet/philosopher who kept his feet planted firmly on the ground, surrounded by notebooks, stage monitors, and his omnipresent bottle of red wine. But in spite of the passage of time, "Porch" remained, as it does to this day, one hell of an exciting way to close out an encore set, even when the band eases into it with an acoustic intro, as they did here.

"Alive"

Pearl Jam came "Alive" in 2009 on Halloween night, October 31, at the Wachovia Spectrum Arena. This was the fourth night of a four-night stand in the "city of brotherly love." The *Ten*-era classic arrived as the ninth song of their eleven-song second encore, making it the forty-first song overall that night. As if to emphasize the point, Eddie tells the audience, "Well, we're still here; we're not going anywhere yet." The shows were becoming Springsteen-esque in length by this point. The audience loudly and enthusiastically sings along on every note here, giving a triumphant air to the proceedings. Appropriately enough, once the song ends, Eddie introduces the band, as if in anticipation of another encore.

"Yellow Ledbetter"

Back to Wuhlheide in Berlin, Germany, on June 30, 2010, for the final track destined for *Live On Ten Legs*. In this case, appropriately enough, "Yellow Ledbetter" was the final song of the second encore. The virtual show that makes up the album, cobbled together over space and time and prettied up in the studio, ends with a solid dose of classic rock. Take a bow, gentlemen.

Third "Legs"?

The advent of Pearl Jam's "official bootlegs" era has certainly lessened the social pressure for curated, compilation-style live releases like 1998's *Live on Two Legs* and 2011's *Live on Ten Legs*. When you can have all of their complete concerts any time you like, why bother with something as dated and artificial as the "Legs" releases? Well, they *do* have their charms, and we can see the arguments on either side. Since the "Legs" albums seem to have coincided with significant moments in Pearl Jam history, we are curious to learn if the 2016 anniversary year will yield another "leg" of live music. There was no official word as of press time, but our best guess is that five years is just too soon. If they do one at all, we're betting they save the next set of "legs" for their thirtieth anniversary.

17

Binaural

The Tale of the Tape

Recorded: From September 1999 through January 2000 at Stone's own Studio Litho

Produced By: Tchad Blake and Pearl Jam

Released: May 16, 2000, on Epic

Singles: "Nothing as It Seems" on April 25, 2000; "Light Years" on July 18, 2000

Billboard: Number two on *Billboard* 200, with 226,000 first-week copies sold; certi-fied Gold by the RIAA but never made it to Platinum. As of 2013, 850,000 copies have been sold, according to Nielsen SoundScan.

Into the Studio

Pearl Jam took some well-deserved time off from band activity for most of 1999, following the success of the *Yield* album and tour. The exception to the rule was Eddie Vedder, who spent a considerable amount of his time playing live with friends Jon Maritheau and Brad Balsley of the band C Average. The experience allowed the Pearl Jam lead singer to scale back to the small clubs and guerilla gigs that had factored prominently in his original vision of the rock and roll lifestyle. Going back to his roots, so to speak, was an act of catharsis for him.

When the time came to go back into the studio to record *Binaural*, Pearl Jam decided that the time was right for a fresh set of ears at the controls and mixing boards. It wasn't as though they were seeking a permanent divorce from their long-time collaborator, Brendan O'Brien; they just thought they ought to play the field and see other people. But sometimes, as the old saying goes, absence makes the heart grow fonder. This was not going to be a clean break. In the final months of the twentieth century, the band reconvened on its home court, Studio Litho in Seattle, to begin work on the new record. The album's proposed title, *Binaural*, is a reference to a recording technique that most closely approximates how the human ear experiences sound. The band was dedicated to advancing beyond the mainstream modern recording experience. In order to employ the technique, the band brought in a new producer. Enter Tchad Blake, the binaural man. The plan was to feature several of the album's tracks in the binaural format. Blake's previous

Binaural

The name says it all, really. The prefix "Bi" means "two," of course. And "aural" has to do with ears, sound, and hearing. So a fair translation of the term would be to "listen with two ears," which strikes us as being an eminently reasonable proposition. Etymology aside, on a more practical level binaural recording employs paired microphones to create a sort of "3D" effect, giving the listener the sensation of actually being in the room with the musicians. Tchad Blake did not invent this technique, which, in its earliest incarnations, can be traced back to the late nineteenth century, long before the advent of commercial broadcast radio. Unfortunately, binaural recordings can only be appreciated by a listener wearing headphones; stereo speakers can't really capture it.

studio credits included work with Suzanne Vega, Tracy Chapman, and Tom Waits, all primarily solo acoustic artists. For the first time since *Ten*, Brendan O'Brien would not be coaching the Pearl Jam team in the studio.

In addition to a new producer and experiments with new recording techniques, the *Binaural* sessions featured a "new" face behind the drum kit, Pearl Jam's old friend Matt Cameron. Cameron, you will recall, came aboard as a replacement for Jack Irons during the *Yield* Tour, and now, with Soundgarden out of the picture for the foreseeable future, he was going to seal the deal by recording an album with Pearl Jam. *Binaural* would thus feature the studio debut of Matt Cameron on drums, where he remains to this day.

The day that Cameron became an official member of Pearl Jam (an event which took place in the midst of the North American legs of the *Yield* Tour) represented the closing of an almost decade-long mythic cycle. The drummer who had long ago helped to create the fabled *Stone Gossard Demos 1990*, which precipitated the birth of Pearl Jam, had returned to man the skins once more. The circle was now complete.

For a guy who had spent much of the previous year surfing and playing informally with friends outside the Pearl Jam family, Eddie surprisingly shifted the mood back toward the dark side. There might have been some yielding going on in general to reach this point, but Ed still possessed some very specific anger. He also had to deal with a case of writer's block. Mike McCready's addictive nature had chased him back into rehab to seek treatment for prescription painkiller abuse, a slip he attributed to going through personal problems—though prescription pain medication is notoriously addictive. To his credit, he dealt with it right away and continued to maintain his abstinence from alcohol and cocaine.

The album cover art features a photo of the Hourglass Nebula and Eagle Nebula taken from the Hubble Space telescope, courtesy of NASA. Faced with the enormity of this imagery, one can't help but understand the underlying message: when you pause to look at the bigger picture, all of our human accomplishments, even Pearl Jam's music, are miniscule by comparison. Using the same songwriting process as on *Yield*, each band member developed their own tracks *before* coming into the studio to initiate recording with the full Pearl Jam contingent.

Overall, the binaural effect seemed to work best on the slower tracks. On the heavier selections, the boys actually brought back Brendan O'Brien for some final mix work at Southern Tracks in Atlanta. It all added up to a conscious distancing from "grunge," whatever that increasingly nebulous term meant. The album navigated between post-punk, folk, and psychedelic rock dalliances throughout, played out primarily under a dark cloud of angst.

The Tunes

Of the thirteen, er, *fourteen* (including "Writer's Block"), total tracks here, just five ("Nothing as It Seems," "Of the Girl," "Rival," "Sleight of Hand," and "Soon Forget") employ binaural recording techniques. Perhaps the album should have been more accurately titled "*Semi-Binaural?*" It is interesting to note that the original track listing contained sixteen songs, including "Sad" (nee "Letter to the Dead"), "Fatal," "In the Moonlight," and "Education," which were cut from the final version and wouldn't see the light of day until the *Lost Dogs* project in 2003. Moreover, the order of the tracks changed significantly, and the song "God's Dice" was added to the final list. Here are the songs that made the cut.

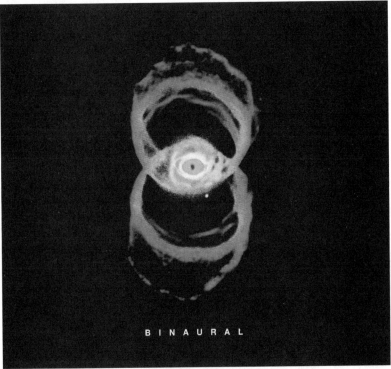

If nothing else, 2000's *Binaural* proved that Pearl Jam was unafraid to experiment and take chances when it came to their artistry. The sessions for the experimental album proved so prolific that they yielded several tracks that would get a new lease on life as a part of the *Lost Dogs* collection. Like the haunting imagery of the Hourglass Nebula on the album cover, Pearl Jam's universe was continually expanding. *Author's collection*

"Breakerfall"

Binaural continues the now classic Pearl Jam pattern of beginning an album with an explosive first track. From Eddie's howl to the opening twin guitar solos of Mike and Stone, "Breakerfall" kicks in hard and doesn't let up—an adrenaline shot that keeps on giving for a 2:19 rush and owes a debt of gratitude to the iconic guitar riff that kick starts the Who's "I Can See For Miles." The subject of the song is the first of several similar chart-toppers that populate the record: a girl close to the edge and emotionally shattered. When faced with despair, love is the only salvation.

"God's Dice"

The assault continues with the next track, "God's Dice." Fully credited to Jeff Ament, the song explores the fundamental question of fate and its inevitability with regard to the relationship between God and Man. The double tracked vocals and fast, hard rocking pace point the listener toward submission. The concept of surrendering to fate represents a transition for Pearl Jam. Here it can be perceived as a coping mechanism to allow mankind to move forward. Ament even goes so far as to invent a word, "Reignore," to describe the act.

"Evacuation"

The title of the next offering is straightforward enough: "Evacuation." The questions of "to where?" and "what to do?" are not so clearly addressed. The fact that Pearl Jam has no immediate answers only increases the album's overall sense of urgency. The music—staccato and halting in its delivery—functions like a siren, a warning to be heeded. It is also the first songwriting credit for Matt Cameron, which is not surprising because of its drummer-friendly, rhythmic pattern. Some fifteen years after its release it has only appeared twenty-nine times on live Pearl Jam set lists. It remains a perplexing tune, even to the diehard doyens of Pearl Jam Nation. Even Eddie Vedder noted the song's idiosyncratic nature when he joked that the song was like Pittsburgh because both had three bridges. Clever.

"Light Years"

Reimagined from an original demo called "Puzzles and Games," "Light Years" is one of the band's most tragically beautiful songs and is dedicated to the memory of their friend, Sony Music's Diana Muus, who passed away at age thirty-three in 1997. In writing the song, Ed made up for the fact that he "never had a chance to say goodbye," as he explained to the audience while introducing the song at Pinkpop 2000. Musically, the song takes on a rising, majestic quality. Lyrically, despite the lament over a profound loss, there remains the hope to rise above.

"Nothing as It Seems"

"Nothing as It Seems" is another solo credit for Jeff, and it features him playing an upright bass. The slow, foreboding, melodic march of the song is punctuated by some vintage Mike McCready pedal dictation, all interwoven by producer Blake's binaural technique. The Pearl Jam bassist cited his rural northern Montana childhood, and some recent reflection that led him to believe that it might not have been as idyllic as he remembered, as the influences that shaped the song's mood. His epiphany was prompted by watching the 1997 Nick Nolte film *Affliction* and by reading Kevin Canty's 1999 novel *Nine Below Zero*. The dirge-like, ominous tone of the track ascends to a higher level by virtue of McCready's wailing, Hendrixian solo turn. The antithesis of "Evacuation," "Nothing as It Seems" is a fan cult favorite. The first single from *Binaural* would have been right at home on a Pink Floyd album.

"Thin Air"

A dramatic shift occurs on the next song. "Thin Air" is as light and accessible musically as "Nothing as It Seems" is heavy and distant. An all-Stone Gossard credit, the song seems to bounce along, with the protagonist pinning all his hopes on his lover's ability to reach out and rescue him from the uncertainty he will otherwise face; simple, but effective.

"Insignificance"

The 1999 Seattle protests targeting the World Trade Organization inspired the song "Insignificance." An all-Vedder credit finds the Pearl Jam lead singer, or at least the protagonist of the song, ultimately feeling powerless. The rolling guitars and galloping drums can only drive the song so far, until they come to an abrupt stop. In the end, does modern society allow him to live, have a voice, and be heard? He's lowered the bar from any utopian dream of changing the world. Can he at least exist in his corner of it?

"Of the Girl"

The seductive, blues influenced "Of the Girl" takes the listener to yet another dark place. The song's subject is desperately seeking an elusive human connection to overcome his loneliness. "Of the Girl" is a Pearl Jam journey to film noir.

"Grievance"

Up next from Ed is "Grievance." A prescient tale from the Internet's nascent period, Vedder takes a cautionary tone. He can see the good, with regard to the convenience that technology provides; the bad, because of the individual's accompanying loss of independence; and, finally, the ugly . . . the increasing loss of human interaction. Fifteen years after its release, "Grievance" can be designated as a reading from the prophet Edward, who seemed to be getting in touch with his inner Marshall McLuhan and Neil Postman at the time.

"Rival"

The 1999 Columbine School massacre in Littleton, Colorado, prompted Stone Gossard's reflection on "Rival." From the growling dog that opens the track, and the hard-edged backbeat, it's a statement of paradise lost. Hope is gone, replaced by a belief in violence born of paranoia. In this world all men are on an island, fighting to defend their turf against all challengers.

"Sleight of Hand"

A man on his own island is the doomed protagonist of "Sleight of Hand." The music exhibits dramatic shifts from the melancholy to the frenetic. The lyrical theme never wavers. This is a wealthy man who long ago got lost in the monotony of his existence. The fact that there is a realization of the deception perpetrated—hence the song title—offers no solace; he is a prisoner of his own existence, nonetheless.

"Soon Forget"

One of Ed's first recorded experiments on ukulele is the sly "Soon Forget." Only Vedder could take on an instrument primarily associated with Hawaiian island reverie and offer a scathing indictment of a corporate tale. On *Binaural*, Vedder asks us to contemplate the fundamental question of material wealth versus spiritual health. In the end, he reminds us that no matter how rich, the subject will soon be forgotten. The song bears a striking musical resemblance to the Who's ukulele ditty, "Blue, Red, and Grey" from *The Who by Numbers*.

PEARL JAM
'BINAURAL'

1. Breakerfall
2. God's Dice
3. Evacuation
4. Light Years
5. Nothing As It Seems
6. Thin Air
7. Insignificance
8. Of The Girl
9. Grievance
10. Rival
11. Sleight Of Hand
12. Soon Forget
13. Parting Ways

EPIC

The final track listing for *Binaural* comprised thirteen tracks, a significant departure from the original track listing, which featured sixteen songs. It is also fascinating to note how the song titles seem to reflect the overall themes suggested by the cover art. Clearly, they put a lot of thought into this project.   *Ryan Byrne*

"Parting Ways" (hidden track: "Writer's Block")

The appropriately titled final song of the album is "Parting Ways." The story of an impending breakup, and how the couple must come to grips with it, plays out lyrically over a musical bed of softly strummed guitars and strings: Pearl Jam's "Moonlight Mile" moment. As with the previous song, "Soon Forget," it is another instance in which the gentle musical atmosphere softens the lyrical impact. In the end, the relationship is severed and the lovers become untethered, all in keeping with the overall message of the album. The tune also contains a reference to Ed's severe case of writer's block during the album's recording sessions, in the form of a hidden track titled, appropriately enough, "Writer's Block." This "song" consists of approximately a half minute of typewriter tapping, and appears at 6:49 during "Parting Ways."

Binaural in the "Rearviewmirror"

In retrospect, the *Binaural* sessions were prolific, in spite of Eddie's writer's block, and the album could easily have been far different musically and harmonically. This fact didn't come clearly into focus until the release of *Lost Dogs* in 2003. That compilation album of outtakes, B-sides, odds and sods, etc., offered a deeper perspective on just how puzzling some of the final song selections were for *Binaural*.

Most significantly, while the band members celebrated the team spirit of *Yield*, *Binaural* was filled with too many "individual songs" (as Stone Gossard noted) that were not successfully executed with the full complement of Pearl Jam's strengths as a musical unit. The fact that Brendan O'Brien was brought back for the final album mix was another indication that this dark-themed record, although having some strong, singular musical moments, was, by the band's own account, not one of their best.

Support Tours

Pearl Jam had given Seattle plenty of attention over the years, so the warm-up gigs for this year's tour gave their fellow Washingtonians in Bellingham an opportunity to check out the band at the tiny Mount Baker Theatre, which only holds around fifteen hundred people. The people of Vancouver got the second warm-up show at the even smaller Commodore Ballroom, which held less than a thousand fans.

Europe

The official first show of the *Binaural* Tour was held on May 23 at Estádio do Restelo in Lisbon, Portugal, and was the first of a scheduled twenty-eight show European leg. This leg of the tour was originally slated to run through July 3 and wrap up at the Ahoy in Rotterdam, the Netherlands. Things went quite smoothly at first, all the way up to and including show twenty-five at Norway's Oslo Spectrum. This show, at the modestly-sized (9,700 capacity) hall, would be Pearl Jam's last normal day for quite a while.

The next day, June 30, found the band in familiar territory, Roskilde, Denmark, for the annual Roskilde Festival, famous for hosting multiple bands on multiple stages in front of six-figure audiences. Pearl Jam had played there before without incident. On this day, however, something went terribly wrong. And before Pearl Jam's set was over, several people would lose their lives, and many others would be seriously injured.

Packing It In

There had been shows scheduled for Werchter, Belgium, and Rotterdam, the Netherlands, on the second and third of July, but in the wake of the Roskilde tragedy, Pearl Jam cancelled the remainder of this leg of the tour and headed home to contemplate their next move. In the aftermath of Roskilde, the members of Pearl Jam seriously contemplated retirement, not to mention their own

Roskilde: A Horror with Echoes of the Who

Months shy of their tenth anniversary, it almost ends for Pearl Jam. Five weeks into the European leg of the *Binaural* Tour, tragedy strikes on June 30 at Roskilde Festival in Denmark. It was the sixth day of the festival, and Pearl Jam played on the Orange Stage. When the band launched into "Daughter," the crowd began to surge toward the stage. What happened next can only be described as a freak accident, analogous to a multi-vehicle pileup on the highway. As near as anyone has been able to piece it together, a number of people fell down onto the ground in the same general area. The ground was wet from rain earlier in the day, which may have been a contributing factor, though no one can say for certain. The pile of people lying facedown on the ground caused a gap in the chain of humanity that typically supports "crowd surfers," enthusiastic fans who lie flat on their backs and are passed overhead by the tightly packed fans standing below them. The crowd surfers began falling into that gap, effectively falling right on top of their fallen fellows. Others have suggested that the forward surge of humanity toward the stage simply washed over the fallen fans like a wave, crushing them. In all likelihood there were several contributing factors, and there is a certain degree of truth in both of the preceding theories. What is irrefutably certain is that nine fans died by asphyxiation that day. Twenty-six other fans were injured, three of them seriously. They were crushed and suffocated, in spite of Vedder's repeated pleas from the stage for the crowd to recede.

Though circumstances differed, the Roskilde incident is reminiscent of the Who's tragedy twenty years earlier, right down to an eerie similarity in the number of fans killed and injured. On December 3, 1979, at a sold-out Riverfront Coliseum in Cincinnati, Ohio, the Who was experimenting with Festival Seating, which meant no assigned seat numbers. Of the 18,348 tickets sold, 14,770 tickets were first come, first seated. Virtually *everyone* showed up early and crowded around the one or two entrance gates that were scheduled to open. During afternoon sound check, the assembled masses surged forward, mistakenly thinking that the concert had begun. In that stampede, eleven fans, ages fifteen to twenty-seven, were trampled to death at the gates, while twenty more sustained serious injuries.

mortality. Early on the morning after the tragedy, Pearl Jam issued the following statement, as quoted by *Rolling Stone's* David Fricke:

> This is so painful . . . I think we are waiting for someone to wake us and say it was just a horrible nightmare . . . And there are absolutely no words to express our anguish in regard to the parents and loved ones of these precious lives that were lost. We have not yet been told what actually occurred, but it seemed random and sickeningly quick . . . it doesn't make sense. When you agree to play a festival of this size and reputation, it is impossible to imagine such a heart-wrenching scenario. Our lives will never be the same, but we know that is nothing compared to the grief of the families and friends of those involved. It is so tragic . . . there are no words. Devastated, Pearl Jam.

Pete Townshend, having been through his own nightmare in Cincinnati, called Eddie Vedder on July 1 to offer his empathy and support. In the Who's

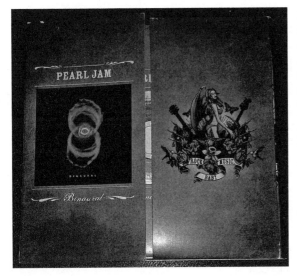

Here, from the personal collection of Ryan Byrne, we see an alternate packaging of *Binaural*, which juxtaposes the official album cover with a motif on the right that is evocative of old-school American tattoo art. As you will read, the European leg of the support tour ended in grim fashion at the Roskilde Festival in Denmark, less than six weeks after the album's release. That June 30th tragedy has left an indelible impression on all of the band members. *Ryan Byrne*

case, Townshend regretted having left the scene too early and not placing enough emphasis on the dead and their grieving families.

After a month of intense soul-searching, during which they seriously contemplated retirement more than once, the band decided to continue their tour as planned. Though it would be a long time before they ever hit the European festival circuit again, they came to the conclusion that the healing process could only begin once they were back playing music in public. As Eddie related to *Spin* magazine's Eric Weisbard, "playing, facing crowds, being together . . . it enabled us to start processing it." In years to come, they would reach out to the families of some of the Roskilde victims and establish enduring relationships with them, but for now they just had to go through their own grieving process the best way they knew how.

East Coast

Toward that end, Pearl Jam began a two-leg, forty-seven-date North American tour on August 3. The first leg ran until September 5 and hit twenty-three locations on the East Coast. Among the highlights was the fact that New Yorkers outside of the Big Apple got several opportunities to enjoy the band, including a three-night run at Jones Beach State Amphitheater, followed by a show at Saratoga Performing Arts Center. Bostonians also got to enjoy a back-to-back at the Tweeter Center.

Midwest/West Coast

After a month off the road, Pearl Jam roared back into action on October fourth for another twenty-four shows, including two in Canada and twenty-two in the States, this time concentrating on venues west of the Mississippi. With the exception of an October 14–15 back-to-back at the Cynthia Woods Mitchell Pavilion in the Woodlands, Texas, the band played hit-and-run across the western United States, performing a single show at each venue.

The *Binaural* Tour wrapped up for good during the first week of November. The grand finale featured two shows at Seattle's KeyArena on the fifth and sixth. The last show of the tour was a marathon three-hour show, with opening appearances by Matt Cameron's side project, Wellwater Conspiracy, and the veteran Red Hot Chili Peppers.

This *lengthy* tour had spanned three seasons, from the second week of May through the first week of November, and it was highlighted by a number of memorable shows along the way. Among them, their coldest show ever (28°F) at Alpine Valley, Wisconsin, that came to be known, appropriately enough, as "the Ice Bowl"; a tenth anniversary celebration of their Mookie Blaylock debut in Las Vegas (where they honored the memory of Andrew Wood by playing "Crown of Thorns" for the first time); and two emotional Seattle homecoming concerts at KeyArena. It was also chronicled on film in the DVD release *Touring Band 2000*, which features twenty-eight songs, nearly three hours of highlights from the two North American legs of the tour, plus some fun-filled bonus materials.

During the final show of the tour they played "Alive" for the first time since the Roskilde tragedy that had marred and cut short the European leg of the tour. It proved to be a cathartic moment, particularly as the song had long since evolved, in the eyes of the fans, from an Eddie Vedder horror story of incest and child abuse into a survivor's anthem of triumph. Eddie recognized that by playing together in front of different audiences and by working together as a team, Pearl Jam—like the Who in Cincinnati many years before them—was able to begin processing what had happened at Roskilde the previous summer. Once again, the old adage applies: that which had not killed them had only made them stronger. The band continues to mourn and honor the young lives so senselessly lost on that day through their generous support of the victims' families. They found a way to put the tragedy of Roskilde into its proper perspective, and bolstered by the strength of the seventy-two shows that did have happy endings, they would continue to tour the world in support of future albums. Still "Alive," after all.

18

Pearl Jam Reads Us the *Riot Act*

The Band It Is A-Changin'

The Tale of the Tape

Recorded: Between February and May of 2002 by Adam Kasper at Studio X in Seattle; "You Are" recorded at Space Studio, also in Seattle

Produced By: Adam Kasper and Pearl Jam

Released: November 12, 2002, on Epic

Singles: "I Am Mine," on October 8, 2002; "Bu$hleaguer," on November 15, 2002; "Save You," on February 11, 2003; and "Love Boat Captain," on February 18, 2003

***Billboard*:** Debuts at number five on the *Billboard* 200, with first week sales of 166,000; RIAA-certified Gold record

A Regular Riot

Beleaguered but far from broken, Pearl Jam again took a step back after the *Binaural* Tour, enjoying a hard-earned and well-deserved one-year break from the road and the studio. It had been a tumultuous, tragic, and ultimately triumphant year on the road. The scabs had finally fallen from the emotional wounds of Roskilde, but they had left indelible scars in their place.

While they were on their self-imposed hiatus, the September 11 terrorist attacks forever changed America and led to more psychological wounds for the band to nurse. Those scars and fresh wounds provided the emotional backdrop for the evolution of the band's next musical sojourn (and perhaps a subconscious inspiration for the album's title). The drummer situation notwithstanding, the core lineup had been intact for more than a decade at this point. The addition of keyboard player Kenneth "Boom" Gaspar marked another musical shift for the band during the recording sessions that would produce *Riot Act*.

Dedicated to the memory of the Who's John Entwistle, Dee Dee Ramone, and Ray Brown, the resulting album is a signature team effort for the band, touching on myriad musical genres with aplomb. This would be the band's most overly political album to date. They had a plethora of psychological pain to process in the studio, and later, out on the road.

Into the Studio

Regrouping at Studio X in Seattle, the band enlisted a new production collaborator. Adam Kasper was welcomed in as the producer for the album that would be called *Riot Act*. The Seattle-based Kasper had worked previously with the Foo Fighters, Soundgarden, and drummer Matt Cameron's side project, Wellwater Conspiracy. The album would also be Pearl Jam's last for Epic Records.

Despite the confluence of both personal and national tragedies, the band members entered the studio revitalized. The wisdom born of pain for Pearl Jam translated into the band having no shortage of material to choose from. Matt Cameron was impressed that each member seemed to have four or five song ideas ready to submit for the rest of the band's blessing. The quality of the submissions was also borne out by the number of songs to make the *Riot Act* cut that needed relatively little development from the demo stage to finished product. Even Eddie was forced to acknowledge what a remarkable asset it was to have *five* songwriters in the band. The overall collaborative level of the album was very strong, and, of course, there was also the new addition to their musical ensemble.

Producer Kasper appreciated the relaxed atmosphere in the recording studio, which allowed the songs to come together quickly. Eddie even kept his typewriter in the studio, so that he could flesh out lyrics right on the spot, should the need arise; talk about immediacy. This was clearly a band heavily invested in their creative processes. They were all excited by the addition of this new dimension to their sound.

The Tunes

All told, fifteen songs made the cut for the final track listing, and the album's running time is north of fifty minutes. The recording sessions had yielded an abundance of material, and as a result, several quality tunes were left off of the official album, only to resurface elsewhere as B-sides for singles and, of course, as "lost dogs." These extra songs included "Down," "Other Side," "Undone," and the Layne Staley lament "4/20/02." For more on these and other "lost dogs," turn to chapter nineteen.

"Can't Keep"

The first track, "Can't Keep," runs counter to the form of all six of the preceding albums, with one exception. Only "Sometimes," the opening track on *No Code*, shares any similarity with this tune being selected for the leadoff spot. The laid-back, trippy swing can be tracked back to the song's origins. "Can't Keep" began as an early Eddie Vedder ukulele experiment. Played in a stripped down form by Vedder during his live solo performances in early 2002, the song underwent a complete metamorphosis in the studio. The fuzzy, three-guitar stomp chugs along, backing Ed's underplayed yet defiant vocals.

"Save You"

"Save You" is highlighted by a high octane Mike McCready guitar riff. The song chronicles the desperation one feels while observing a loved one in the throes of addiction. Eddie howls with urgency, as his vocals take a 180-degree turn from the opening track. Drummer Matt Cameron lost his headphones during the recording, which left him in full improvisational mode. Ultimately, Eddie's lyrics are universally relatable. He is absolutely right: everyone *does* desperately want to help those who are so close yet so far removed from the here and now by their demons. It is a feeling of profound helplessness for the would-be saviors.

"Love Boat Captain"

A remote corner of the Hawaiian Islands gave birth to the purifying "Love Boat Captain." Originally an eleven-minute demo opus dubbed "Boom B3," it is unquestionably the showcase piece for Boom Gaspar, the newest member of the band. "Love Boat Captain" takes on a prayerful tone of reflection for the nine fans killed during the horrific events at Roskilde and their grieving families. The youth of those lost was certainly not lost on the members of Pearl Jam. The conclusion of the song contains a rather obvious nod to the Beatles' 1967 classic, "All You Need Is Love," proving, once again, that

Here Comes "The Boom"

In keeping with the spirit of Pearl Jam's origin story and its inherent surfer mythology, it is entirely fitting that Eddie should have discovered Kenneth "Boom" Gaspar on a remote Hawaiian island. While on sabbatical from the band, Ed retreated to a particularly secluded Hawaiian outpost. Rarely mingling socially, Vedder had the good fortune of meeting Gaspar at a wake for a young man who had recorded some of the local musicians. As music mixed in with the mourning, Eddie couldn't help but notice that here, right before his eyes, was a guy playing a world class Hammond B3 organ. Eddie was just blown away. It seemed as though they were destined to meet, and subsequently they agreed to play together.

Their first musical collaboration turned into the Pearl Jam song "Love Boat Captain," which should give you some indication of how easily the duo clicked. There was no threat of Gaspar being starstruck because he had never even *heard* of Pearl Jam before. Boom's ability to expand the Pearl Jam instrumental sound made him an excellent veteran free agent signing for the Pearl Jam team. Mike McCready, long a proponent of adding keyboards, was particularly happy with Boom and his Hammond B3. "Crazy Mary" would never be the same live with the guitar and organ duels between the two.

This extraordinary musician would prove to be a significant and expansive addition to the Pearl Jam sound. When you consider the addition of an accomplished, older musician from a different cultural background as a theme, you cannot help but be reminded of Jefferson Airplane and Hot Tuna's association with fiddle player Papa John Creach.

such good advice is timeless. Music is still the only way out of unspeakable tragedy, and it offers us a glimmer of hope. Ironically, it is, in many ways, one of the band's most optimistic observations.

"Cropduster"

The tables are turned on "Cropduster," a musical contribution by Matt Cameron. Any thoughts about control, or having a human impact, are removed. Vedder's lyrics reveal the ruse with resignation. The musical backdrop is muscled up all around, with all of the instruments cranking at one point or another. Hey, you can take the drummer out of Soundgarden, but you can't take Soundgarden out of the drummer.

"Ghost"

Jeff Ament is the next member to take center stage with "Ghost," where he is credited with writing the music and cowriting the lyrics with Vedder. On "Ghost," the burly Pearl Jam bassist rocks straight down the highway, seeking escapes. The "ghosts," in the form of memories, are tangible, but the protagonist has confidence that he will find a way out.

"I Am Mine"

The existential recognition of "I Am Mine" is overwhelmingly poignant in its simplicity. Vedder wrote the song in his Virginia Beach hotel room the night before the band's first post-Roskilde show, as a means of reassuring himself that music remained the best way for him to move forward. It stands today as a signature Pearl Jam epic.

The subtle references to the band's experiences at the Danish festival and the implicit acknowledgement of human mortality—we are all born, we all die, it's up to each individual to determine the in-between—gives Vedder, and all of *us*, a reason to believe, despite the obstacles that life places in our respective paths.

An emotive McCready guitar solo and solid work from the rhythm section of Ament and Cameron elevate the track to the Pearl Jam pantheon. With a hint of an homage to his friend Michael Stipe and REM's sound, you can almost see Vedder leaving the hotel room confident that this is his life's calling. Abandoning this path would be disingenuous.

"Thumbing My Way"

"Thumbing My Way" takes a softer approach. The song is an all-Ed effort that came together quickly. The lilting number ranks among the most beautiful songs of Pearl Jam's career. In a musical departure for the band, the song combines acoustic guitars, an understated organ, an upright bass, and brushed drums to create a hopeful light at the end of the tunnel of heartbreak. Vedder's vocal infection exhibits both the pain and the promise of a better day. Thanks to the valiant efforts of producer Adam Kasper, the band managed to capture the song on virtually the first take. For all intents and purposes, the resulting song was a live performance, as Stone Gossard has often noted.

"You Are"

The record takes another sojourn to uncharted territory on the next track. The ethereal "You Are" makes use of a new toy that Matt Cameron had recently acquired. A drum machine filters the guitar track to create a reverb-heavy, faux techno beat, reminiscent of the Smiths' guitarist Johnny Marr's chunky riff on their epic "How Soon Is Now?" Vedder showcases his vocal range by interspersing a multi-tracked falsetto. An eerie, haunting song. Today, as we approach the quarter century mark of the band's history, it stands as arguably their quirkiest musical moment.

"Get Right"

Its back to familiar rock and roll ground on the all-Matt Cameron tune "Get Right," or "Wanted to Get Right," as it appears on the album's liner notes. A back-to-basics riff looks to land the subject back with his lover. Jeff Ament's funky bass line urges the song forward, in tandem with Cameron's propulsive drums. The rhythm section provides Mike with an opportunity to cut loose with a killer guitar lead.

"Green Disease"

"Green Disease" is another *Riot Act* track that veers in a different sonic direction. Exploding out of the gate at a breakneck, punked-up pace, "Green Disease" mounts an offensive directly against corporate America and all of its bloated, excessive glory. If not the root of *all* evil, it certainly bears the responsibility for a high percentage of it, from Vedder's perspective. The "green" is greed, of course, and it's *not* good (apologies to Gordon Gecko). The song stands as the most new wave-inspired in the Pearl Jam canon, and it is handled with customary aplomb.

"Help, Help"

On the next track, "Help, Help," it is Jeff Ament's turn to get political. An expansion on the "crimes of corporate America" theme articulated in the prior song, "Help, Help" addresses the delusion perpetuated by a corrupt society that conquers by continuing to divide, particularly with regard to the subject of race relations. The singer yearns for the truth but doubts if it exists amidst the preponderance of *untruth*. If he somehow manages to untangle the truth, can he handle it? Musically, the song negotiates some dramatic mood swings, and it is a metaphoric comparison, showcasing the eternal dichotomy between truth and lies.

"Bu$hleaguer"

There is no doubt whatsoever about the subject, or *target*, of "Bu$hleaguer," a satirical skewering of the (then) sitting forty-third President of the United States, George W. Bush. Vedder vented his frustrations, as all artists have done for time eternal,

Though recorded shortly after September 11th and nearly two years after the life-altering tragedy at Roskilde, *Riot Act* does not *explicitly* reference either event. With the exception of the satirical "Bu$hleaguer," Pearl Jam take a subtler approach, with the result that those painful memories become inherent in the overall atmosphere and theme of the album.   *Author's collection*

through his art. Grounded by an offbeat (for Pearl Jam) Matt Cameron four-on-the-floor rhythmic base, the song creates an ominous, foreboding atmosphere, the ideal background for Eddie Vedder's state of the union address.

The song's title also references an archaic term for the lowest level of baseball's minor league system. "Bush league" is also used as a derogatory term to describe a person or their actions. The fact that George W. Bush owned Major League Baseball's Texas Rangers prior to becoming governor of Texas was a perfect storm for Ed's lyrical collaboration with Stone Gossard. When you factor in that his father, former president George H.W. Bush, was once a Yale baseball captain and first baseman, the metaphorical "diamond" was set for the scathing, spoken-word delivery of this volatile political attack.

"½ Full"

Pearl Jam traverses a bluesy road leading toward Led Zeppelin on "½ Full." From Matt's robust rhythmic foundation to the snarling, three-guitar interplay of Vedder, McCready, and Gossard, "½ Full" completes the thematic outrage that began with "Green Disease." The subject here is the damage that man has done to the ecosystem and the band's hope that the damage is not irreparable. Musically, it remains, indisputably, Pearl Jam's heaviest blues journey.

"Arc"

"Arc" is a moving tribute to the victims of the Roskilde tragedy. Eddie drew inspiration from the late Nusrat Fateh Ali Khan, the legendary Pakistani musician who had earlier worked with Peter Gabriel on the soundtrack for *The Last Temptation of Christ*, and whose work also appears on the *Dead Man Walking* soundtrack. Ed uses the power of his voice to connect nine continuous loops of wordless vocalization to honor the nine fans that so senselessly perished. This was an ideal form of expression for Eddie, who was definitely at a loss for words to describe the pain he felt. In a tacit tribute to the fallen nine, the band played "Arc" precisely *nine* times during the 2003 tour, in spite of the inherent difficulties of performing such a song live.

"All or None"

The album's closer, "All or None," takes a mellow, melodic turn. Co-written by Eddie and Stone, the lyrics encapsulate the sum total of all the album's many conflicts. In so doing, they revisit a recurring Pearl Jam theme: *is* there a way out? The stakes have been raised, exponentially. As a result, there can be no halfway; it's an all or nothing proposition. To a band now a decade old, whose members were flirting with forty, the questions of existentialism and mortality had taken on new meaning. Gaspar again steps up with his Hammond B3 play, enhancing the quiet strumming of the acoustic guitars.

When the Dust of the Riot Settled

Overall, *Riot Act* took Pearl Jam to a multitude of new musical places with favorable results. This was not a band afraid to take risks in their artistic development. The cover art features the forged metal figurines of a skeletal king and queen sitting among barren rocks. The figurines represent the work of blacksmith Kelly Gilliam; the cover features Gilliam's figurines as photographed by Jeff Ament. This bleak tableau can perhaps be interpreted as the band's acknowledgment that fame is fleeting; ashes to ashes, dust to dust, as it were.

With over a decade in their rearview mirror, and having survived the Ticketmaster War, the Roskilde tragedy, and the inevitable backlash to a grunge scene that never accurately described their sound, Pearl Jam had also survived their own personal identity crisis. They now knew what the "in between" was all about, and they emerged from these experiences ready to embrace it as a far more content musical force.

Support Tours

Just weeks after the release of *Riot Act* on November 12, Pearl Jam booked some warm-up shows to loosen them up for the upcoming 2003 tour. On previous tours,

The Tour That Never Was

After consulting with and receiving the blessing of Pete Townshend, Joe Strummer and the Mescaleros agreed to open for Pearl Jam on the upcoming North American leg of the 2003 *Riot Act* Tour. Sadly, Strummer died of a sudden heart attack on December 22, 2002, just three days before Christmas, resulting in The Tour That Never Was. The Clash front man was one of the first of Eddie's idols that he actually met and snapped a Polaroid with in San Diego, so the pairing was symbolic of Eddie's career having come full circle, from eager volunteer roadie to headlining superstar. The profound influence of "the only band that matters" on Pearl Jam, in terms of music and social consciousness, cannot be overstated. What a shame.

their custom had been to play a couple of small club dates immediately before hitting the road for the official tour. This time around, there would be a gap in the schedule. On December 5 and 6, the band hit the familiar environs of the Showbox to start things off in a more intimate setting. Two days later, on December 8, they began a back-to-back in front of capacity crowds at KeyArena. Seattle fans had gotten a taste of what was to come, but it would be another two months before the official start of the Australian and Japanese legs of the tour. It was during this period that Joe Strummer passed away.

Australia

From February 8 through February 23, Pearl Jam barnstormed across Australia, bringing the Aussies a healthy dose of live music spread out across ten shows in five different cities. Sydney and Melbourne were the winners this time, with three apiece.

Japan

Pearl Jam left Oceania without performing in New Zealand. Instead, they headed for the traditionally music-friendly shores of Japan. Between February 28 and March 6, they played five shows in five different Japanese cities. Pearl Jam wrapped up this mini tour of Japan at Nagoyashi Kokaido in Nagoya. After the show, the band would have nearly a full month off to rest before the grueling first leg of the North American tour began.

On Tour During Wartime

The North American tour to support *Riot Act* would include a number of milestone moments and some infamous ones, too. Pearl Jam's set lists began to grow exponentially, and the shows seemed to be getting longer and longer. A three hour, thirty-eight minute epic show at Penn State set a new standard for length and resulted in a *three*-CD live bootleg. The three shows at the Tweeter Center in Mansfield, Massachusetts became "The Experiment," as the band attempted to perform its entire 100-song-plus catalogue without a repeat over the three nights. The two Madison Square Garden shows literally *shook* the iconic building in New York City, placing Pearl Jam in the elite company of the Grateful Dead, Bruce Springsteen, and Iron Maiden. The sheer number of "firsts," the variety of special guests, and the ironic opening acts, made the *Riot Act* Tour a Pearl Jam triumph.

North America: First Leg

The first leg of the *Riot Act* North American Tour started off in the Midwest, headed down to the Gulf of Mexico, and then headed east. The month-long leg kicked off on April Fools Day at the Pepsi Center in Denver, Colorado, and would run until May 3. From Denver, the tour would hit twenty-two more stops over the course of a single month, finishing up at Penn State's Bryce Jordan Center in University Park.

North America: Second Leg

The second leg of the North American *Riot Act* Tour was an absolute monster, with thirty-six scheduled shows spread out from coast to coast and extending north into Canada and south into Mexico. Less than four weeks after wrapping up in Pennsylvania, Pearl Jam was back out on the road, logging all sorts of miles. This time around, they kicked things off on May 28 in Jeff Ament's neck of the woods, the University of Montana's Adam's Fieldhouse in Missoula. From this point forward, they would be on the road for nearly two straight months, and the precious few days off between shows would mostly be devoted to traveling from one gig to the next. Finally, after seventy-three shows and seven months on and off the road, the expansive *Riot Act* Tour had finally been quelled.

Bushed

It was here, at Nassau Coliseum, that Eddie's "Bu$hleaguer" shtick led to a chorus of boos and chants of "U-S-A! U-S-A!" from disgruntled members of the audience. In the available film footage, it appears as though the audience is reacting to Eddie's interactions with the rubber George W. Bush mask that he had been using as a prop during performances of the song. He can be seen draping it over the microphone stand and pouring wine into its mouth. When the song ends, Eddie spends the next two minutes provoking the audience with taunts about the president and assumptions about their reasons for liking him. The band appears as though they are ready to crawl underneath the stage. Matt Cameron fidgets from his drum stool, while Jeff and Stone face awkwardly toward the back of the stage.

Eddie then turns the near-riot into an opportunity to defend his rights to free speech and artistic expression and an attempt to engage a KeyArena full of people in productive political debate; an awkward moment, to say the least. At this point, there was nothing left for Pearl Jam to do but perform a cover of the Clash's "Know Your Rights," and the show went on as if nothing had happened. Besides, the people who were *really* offended had already left by this point!

Merchandising

The *Riot Act* Tour also facilitated the production of some fun collectibles. The DVD, *Live at the Showbox*, chronicles the band's warm-up concert in Seattle on December 6, 2002. It provided all of us non-locals the opportunity to see what we'd been missing all these years. At the other end of the spectrum, and at the other end of the tour, Pearl Jam filmed the Madison Square Garden shows, releasing the one from July 8 as the aptly titled DVD, *Live at the Garden*.

By this point, the band was making audio recordings of *all* of their shows available to their fans through their website as official bootlegs, either in digital format or on compact disc. In a select few cases, they packaged and released them in stores. On the *Riot Act* Tour, these extra special official bootlegs included the Burswood Dome show in Perth, Australia, on February 23, and the Nippon Budokan show in Tokyo on March 3. Stateside, the May 3 show at Penn State's Bryce Jordan Center closed out the first leg of the North American tour in style, lasting well over three hours and resulting in the show being released to stores as a rare *three* CD official bootleg.

During the second leg of the tour, both Madison Square Garden shows were released in this manner. The show on July 8 (the one that was also featured in the *Live at the Garden* DVD) resulted in another three-CD set, while the July 9 show became a more typical double-CD release. Finally, the last show of "The Experiment" at the Tweeter Center in Boston on July 11 produced yet *another* three-CD official bootleg. This show eclipsed the Penn State show in length by more than twenty minutes, and at over three hours and forty minutes, it remains the longest Pearl Jam concert to date. And in case anyone was wondering how "The Experiment" turned out, the answer is: pretty well. Out of ninety-four tunes played over the three dates at the Tweeter Center, a dozen were covers, eighty-two were originals, and the only repeat was "Yellow Ledbetter." And since it obviously would have been very easy for them to avoid this single repeat, we consider "The Experiment" and the *Riot Act* Tour, in general, to have been an overwhelming success.

19

Lost Dogs

Out of the Pound

The Tale of the Tape

Recorded: Between 1991 and 2003

Produced By: Tchad Blake, Stone Gossard, Adam Kasper, Brendan O'Brien, Rick Parashar, Pearl Jam, Eddie Vedder, and Westwood One Broadcast

Released: On November 11, 2003

Billboard: Debuted at number fifteen on the *Billboard* 200, with 89,500 first-week copies sold; RIAA-certified Gold album

Something Lost, but Something Gained

The release of *Lost Dogs* offers us a rare insight into what might have been. This collection of thirty tracks (*thirty-one*, counting the discreetly hidden Layne Staley tribute, "4/20/02") that, for a variety of reasons, never made the cut for an official Pearl Jam release, includes eleven songs that had never been released at *all*. The others had previously been included on various benefit albums, movie soundtracks, Christmas singles, and B-sides.

The overall effect of the compilation provides compelling insight into the band's musical evolution from 1991 through 2002, spanning their first seven studio albums. Individual albums would have sounded dramatically different, and in some cases perhaps more "commercial," with the inclusion and substitution of some of these "dogs" that were lost or, more accurately, misplaced. *Lost Dogs* is an invaluable piece of work, not to mention one of our personal favorites, with a number of special musical moments. On stage, Eddie will often make reference to "one for the serious collectors." Several of these tracks qualify for that distinction. At this point in the band's history, the Sony Music/Epic Records chapter came to a close. Let's meet the "dogs."

"All Night"

This unreleased outtake is from the tense *No Code* sessions in Chicago, post-Soldier Field, during the horrific 1995 heat wave that claimed the lives of many people. The song may be either an antidote to, or acknowledgment of, that horrific weather event. This was one of Jack Iron's first studio sessions with the band and

In the spirit of Bruce Springsteen's 1998 compilation set, *Tracks*, Pearl Jam released *Lost Dogs* in 2003. The collection of thirty studio outtakes, B-sides, and alternate versions which otherwise may never have seen the light of day proved to be a delight for the band's increasingly discerning and fervent fan base. Serious collectors indeed.
Author's collection

producer Brendan O'Brien. It was also one of their first experiments with multi-tracked vocals. "All Night" was on the original track listing for *No Code* but did not make the final cut.

Lyrically, "All Night" seems optimistic and conveys the sense that the world is wide open. Musically, it rocks hard, chugs ahead aggressively, and features some ominous-sounding vocals. If anything, Matt Cameron seems to pick up the tempo halfway through, as the vocals become haunting and drawn out.

"Sad"

Originally titled "A Letter to the Dead," "Sad" is an unreleased song that failed to make the cut for *Binaural*—the first of *many* such Tchad Blake-produced outtakes from *Binaural* in this collection, as it turns out. The guitar riff which repeats throughout is ethereal and almost Middle Eastern-sounding—a nervous and very exotic sputter. Lyrically, the song tackles the theme of grief and the process of mourning. This is an all-Ed affair, both lyrically and musically. "Sad" is the other side of "Other Side," as Eddie notes in the album's liner notes. In a sense, the song is almost an example of power pop. Jeff Ament certainly considered it a pop song. These types of songs have often gotten cut from Pearl Jam's studio sessions since they don't fit into the overarching scheme of things and since Pearl Jam is not considered a pop-centric band; what a shame, because this song is excellent. Mitchell Froom was in the room and played keyboards here, pre-Boom.

"Down"

Produced by Adam Kasper, "Down" originally saw the light of day as the B-side of the "I Am Mine" single from 2002's *Riot Act* . . . well, of *one* version of the single, anyway. Another version of "I Am Mine" featured "Undone" as the B-side, a littermate of "Down," which also appears on disc one of *Lost Dogs*.

Inspired by the work of Bernie Corbett's old Boston University professor, Howard Zinn, "Down" is credited to Mike, Stone, and Eddie. Mike was inspired to write this song after seeing a Social Distortion concert in Los Angeles with his bandmates, Stone and Ed. The song is evocative of the Replacements, with its strumming, major key melody. As Eddie mentions in the liner notes, "This should have been the single." The liner notes also acknowledge the Howard Zinn connection: "Inspired by the writings of, and friendship with, historian/activist, Howard Zinn."

"Hitchhiker"

This is another *Binaural* outtake. Could the inclusion of so many *Binaural* outtakes here be a sign that the boys were listening to their Tchad Blake-era work with a fresh set of ears? This simple, angry tune finds the protagonist lashing out at someone, a "hitchhiker," who is taking advantage of his good nature and imposing on his time and resources—a common experience among the newly wealthy and successful, unfortunately.

Eddie was inspired to write this song during a hike with his brother. The pair noticed that a large number of prickly burs had attached themselves to their legs along the trail, and that provided the perfect metaphor. A particular target of Vedder's wrath here are those opportunistic autograph hounds, the "blue penners," who ask for autographs only to turn right around and sell them to the highest bidder.

"Don't Gimme No Lip"

This is a Stone tune, left off of *No Code*, and produced by Brendan O'Brien during the New Orleans sessions, pre-Chicago, during 1995. This was Stone's first turn at the microphone, singing lead. "Don't Gimme No Lip" is a simple, straightforward, mid-tempo punk rock song that begins with a rhythmically distorted guitar riff. Lyrically, the song consists primarily of repetitions of the song's title, so there are no great mysteries to ponder here. If anything, the song's protagonist sounds like a vexed authority figure attempting to regain control.

"Alone"

Try to follow this one. "Alone," primarily written by Stone Gossard and produced by Rick Parashar, first appeared on the scene as the B-side of "Go," the first single from the band's second album, *Vs.* Dave Krusen appears on the drums here. This, however, is not *that* version of "Alone." This version cobbles together alternate lyrics and, of course, a new vocal track, with instrumental tracks from the *Ten* sessions, which means that there's some Rick Parashar influence here. Lyrically, the song chronicles the plight of a protagonist who is trying to cope with living alone in the wake of a broken relationship. Musically, the song is reminiscent of mid-seventies era Black Sabbath (or more contemporary Soundgarden) and the vocal delivery conveys more of a sense of anger than it does of sadness, loss, or regret. The mid-tempo rocker features an impressive vocal turn from Vedder. "Alone" has always been one of Mike McCready's favorites, as he was able to use a glass bottle as a slide during his guitar solo. With origins dating back to *Stone Gossard Demos 1990*, this song wouldn't have been out of place on the *Singles* soundtrack.

"In the Moonlight"

A *Binaural* outtake, "In the Moonlight" has a really infectious groove to it, punctuated by some vintage McCready acid rock guitar solo work. Lyrically, the image of an omnipresent "night bird" is a bit chilling and may be yet another metaphor for the sudden fame that haunted the band during their early years. Drummer Matt Cameron wrote the song and also plays guitar here. Mitchell Froom is on the keys. This is a very "grungy" and slow tune, as Matt observed. The spooky song wouldn't sound out of place on a Led Zeppelin album.

"Education"

Yet another *Binaural* outtake, "Education" comes across lyrically as almost a protest song. The song's protagonist seems concerned that he's been the victim of propaganda and misinformation, and is committed to a search for the truth. This is another all-Eddie song that questions the establishment, which is arguably a microcosm of what Pearl Jam is all about. "Education" also features Mitch Froom on keys and Mike McCready stretching his musical repertoire on the piano. Initially, Ed began writing this song while on vacation with Matt Cameron and his family, until the bandmates came to their senses and decided to just relax and enjoy themselves. They would complete their "Education" at a later date.

"Black, Red, Yellow"

Here's where the linguistics expression "dead metaphor" comes into play, with the term "B-side" being the metaphor in question. "Black, Red, Yellow" began life as the B-side on the "Hail Hail" single. However, "Hail Hail" was a *CD* single only (no vinyl 45), so, strictly speaking, it didn't *have* a "B-side." "Black, Red, Yellow" simply followed after "Hail Hail," with both songs appearing on the *same* side. What can we say? We're sticklers for accuracy. Remember this example of "dead metaphor" the next time someone asks you to "turn the channel" or "dial a phone number." Anyway, this is not the version from the so-called B-side. This is a longer version of the song.

Eddie Vedder plays guitar here, with Brendan O'Brien at the control board. Vedder's vocal delivery is reminiscent of classic Lou Reed, bordering on spoken-word poetry. Some say the song was written for super fan Dennis Rodman and that the song's title refers to Rodman's race, the yellow hair dye he has used in the past, and the red Pearl Jam logo he dyed into his hair during the NBA Playoffs one year. And yes, that *is* Rodman's voice—as recorded on Eddie Vedder's telephone answering machine—that appears in the middle of the song.

"U"

Though for some reason it is spelled "You" on the album cover, "U" was originally one of two B-sides for "Wishlist," a single from the *Yield* album. "U" was followed on most versions of the single by a live version of "Brain of J.," which would be, what, the "C-side?" Eddie wrote the lyrics, the music, and played guitar. This is a buoyant power pop song with ironic lyrics and could almost be a cousin to "Sad." Once again, the odd pop song was left out of the final track listing. According to Eddie, this song was written in a car during a ten-minute drive. Had it been a longer drive, it might have been a more complex song.

"Leaving Here"

Wow, talk about a tune with a backstory. As the story behind "Leaving Here" illustrates, oftentimes it is the cover songs that are the most interesting. "Leaving Here" is an old Motown song, originally released in 1963 by Eddie Holland. Two years later, a British band called the Birds (not to be confused with American legends, the Byrds) recorded their own version. These Birds of a different feather didn't have Roger McGuinn, but they *did* feature a young guitarist you may have heard of in the years since, a guy named Ronnie Wood. And the story just gets weirder from there.

Among the Birds' fans was a guy named Ian "Lemmy" Kilmister, who liked "Leaving Here" so much that it became the first single for his new band, Motörhead, in 1977. Meanwhile, the Who had recorded "Leaving Here" in 1965, not once, but *three times* (two studio versions, plus one for BBC Radio), but never released any of them. Fast-forward twenty years, and the Who released "Leaving Here" on their 1985 compilation album, the cleverly titled *Who's Missing*. Fast-forward another nine years, and an alternate take appeared on their 1994 deluxe box set, *Thirty Years of Maximum R&B*, and yet *again* on the 1998 remastered version of their original compilation, 1974's *Odds & Sods*. Finally (or so we *think*), another version appeared on the 2002 remastered version of the album *My Generation*.

The Rationals released singles versions in 1967 and 1968 with an alternate spelling, "Leavin' Here." About ten years later, an English garage band called the Bugs released their version of "Leaving Here" on their 1987 debut EP. Two years later, Tinsley Ellis recorded it as "Leavin' Here" for his 1989 debut album, *Fanning the Flames*. As for where *Pearl Jam* first heard the song, it's probably a tossup between *Who's Missing* and the Motörhead version.

Pearl Jam's version first appeared on a 1996 benefit compilation album titled *Home Alive: The Art of Self Defense*, the proceeds of which went toward funding self-defense classes for women. It featured Eddie as a third guitarist, prompting Mike McCready to wonder in the liner notes, "Who takes the first lead when we play live? Kick ass!"

A few years later, a band called Lars Frederiksen and the Bastards recorded it for their eponymous debut album in 2001. That very same year, a certain former "Bird" and long-time Rolling Stone named Ronnie Wood returned to re-feather an old nest, releasing (or would it be re-releasing in this case?) "Leaving Here" for *his* 2001 solo album, *Not for Beginners*.

Lost Dogs, of course, was released in 2003, and that brings the conversation back to where we are right *now*. As if anyone needed any more evidence that the song "Leaving Here" had some legs, Irish rockers the Strypes (perhaps influenced by Pearl Jam?) recorded a version for their 2012 EP, *Young, Gifted & Blue*, forty-nine years after Eddie Holland, and damn near a fifty-year anniversary for a song that just keeps coming back. Say one thing for Pearl Jam, they know how to pick a good cover song.

"Gremmie Out of Control"

Here's a Silly Surfers cover tune originally released on a benefit compilation album *Music for Our Mother Ocean, Vol. 1* on Surfrider Records, for the benefit of one of Eddie's favorite 501(c)(3)s, the Surfrider Foundation. "Gremmie" is surfer slang for a newbie surfer. Stone is credited with providing the Gremmie vocals, and the versatile Brendan O'Brien, the prince of surf guitar, appears here on rhythm. The sound really does harken back to the classic surf music sound of the 1960s. Lots of fun.

"Whale Song"

Jack Irons penned this one, which appears on *Music for Our Mother Ocean, Vol. 3*. "Whale Song" is a serene, emotive, spacy, and trippy tune, with a real communing-with-nature vibe. Jack Irons wrote the song, and he also sings and plays guitar here. According to Ed, Jack couldn't believe it when he learned that the heart of a whale was the size of a Volkswagen. The song also features an almost spoken-word, Lou Reed-style of vocal delivery, interspersed with sonic effects that mimic the sounds of actual whale songs.

"Undone"

"Undone" is the Eddie Vedder tune that was the *other* "B-side" from the 2002 *Riot Act* "I Am Mine" single. A great riff sets the tone for this Adam Kasper-produced tune, which is yet another one of Pearl Jam's studio forays into the world of power pop. Eddie wrote the lyrics and the music for this song, which, according to him,

Many of the tracks on *Lost Dogs* have compelling backstories, and we explore many of these in detail. Here is disc 2, featuring an impressive array of tunes. The art here is evocative of the old milk carton "missing children" motifs of the late 1970s and early 1980s, when the band members were still children themselves.   *Author's collection*

sounds best when listened to in the car while traveling down the road. Lyrically, the song is filled with Vedder's familiar imagery and themes: waves, pendulums, and fighting the system.

"Hold On"

Here is another *Ten* outtake. A typo on the liner notes indicates that it is a *Vs.* outtake, but the matter is clarified on pearljam.com. With lyrics by Ed, music by Stone, and production by Rick Parashar, "Hold On" features a chorus you won't be able to get out of your head and a lyrical sentiment that we can all relate to. Musically, it sounds as though it would have fit right in on *Ten*, but it is perhaps a bit more slow and deliberate—a heavy, "grungy" type of sound reminiscent of Soundgarden. "Hold On" is a distant relative of "Alone." Neither song made the cut for *Ten*, but the two songs have a lot in common. They are kindred musical spirits.

"Yellow Ledbetter"

Another Rick Parashar-produced outtake from *Ten* that has become something of a Pearl Jam classic and fan favorite, "Yellow Ledbetter" was one of the two available B-sides of the 1992 "Jeremy" single ("Footsteps" being the other). The song is lyrically ambiguous (like the most-recorded rock and roll song in history, "Louie Louie"). Nobody seems to know what the words are, and our enigmatic Eddie does nothing to help unravel the mystery. Nevertheless, it resonates with fans. As Ten Clubber Jeff Wilder told us, "It's one song that I loved from the time I heard it, and I have yet to tire of it. The guitar solo on it is killer, and the way Vedder sings it makes it hit home."

"Yellow Ledbetter" has an almost Hendrixian blues bent to it, as if Mike McCready is under the spell of the "Voodoo Chile" himself. The song was number two on *Rolling Stone's* online Pearl Jam fan survey, "The Ten Best Pearl Jam Deep Cuts." In a listener survey, out of KISW's top ninety-nine Pearl Jam songs, "Yellow Ledbetter" came in at number five. Clearly, this song is a fan favorite. The perennial live tune has closed many a set and has been an encore on many occasions. The often indecipherable, ever-evolving and devolving lyrics make the crowd sing-alongs a comedic exercise. *Rolling Stone's* Andy Greene wrote that the song was so good that everyone found it, even though Pearl Jam had initially tucked it away. It was too good to hide.

"Fatal"

Another in our long list of *Binaural* outtakes, "Fatal" is a Stone tune that kicks off disc two. This is a smoldering acoustic song, a favorite of Tchad Blake's. Mitchell Froom appears on keys once again. According to Eddie, the original chorus mentioned the ancient Greek philosopher Plato, but they were afraid that people would hear the word "Play-Doh" instead. The song's title is reflected in the melancholy, sad atmosphere of the song, which paints a bleak picture. Pearl Jam gave the song its live debut during the acoustic show at Benaroya Hall, which was later immortalized on CD.

"Other Side"

We *love* the title of this one, because it was the "B-side" of the second single from *Riot Act*, "Save You," a 2003 CD single. *Other* side indeed. "Other Side" is a bittersweet tune, a lament full of aching and longing. Adam Kasper produced the track. Jeff wrote the words and the music, and he plays guitar here. It started off being written as a song for Jeff's parents, married for over forty years at the time, and it evolved over a couple of years and revisions to have a different meaning entirely. The song is now primarily about Jeff's partnership with his bandmates. In the liner notes, Eddie describes this song as capturing what it is like to remain behind on shore while your partner is out at sea.

"Hard to Imagine"

An alternate take on a tune that originally appeared on the *Chicago Cab* soundtrack, this one was recorded during the *Vs.* sessions. It just goes to show you that, when your band is raking in the dough, you can afford more studio time, and that's when the outtakes really start to pile up. This one almost made the cut for a couple of different albums but remained on the sidelines. "Hard to Imagine" is a great show opener and has been become a Pearl Jam fan cult classic (particularly among those fans who never saw *Chicago Cab*).

"Footsteps"

Here's a live version of the old "Momma-Son" trilogy song, which first saw the light of day as a studio version on one of the B-sides for the 1992 "Jeremy" single. This one was from the band's live May 11, 1992, appearance on Bob Coburn's *Rockline*. The song is a favorite of Ten Clubber Jessica Seyfarth, who told us, "'Footsteps' is my favorite because it is one of those songs that takes me back to a moment in time when I can visualize exactly how I was feeling at the time and people I was with when I heard the song for the first time." Such is the power of a great song, Jessica. Terri McNelly, of Dallas, Texas, has an interesting take on the song. She told us, "Sad, longing, intense pain, but even though the lyrics don't depict it, there's an illusion (maybe from the harmonica?) that positive things are to come."

That harmonica part that McNelly mentions was added specifically for the *Rockline* appearance. The song, of course, evolved from "Times of Trouble," the Temple of the Dog song. The stripped down version here features Stone on guitar and Ed on vocals and harmonica. The footsteps in the song represent a psychological journey, one tentative step at a time, like a Rorschach image of Eddie's mind.

"Wash"

Depending on which way you score it, "Wash" was an appendage on the European version of *Ten* or (in an alternate version) an alternate B-side to the 1991 "Alive" single. Either way, that makes it a "golden oldie" in Pearl Jam circles. Rick Parashar was at the controls for this, one of the band's earliest collaborative compositions, and it came together very quickly. "Wash" has a cleansing, cathartic quality to it, lending credence to its title.

"Dead Man"

The story goes that Eddie wrote this one for the *Dead Man Walking* soundtrack, but the song was bumped by "The Boss"; Bruce Springsteen's "Dead Man Walkin'" won out. This "Dead Man" was resurrected for a new life as the B-side for the 1995 "Off He Goes" single. "Dead Man" also dates back to the New Orleans sessions for *No Code*. So this song had two strikes against it before it found its way to the *Lost Dogs* collection and was given new life. This sparse version features Ed on vocals and guitar, Jeff on bass, and Jack Irons on percussion. In retrospect, Stone felt that this song should never have been a B-side and that it should have definitely made the cut for the film soundtrack. The dirge-like song really conveys the visual imagery of the death march of the condemned man.

"Strangest Tribe"

Stone's tune is from 1999's fan club Christmas single. "Strangest Tribe" was produced by Stone and Ed and features words and music written by Stone. Stone also plays percussion here, while Ed tickles the ivories on piano. The song finds Stone filled—by his own admission—with the Christmas spirit. Atmospherically, it perfectly captures the melancholy of a deep winter's day.

"Drifting"

An alternate take on the companion piece to "Strangest Tribe" from the 1999 fan club Christmas single, "Drifting" is an Eddie tune and yet another song produced by Stone and Ed. It was recorded at the same time as "Strangest Tribe" in 1999. The song was written, during a long drive to Neil Young's house, on the back of an airplane ticket.

"Let Me Sleep (It's Christmastime)"

Truly the first Noel, "Let Me Sleep" was the original fan club Christmas single in 1991. So, stuff *that* in your stockings. When you're a kid, you *can't* sleep at Christmastime, in spite of repeated family exhortations to sleep, lest Santa Claus not visit you. As an adult, it seems as though sleeping is all you want to do at Christmastime. This was the first songwriting collaboration between Mike and Ed. Mike used open tuning on the spontaneously written tune. Eddie was inspired to write the sad and touching lyrics one day when he found himself locked outside of Jeff's apartment, thinking about the homeless and indigent.

"Last Kiss"

Pearl Jam recorded this one for their 1998 fan club Christmas single, and later it appeared on the 1999 benefit album *No Boundaries: A Benefit for the Kosovar Refugees*. But somewhere in the middle of those two releases, the song—quite unexpectedly—became a huge radio hit for them, and they had to release it as a single for *all* their fans (proceeds were donated to the Kosovar refugees). Between the wide-release single and the 1999 benefit compilation, Pearl Jam raised in excess of $10 *million* for the worthy cause. If only Wayne Cochran had been so lucky. If you are asking, "Huh?" then a history lesson may be in order.

Another one of those cover tunes with a fascinating backstory, "Last Kiss" is older than all of the members of Pearl Jam (except for "Boom"). Loosely based on a true story, it tells the tragic tale of a young girl killed by a truck during her first date with her sweetheart, who cradles her in his arms for one last kiss before she dies. The true story was, if anything, even *more* horrific because three young couples drove straight into a logging truck (or a train; accounts vary) and were killed instantly. James Lafayette Tarver wrote the song in memory of his daughter Carol Ann, who was one of the crash victims. The trusting soul shopped the song around, and it was promptly "stolen" by unscrupulous industry types who rearranged it.

One thing led to another and it wound up in the hands of Wayne Cochran, who got a songwriting credit, along with Joe Carpenter, Randall Hoyal, and Bobby McGlon. Let's call it "group plagiarism." Wayne Cochran recorded the song for Gala Records in 1961, but it kind of fizzled out. Undaunted, Cochran took another swing at it two years later, in 1963, on King Records, but the single still went nowhere. Strike two.

Against all odds, "Last Kiss" was then covered by another band when J. Frank Wilson and the Cavaliers recorded it in 1964 (though the discography on their website lists a single date of 1961 and an album release date of 1964). What is undisputed is that Cochran recorded it first.

Then, as fate would have it, an odd character named Sonely Roush became the divine intermediary. Roush was obsessed with the song and brought it to J. Frank Wilson, insisting that his band, the Cavaliers, learn it and play it. They obliged and played it whenever Roush was around. But Roush wanted to take it to another level. He contracted for studio time, got the band in there to record the song, and even acted as producer, reportedly annoying the band in the process. And then, wonder of wonders, J. Frank Wilson and the Cavaliers became "One Hit Wonders." "Last Kiss" was a smash hit.

Unfortunately, the success went right to Wilson's head, and he became a total mess, boozing and womanizing to the point where the band kicked him out. Here's where the story gets *really* wacky. Wilson was not content to sit on the sidelines, so he formed a *new* group of competing Cavaliers and went out on the road with that act, hiring Roush as his manager. In a cautionary tale infused with incredibly cruel irony, Roush was driving Wilson to a gig in Ohio one night when he fell asleep behind the wheel and got them into a head-on collision, killing himself and injuring Wilson.

Give Wilson credit for perseverance; he kept on playing and recording as "the Cavaliers" in spite of the fact that the band that ditched him was still using the same name. He kept recording until the 1970s. His song "Hot Little One" only hit eighty-five on the charts, and that was all she wrote. He never hit the charts again, but he did hit the *bottle*, drinking himself to death after eight failed marriages at the age of forty-nine. Coincidentally, he died in 1991, just as Pearl Jam was being born. Eddie supposedly first stumbled upon the song on an old record he found in an antique shop in Seattle, and he convinced his bandmates to give it a shot. Good call, Ed.

"Sweet Lew"

Jeff Ament wrote the music and lyrics for "Sweet Lew," another *Binaural* outtake, with Tchad Blake producing. Jeff, Pearl Jam's resident basketball gym rat, offers a tongue-in-cheek homage to the life and times of NBA Hall of Famer Lew Alcindor, better known as Kareem Abdul-Jabbar, a man he had idolized since he was seven years old. The burly bass player sings lead here, and the track also features Tchad Blake getting in on the act by playing the Wurlitzer. Meanwhile, Eddie sat on the bench for this one, relegated to the role of sixth man.

"Dirty Frank"

"Dirty Frank" (great song title, by the way) was the B-side from the "Even Flow" single and was yet another "appendage" on the European version of *Ten* (how

Here, beside an array of handwritten "lost dog" flyers, is the full track listing. A quick perusal of the song titles confirms that once they may have *been* lost, but now they are unquestionably found. A number of these songs have become Pearl Jam concert staples, much to the delight of the faithful.   *Author's collection*

come the European fans get all the bonus tracks, anyway?). In any case, this is a different version of "Dirty Frank," a favorite of Matt Spitz, guitarist of the Lost Dogs: A Tribute to Pearl Jam, who said, "'Dirty Frank' is out-of-character funky, and I love it. The lyrics are pretty great, too: 'Where's Mike McCready? My God, he's been ate!'"

With lyrics by Eddie, music credited to the rest of the band, and Tchad Blake producing, "Dirty Frank" is a humorous homage to a scary-looking bus driver the band employed during their 1991 tour. During the long rides to gigs, the boys began to fantasize that the bus driver might really be a cannibalistic serial killer, like Jeffrey Dahmer. Naturally, he would want to eat Mike McCready first because the guitarist was so scrawny at that time. Musically, the song is clearly influenced the Red Hot Chili Peppers' outrageous funk style.

"Brother"

This is an instrumental version of "Brother" and another outtake from the *Ten* sessions, featuring a new lead guitar overlay by Mike. The music is credited to Stone. This track is a favorite of Ten Clubber John Cafarella, a fellow native of Bernie Corbett's Massachusetts: "The song rocks. I love that it is an instrumental;

it doesn't need any words. It shows off the talent of the band. And the guitar solo in it is killer. I believe it to be their hardest rocker." "Brother" offers a rare glimpse inside the band dynamic, just jamming and riffing in the studio. But this is a jam with a purpose, featuring each band member playing to his strengths. The song was an early candidate for *Ten*, but it didn't make the cut.

Roughly six years later, in 1997, Eddie wrote lyrics and added his vocals to the song, but that version wouldn't see the light of day until 2009, when it was included on the deluxe edition of the *Ten* reissue. It went to number one the *Billboard* Modern Rock Chart (which tracks radio plays, not sales) eighteen years after it was originally written as an instrumental.

"Bee Girl" (includes "hidden" track "4/20/02")

"Bee Girl" is an unreleased live recording from *Rockline*, which (sort of) pays homage to Heather DeLoach, the little girl dancing around in the bee costume in Blind Melon's 1992 "No Rain" video. In true Pearl Jam tradition, this track also includes a "hidden" track, "4/20/02," which pays tribute to the memory of old Alice in Chains friend Layne Staley. The song title supposedly refers to the fact that Staley's body was found on this date, though other accounts have the body being found on the nineteenth. If that is the case, then perhaps the song title refers to the memorial held for Staley on April 20 at the Seattle Center. In any case, he is thought to have died on April 5, two weeks earlier, from (what else?) a drug overdose—another tragic ending for yet another talented individual.

"Bee Girl" was produced by Westwood One and taken directly from the October 18, 1993 *Rockline* live broadcast. It features Jeff on guitar and Ed on vocals. Apparently they just made the song up on the spot while they were there for an interview, and it was inspired by some notes and a couple bottles of cheap red wine. During a commercial break, Eddie turned to Jeff and asked him if he had anything, song-wise, and he just began to play. This is improvisation in its purest form. As for the "hidden" track, Eddie wrote "4/20/02" on the night he found out about Layne Staley's death. It is a haunting, emotionally raw song that sends shivers up the listener's spine. Even the electric guitar sounds haunted by this lament to the memory of yet another lost friend. It has been said that all dogs, lost or otherwise, go to heaven. "4/20/02" makes one believe that somehow Staley is up there with them, finally at peace. A beautiful way to close out this collection.

20

Pearl Jam

The "Avocado Album" Is *Far* from the Pits!

The Tale of the Tape

Recorded: From February 2005 through 2006 by Adam Kasper at Studio X in Seattle, Washington

Produced By: Adam Kasper and Pearl Jam

Released: May 2, 2006, on J. Records

Singles: "World Wide Suicide," "Life Wasted," and "Gone"

Billboard: Debuted at number two on the *Billboard* 200

Eponymous, but Not Anonymous

In the aftermath of the 2004 presidential election—a crushing disappointment for the band members and Eddie in particular—Pearl Jam returned to the friendly confines of Studio X in Seattle to begin work on what would become the eighth studio album of their career. Ralph Nader's loss during the 2000 election had really been a foregone conclusion, but this time around the band believed, as did many others, that John Kerry had a good shot at defeating George W. Bush. Pearl Jam had exerted a great deal of effort and energy toward achieving that end, too. Between participating in the Vote for Change Tour and their own provocative performances of "Bu$hleaguer" in concert, the election had never been far from their thoughts. But now that it was over, rather than sit around moping about Bush's reelection, they decided to follow Bruce Springsteen's example and get back to work.

Into the Studio

The freedom of having no traditional contractual obligations resonated in the self-titled album *Pearl Jam* (also known as the "Avocado Album" because of the cover artwork, which features a photograph of—drumroll, please—an avocado!). They had fulfilled their obligation to Epic Records with the 2004 release of a greatest hits collection, *Rearviewmirror (Greatest Hits 1991–2003)*, so *Pearl Jam* would be

Eponymous, but never anonymous. Aside from potentially induc-
ing hunger pangs, the cover of 2006's *Pearl Jam* largely failed to
capture critics' imaginations. But the band remains unapologetic, and the unusual motif clearly caught on among the fans.
Besides, the music really speaks for itself; it's fast, hard, and *loud*.
Author's collection

released on Clive Davis' new label, J. Records, which turned out to be a one-time-
only deal. Many acknowledged the album as a welcome return to the band's earlier
sound. It reminded Mike McCready of *Vs.* Jeff Ament was pleased that the album
managed to capture a vibe of immediacy, which was their primary objective heading into the project. This time around, the band members did not show up to the
studio with completed songs. They collaborated throughout the creative songwriting process, which really helped the group communication. The overall tone of
the album is fast-paced and aggressive, and many of the tracks begin with a guitar
riff.

The Tunes

The studio sessions were so productive that they wound up recording twenty-five
songs, which they whittled down to thirteen for the official release. The remaining twelve tracks would not go to waste, however. Several years down the road,
they would begin playing "Of the Earth" live, and "The Forest" appeared on Jeff
Ament's 2008 solo album, *Tone*. Who knows, maybe these outtakes will form the
basis for *Lost Dogs, Volume II* at some point.

The first single, "World Wide Suicide," would become a number one hit, highlighting the band's uncanny ability to capture the spirit of the nation (or at least *half* of it!) at any given moment. The album features a pointed criticism of the Iraq War and the overall direction of US foreign policy. In fact, the album was so focused that it bordered on being a "concept" album, with a common "state of the union" thread that seemed to connect much of the material. Even though his idol, Pete Townshend of the Who, was the godfather of the concept album, Eddie, true to form, seemed conflicted about the idea. Eddie's angst aside, *Pearl Jam*, aka the "Avocado Album," featured a more sonically accessible and lyrically direct Pearl Jam in comparison with their last two Epic releases.

"Life Wasted"

"Avocado" opens up with the gut-punching "Life Wasted," which combines a Stone Gossard guitar riff that was rooted in an improv song from a live show in Charlotte, North Carolina, back in 2000, with Ed's poignant, emotionally charged reflection on his friend and political polar opposite, Johnny Ramone. *Spin* magazine paid Stone the ultimate compliment when it referred to the riff as the best one that "Pete Townshend never wrote." Vedder talked about the lyrical inspiration tracing back to the funereal energy that allows a person to feel a "renewed approach" for life in the immediate aftermath before you get back into your own daily routine of living. The ultimate lesson to be learned is: "Live life to the fullest. I wasn't going to let this deep loss go without recognition." No, Vedder most assuredly wouldn't, citing Ramone's frequent tutorials of rock and roll history as playing a major role on the record overall, well beyond this one track that offers the most direct reference. It was, in Ed's opinion, indisputable that the late Ramones guitarist's influence raised the bar for the band on *Pearl Jam*.

"Life Wasted" on the Small Screen

An elaborately realized video accompanied "Life Wasted." Filmed over a ten-month period in multiple locations, director Fernando Apodaca took life casts of each of the band members' heads to create busts. The heads are subjected to various indignities: fire, water, insects, and interspersed with footage of Pearl Jam playing the song. Apodaca referenced "the ambiguities of consumerism, obsolescence, determination, and growth" as a thematic basis for his video presentation. The first Pearl Jam conceptual video release since "Do the Evolution" back in 1988, "Life Wasted" was nominated for a 2006 MTV Video Award for Best Special Effects.

"World Wide Suicide"

Vedder and the band embrace their personal moment of Dylanesque musical protest on "World Wide Suicide." Look no further than the morning newspaper reporting another military casualty from Iraq in order to understand this song. There is a moment of recognition for the narrator that forces him to vent his anger. Helpless to the loss of life, he can only pray that somehow hope is kept alive and that the wrong of this latest war can be righted before another life is taken. The cannonballs are indeed still flying and the answer is still blowin' in the wind. Over a screeching guitar attack and

The first single released from *Pearl Jam*—also known, for fairly obvious reasons, as "the Avocado album"—was "World Wide Suicide," a snarling return to form for Eddie Vedder's early punk rock sensibilities. The rousing single also prompted the band to return to the medium of music video for the first time in the better part of a decade.

Author's collection

pulsating rhythm section, Vedder snarls his anger-infused vocals. It is raw, and it delivers.

"Comatose"

"Comatose" continues the sonic onslaught with a crash and burn fury. If there was any doubt about a band now on the cusp of twenty losing their fastball, this song refutes it in a warp speed of 2:19. Worthy of recognition on both sides of the Atlantic—with echoes of the Clash and Ramones and all the way to the more contemporary proponents of classic punk—"Comatose" is far from it.

"Severed Hand"

Where "World Wide Suicide" explores the tragic ending of the common foot soldier in Iraq, "Severed Hand" offers the perspective of the same soldier's day-to-day life in the desert. In this case, the soldier seeks escape from the reality that surrounds him. The only way out is to suspend his reality with the abuse of drugs. Falling deeper into a state of dependence makes for an existence that has become another form of tragedy—the living kind—for escaping the abyss of the war-torn desert proves impossible, no matter how he seeks to numb the pain.

"Marker in the Sand"

The frenetic five-song opening attack culminates with another trip to the front lines. "Marker in the Sand" finds Vedder questioning the existence of God when forced with yet another conflict where both sides state their claim of righteousness in His name. A moral question posed since time eternal, still with no definitive answer. All that the protagonist can see is destruction, a death wish fulfilled by both sides in the name of God. Ed's vocals cry out with urgent inflection through Mike and Stone's raging guitar duel, layered over the rock steady foundation of Matt recalling his Soundgarden physicality in perfect sync with the thunder of Jeff's bass line.

"Parachutes"

The opening salvo finally subsides and takes a melodious turn with Stone's "Parachutes." The acoustic ballad offers up a mainstream tale of lament and love. The seamless interplay of the guitar tandem with Vedder's vocals ups the ante and raises the song above what could have been a mundane offering. Following the preceding tracks, the effect makes for an emotive interlude.

"Unemployable"

It's back to the battles waged at home with "Unemployable." A stark commentary on the state of the American economy, the central character is a God-fearing family man who has been cast aside like any expendable piece of equipment. In our modern society dominated by corporations, everyone is a day removed from being deemed a spare part. There is no loyalty or consideration of the blue-collar everyman who was once the backbone of our country. From the front lines of the Iraq desert to the streets of the US, the song remains the same to a large percentage of the American populace.

"Big Wave"

"Big Wave" employs one of Vedder's most frequent metaphors, the ocean, to offer a feeling of simple joy that rises to euphoria. The song is the album's mood swing moment. The vastness of the ocean and the power of nature provide the point of release for the singer. When measured against the issues that have come before and are to follow on the record, the only true escape can be found on a surfboard, catching a little bit of heaven while riding the perfect wave. To Vedder, an accomplished surfer, surfing is a religious experience.

"Gone"

"Gone" articulates the desire for a new beginning, in spite of long odds. Reflecting sentiments similar to previous "car" songs, such as "Rearviewmirror," the subject here could be the desperate man from "Unemployable." What is undeniable is the recurring theme of subject as victim. The American Dream has turned into a nightmare. It's not working, and it must somehow change. The song's origin was certainly unique. Vedder outlined the specifics of writing the song in room 1152 of the Borgata Hotel in Atlantic City and debuting the song the next night in a solo preset. Vedder thanked Pete Townshend in the liner notes to the song for his appropriation of the lyric "nothing is everything," originally found in Pete's 1972 solo tune "Let's See Action." The observation was a fundamental tenet of Meher Baba (Townshend's spiritual guide)'s teachings: "Desire nothing but desirelessness."

"Wasted Reprise"

With "Wasted Reprise" inserted next, the overall traumatic stream of the record is reinforced, setting up the final three tracks.

"Army Reserve"

It's back to the realities of war, specifically for those left behind, on "Army Reserve," one of Vedder's most soulful vocal interpretations. The song succeeds in conveying the sense of foreboding felt by the wives, sons, and daughters of those that serve and that sometimes make the ultimate sacrifice in the name of preserving our freedoms. The Jeff Ament 60s retro musical contribution invokes an ominous sonic atmosphere. Damien Echols, one of the West Memphis Three, is credited as a cowriter of the lyrics with Vedder.

"Come Back"

A little bit of rhythm and blues meets country on "Come Back." Somewhat of a stylistic departure for Pearl Jam—getting in touch with their soulful side—Vedder carries the tune with his longing vocals. Musically, Boom Gaspar enhances the heartbreak with his piano front and center. Not to be dismissed is an evocative Gossard guitar moment. The end result, as throughout the record, is the band feeling right at home at another musical stop on the road.

"Inside Job"

For all the despair and hard realities of the "Avocado Album," there is a light that shines in the end. The final track, "Inside Job," maintains a sense of hope that must come from within. The spirit must remain indomitable, despite everything, in order for change to remain possible. There is defiance amidst the pain, reminiscent of "Indifference" or Springsteen's "Reason to Believe." With a shared musical credit (with Vedder) and his first lyrical effort, kudos to Mike McCready for this uplifting finale to a mature record that is not afraid to ask the tough questions facing Americans both at home and in distant foreign lands.

Avocado: What a Concept

Upon completion, Vedder openly questioned whether he had unintentionally created a "concept album." For a lifelong disciple of the Who and Pete Townshend, creator of *Tommy* and *Quadrophenia*, maybe it wasn't such a happenstance. As he recounted in *Pearl Jam 20*:

> It wasn't a conscious approach. It just started to happen. Because there was so much music and because the other guys hadn't brought in finished lyrics, there was a big, giant obelisk of clay ready to be molded, which was the music. It seemed like, wow, you could really make a sculpture out of this . . . Basically this has potential to be a concept record.

After an initial sequencing attempt, the album settled on its eventual batting order, which seemed to work. The critics agreed, with generally favorable reviews, and several hailed *Pearl Jam* as the band's best overall work in a decade. In retrospect, the album was the first in the triumvirate of consistent, versatile studio records that Pearl Jam has spread out over the past decade. An epiphany regarding their current position as the torchbearers for their 1960s heroes has been delivered with passion through their recent creative endeavors.

The album cover became an anti-cover; why *not* an avocado with a pit on the front and an avocado without a pit on back? Vedder felt the song titles spoke for themselves and that adding another title to the record was unnecessary, referring to it as "Nothing" by Pearl Jam, although he had suggested "Super Unowned," a wordplay on Soundgarden's 1994 blockbuster album, *Superunknown*. By any other name . . . Pearl Jam was back, unafraid to address the state of George Bush's America with their populist politics and, above all, the power of their music.

Support Tours 2006: London Calling

No, the *Pearl Jam* Tour did not kick off in London, but British fans were treated to a pre-tour warm-up concert at the 2,000-seat London Astoria on April 20. The 2006 tour proper was scheduled to be more of a May–December affair.

North America

This time around, rather than making Canadian fans wait, Pearl Jam kicked things off with a back-to-back in Toronto at the beautiful, modern Air Canada Centre on May 9 and 10, and wound up at Continental Airlines Arena in East Rutherford, New Jersey, on June 3, sixteen shows later.

Pearl Jam enjoyed a break in the action after the shows at "the Meadowlands" until June 23, when they reconvened in Pittsburgh, Pennsylvania, for a gig at the Mellon Arena to begin another sixteen show run. To wrap up the second leg, the band played a back-to-back at the site of some of their most legendary performances, the Gorge Amphitheatre in George, Washington. These two shows, along with an earlier Gorge appearance from 2005, would later be released as a seven-CD boxed set called *Live at the Gorge 05/06*.

Europe Beckons

Not counting the *Pearl Jam* Tour warm-up gig in London on April 20, 2006, the band hadn't been on tour in Europe since the *Binaural* Tour in 2000. In fact, the last gig they had played there devolved into the infamous Roskilde tragedy. It was time to get back on the horse, and what better way to kick off a European tour leg than a gig at the Point Depot in Dublin, Ireland, on August 23? Two days later, Pearl Jam trod the Who's turf with a concert in Leeds, at Bramham Park, and then hit Reading for a show at Little John's Farm. It is important to point out that these last two shows were the Leeds and Reading *Festivals*. After the nightmare at Roskilde, Pearl Jam said they were done with festivals. Evidently, time does heal. Never say never. Pearl Jam wrapped up the twenty-three show European leg of the tour, which was highlighted by five shows in Italy, by following in the footsteps of the ancient Greek philosophers in Athens, where they played the OAKA Sports Hall.

Australia

Pearl Jam enjoyed roughly five weeks off the road after the gig at OAKA Sports Hall. Then they returned to Australia, which seems to have become one of their favorite touring destinations by this point in their career. They hit their old familiar haunts, starting with a back-to-back at Sydney's Acer Arena on November 7 and 8, kicking off a run of a dozen shows that culminated at the Subiaco Oval in Perth on November 25. There would be no New Zealand shows this time around.

So Long, and Mahalo, U2

A week after they wrapped up operations in Perth, Pearl Jam hit the Neal S. Blaisdell Center in Honolulu, Hawaii, on December 2. The fiftieth state was becoming a real base of operations for Eddie by this point, and hey, this is where he found Boom, let's not forget. While the show on December 2 was the last official stop on the *Pearl Jam* 2006 world tour, the band was in no hurry to pack up and leave Hawaii. A week later, on December 9, Pearl Jam helped the legendary U2 wrap up their *Vertigo* Tour, by serving as the opening act. During U2's set, Eddie and Mike joined the Irish veterans for a jam on Neil Young's "Rockin' in the Free World." What better way to celebrate the end of your successful world tour than by helping your friends and colleagues celebrate the end of *their* successful world tour? And the Pearl Jam tour was certainly successful. While Pearl Jam's sixty-eight-show itinerary may have paled in comparison with the one hundred and thirty one show tour that U2 was just wrapping up, it had been a smooth ride. There were no cancellations, no unforeseen tragedies, and, best of all, they had lifted their self-imposed moratorium on playing outdoor festivals. The album cover may have featured an avocado, but this tour was anything but the pits. Pearl Jam was back and in better shape than ever.

21

Backspacer

A "Monkeywrench" in Rock and Roll's Gears

The Tale of the Tape

Recorded: Between February 16 and April 30, 2008, by Nick DiDia (with help from Tom Syrowski) at Henson Recording Studios in Hollywood, California, and at Southern Tracks Recording and Doppler in Atlanta, Georgia (with help from Steve Morrison)

Produced By: Brendan O'Brien (He's back!)

Released: September 20, 2009, on Monkeywrench Records

Singles: "The Fixer" on August 24, 2009; "Got Some"/"Just Breathe" on October 31, 2009; and "Amongst the Waves" on May 17, 2010

Billboard: Number one on *Billboard* 200 with 189,000 first week sales

Into the Studio

It was a reunion that began with a soundtrack. When the boys were asked to cover the Who's "Love, Reign O'er Me" for the 2007 film *Reign over Me*, they immediately thought of their old friend Brendan O'Brien. They hadn't worked together on a studio album since *Yield*, and working on the Who cover together rekindled the old flames of collaboration. Afterward, O'Brien remixed and remastered Pearl Jam's debut album, *Ten*, for a 2009 reissue.

Pearl Jam tweaked their game plan this time around by rehearsing ahead of time, instead of just showing up at the studio with individual song ideas. Band members made good use of Jeff Ament's Montana home studio for rehearsals. By doing so, they were able to provide Eddie with an array of demos that needed lyrics and a vocal strategy.

O'Brien possessed a keen, discerning ear, he had a knack for arrangement, and, of course, he was also a versatile musician who could contribute his talents whenever the need arose. He has arguably more influence than ever on *Backspacer*; in keeping with the familiar idiom, his absence the past few years had clearly made the band's hearts grow fonder.

gonna see my friend
got some
the fixer
johnny guitar
just breathe
amongst the waves
unthought known
supersonic
speed of sound
force of nature
the end

Pearl Jam released 2009's *Backspacer* on its *own* label, Monkeywrench Records. At 36:38, the album's concise running time calls to mind the temporal constraints of the pre-compact disc era. And the backstory behind Dan Perkins's striking cover art is a compelling tale in its own right.

Author's collection

Lyrically, this was a kinder, gentler Eddie Vedder on *Backspacer*. The biting social commentary that set the tone on much of the band's recent work had, for the most part, receded. Vedder's post *Into the Wild* persona seemed more comfortable being reflective and, in some cases, more thematically conventional. He was now a grounded family man, who often said how lucky he was to be fronting a band that appeared to be more in tune with exactly who they are—comfortable in their own skin, blemishes and all.

The album title conjured up a large dose of nostalgia, particularly for Vedder. The "backspace key" is commonly found on typewriters. Metaphorically, the term "backspace" implies reflection, a look back into the past. Vedder preferred using a typewriter, both for personal correspondence and lyric writing. All told there is a degree of wistful reminiscence throughout the record.

The album's unique cover art is a story unto itself. Vedder had become friends with political cartoonist Don Perkins—known professionally as "Tom Tomorrow" for his *This Modern World* comic strip—during the 2000 Ralph Nader presidential campaign. Ed recruited Perkins to design the *Backspacer* cover. The tic-tac-toe board effect contains nine images created by Perkins. In late July, the album artwork was released via the Internet and went viral. The fans were invited to participate in an online scavenger hunt of various websites to find all nine Backspacer album cover panels. Winners received a demo of the track, "Speed of Sound," from the forthcoming album. All nine images evoke a dream-like, hallucinogenic quality, particularly the image of the drum-playing astronaut floating above the Earth. The image appears elsewhere in the album's promotional material and is a visual metaphor for the band's independent status on their Monkeywrench label. And *Backspacer* serves notice right out of the gate that Pearl Jam is about to take the audience on a frenetic ride.

The Tunes

Vedder's ear for each song's potential as a live performance, combined with O'Brien's intuitive approach, proved vital in creating an album that checked in at a lean, mean, Ramonesesque eleven songs over thirty-seven minutes. This hurry-up offense calls to mind Vedder's mantra that if you think, you stink; just roll up your sleeves and get it done. Stone Gossard shared this sentiment, and the results speak for themselves. Here are the chosen eleven.

"Gonna See My Friend"

The pattern of opening their albums with a haymaker continues. "Gonna See My Friend" surges forward with the manic energy of its subject. The rhythm section of Jeff and Matt firmly lays the groundwork, with the guitar interplay of Stone and Mike pushing the pace forward at double speed. Eddie reaches down to provide howling vocals. On the surface, the song appears to be drug related, but not in a traditional sense of the friend being the dealer. In this case the friend is the savior, the positive antidrug influence. The only one hooked here is the listener, to the sound of the blistering album opener.

"Got Some"

There is no letup on "Got Some," a great example of how the best rock and roll can often be the most spare. The tune is kick-started and subsequently propelled by an exemplary Matt Cameron effect, and the initial familiarity level is almost immediate. It remains a song that is impossible to get out of your head, not that one would ever want that to happen.

There is a clear and present snap and crackle to accompany the delicious hooks and pop flourishes, all delivered with Pearl Jam's requisite muscle. You can imagine the same subject of the opening song literally (and figuratively) walking the line between seeing his virtuous friend on the album opener, or drifting over to the dark side with the sinister figure attempting to lead him into temptation found on "Got Some."

"The Fixer"

The energy remains high on "The Fixer." Originally titled "Need to Know" in a much longer form, this is arguably the most accessible, blatantly "single" material in the band's canon. And it works with its dose of optimism, right down to Ed's Beatlesesque "yeah yeah yeahs." The entire band, supplemented by Brendan O'Brien's piano, is at the top of its game. If great coaching is simply putting players in their best position to win, credit O'Brien for making everyone feel right at home in their respective roles here.

The song can be interpreted on many levels. The big picture showcases a healing influence, an elixir for what may ail you. Vedder makes reference to the importance of listening in a relationship. Stone characterizes Ed's chief role in the band's creative process as his ability—to paraphrase the Beatles—to take the

Here, from the personal collection of Canadian Ten Clubber Jeremy Mahn, we see a beautiful white vinyl pressing of *Backspacer*. Later, in "The Legend Live" chapter, Jeremy will recount for us his adventures during the PJ20 celebration. In a book about Pearl Jam, there can never be enough guys named "Jeremy."
Jeremy Mahn

sad songs the band brings him and make them better. Any way you spin it, "The Fixer" is an irresistible moment of good, clean fun.

"Johnny Guitar"

The nine-minute, high-voltage, triple play that opens the album turns, ever so slightly, with the more significant narrative twist of "Johnny Guitar." Inspired by a framed album cover on the bathroom wall at the band's rehearsal space, Vedder weaves the story of Johnny "Guitar" Watson from the cover photo of his 1979 album, *What the Hell Is This?* The cover features Watson surrounded by a bevy of attractive women, not an unusual scenario in the world of rock and roll. Ed's yarn is spun from the perspective of a man who can't understand why the woman he is interested in rejected his offer for her to become one of the many in his world. To paraphrase Neil Young's universally relatable question from his song "Cowgirl in the Sand": *is* it the same, really, when so many people love you? There may be safety in being one of Johnny's many and not committed to the song's suitor. It's a stylistic departure for Vedder, who sings faster to emulate the song's protagonist.

"Just Breathe"

If anyone bet against Pearl Jam ever writing a prom or wedding song anytime during its career, you lose. Ed gets the band in touch with its sensitive side on, arguably, the single most beautiful song they have ever recorded. Leaning specifically on the *Into the Wild* soundtrack number "Tuolumne," "Just Breathe" allows producer O'Brien to interject orchestral elements, such as strings and violins, with great effect. The romantic interlude is akin to the best of the rocking opening combination punches in its conspicuous simplicity. The title itself is a fundamental testament to life: we breathe or die.

"Amongst the Waves"

It's back to a familiar setting for Vedder on the next track. "Amongst the Waves" finds him in his element, out on the ocean, riding his surfboard. The vocal narrative speaks to the education of a novice surfer. It could almost be Ed in an introspective moment, looking back on his early surfing days at Pacific Beach in San Diego. There is no doubt about where he is now. It's a life affirming moment, the joy building to a crescendo, like a wave pounding the shoreline. This surf song is euphoric and triumphant in tone.

"Unthought Known"

"Unthought Known" is about as deep a psychological examination as any in rock history. The sparse musical opening draws the listener in and immediately transfers all of the focus to Vedder's vocal. This allows the band to cut loose and crank it up as the album's longest song (4:08) detonates like an exploding bomb. The pacing forms a dead-on counterpoint to the lyrical message of letting go. The first step toward achieving contentment is to not overthink things.

"Supersonic"

Just when you might have thought that Pearl Jam was staying in the travel lane for the rest of this musical trip down the highway, they spring back with "Supersonic." Yet another offering on *Backspacer* that draws primarily from the punk side of the band, "Supersonic" succeeds in pulling anyone with a pulse up onto the dance floor or perhaps into the mosh pit. The breakneck pace finds Vedder achieving screeching perfection as he describes the subject's regrets. The halting moment in the middle showcases Gossard's and, in particular, McCready's guitar work at full, quick-strike power.

"Speed of Sound"

"Speed of Sound" is presented in sharp contrast to its name. It is trippy and meandering, evocative of its subject, a rudderless man in a bar. The song was originally written for Rolling Stone Ron Wood's 2010 solo album, *I Feel Like Playing* (wherein Vedder sings backup vocals on the song "Lucky Man"). It wound up on *Backspacer* instead. O'Brien takes the ballad route, reinforcing the track with piano and a sedate Matt Cameron. Despite a downbeat theme there is a tomorrow-is-another-day glimmer of hope at the end. The character from "Supersonic" could also easily be the guy here on an alcohol-fueled manic-depressive flip side.

"Force of Nature"

On "Force of Nature," Pearl Jam returns to the album's predominant approach. Launched from a catchy guitar riff, the song fits the familiar model of the more explosive rockers in the Pearl Jam catalogue. Lyrically, it provides yet another example of the record's optimism. The longer implications of nature's forces are reduced to how personal relationships can be navigated successfully with a little tolerance amidst the turbulence

"The End"

It took almost an entire album—albeit only a Ramones-like thirty-three minutes—for Pearl Jam to descend into darkness. "The End," the final selection on *Backspacer*, arrives at the abyss. An ode to a dying man filled with regret, it serves as a haunting existential reminder of our life's journey: dust-to-dust, ashes to ashes. The overall optimistic feeling of the album is swallowed up in this haunting arrangement, complete with strings and signature vocals from Vedder—still one of the best weapons in the band's arsenal. As a result of the album's prevailing up-tempo energy, "The End" becomes all the more impactful as the closer.

Backspacer Hits the Shelves

The release of *Backspacer* in 2009 officially marked "independence day" for Pearl Jam. Their short-term deal with J. Records had expired and was not renewed. Thus the band's latest studio offering was released exclusively on their own label, Monkeywrench Records, in the United States. *Backspacer* was the first Pearl Jam album to debut at number one on the *Billboard* charts since *No Code* in 1996. Predictably, their thoughts soon turned to the road.

　With a nod to local tradition, Pearl Jam would play two triumphant "home games" at KeyArena in Seattle to coincide with the album drop in September, debuting half of the *Backspacer* material live in concert.

Support Tours

In a break with tradition, live Pearl Jam activity during 2009 actually predated the release of *Backspacer* by more than a month. When the band took the stage at Canada Olympic Park in Calgary, Alberta, Canada, on August 8, 2009, it was the first time they had appeared on stage together as a band since they played at UCLA's Pauley Pavilion in Los Angeles on July 12, 2008, when they appeared at *VH1 Rock Honors: The Who*, to help celebrate their idols. It had been more than a year, and with a major tour on the horizon, now was the time to shake off the rust and maybe give the fans a few teasers in the bargain. On this night at the Virgin

Festival, fans were in for a treat, as Pearl Jam previewed two of the songs from the forthcoming *Backspacer*, "Got Some" and "The Fixer." This, for all intents and purposes, was the warm-up gig for the *Backspacer* Tour, and the August 11 show at Shepherd's Bush Empire in London—the first of five on a brief, European teaser run—is considered the first official show of the *Backspacer* Tour.

Anticipation for the album grew as Pearl Jam offered four more August previews stateside, culminating at Golden Gate Park for the Outside Lands Music and Arts Festival on August 28. The band took a break and kept its fans in suspense for nearly another month.

North America

Backspacer was released on September 20 to the delight of Pearl Jam fans everywhere. The band resumed touring activities the following day with a run of fifteen shows that would culminate with the last of a four-in-a-row at Philadelphia's Wachovia Spectrum on Halloween night (the final show in the storied venue's thirty-two year history). In the spirit of Halloween, Pearl Jam dressed up in full Devo costumes to play a cover of "Whip It," much to the delight of the assembled. But the true highlight of this run was October 4, 2009, a proud moment in Pearl Jam history as the band headlined the prestigious Austin City Limits at Zilker Park, a momentous occasion we cover in our "Bad Television" chapter.

Oceania

During the second half of November, Pearl Jam visited Oceania for a run of seven shows: five for Australia and two for New Zealand. The final show in Christchurch, New Zealand, put the proverbial "Amen" to the Oceania leg of the tour, giving the boys a break that would take them straight through the holidays and on into May of 2010.

North America

Pearl Jam kicked off the fourth leg of the tour in "The Big Easy," breaking new ground by participating in the New Orleans Jazz Festival. The merry month of May featured a baker's dozen worth of shows in the eastern half of the United States, highlighted by the band's triumphant return to Madison Square Garden, where they gave New York Jammers a back-to-back on May 20 and 21.

Europe

A month later, the fifth and final leg of the *Backspacer* Tour got underway in the music-friendly environs of Dublin, Ireland, where Pearl Jam played at the O2 Arena. After a second arena show in Belfast, the band was back on the European festival circuit, hitting nine countries between June 25 and July 10. On that day, Pearl Jam wrapped up the fifth and *final* leg of the *Backspacer* Tour in grand style at Passeio Marítimo de Alges in Oeris, Portugal (just west of Lisbon), where they graced the "Optimus Stage" at an annual festival known at the time as Optimus Alive (rebranded in 2014 as NOS Alive).

Backspaced

It had been a long and eventful eleven months between August 13, 2009, and July 10, 2010, and the band had logged many miles in the air and on the ground. The *Backspacer* Tour was a rousing success, with fifty-six concerts all over the planet at a nice, leisurely pace, and regular breaks in between legs of the tour. There were no cancellations or tragic events to ruin the experience; it looked as though the band was really hitting its stride. The only thing left on the concert calendar for 2010 was the Bridge School Benefit in October,

Meanwhile, Back in Pearl Jam World

"Break," of course, is a relative term. In between legs of the *Backspacer* Tour, the band members kept busy with solo projects. Eddie sat in with the Who for *Quadrophenia*, Pearl Jam were the musical guests on *Saturday Night Live* for the *fourth* time, Mike jammed with the Roots on *Late Night with Jimmy Fallon*, and, oh yeah, Soundgarden came back from the dead after fourteen years. They performed at the Showbox on April 16, with Matt Cameron manning the skins (nice work if you can get it). Just another typical vacation in the life of a world class rock and roll band.

where Pearl Jam played short sets on both days, October 23 and 24. They would enjoy a long break from the stage at this point, as they geared up to celebrate their twentieth anniversary, coming up in 2011.

22

Pearl Jam at Twenty

A Happy Anniversary

Start the Clock

How best to mark a band's anniversary? In the case of the band that would become Pearl Jam, one can make the case for a number of different dates as the proper place to start the clock. The first of these dates is October 8, 1990, the day Eddie Vedder got off a plane in Seattle and went into the studio with Jeff, Stone, Mike, and fellow new recruit Dave Krusen to play music together for the first time. If that is were you start the clock, then the band's twentieth anniversary was October 8, 2010, and pretty anticlimactic; they weren't on the road at the time.

Others point to October 22, 1990—the date the newly formed band first performed live at the Off Ramp Café in Seattle—as being their true birth date. This logic is reminiscent of Deadheads who trace the birth of the Grateful Dead back to the Warlocks, or Mother McCree's Uptown Jug Champions, and their first performances. Here again, the by-the-date anniversary was pretty quiet. There was no show on that date, either, but they would be busy the next two days.

The Bridge School

Twenty years and one day after their first performance as Mookie Blaylock, Pearl Jam found itself in familiar surroundings: playing live at the annual Bridge School Benefit hosted by Neil Young at the Shoreline Amphitheater in Mountainview, California, on October 23 and 24. As quoted in *PJ20* and elsewhere, Vedder poignantly acknowledged that the band "wouldn't have made it past the first five or six years of its existence without the friendship of 'Uncle Neil.'"

Name Day

As detailed in chapter two, in spite of conflicting evidence in the schedule, we have determined within a reasonable doubt that the name "Pearl Jam" was first uttered by Jeff Ament at Nassau Coliseum on February 22, 1991, at a Neil Young, Sonic Youth, and Social Distortion show he attended with Stone and Eddie, courtesy of Epic Records, though they would continue to play their next three shows as Mookie Blaylock.

They formally announced their new name during an interview on Seattle's KISW on March 10, and played their first show as Pearl Jam a little over two months later, on May 15, 1991, at the Union Trade Hall of Woodmen of the World in Eugene, Oregon. They broke out their new name on the home court, Seattle's Off Ramp Café two days later, and the rest, as they say, is history. Fascinatingly, no matter where you choose to start your Pearl Jam clock, nothing noteworthy happened on the day of their twentieth anniversary. As it turned out, they had been busy, contributing to a book and a film in commemoration of the milestone. They were saving the real party for summer's end, and then they would be taking the show on the road. Plans were announced for a Labor Day weekend festival, followed

Though stateside concert activity was largely confined to that now legendary weekend at Alpine Valley, Pearl Jam celebrated its twentieth anniversary through every medium imaginable, from book to film to good old reliable radio. We suspect that many more such milestone celebrations lie ahead.   *Author's collection*

by a tour of Canada. Later, the plans grew to include nine south-of-the-border shows, which grew to ten when a second date was added for Sao Paolo, Brazil.

A Real Labor (Day Weekend) of Love

On Labor Day weekend, September 3 and 4, 2011, Pearl Jam hosted their own belated twentieth birthday party in the form of an ambitious, joyous, raucous, rock and roll festival at the Alpine Valley Music Theater in East Troy, Wisconsin, the scene of several of the band's most memorable concerts.

The weekend celebration, known as PJ20, manifested itself exactly as the band had envisioned: an intimate gathering of their most ardent followers from around the world. The weekend even featured a side stage, in the old spirit of Lollapalooza. Among the side stage acts were Irish singer Glen Hansard, Ohio singer-songwriter Joseph Arthur, old Betchadupa friend Liam Finn, John Doe of X, and thenewno2, a British alternative band led by Beatles' progeny Dhani Harrison, son of George.

With main stage acts such as the Strokes, Queens of the Stone Age, and longtime Seattle favorites Mudhoney, the event was a rousing success, a love letter shared between the band and nearly 75,000 members of their extended family over the course of two days. The two Pearl Jam sets provided a sharp contrast. The first night was a more mainstream set list, while the second became one for "the serious collectors." The appearances, both days, by special guest Chris Cornell, brought the proceedings full circle back to Seattle, circa 1990, for Vedder and his bandmates. Curiously, the PJ20 shows have yet to be officially released by the band. But there will be plenty of other souvenirs to choose from.

Taking Off for the Great White North

The PJ20 Festival at Alpine Valley would have been a tough act to follow in the United States, so Pearl Jam took the party north of the border for ten shows in Canada, beginning in Montreal on September 7 at the Bell Centre, home of the NHL's Montreal Canadiens. They took Mudhoney along with them to serve as the opening act. The Canadian leg wrapped up in Vancouver, British Columbia, at Pacific Coliseum on September 25.

Jammin' South of the Border

After a break during the month of October, Pearl Jam once again hit the road in celebration of their twentieth anniversary year, this time taking X along with them as an opening act for ten shows, hitting Brazil, Argentina, Chile, and Peru. From there, the tour headed northward. Though south of the United States' borders, Costa Rica and Mexico are part of the North American continent. Being well-traveled by this point, the Pearl Jam anniversary party knew the way to Costa Rica's San José on November 20. The *Pearl Jam Twenty* Tour wrapped up for good in Mexico City, Mexico, at the 55,000 seat Foro Sol on November 24. Foro Sol is a rare and noteworthy venue in the sense that it is one of the few on the planet to be built *specifically* for the purpose of hosting big, outdoor concerts. Though by this time it was also being used for baseball games, it was and remains an exceptional concert venue, and it was the perfect place for Pearl Jam to bring their anniversary party to a close.

Now it was time to head home for the holidays. And while Pearl Jam would tour Europe the following summer, followed by four East Coast dates in the United States, for the most part American fans would have to wait until the *Lightning Bolt* Tour of 2013–2014 to see their heroes perform again. Fortunately the *Pearl Jam Twenty* Tour had yielded a treasure trove of souvenirs to keep them busy.

Pearl Jam Twenty: The Book

Pearl Jam Twenty was published on September 13, 2011, just two days after the theatrical release of the film. Part family photo album, part guidebook, part journal, the highly anticipated *PJ20* is a big, beautiful coffee-table book and a feast for the senses. Though the publication information credits Pearl Jam itself with authorship, a cursory glance at the Acknowledgments section in the back of the book reveals the proverbial men-behind-the-curtain, Jonathan Cohen and Mark Wilkerson. While everyone in Pearl Jam's inner circle evidently played a role in the production of this extraordinary book (heck, even Regan Hagar gets a design credit!), Cohen and Wilkerson are evidently the two who did the heavy lifting and tied the entire project together.

Cameron Crowe's foreword to the book, composed in January 2011, is a highlight of the project for any true fan of rock and roll history. The journalist turned filmmaker clearly retained his analog-era writer's penchant for maintaining voluminous files, and those instincts served him well when it came time to put together the multimedia *PJ20* project. His foreword is as artful an articulation of the entire Pearl Jam mythos as one is likely to find, and it should be required reading for any fan of the band.

Brief biographical sketches of Ament, Cameron, Gossard, McCready, and Vedder, the current and "classic" lineup, follow. They provide no such biographical sketches for erstwhile skinsmen Dave Krusen, Matt Chamberlain, Dave Abbruzzese, or Jack Irons, not to mention the elder statesman utility player, keyboardist Kenneth "Boom" Gaspar. Here, as in the film version, the Dave Abbruzzese situation is more or less glossed over, leaving inquisitive fans with more questions than answers.

The first chapter is unlike any of the others in that, ostensibly, at least, it encapsulates a period of time from 1962 through 1989. The chapter makes no mention of 1962, nor any of the other ensuing years until 1984, but that curious omission does little to diminish this narrative of the band members' backstories and early bands.

Beginning with the second chapter, "Chapter 1990," a pattern begins to emerge. Each chapter is named for a specific year and begins with a pithy paragraph encapsulating the events of that year. The text is laid out as a series of journal entries, the first of these being "February 11." These journal entries chronicle what the band members and curators determined to be the most significant dates and events of any given year. Whenever applicable, a chapter will end with an extended essay on an album. "Chapter 1990," for example, ends with a section devoted to *Temple of the Dog*. That pattern remains consistent through the final chapter, "Chapter 2010," the last journal entry for which is "December 1," and contains quotes from Stone, Jeff, and Eddie about the success of *Backspacer*, with an eye toward the future.

The other element that makes *PJ20* so compelling is the visual imagery. Virtually every single page is artfully adorned with graphics, and the book is full of hundreds upon hundreds of photographs—black-and-white, color, sepia, and a host of filtered renderings. The photographs are not rendered in high-definition clarity, but rather with a subtly distorted, brushed appearance, which gives the images a timeless quality. That keen aesthetic sensibility was brought to vivid life as the *PJ20* project manifested itself on film.

Pearl Jam Twenty: The Rockumentary Film

The band's twentieth anniversary not only provided fans with an opportunity to celebrate two decades of Pearl Jam (and to put a beautiful book on their coffee tables), it also provided yet another opportunity to showcase the filmmaking genius of Cameron Crowe. The erstwhile rock journalism prodigy turned filmmaker was one of the original Pearl Jam fans, so who better to capture the spirit of the band's milestone year on film? We can think of no one.

In his song "Like a Rock," Bob Seger wonders where the last twenty years have gone. After its own first twenty years had elapsed, Pearl Jam took the initiative and answered that same question in definitive, multi-media fashion. An argument can be made that *PJ20* is among the best "rockumentaries" of all time. *Author's collection*

New footage for the two-hour film was shot between June 2010 and April 2011. It is said that Crowe then combed through an astonishing twelve *thousand* hours of film footage to create the definitive Pearl Jam documentary. The film cobbles together a wealth of performance footage, new interviews conducted specifically for the film, TV appearances, media coverage of the band from around the world, and home movies, into a visually stunning, cohesive narrative. The film saw a limited theatrical release in September 2011, was aired on PBS, and was released on DVD and Blu-Ray in October of the same year. The DVD became a best seller and was certified Platinum in the US and Australia. In addition to one of the best rock documentaries of all time, the deluxe version provides hours of worthwhile bonus materials.

All of the defining moments of Pearl Jam history are at least touched upon here, though the film medium doesn't really lend itself to in-depth analyses and reflection. Here again, the Dave Abbruzzese situation is glossed over (no rebuttal from Abbruzzese), as Eddie plays addled rock star and punts the question over to Mike, who dutifully encapsulates the band's drummer history in about two sentences.

Eddie Vedder is portrayed in the film as appearing on the Seattle scene as a "shy outsider," a characterization that is belied by the mercurial singer's rapid ascent to the helm of the band. While it is clear that Eddie did not crave the spotlight, he appears to have had no qualms when it came to matters of control.

Here, as in the book, one gets the sense that all of the creative forces in the band gradually evolved to the point where they are able work together harmoniously, both in the studio and on the stage. The song "Alive" serves as a framing element for the narrative arc of the film. As discussed earlier in this narrative, "Alive" evolved from a gruesome tale of incest and child abuse into a survivors' anthem, and the song also evolved into a metaphor for the band itself. As the song plays during the film's climactic finale, with two decades of memories streaking across the screen at lightning speed, it is impossible not to get caught up in the moment. At a pivotal point, a more wizened and seasoned Vedder gestures to his audience and says, "We're *all* still alive," a departure not only from the lyrics, but from the original intended meaning of the song; the fans had made it their own. With Pearl Jam approaching yet another milestone anniversary, it is clear that they are nothing if not resilient. Like "Alive," the whole has become greater than the sum of its parts; the band no longer belongs to itself, they belong to the world.

Pearl Jam Twenty: **The Soundtrack**

While compilation albums—particularly *double* compilation albums—can be a tough sell, the *Pearl Jam Twenty* soundtrack album has a lot going for it, and it is a must-have for any serious collector. Isolated from the visual pastiche of the film, the music takes center stage here. Twenty-nine of the live tracks and demos from the film are presented here in their entirety, making the soundtrack album more than eight minutes longer than the film itself. The soundtrack charted in more than twenty countries and even hit number one in Portugal.

Just Hitting Their Stride?

When all of the dust from the twentieth anniversary celebration settled down, 2011 was over. Any arguments among Ten Clubbers over whether the *true* anniversary should have been on October 22, 2010 were rendered moot. The book, the film, and the corresponding soundtrack were as much navel-gazing as the band was willing to do. They had laid their cards on the table and were now content to sit back and let the public make of it what they would.

In 2012, the band would be back to business as usual, touring, recording, and being Pearl Jam. The future was wide open.

23

Lightning Bolt Strikes

The Tenth, Including *Ten*

The Tale of the Tape

Recorded: Between 2011 and 2013 at Henson Recording Studios in Los Angeles, California, and Studio X and Studio Litho in Seattle, Washington

Produced By: Brendan O'Brien

Released: October 11, 2013, on Monkeywrench Records in conjunction with Republic Records

Singles: "Mind Your Manners" on July 11, 2013; "Sirens" on September 18, 2013; "Lightning Bolt" on March 4, 2014

Billboard: Debuted at number one on the *Billboard* 200, with first-week sales of 166,000 copies

Into the Studio

With Brendan O'Brien once again producing, Pearl Jam stuck to the same format as *Backspacer*, shifting from their home in Seattle to work at O'Brien's base of operation, Henson Studios in Los Angeles. The veteran production guru observed in a *Rolling Stone* interview a unique aspect of the band: their ability to work independently, cut their own demos, and then present them to the rest of the group to create the finished product. For O'Brien, this democratic creative approach epitomized what it meant to be a band.

The initial game plan, post-*Backspacer*, was to get the next record out quickly, capitalizing on the overwhelmingly positive experience of those recording sessions. The twelve new tracks rock hard and effectively encapsulate the many rock and roll genres that Pearl Jam has mastered during the course of its career.

During the gap between studio sessions, the band members traveled many different roads. For Eddie, it was an acoustic solo side tour. Stone played with Brad. Jeff played with RNDM. Mike played with his fledgling Walking Papers and revisited Mad Season. And, most prominently of all, Matt returned to the drum riser for Soundgarden's triumphant reunion. These assorted side projects seemed to invigorate each of Pearl Jam's members and helped them to appreciate their own recording sessions even more. They all shared Eddie's belief that each recording opportunity for Pearl Jam should aspire to a higher level than that which preceded it.

Tenth time is the charm? By the time *Lightning Bolt* was released in October of 2013, Pearl Jam had long since become a well-oiled, fine-tuned machine in terms of their songwriting and efficiency in the studio, and that is evident here from the first drop of the proverbial needle. This is a truly collaborative effort and an album that all of the band members can be proud of.   *Author's collection*

The Tunes

The two universally accepted topics to stay away from have been for time eternal politics and religion. Pearl Jam has spent significant time and effort exploring political issues with their music throughout their career. The subject of religion had rarely, if ever, been touched upon until the opening track of *Lightning Bolt*. The theme recurs elsewhere on the album, as well.

"Getaway"

"Getaway" offers an indictment of the propensity of organized religious dogma to lead directly from blind faith to bad faith. Backed up by a prominent Jeff Ament supporting bass line, Vedder preaches his gospel over the cacophony of the dual guitar attack of Gossard and McCready. The message: find your answers within yourself and let your personal discovery take precedence. There is no right or wrong for any individual's belief system.

"Mind Your Manners"

There was no mystery attached to why the band chose "Mind Your Manners" as the album's first single. A manic-paced, full-blown assault on the senses, "Manners" continues the line of religious questioning from "Getaway." Now that the subject of the opening track has found a path that works for him, here come the obstacles. In the name of hypocrisy, organized religion returns to the forefront. Killing in the name of God is a pattern as old as recorded history. The misguided, misplaced sensibility at the core of the song creates the polar opposite result. Mike McCready's stinging lead is the engine that drives the track forward, while the rhythm section of Ament and Cameron play out their staccato punk rock fantasy. McCready gave a shout out to East Bay Ray, the Dead Kennedy's guitarist for providing inspiration.

"My Father's Son"

Vedder steps back to revisit some early prevalent autobiographical themes on "My Father's Son." A disguised yet relentless melody hammers away at the listener as Ed spins a tale of multi-generational madness far beyond any drawn from his own experience. The desperate subject here harkens back to the ticking time bomb in "Once." How do you . . . how *can* you escape your DNA?

"Sirens"

Inspired by Roger Waters's performance of *The Wall* on his epic solo tour (as Bernie Corbett experienced it in front of the left field wall at Fenway Park during the summer of 2012), Mike McCready wrote a musical piece that challenged the majesty of Pink Floyd's masterpiece. The story of love, its fragility, and the ultimate mortality we all face combine in Vedder's lyrics to form a Pearl Jam instant classic. "Sirens" features yet another emotive Vedder vocal where the honesty trumps all; it is a ballad of epic proportions that is proudly anarchistic, featuring yet another signature guitar hero moment for McCready.

"Lightning Bolt"

The title track, "Lightning Bolt," will always hold a special place in the hearts of all the lucky Pearl Jam fans that shared in the Wrigley Field experience; after all, what could be more poetic than a *Lightning Bolt* concert being delayed by a lightning storm? That's perfect poetry. The coincidence has an almost surreal quality to it. Truth is stranger than fiction indeed. The "lightning bolt" in this case is a metaphor for the object of the singer's affection, a beautiful, untamed woman. For Pearl Jam's male audience there is a ubiquitous relatable quality. Most of us have been struck. For the female population: you know who you are; in accordance with the lyrics you are rock and roll personified. And so is this tune, with its soaring, classic rock guitar line and a pacing that varies from restraint and anticipation to full-blown fury. "Lightning Bolt" is a joyous ride from start to finish.

"Infallible"

Vedder broadens the scope of his focus on "Infallible," a quirky but ultimately catchy tune that rises and falls like a day on Coney Island's famed Cyclone rollercoaster. "Infallible" is a lyrical cautionary tale, offering a multitude of reminders that we ought to be mindful of all that is going on in the world around us. Just because one may have escaped a natural disaster this time around doesn't mean one is infallible. Don't think it can't happen to you because it certainly can. Eddie reminds us that the first step is to be aware. In spite of what many of us evidently believe, none of us are truly "Infallible." The song unfolds at a measured pace, and allows the densely rich musical tapestry to unfold in a manner that not only gives the lyrics added emphasis, it also allows all of the individual instruments an opportunity to shine. This arrangement gives "Infallible" an almost progressive rock feel, which provides a nice contrast to some of their punkier hard rockers.

"Pendulum"

The mortality you've spun on "Pendulum" was originally slated for *Backspacer*, but its ominous tone is a perfect fit here. The song features a sedated opening, punctuated by haunting keyboard notes. Then the band expands the musical arrangement, with Stone surrendering to his inner beatnik on bongos and Jeff credited with a turn on both bowed guitar and keyboard. The song's sparse, near-barren musical backdrop made it a perfect opening song in concert; after all, what better way to build up the tension and anticipation than with a mellow opener? "Pendulum" opened many a Pearl Jam show during 2013 and 2014. The ephemeral quality of life theme is articulated in the lyrics with a literary nod to Edgar Allan Poe. There is a sense of powerlessness in these words, as if we are not fully in control of our own fates. If the legendary Poe were alive today, we think he'd be a Pearl Jam fan or at least admire Eddie Vedder's own unique perspective on the human condition.

"Swallowed Whole"

The mood is elevated considerably on "Swallowed Whole." Ed is back on his surfboard here, celebrating nature through the power of the ocean. There is a hopeful, life-affirming quality inherent in this song. The man who had to get away on the album's opening track has now arrived and is blissfully taking it all in with some guitar strumming that clearly evokes the spirit of Pete Townshend and the Who.

"Let the Records Play"

The ultimate redemptive quality on the next track is the music. Although the story Vedder tells here seems to be autobiographical, it could definitely fit any of the band members, all passionate fans long before achieving rock icon status in their own right. "Let the Records Play" is a bluesy, simple answer to all of life's difficult questions. As Ed's adopted father figure, Pete Townshend, famously said, "Rock and roll may not solve all your problems but it will allow you to dance around them." Over Stone's deep groove, Ed exults in the power of rock and roll's shot of salvation that we all crave. Music can really heal. Relax, turn it up and let it loose.

"Sleeping by Myself"

A tune from Vedder's acclaimed solo effort, *Ukulele Songs*, "Sleeping by Myself" gets the full band treatment here. "Sleeping by Myself" remains stripped down, in the spirit of "Soon Forget," but the band soon picks up the tempo considerably, at least compared with the solo original. A comparison of the two versions of the song serves as a poignant reminder how different arrangements can alter the entire atmosphere of a song. Nevertheless, the love, loss, and heartbreak remain intact, and the lamenting subject is left alone to ponder his fate.

"Yellow Moon"

"Yellow Moon" achingly summons the sweet hereafter. The mortality theme is once again in the foreground, as the song carries the listener to a place far from the city or suburbia. Lyrically, the song borrows a line from Neil Young's classic, "Helpless," in apparent homage to the legend's influence on the band. Here, the yellow moon's ascent is symbolic of the rising spirit of the departed. One can almost picture Mike McCready's guitar solo bringing a smile to Neil Young's face, as he accentuates this spiritual ascent. This is among Pearl Jam's most ethereal and atmospheric songs.

"Future Days"

As was the case with *Backspacer's* "The End," the final track on *Lightning Bolt* also returns to balladry. The haunting "Future Days" takes on a hopeful tone. The subject has found someone he can believe in, and that is enough for him to weather any storm. A Brendan O'Brien keyboard opening—evocative of "Professor" Roy Bittan of Bruce Springsteen's E Street Band on "Jungleland"—draws the listener into a simple story of love being all you need, and "Future Days" is yet another in a long list of Pearl Jam's reminders about how fleeting life can be. The accidental drowning of the Frogs' Dennis Flemion—a close friend of Vedder's, whose hand-written note inspired the song "Smile" from *No Code*—gave Eddie the inspiration for this song and a renewed appreciation for life in general. Pearl Jam seems to be reminding us to take nothing for granted.

The *Lightning Bolt* Storm

At skateboard enthusiast Jeff Ament's request, Don Pendleton, a graphic artist best known for his skateboard-related work, created the logo for the

To our eyes, Don Pendleton's vivid album cover art on *Lightning Bolt* has the potential to become as ubiquitous and iconic as the Rolling Stone's "tongue" and the Grateful Dead's "Steal Your Face." Like those timeless classics, the *Lightning Bolt* motif lends itself effortlessly to almost any medium or context. Here the album's iconography adorns a wristband.   *Ryan Byrne*

album cover. Pendleton's image of an eye with a lightning bolt was the first one that the Pearl Jam bassist received, and it stuck. From that point forward, the two artists and skateboarders formed a close working relationship. Jeff kept the artist informed of the album's song listing and lyrical content, and Pendleton created drawings accordingly. Pendleton's dedication and hard work paid off when the album was recognized at the 2015 Grammy Awards with an award for Best Recording Package. Moreover, the *Lightning Bolt* artwork has already become iconic in the Pearl Jam fan community, adorning T-shirts, tattoos, and many other contexts.

Lightning Strikes

Emerging from their most lengthy hiatus between studio albums, a full *four* years, Pearl Jam released *Lightning Bolt* in October of 2013. The band's tenth studio album has received overwhelming critical acclaim and makes a compelling case for Pearl Jam's continued musical relevance and overall standing as one of the last guardians at the gate of rock and roll.

Lightning Bolt became the second studio release on the band's Monkeywrench Records. The October album drop was preceded by a three-month promotional campaign and the release of two singles, "Mind Your Manners" and "Sirens." The band harnessed the power of social media to create a buzz of anticipation for the album, and it became the fifth Pearl Jam record to reach number one straight out of the gate.

The overall success of *Lightning Bolt*, along with its sense of purpose, thematic maturity, and unquestioned dedication to the true spirit of rock and roll, augurs well for the future of Pearl Jam.

Support Tours

As per their custom, Pearl Jam prepared themselves for the upcoming *Lightning Bolt* Tour with a couple of warm-up shows. Oddly, these two particular shows took place a good three *months* before the onset of the actual tour. The first took place on July 16 in Canada, at Budweiser Gardens in London, Ontario, which seats a modest 9,000 fans for a concert. The second one, held at Chicago's legendary Wrigley Field on July 19, kind of took on a life of its own. The show, chronicled in

Wristbands, keychains, hats, T-shirts, you name it. Barely two years old at press time, the *Lightning Bolt* iconography suddenly seems to be everywhere. Ten albums in, Pearl Jam may have finally found its defining visual motif.

Ryan Byrne

The Legend Live chapter, was interrupted for more than two hours by a thunderstorm, of all things. That's right, lightning *struck*! It is also noteworthy for being the fastest selling concert in the storied venue's long history.

North America 2013, First Leg

The first leg of the North American tour officially kicked off at the Consol Energy Center in Pittsburgh on October 11, and ran through November 1. The highlight of this leg found the band making their Brooklyn debut with a back-to-back at the sparkling new Barclays Center on October 18 and 19. They finished up this leg by headlining the opening day of the Voodoo Music + Arts Experience in New Orleans. This highly regarded festival was the perfect way for them to wrap things up, and from there they headed into two weeks off the road.

North America 2013, Second Leg

The *Lightning Bolt* Tour resumed on November 15 at the American Airlines Arena in Dallas, and from there this tour would stick to points west of the Mississippi. Pearl Jam finished up the second North American leg of the tour on their home court at Seattle's KeyArena on December 6, the forty-fourth anniversary of the Rolling Stones' infamous free concert at Altamont Speedway. This was a festive occasion, as the boys were joined onstage for an all-star jam on MC5's "Kick Out the Jams" by Green River alumni Mark Arm and Steve Turner (of Mudhoney), and another old friend, guitarist Kim Thayil of Soundgarden. It was like "old home week" in Seattle. By this point in their careers, they could afford to take the holidays off to enjoy time with their families, so they did.

Oceania 2014

Pearl Jam kicked off the third leg of the *Lightning Bolt* Tour in Oceania, specifically in the oft-overlooked Auckland, New Zealand, where they played at the hulking Western Springs Stadium, a rugby venue that holds well above 50,000 fans when used for concerts. It was one-and-done for New Zealand, as the band winged on over to Australia for a mini tour that took them across Australia at a leisurely pace, with plenty of time off between gigs for surfing, sightseeing, and other activities. The New Zealand show and all five of the Australian shows were part of the Big Day Out Festival. Pearl Jam wrapped up the Oceania leg of the tour at the Claremont Showgrounds in Perth on February 2.

Europe 2014

Four long months later, on June 16, Pearl Jam kicked off the European leg of the *Lightning Bolt* Tour with a back-to-back in the Netherlands at Amsterdam's Ziggo Dome. These were the first of twelve shows that would take the band through July 11, and found them back on the European Festival circuit.

American Midwest

A little less than three months later, Pearl Jam kicked off the fifth and final leg of the *Lightning Bolt* Tour, back in North America for a dozen full concerts that took them through Ohio, Missouri, Texas, Oklahoma, Nebraska, Tennessee, Michigan, Illinois, Minnesota, Wisconsin, and Colorado. Pearl Jam concluded concert activities for 2014 and brought the *Lightning Bolt* Tour to an official close with two short sets at the annual Bridge School Benefit, which was held, as always, at the Shoreline Amphitheatre in Mountain View California. It was time to visit Neil Young and do some good works, in keeping with the Pearl Jam way. Weighing in at about fifty-four weeks, the *Lightning Bolt* Tour took Pearl Jam around the world in fifty-seven stops, thirty-nine of which were in the continental United States, where fans were finally getting their full share of Pearl Jam concerts.

24

A Little Something on the Side

Pearl Jam Side Projects

Playing in the Band

Under the best of circumstances, being a member of a band can be a series of satisfying collaborative creative experiences. We feel that it is safe to say that the members of Pearl Jam have grown and matured to the point where they are comfortable working together. It took them a long time, but some bands never seem to get that right.

One of the best ways a member of a famous rock and roll band can balance his or her need for individual expression with their responsibilities to the band is by working side projects. Take the case of the Beatles' guitarist, George Harrison. While George did work on a soundtrack album and some instrumental music during the latter years of the Beatles, he never really had that creative outlet for his songwriting skills while he was a member of the Fab Four. John Lennon and Paul McCartney's compositions dominated the Beatles' albums, allowing George maybe a song or two on each. But once the band broke up, the floodgates were open. In November of 1970, George released a *triple*-album set called *All Things Must Pass*. It was a bit of a wakeup call, as Robert Rodriguez notes in *Fab Four FAQ 2.0*. He writes:

> The sheer volume of high-quality original compositions was revelatory, helping the public begin to understand that, with a talent this big alongside two acknowledged geniuses, no wonder the group could not remain intact.

Circumstances were somewhat different for the members of Pearl Jam, as the band was not their first rodeo. Each member had been in bands before, some dating back to middle school. So it stands to reason that each of the members of Pearl Jam has always enjoyed a healthy musical life outside the context of the band, and they continue to do so to this day. Each of them enjoys a little something on the side.

Stone Gossard

We will begin with Stone Gossard, the Seattle native whose post-Mother Love Bone activities put into motion the series of events that would lead to the birth of Pearl Jam. Arguably, Stone was the band member most in need of additional outlets for his creativity. Eddie Vedder's enormous talents as a singer and prolific songwriter contributed to the social pressure for Stone's side projects. By way of analogy, it would be as if George Harrison had created the Beatles, and was then faced with the enormity of Lennon and McCartney's talents. No wonder Stone determined that he needed to create side projects to get his own music out there.

Bayleaf

Stone Gossard released a solo album named after an herb (no, not *that* one). *Bayleaf* was released on an infamous date, September 11, 2001. The album is almost a perfect blend of Stone doing a McCartney-like one-man-band thing, singing and playing every instrument, and a Ringo Starr-like, the-more-the-merrier approach, featuring lots of special guests. Among the notables were former Pearl Jam drummer Matt Chamberlain (the one who left to go to *Saturday Night Live*, remember?), who drums on the songs "Bore Me" and "Fits," and Seattle artist Pete Droge.

As is often the case with side projects, *Bayleaf* took many years to come to fruition, between ideation, songwriting, recording, and release. The album involved four or five years of songwriting and more than two years of studio time, on and off. The project was an artistically satisfying one for Stone, who took the opportunity to showcase his musical skills outside of his usual realm of rhythm guitar. Here, he can be heard playing piano, bass, and even drums. He sang lead vocals on seven of the album's ten tracks.

For musicians who are in a band with a force of nature like Eddie Vedder, it is always healthy to have outlets like this one. And *Bayleaf* fared pretty well, all things considered, hitting number thirty-seven on the *Billboard* Top Heatseekers' chart.

Moonlander

In 2003, Stone began recordings for a second solo album, *Moonlander*, but it was not released until June 25, 2013. After ten years on and off in the studio, and some songs being made available on the Pearl Jam website as early as 2008, the album may as well have been released on the moon. It didn't make much of an impact.

Brad

Stone has been a part of Brad for so long now that it is more like an alter ego than it is a side project. The band formed back in 1992, when Stone teamed up with Shawn Smith and Malfunkshun alumnus Regan Hagar, both now members of the band Satchel. Shawn Smith handles lead vocal duties and plays piano. With his long hair, beard, and omnipresent hat, Smith looks and sounds, for all the world, like the musical progeny of Greg Allman and Dr. John. The multitalented Hagar is the drummer, and Stone plays guitar. The bass player is Jeremy Toback.

As is often the case with solo albums from members of high-profile bands, Stone Gossard's 2001 inaugural effort took about five years to come together, between songwriting and production. The only other member of the Pearl Jam team to participate in the project was drummer alumnus Matt Chamberlain, who appears on two of the songs. *Bayleaf* was an outlet for Stone's creativity, so commercial success was always sort of beside the point.   *Author's collection*

In case you were wondering about the name of the band, we should point out that "Shame" was their first choice of group moniker, but someone had already beaten them to it, so they used that name as the title of their first album instead. As albums go, *Shame* came together fairly quickly. It was recorded in less than three weeks, mixed by the ever-reliable Brendan O'Brien, and released on April 27, 1993, on Epic. It charted at number fourteen on *Billboard*'s Top Heatseekers, but critics were ambivalent about it. It would be four years until the next one.

On June 24, 1997, Brad returned with its sophomore effort, *Interiors*, which garnered a lot more critical praise, but it didn't sell very well (ah, the paradoxes of the music business). It charted at number thirty on *Billboard*'s Top Heatseekers, sixteen places worse than its predecessor. Mike McCready made a guest appearance on the album, lending his fellow Pearl Jam guitarist a hand on the "The Day Brings." Brendan O'Brien was on the team once more, and fellow studio wizard Nick DiDia joined him at the mixing board.

In spite of the album's poor sales, fans began to take notice, enough so that they were able to take this show on the road, with tours in North America in 1997 and in Oceania the following year. And let's face it; that's what really matters to

In Jeff Ament's world, good things evidently come in threes. His side project, Three Fish, dates back to 1994, and this is the back cover, featuring the track titles, of their self-titled 1996 debut album. After releasing a second album with Three Fish, *The Quiet Table*, in 1999, Ament and Richard Stuverud went on to form Tres Mts. in 2001, and yet *another* trio, RNDM, in 2012, with a talented young singer/songwriter named Joseph Arthur.   *Author's collection*

musicians. Big album sales are nice, but nothing is more satisfying than performing before an appreciative audience.

Five years passed before the release of the third album, *Welcome to Discovery Park*, on August 13, 2002. Bassist Mike Berg was added to the mix, not only replacing Toback on the road but working with the band in the studio, too. This time around, Stone and his cohorts handled most of the mixing duties at his Studio Litho, with some production help from Phil Nicolo and Skip Drinkwater, and mixing help from Matt Bayles. They took their time with this one, spending ten months on and off in the studio. All of the time and attention to detail did little to improve sales or critical acclaim, as it debuted at number forty-six on Top Heatseekers, to tepid reviews.

Three years later, the compilation album *Brad vs. Satchel* was released on July 26, 2005, and featured outtakes from these sessions, along with leftovers from Satchel's studio work. It was also around this time that Satchel stopped being a band in its own right and was incorporated into Brad (they were three-fourths the same band, anyway, so the decision was an easy one to make).

Brad hit the studio again in 2003 to record the album *Best Friends?* Instead of releasing it right away, they kept it in the can for several years. When they finally did release it, on August 10, 2010, it was only available for purchase through Pearl Jam's official website. In the intervening years they appeared on Jimmy Fallon on October 11, 2004. Kevin Wood, Andy's brother, joined the group on the road, and they performed live several time during 2007 and 2008.

The following year, 2011, Brad decided to get serious. They signed a contract with Razor & Tie, and hit the studio to record their fifth album, *United We Stand.* The album hit the shelves on April 28, 2012, and they hit the road in North America for their twentieth anniversary year. In the following year, 2013, Brad took their show on the road again, hitting Europe for the first time.

Jeff Ament

Jeff Ament is another member of Pearl Jam who likes to keep busy. Recall how quick he was to pick up his instrument and start jamming with War Babies and other bands while still mourning the loss of Andrew Wood. Like his artwork, music is simply what Jeff *does*. Here are some of his extracurricular activities.

Three Fish

While not precisely a "Super Group," Three Fish featured Tribe After Tribe's charismatic leader Robbi Robb on vocals and guitar, the Fastbacks' Richard Stuverud (formerly of War Babies) on drums, and Jeff, of course, on bass. The roots of the project date back to Tribe After Tribe opening for Pearl Jam in 1992. Within three years, they had gotten it together in the studio with producer John Goodmanson and released their eponymous debut, *Three Fish*, on June 11, 1996. Like George Harrison and Robert Plant before them, Robb, Ament, and Stuverud were clearly influenced by the ethereal sounds of "Eastern" music. That term encompasses a big pool of musical styles, and these Three Fish proved more than capable of swimming in it. This was a big album, eighteen songs and nearly an hour in length. The final track, "Laced," was released as a single. The album, like the single, was critically acclaimed, but did not sell well.

Fittingly enough, it would be three years before the follow-up, *The Quiet Table*, was released on June 1, 1999. Again, the album was critically praised but didn't move a lot of units. But this time around, with no official single but a receptive audience, they took the show out on the road for a tour during 1999.

Tres Mts.

Ament's collaborative spirit shone through again in 2011, when he got together with fellow bassist Doug Pinnick of King's X, (who often bills himself as dUg, for some reason), and brought his Three Fish bandmate Richard Stuverud along for the ride. With the "three" motif firmly in place, the group released their debut, *Three Mountains*, in March of 2011. Four may well *be* a crowd in a trio, but fellow

Pearl Jammer Mike McCready certainly contributed a lot to the album, playing on four of the tracks and making him a de facto fourth member.

The resulting thirteen-track record has a heavy sound, with a nod to the blues-based rock of the 1960s and 1970s bands they grew up on. "Makes Me Feel"—a rhythmic ballad in direct contrast to the thunderous three minute lead single, "My Baby"—got a lot of critical attention, During March of 2011, Tres Mts., with McCready in tow, hit the road for a tour, beginning at the Showbox in Seattle on March 16. They hit Stubbs at South by Southwest down in Austin, Texas, three days later, before hitting all the major points as they moved eastward and northward through Washington, D.C., Philly, New York, and Boston, pausing along the way for an appearance with Pearl Jam aficionado, Jimmy Fallon.

RNDM

The Ament and Stuverud sideshow sought out other pastures in 2012 when the two teamed up with singer-songwriter Joseph Arthur, a "discovery" of former Genesis front man Peter Gabriel's, to form RNDM. The project was not as spur-of-the-moment as it may have appeared to the general public. Ament, Stuverud, and Arthur had all known one another for many years and had been talking about doing something together for more than a decade. The resulting album sounds as though it could easily have come out during the early 1990s heyday of the "Seattle Scene"; unfortunately this made it sound like something of an anachronism in 2012. On Halloween Eve, 2012, they released their twelve-song debut album *Acts*, which was reportedly recorded in just *four* days. "What You Can't Control" is one of the stand-out tracks, and it showcases how the rhythmic stylings of longtime collaborators Ament and Stuverud helped to flesh out the folk-like works of Arthur. The trio did a triad of shows in May of 2013,

Mike McCready's heart was certainly in the right place when, fresh out of rehab, he formed a side project, Mad Season, with Screaming Trees' Barrett Martin, rehab buddy John Baker Saunders, and Alice in Chains' lead singer, Layne Staley. The underlying premise of strength through group sobriety was unquestionably a noble one, but Saunders and Staley were unable to keep their demons at bay for very long. Though brimming with talent and potential, this 1995 album, *Above*, would be the original lineup's sole studio output.   *Author's collection*

hitting Seattle's Tractor Tavern, the Bootleg Theater in Los Angeles, and Bottle Rock in Napa Valley.

Tone

Like his longtime collaborator Stone Gossard, Jeff Ament also had a solo album in him that took more than a decade to evolve. When it finally came out on September 16, 1998, the ten-song album had been a dozen years in the making, including eight years of on-and-off studio work at Jeff's own studio, Horseback Court, in Blue Mountain, Montana. The initial pressing was limited to 3,000 copies, which were sold only through independent record stores, such as Pearl Jam's local Seattle favorite, Easy Street. Later it was made available as a digital download on Pearl Jam's official website.

As one would expect, Richard Stuverud and Doug Pinnick are represented on the album, and old friend Brett Eliason did the mixing. One track, "The Forest" is noteworthy for having been recorded as an instrumental by Pearl Jam. Because of its limited and unorthodox release, there were no Billboard chart implications for *Tone*.

While My Heart Beats

Ament's sophomore effort, *While My Heart Beats*, appeared just four years later, on June 12, 2012. The nod to mortality inherent in the title was apparently inspired by the bass player having entered his fiftieth year and approaching that milestone birthday. The album features a who's who of Ament's musical friends. Richard Stuverud is here again, along with Matt Cameron on a few tracks, Mike McCready, and Joseph Arthur. Once again, Ament used the home studio in Blue Mountain, and Brett Eliason handled the recording and mixing.

Mike McCready

As every Pearl Jam fan knows, Mike McCready has been playing in bands since he was a skinny little middle school kid, so it should come as no surprise that he also likes to keep busy between Pearl Jam projects. We've just seen how he contributed to several of Jeff Ament's side projects, and he has a few of his own, too.

Mad Season

You might say that Mad Season owes its existence to the excesses of the rock and roll lifestyle, or to atonement from those excesses, at any rate. While he was in rehab for substance abuse issues, Mike met a fellow musician named John Baker Saunders, Jr., who was then the bass player for the Lamont Cranston Band, a veteran outfit from Minnesota. Saunders and McCready agreed to collaborate upon completion of their programs. They certainly aimed high when it came to rounding out the band, for they recruited none other than Layne Staley of Alice in Chains as lead vocalist, and Barrett Martin, the drummer of Screaming Trees. Saunders's resume also included Seattle's own, the Walkabouts, so this band could very well be considered a supergroup. They were originally called the Gacy Bunch, the name of which fused *The Brady Bunch* with serial killer John Wayne Gacy, but they soon changed the name to Mad Season.

They released their debut album, *Above*, on March 14, 1995. It was produced by Brett Eliason and included the critically acclaimed hit "River of Deceit." *Above* steadily rose on the *Billboard* 200 and peaked at twenty-four. Sadly, Saunders soon became reacquainted with heroin, and he died in 1999 at age forty-four. Staley would follow in his footsteps three years later in 2002. They have since milked the short-lived band's legacy to death with boxed sets, DVDs, and re-releases.

Flight to Mars

Mike McCready was always a huge fan of UFO, and Flight to Mars was a Seattle-based UFO tribute band founded in 2003 that Mike played with. In case anyone was wondering, UFO was (*is*) a British heavy metal band from the same generation as Black Sabbath. They are perhaps most famous for their fleet-fingered lead guitarist, Michael Schenker, who left to begin a solo career in 1978 but would return periodically for reunions. Schenker was clearly the band's main source of appeal for the young Mike McCready.

The Rockfords

The Rockfords were named after James Garner's 1970s cop drama, *The Rockford Files*, which happened to be one of Mike's favorite TV shows growing up. For all practical purposes, the band was a jobs program for Mike's childhood friends from his band Shadow. In addition to McCready, the lineup included Shadow veterans the Friel brothers, Chris and Rick; Danny Newcomb from the band Goodness; and Goodness' vocalist Carrie Akre, the lone female of the five.

The band released their debut album, *The Rockfords*, on February 1, 2000. It would be their only full-fledged studio release and featured a cameo appearance by the legendary Nancy Wilson of Heart on one track, "Riverwide." They supported the album with a mini tour of five local Seattle spots before going back to their main gigs.

Three years later, the Rockfords regrouped and started gigging around Seattle, resulting in the inevitable: a live album called *Live Seattle WA 12/12/03*. While they were together, they came up with some new material, which resulted in a four-song EP called *Waiting*, released the following year in 2004. As for a follow-up LP, well, we are still "waiting."

Walking Papers

Walking Papers features another collaboration between Mike and Screaming Trees' Barrett Martin, and they are joined here by another superstar, Duff McKagan of Guns N' Roses, and singer Jeff Angell. The quartet released their eponymous debut album on August 6, 2013, to critical acclaim but quiet sales. They sound an awful lot like Black Sabbath or Deep Purple in their prime—a real heavy, bluesy, throwback sound. We wouldn't be surprised if we haven't heard the last from them.

Soundtrack Album Contributions

Anyone can belong to a side band, but how about a *fictional* band? Mike McCready did just that as a "member" of Stillwater, the band at the heart of Cameron Crowe's quasi-autobiographical film, *Almost Famous*. Heart's Nancy Wilson wrote the tune "Fever Dog," and Mike played the guitar part. "Zeppelinesque" by design, one can't help but hear "When the Levee Breaks," albeit shorter and with no harmonica part.

Live Appearances

On March 15, 2004, Mike jammed with the Roots on Jimmy Fallon's show.

Matt Cameron

When you talk about busy musicians, few are busier than Matt Cameron, drummer for not one but *two* of the biggest bands to ever come out of Seattle, Soundgarden and Pearl Jam.

Tone Dogs

Before Pearl Jam existed, a jazz band named Tone Dogs asked Matt to play drums on their debut album, *Ankety Low Day*.

Hater

Hater was the brainchild of Soundgarden's bass player, Ben Shepherd, who had the presence of mind to recruit his rhythm section partner, the always-in-demand Matt Cameron, to man the skins. Like many guys in their age group, Shepherd and Cameron have a love for the old school sounds of garage rock, and this side project allowed them to flex those muscles. Shepherd took this opportunity to sing lead vocals, play guitar, and write songs. They added John McBain of Monster Magnet to play guitar, John Waterman to play bass, and Brian Wood (another of the late Andrew Wood's talented siblings) to sing lead vocals.

The eponymous debut album, *Hater*, was released on September 21, 1993, long before Cameron even joined Pearl Jam. Two years later, after replacing John Waterman with Alan Davis on bass, Shepherd was ready for round two, and the band headed into the studio to record a follow-up album. During this period they also contributed the tune "Convicted" to what they deemed to be a worthy cause at the time, a benefit compilation album called *Hempilation: Freedom Is NORML*, which advocated the legalization of marijuana. The new album was in the can, but it would *stay* in the can for a decade. In the interim, Hater officially broke up in 1997, and the guys moved on to other projects.

Finally, on April 26, 2005, long after their demise, *Hater* released their second album, with the well-thought-out title *2nd*.

Wellwater Conspiracy

One of the aforementioned "other projects," Wellwater Conspiracy, like Hater, was formed in 1993 and consisted of Ben Shepherd, Matt Cameron, and John McBain. It, too, revolved around the garage rock sound, or perhaps "basement rock" would be the more appropriate term since the band's first few singles were recorded in Cameron's basement studio at home. It took them a few years, but the trio finally released their debut album, *Declaration of Conformity*, on June 17, 1997, just before Matt began his tenure in Pearl Jam.

Oddly, the album is anything but conformist in its sound, which is reminiscent of early Pink Floyd in all its psychedelic glory. As if to emphasize this point, they even cover one of Pink Floyd founder Syd Barrett's solo songs, "Lucy Leave." Shepherd packed it in after this album, but Cameron and McBain decided to keep the band alive as a duet, with frequent guest appearances by their musician friends.

The band's subsequent releases are similar in their focus on that throwback—1960s garage rock psychedelia—and are worth owning for the album titles alone. The sophomore release, *Brotherhood of Electric: Operational Directives*, came out on February 9, 1999, with a guest vocal and guitar appearance by Josh Homme of Queens of the Stone Age.

Barely two-and-a-half years later, they released *The Scroll and Its Combinations* on May 22, 2001. This time, Ben Shepherd guested, along with Eddie Vedder and Soundgarden's Kim Thayil. If you're looking for the eponymous album, fast-forward another two years.

Wellwater Conspiracy was released on September 9, 2003, and was more of a home team effort without significant guest appearances. But this side project had run its course, and Wellwater Conspiracy was shelved in 2004. As to whether that shelving will remain permanent, only Cameron and McBain know for sure.

Eddie Vedder

Last but never least, there is the matter of Eddie Vedder and his side projects. Perhaps due to his overwhelming popularity, Eddie's solo projects have been somewhat different from those of his peers. He doesn't have the luxury of throwing a band together and playing small clubs in relative anonymity, although that is precisely what he would love to do if given the chance. His somewhat unique circumstances mean that he has to pick his spots more carefully. So he does soundtrack work, appears on other artists' albums, and, in more recent years, plays solo shows.

"Watt" Are Friends For?

On February 28, 1995, Eddie Vedder sang lead vocals on "Against the 70s," a track on Mike Watt's solo album *Ballhog or Tugboat?* Watt was the creative force behind Minutemen and Firehose and was clearly a popular figure among his musical brethren; Eddie was one of about fifty guests on this album, including Henry Rollins, Flea, Dave Grohl, and Krist Novoselic. On April 28, 1995, he

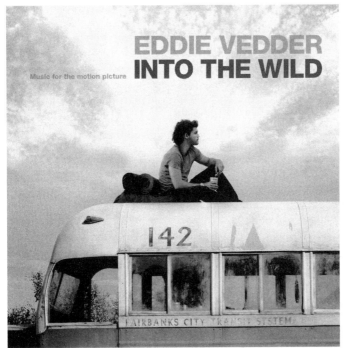

It has been said that Eddie Vedder had just *one* viewing of a rough cut of Sean Penn's film *Into the Wild* before diving into the studio with Adam Kasper to create the film's soundtrack. This 2007 project became, in essence, Eddie's first solo album, and he took the matter very seriously. In the years since, the film, the soundtrack album, and the Jon Krakauer book that started the whole thing have all become staples in the collections of serious Pearl Jam fans.   *Author's collection*

appeared on the Jon Stewart Show, along with Dave Grohl and Pat Smear, to back up Mike Watt on "Big Train" and "The Red and the Black."

Soundtracks

Eddie has made valuable musical contributions to numerous film soundtracks, beginning with "Face of Love" and "The Long Road," a pair of duets with Nusrat Fateh Ali Khan on the soundtrack for Sean Penn's 1995 film *Dead Man Walking*. Six years later, he rekindled his relationship with Penn on 2001's *I Am Sam* soundtrack, a star-studded album which featured Eddie on a cover of the Beatles' "You've Got to Hide Your Love Away." In 2004, Eddie helped to honor his surfing brethren with the song "Goodbye," his contribution to the soundtrack for the surfer film *A Brokedown Melody*. To date, Eddie's banner year for soundtrack work has to be 2007. That year, he and Pearl Jam as a whole contributed to the Tomas Young Iraqi war documentary *Body of War*. Eddie and Ben Harper collaborated on "No More," while Pearl Jam contributed their cover of Bob Dylan's "Masters of War." Eddie and Pearl Jam manager Kelly Curtis are credited as two of the album's seven co-producers.

Into the Wild, 2007

Eddie's work on the soundtrack for the 2007 Sean Penn film *Into the Wild* almost gives new meaning to the term "solo project." He really did have a hand in everything. In addition to writing the majority of the songs, along with co-producing and co-mixing with Adam Kaspar, Eddie did the Jeff Ament thing by creating the design and layout, and the Paul McCartney thing by playing *all* of the instruments: drums, piano, organ, guitar, bass, banjo, and mandolin. Oh, and as one would expect, he *sang*, too.

His stewardship was enough to land the album, which moved nearly 40,000 units in its first week, in the eleventh spot on the *Billboard* 200. And awards followed. The song "Guaranteed" earned the 2008 Golden Globe for Best Original Song and was nominated for a Grammy. Eddie also garnered a 2009 Grammy nomination for Best Rock Vocal Performance for "Rise." He had some help from Sleater-Kinney's Corin Tucker on the Gordon Petersen (aka "Indio") song "Hard Sun."

In April of 2008, Eddie hit the road for his first solo tour, in support of his first solo album, the *Into the Wild* soundtrack. Appropriately enough, Eddie dubbed it "The April Fools Tour." He started at The Centre in Vancouver, British Columbia, Canada, before heading south for nine more dates along the West Coast of the US. Who says the man doesn't have a sentimental side? When Eddie Vedder performed his first live solo show on the tour, he donned the same Butthole Surfers T-shirt he had worn years earlier on October 22, 1990, during Mookie Blaylock's debut at Seattle's Off Ramp Café.

That same year, Pearl Jam contributed to the Binder brothers' Adam Sandler comedy-drama *Reign over Me* with a cover of the Who's "Love, Reign O'er Me." It was also the year Eddie took things a step further by creating a film soundtrack from start to finish for Sean Penn's *Into the Wild*.

On the Big Screen

In addition to his extensive work on film soundtracks, Eddie has also enjoyed more screen time than his bandmates. Aside from *Singles* and *Walk Hard: The Dewey Cox Story*, which we discussed earlier in this narrative, he has appeared in documentaries about the Ramones (*End of the Century: The Story of the Ramones*, 2003), Tom Petty (*Runnin' Down a Dream*, 2007), and, not surprisingly, "grunge" (*Hype!* 1996). Political documentarians, such as Michael Moore, sought him out for 2008's *Slacker Uprising*, as did Howard Zinn for 2009's *The People Speak*. He appeared in the 2012 documentary *West of Memphis* because of his tireless advocacy for The West Memphis Three.

C Average

Eddie's collaborations with the band C Average in the late 1990s, in which he sometimes wore a Roger Daltrey disguise and sang Who songs, are indicative of his desire to return to a simpler time when he could just be "one of the guys" in the band and play at small clubs without creating a scene.

Ukulele Songs

As if to emphasize that his fascination with the ukulele wasn't merely some strange affectation borne of spending too much time in Hawaii, Eddie made it official on May 31, 2011, when he released his second solo album, *Ukulele Songs*. In a stroke of marketing genius, the album's release coincided with the release of a DVD (filmed in Washington, D.C. during his 2008 solo tour) called *Water on the Road*. *Ukulele*

Songs features an impressive array of ten original compositions, bolstered by five cover songs, and was surprisingly well received. Eddie booked a series of small theater dates in June and July of 2011 to showcase the new material.

The Alumnus: Jack Irons

Jack Irons's 2004 solo album *Attention Dimension* may have been released long after his tenure in Pearl Jam had ended, but the fact that Stone, Jeff, and Eddie all appear on the album to lend their skills shows you that he, at least, remains an alumnus in good standing.

25

Odds and Sods

Holiday Singles, Soundtracks, and Benefits

The Ten Club "Christmas" Singles

A mong the many perks of being a member of the Ten Club is the anticipation that comes from waiting by your mailbox for the latest members-only holiday singles. What could be more nostalgic, particularly now in the twenty-first century, than unwrapping a brand-new vinyl 45? For the most part, as we will see, Ten Clubbers have enjoyed this perk on an annual basis.

The first Christmas single, *Christmas 1991*, featured "Let Me Sleep (It's Christmastime)" and "Ramblings." It wasn't released until December 31, 1991, so somebody may have overslept after all. But the December 31 release date became something of a tradition from that point forward. During most years, Pearl Jam would reward Ten Club members with these exclusive singles. *Christmas 1992 (Who Killed Rudolph?)* featured their favorite Dead Boys' cover, "Sonic Reducer," backed by "Ramblings Continued." *Christmas 1993* featured "Angel" backed by "Ramblings aka F*** Me in the Brain."

The Grinch must have been around in 1994, for there was no Christmas single under the tree that year. But Pearl Jam made it up to the club with *two* singles for *Christmas 1995*: "History Never Repeats" backed by "Sonic Reducer (Christmas Single Reprise)"—featuring Joey Ramone as a guest—and the second single featured "Swallow My Pride" backed by a cover of Frank Sinatra's "My Way" (yes, *really*). Next year's lofty title was *Christmas 1996 (Pearl Jam Plays and Sings: Olympic Platinum)*, which featured "Olympic Platinum" backed by "Smile." Christmas 1997 featured "Happy When I'm Crying" backed by the surprise B-side, R.E.M.'s "Live for Today." *Christmas 1998* featured two covers, Arthur Alexander's "Soldier of Love," backed with the ever-popular "Last Kiss," by Wayne Cochran & the C.C. Riders (and many others, as discussed elsewhere in this narrative).

Christmas 1999 heralded a return to originals with "Strangest Tribe" and "Drifting." The new millennium brought out Pearl Jam's sentimental side on *Christmas 2000 (9 Stars Watching over Us)*, which featured a live cover of Mother Love Bone's "Crown of Thorns" backed by a live Elvis Presley cover, "Can't Help Falling in Love." They returned with more live material and a double dose of singles for *Christmas 2001*, the first single featuring "Last Soldier" and a jam with Ben Harper on "Indifference," and the second single featuring John Lennon's "Gimme Some

Truth" backed by a studio version of Jeff Ament performing the Ramones' "I Just Wanna Have Something to Do."

PJ Merry Christmas 2002 was back to a *single* single, a cover of the Sonics' "Don't Believe in Christmas" backed by a live cover of the Everly Brothers' tune "Sleepless Nights." The Christmas Singles titles reached their most elaborate in 2003 with *PJ 03 Xmas (Come Back! It's Christmas . . . I Can Change, I'll Show You . . . I . . . Love . . .)*. This featured a rare live Temple of the Dog song, "Reach Down," backed by a live cover of the Ramones' "I Believe in Miracles." *Christmas 2004* featured Stevie Wonder's "Someday at Christmas" backed by Eddie Vedder performing "Better Man" with the Weimer High School Choir of Port Elizabeth, South Africa.

Christmas 2005 was a real treat: a live cover of Elvis Presley's "Little Sister," with guest Robert Plant, backed by a demo of "Gone." *Christmas 2006* featured Pearl Jam's cover of the Who's "Love, Reign O'er Me" backed by a raucous live cover of Neil Young's "Rockin' in the Free World," with special guests Bono and The Edge of U2. After 2006, the time line for the releases began to move all over the map. *Christmas 2007*, the last such release to use the term "Christmas," was actually released on Christmas Day, 2007. It featured "Santa God" backed by Mike McCready's solo take on "Jingle Bells." The following year, 2008, and thereafter, there were no more Christmas Singles. Bu t in May of 2009, there appeared something called *2008 Annual Holiday Release*, featuring a new tune called "Santa Cruz" backed by an Eddie Vedder and Corin Tucker duet cover of John Doe's "Golden State." The *2009 Annual Holiday Release* did not appear until June of 2010 and featured "Turning Mist" backed by a live cover of the late Israel Kamakawiwoʻole's "Hawaii '78." Kamakawiwoʻole was perhaps best known for his 1993 album, *Facing Future*, and his medley/mashup of "Somewhere over the Rainbow/What a Wonderful World." The following year, fans had to wait until September of 2011 for *2010 Annual Holiday Release*, which featured "No Jeremy"—a different, slower paced arrangement of the original "Jeremy"—backed by "Falling Down," both live from Red Rocks, June 20, 1995. Change was in the air once more the following year, as June of 2012 saw the release of *Ten Club Stereo 2011*. This oddly named single featured a cover of the Kinks' hit "Better Things" backed by Eddie Vedder and X doing X's tune "Devil Doll." The strange evolution of these releases continued the following year, as *2012 Annual 10 Club Single: Live from Alpine Valley 2011* was released in March 2013. It featured Liam Finn, Glen Hansard, and Joseph Arthur in a guest jam on "All Night" backed by Queens of the Stone Age's Josh Homme's guest turn on "In the Moonlight."

Things returned to a more familiar pattern at year's end with *Holiday Single 2013*, released *before* Christmas, on December 20, 2013. It featured a live Pearl Jam and Jay-Z take on Jay's "99 Problems" backed by Eddie and Jean Tripplehorn's cover of the Stones' "Shattered." Then 2014 came and went without any single at all ("Holiday," "Christmas," "Ten Club," or otherwise).

On February 2, 2015, two months *after* the 2014 holidays, Ten Clubbers were treated to *Holiday Single 2014*. This long-awaited single featured Eddie doing a live cover of John Lennon's "Imagine" backed by a Jeff Ament bass solo, "Pendulumorphosis." As of press time, there is no way of telling whether Pearl

Jam's 2015 holiday plans include a new single for the faithful, but you never know. This band is nothing if not full of surprises.

Soundtracks

You are already familiar with the more obvious ones, such as 1992's *Singles*, the soundtrack for *Pearl Jam Twenty*, and Eddie's stellar work on *Into the Wild*, but Pearl Jam's music has also been a part of many other film soundtracks, including documentaries. *Judgment Night* arrived in 1993, and the soundtrack found Pearl Jam collaborating with Cypress Hill on the final track, "Real Thing." Two years later, in 1995, Pearl Jam contributed to *The Basketball Diaries: Original Motion Picture Soundtrack* by collaborating with the real-life protagonist Jim Carroll, author of the autobiography that spawned the film, on the song "Catholic Boy." The following year, the Pearl Jam song "Not For You" was included on *Hype!: The Motion Picture Soundtrack*; the documentary film chronicled the "grunge" era.

1998's *Chicago Cab* featured an obscure Pearl Jam track called "Hard to Imagine." The song has become a cult classic. Pearl Jam's trippy "Who You Are" also makes an appearance. And Brad gets in on the fun with "Secret Girl."

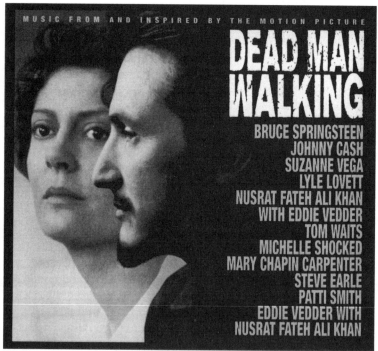

Many years before *Into the Wild*, it was Eddie Vedder's contributions to the 1996 soundtrack for Sean Penn's *Dead Man Walking* that planted the seed for further collaborations between the two artists. Over the years, the music of Pearl Jam's members, whether collectively or individually, has appeared in a host of film and television contexts. And you can bet that there will be more to come.   *Author's collection*

Five years down the road, in 2003, Pearl Jam's "Man of the Hour" was the opening track on *Big Fish: Music from the Motion Picture*. While technically not a "soundtrack" album, 2004's *Songs and Artists That Inspired Fahrenheit 9/11*, features Pearl Jam's cover of Dylan's "Masters of War" as part of a roster of artists and songs that inspired Michael Moore as he created the controversial documentary film. That same year, Pearl Jam's "Go" appeared on *Riding Giants: Music from the Motion Picture*, the soundtrack to the documentary film by legendary surfer and skateboarder Stacy Peralta.

"Masters of War" made another appearance in 2007, this time in the documentary film *Body of War*. The soundtrack album, *Body of War: Songs That Inspired an Iraq War Veteran*, was released the following year in 2008. Not only did it include the live Pearl Jam version of "Masters of War," it also featured Eddie Vedder and Ben Harper's live rendition of "No More," which was recorded specifically for the film.

They revisited the surfing theme in 2008 when "Big Wave" appeared on *Surf's Up: Music from the Motion Picture*.

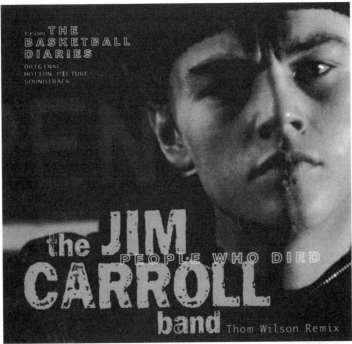

Pearl Jam made a name for itself early on in their film soundtrack career by collaborating on *The Basketball Diaries Original Motion Picture Soundtrack* with the author/protagonist himself, Jim Carroll, on the opening song, "Catholic Boy." And just to add a little Seattle-style "bookending" to the project, their old friends Soundgarden wrap things up with the final song, "Blind Dogs." Soon enough their musical contributions would be in wide demand.   *Author's collection*

Notable Benefit Concerts

Benefit concerts have long been a staple of the rock and roll community, and they provide artists with a forum for raising awareness and donating to the causes they deem worthy. Whether collectively or as individuals, the members of Pearl Jam have participated in many of these events over the years and have created countless others. Strictly speaking, since the creation of the Vitalogy Foundation, *all* Pearl Jam concerts have been benefit concerts, with the foundation serving as the clearinghouse for each band member's personal charities. Here are some of the highlights.

Just a Drop in the Park: Pearl Jam Rocks the Vote!

As discussed earlier in this narrative, Pearl Jam's first collective effort as a band was a free concert dubbed *A Drop in the Park*. It was not a fundraiser per se, but it had a more pragmatic purpose: getting young people politically motivated by registering them to vote, in support of Rock the Vote's efforts. Delayed from its original May 18 date because of skittish city officials withholding the permits, the event was finally held on September 20, 1992, at Seattle's Warren G. Magnusson Park, and attracted a crowd of 33,000 concertgoers. Several fellow artists joined Pearl Jam in their efforts, including Seaweed, Pete Droge, Cypress Hill, and the Jim Rose Circus Sideshow. When all was said and done, about ten percent of the audience members (roughly 3,000) registered as first-time voters that day. Not too shabby.

Vote for Change: With a Little Help from Our Friends

From the very beginning, and for nearly a quarter of a century since, Pearl Jam has been at the forefront of social and political activism. At one point, Eddie was one of twenty-five artists chosen to write essays for *Rolling Stone* magazine about the significance of the Bush vs. Kerry decision facing the American electorate. Never was Pearl Jam's political idealism more evident than in 2004. The difference was that this time Pearl Jam would have plenty of elite company, with each band and artist doing their own part. Bruce Springsteen and the E Street Band, R.E.M., John Fogerty, and John Mellencamp (among others) all joined forces for a common cause, leading up to the 2004 election. Pearl Jam contributed the proceeds of a series of seven concerts to America Coming Together (ACT), beginning with a nearly two-and-half hour marathon on October 1 at the Sovereign Center in Reading, Pennsylvania. From there, the tour swung through the Sports Arena in Toledo, Ohio, on the second; the DeltaPlex in Grand Rapids, Michigan, on the third; the Fox Theatre in Saint Louis, Missouri, on the fifth; the Civic Center in Asheville, North Carolina, on the sixth; and Silver Spurs Arena in Kissimmee, Florida, on the eighth. The grand finale came on the eleventh at the MCI Center in Washington DC. This classic-style packet show brought together all of the artists participating in the Vote for Change Tour under one roof, with different genres and generations doing their part. In addition to Pearl Jam, who turned in a taut, five-song set, the bill featured R.E.M., Kenneth "Babyface" Edmonds, Keb Mo, Jurassic 5, Jackson Browne, John Mellencamp, John Fogerty, the Dave Matthews

Band, the Dixie Chicks, Bruce Springsteen and the E Street Band, and Bonnie Raitt. The combined tours raised in excess of $15 million.

The Annual Bridge School Benefit Concerts

Whether their continued involvement is a direct result of their loyalty to Neil Young or not, Pearl Jam first appeared at this event in 1992, hot off the concert trail from their first Lollapalooza, and they continue to contribute their artistry to the cause to this day. The brief, all-acoustic sets they play at the Shoreline Amphitheater are a welcome musical change of pace for the band, and they turn up there like clockwork every two or three years.

November 1, 1992. On their first go-around at The Bridge School Benefit Concert, Pearl Jam offered seven songs: "Footsteps," "Jeremy," "Black," "Alive," the debut of "Daughter," "Angel," and Little Steven's "I Am a Patriot." Evidently they made a good impression on Neil Young that night because it was not long after that he asked them to tour Europe with him.

Joining a truly eclectic roster of veteran artists, Pearl Jam holds its own among such luminaries as David Bowie, Simon & Garfunkel, Bonnie Raitt, Tracy Chapman, the Pretenders, Beck, the Lovemongers, Don Henley, Ministry, Nils Lofgren, Elvis Costello, and "Uncle Neil" Young himself. Their live version of "Nothingman" retains its emotive power decades later.

Author's collection

The Great Turtle Race

Sometimes activism can really be a great deal of fun, as evidenced by this unusual and innovative event in mid-April of 2009. Pearl Jam joined a coalition of eleven like-minded groups and individuals in sponsoring a leatherback sea turtle in a race from Nova Scotia to the Caribbean, or to put it another way, from their feeding grounds to their spawning grounds, 3,700 miles south. Why sea turtles feel the need to separate these two activities by such a great distance is one of those mysteries of nature we'll leave to the marine biologists. The cool part about this event was that the turtles were tagged and tracked by satellite during their eight-day journey. Pearl Jam sponsored a female leatherback they dubbed "Backspacer," who, in spite of her name, crossed the virtual finish line ahead of her marine reptile colleagues, winning the day for Pearl Jam and raising awareness and needed funds for the oceans in the process.

October 1 and 2, 1994. The next time around, less than two years later, Pearl Jam appeared on the bill both nights, throwing in Young's "Tonight's the Night" during the second night. The pattern continued during the 1996 shows on October 19 and 20, when they were billed second only to Neil Young and Crazy Horse, and ahead of such notables as David Bowie and Patti Smith.

After ten years of benefit concerts for the Bridge School, Neil Young evidently felt that the time was right to add another revenue stream to the fundraising efforts, and what better way to capture the spirit of the event than to release a compilation album? The album, *The Bridge School Concerts, Vol. 1*, was released on November 18, 1997, and features Pearl Jam's performance of "Nothingman."

Pearl Jam returned for the 1999 benefit, held on Halloween, with a brief, seven-song set. Interestingly enough, this was their only live concert appearance for the year, though a grueling schedule awaited them, mostly during the second half of 2000. They returned with a more robust two-day appearance on October 20 and 21, 2001, though they had slipped to third in the billing, after Dave Matthews. Two years later, on October 25 and 26, 2003, Pearl Jam again appeared third on the bill, behind a Crosby, Stills, Nash, and Young reunion set and the legendary Willie Nelson. Pearl Jam covered Dylan's "Masters of War" both nights and upped the fun factor with a parody song, "Old Dick Cheney," to the tune of the children's classic "Old McDonald." In a departure from the usual pattern, Eddie Vedder returned the following year, performing solo on October 23 and 24 of 2004.

The next full Pearl Jam appearance at the Bridge School came two years later on October 21 and 22, 2006, when they regained second place in the billing, over the returning Dave Matthews. They would not return to the Bridge School stage until four years later on October 23 and 24, 2010.

The following year, the Bridge School would hit the quarter-century mark, so the time was right for another benefit compilation album. *The Bridge School Concerts: 25th Anniversary* was released on October 21, 2011, and features Pearl Jam doing the song Eddie famously almost gave away, "Better Man."

Most recently, Pearl Jam appeared at the Bridge School Benefit on October 25 and 26, 2014, where they wrapped up their 2014 fall tour.

The Mount Graham Coalition

On November 6 and 7, 1993, Pearl Jam performed two benefit concerts for the Mount Graham Coalition, originally donating one dollar from each ticket sold to the cause. Mount Graham, as discussed in chapter six, is sacred land for the Apache, and the band was trying to help the coalition prevent the University of Arizona from building space observatories atop it.

The memorable moments came during the second show, on November 7. Eddie announced that after visiting the mountain with Apache leaders, he and the other members of Pearl Jam agreed to donate all of the proceeds to the Mount Graham Coalition. When someone threw a University of Arizona sweatshirt onto the stage, Eddie made his feelings known by setting it on *fire*!

The Louis Warschaw Prostate Cancer Center Benefit Goes to the Dogs

On October 28, 2003, at the Santa Barbara Bowl in California, Pearl Jam invited a who's who of their friends to perform a very special benefit concert for the Louis Warschaw Prostate Cancer Center at Cedars-Sinai Medical Center. The show was Pearl Jam's way of honoring a request from the legendary Johnny Ramone, who was dying of prostate cancer at the time. Among the special guests were Red Hot Chili Peppers' guitarist John Frusciante, founding Pepper and former Pearl Jammer Jack Irons, Jack Johnson, Lyle Workman, and last but *never* least, Chris Cornell. Each of the guests had their turn onstage with Pearl Jam, with Jack Irons manning the skins on the *No Code* tunes "Hail Hail" and "In My Tree," which he cowrote with Stone and Eddie. Pearl Jam turned the stage over to their early patron and friend Chris Cornell for a brief solo set, which led into a full-fledged Temple of the Dog alumni reunion. They played "Hunger Strike" and "Reach Down" to close out the show. The hootenanny-style encore got *everybody* out on stage together for a festive cover of the Byrds' classic, "So You Want to Be a Rock 'n' Roll Star." The fundraiser was a success, both financially and artistically, and a loving tribute to the ailing Ramone. As fate would have it, this proved to be the last time Johnny Ramone would ever see Pearl Jam perform, so it is gratifying to know that Pearl Jam and their friends left it all on the court.

When the Levees Broke

Hurricane Katrina brought out the best in many artists. Pearl Jam did their part at the world renowned House of Blues in Eddie's hometown of Chicago. Proceeds from the October 5, 2005 gig were divided among Habitat for Humanity, the American Red Cross, and the Jazz Foundation of America.

On July 1, 2008, Pearl Jam entertained a capacity crowd of well-heeled fans at New York's legendary Beacon Theater, just before the beloved venue closed for a seven-month round of badly needed renovations. The goal of this show was to raise funds for NYC's Robin Hood Foundation, and it proved to be a smashing success, to the tune of $3 million.

Benefit Compilation Albums

Pearl Jam's earliest contribution to a benefit album was in 1993, when they contributed to *Sweet Relief: A Benefit for Victoria Williams*. Williams was a fellow artist who had been diagnosed with multiple sclerosis. Pearl Jam joined the artist on her song "Crazy Mary."

Three years later, in 1996, Pearl Jam contributed their cover of Eddie Holland's "Leaving Here" to *Home Alive: The Art of Self Defense* in the interest of helping to promote women's safety. That same year, they contributed a cover of the Silly Surfers' "Gremmie Out of Control" to *M.O.M., Vol. 1: Music for Our Mother Ocean*. This was a three-album series produced by Surfdog Records for the benefit of the Surfrider Foundation, one of Ed's favorite charities. Pearl Jam didn't contribute to the second one, but in 1999 they contributed former drummer Jack Irons's "Whale Song" to *M.O.M., Vol. 3: Music for Our Mother Ocean*.

During 1997, Pearl Jam contributed songs to two benefit compilations, one for the Bridge School, and the other a sampler from the Tibetan Freedom Concert. They offered their Bridge School Benefit Concert performance of "Nothingman" for *The Bridge School Concerts, Vol. 1*. Several years down the road, they contributed their performance of "Better Man" for *The Bridge School Concerts 25th Anniversary Edition* in 2011. Though the Tibetan Freedom concerts spanned a period of time between 1996 and 2001, 1997's *Tibetan Freedom Concert* album focused specifically on the 1997 New York City concert, during which Pearl Jam's Mike McCready and Eddie Vedder performed "Yellow Ledbetter."

Two years later, Pearl Jam went from fighting for freedom to protecting the displaced. 1999's *No Boundaries: A Benefit for the Kosovar Refugees* featured two Pearl Jam songs: the ever-popular cover song "Last Kiss" to open the album, and a cover of Buzz Cason and Tony Moon's 1962 composition "Soldier of Love (Lay Down Your Arms)" as the closing track.

Freedom became the theme of the day once more in 2004, when Pearl Jam joined more than twenty-five of their fellow artists in contributing to *For the Lady*, a benefit album for Aung San Suu Kyi, a Burmese opposition leader and political prisoner at the time. Pearl Jam provided a live recording of "Better Man." Proceeds from sales of the double-album CD were funneled to a 501(c)(3), U.S. Campaign for Burma. That same year, Pearl Jam contributed one of their most controversial concert moments—the April Fool's Day 2003 version of "Bu$hleaguer" from the Denver Pepsi Center show that caused a fan walkout during the first encore set—to *Hot Stove, Cool Music, Vol. 1*. Proceeds from the album were allocated to the Jimmy Fund, in support of the Dana-Farber Cancer Institute in Boston, Massachusetts. If Pearl Jam's history teaches us anything, we can expect the band to contribute to more benefit compilation albums in the years ahead.

26

The Legend Live

Memorable Pearl Jam Concerts

They're Better "Live"

T he Pearl Jam fan base was created by, and subsequently sustained by, the live concert experience. This chapter will examine some of the most memorable live performances by the band, an exercise that is by its very nature subjective. We hold out no hope for attaining a consensus among the Pearl Jam faithful. The best Pearl Jam concerts will always be the ones you attended and never the ones that you missed. Nevertheless, there are certain shows that stand out for us because of their significance in the band's evolution. With that in mind, we will discuss some of these milestone concerts.

Next, a special section will chronicle some of the highlights of co-author Bernard M. Corbett's nearly two decades of Pearl Jam concert experiences. The often quixotic and eternally youthful sportscaster lets no obstacle stand in his way when he is determined to see a show. While certainly there are Pearl Jam fans out there who go back further in the band's history, and who have seen more shows, Bernie has somehow managed to be present for many of the band's most memorable performances. Working around his hectic broadcasting schedule, his quests for live Pearl Jam have taken him from coast to coast, and up above the border into Canada.

Finally, it will conclude with brief vignettes from some of the band's most loyal fans, the Ten Clubbers we have come to know along the way, as they recall their favorite Pearl Jam concert memories.

The Pinkpop Festival 1992

June 8, 1992. Landgraaf, the Netherlands. Pearl Jam's performance at the 1992 Pinkpop Festival is memorable for a number of reasons, not the least of which is because it was broadcast live on television and preserved on film, giving new meaning to the term "Dutch treat." Thanks to this film, the world learned of Eddie's unusual penchant for taking Polaroid photographs of the band's audiences. Pinkpop 1992 was not Pearl Jam's first festival (they had already appeared at Germany's Rock Am Festival on June 5, and at London's Finsbury Park Festival on June 6), but it was their first time on the European festival circuit, and certainly their largest audience to date, which clearly made an impression on the band.

The boys were already, as Jeff might phrase it, "stoked" to be sharing the bill with their friends, Soundgarden, and legends like David Byrne and Lou Reed, but the sight of this enormous audience pushed their performance pedals to the metal. Eddie took to the stage wearing a hat and his soon-to-be iconic brown corduroy jacket over a Tivoli T-shirt but shed them within minutes as he became soaked with sweat. Dave pounded away furiously, in rhythmic sync with Jeff and Stone. Mike appeared at times to be lost in a trance, switching guitars and gears as he channeled Hendrix, Tony Iommi, and all of the other guitar gods crowding his mind. All three of the axmen were in perpetual motion throughout the set, running, jumping, bouncing, and spinning on the floor as if enraptured. In less than forty-four minutes, Pearl Jam delivered thirteen songs with a ferocity that is beautiful to behold, to the delight of the chilly, fog-drenched crowd below. Thrilling as it was, the encore set of Fugazi's "Suggestion," the Talking Heads' "Pulled Up," and Neil Young's "Rockin' in the Free World" takes second place. The spiritual climax of the whirlwind set came during "Porch," when Eddie commandeered a camera boom and dove off of it into the manic crowd waiting below. It was a show for the ages, a volcanic performance that captured the band at the height of their youthful beauty and power.

A Drop in the Park

September 20, 1992. Warren G. Magnuson Park, Seattle, Washington. Mentioned elsewhere in this narrative for its significance in the context of the so-called Ticketmaster War, and again for its success as a voter registration drive, A Drop in the Park is also noteworthy for having been one terrific live show, a veritable miniature West Coast Woodstock organized and run by the band before a modest but appreciative crowd of 30,000 fans.

During "Porch," Eddie at first appeared content to keep his feet planted on the ground. He amused himself by playing catch with the audience, who were busily throwing articles of clothing and other objects onto the stage. But it wouldn't last. Eddie began to use his microphone, which fortunately was attached to a very long cable, as a lasso, and after several attempts he finally managed to loop his microphone around the scaffolding about forty feet above the stage. This was all the incentive he needed to go climbing.

Vaulting atop a speaker column, he proceeded to climb up the scaffolding and out across to the middle of the stage like a hyperactive grade school kid on a really large jungle gym. After dangling by his hands to sing into the hanging microphone, and other nerve-wracking stunts, Eddie upped the ante by lowering the microphone over the beam to a waiting roadie below, effectively doubling the thickness of the microphone cable. He then slid down the cable to the stage like a fireman as the crowd roared appreciatively. But he wasn't done yet. He then proceeded to use the microphone cable like one of Tarzan's vines and swung out over the audience. Naturally, at one point he just stage dove into the audience altogether. After a few tense moments, and some help from a couple of stagehands, they returned him unscathed. The home crowd went wild.

"The Ice Bowl"

October 8, 2000. Alpine Valley. East Troy, Wisconsin. Many are cold, but few are frozen. In the 28°F Wisconsin night, Pearl Jam turned in a twenty-song first set followed by a nine-song encore. This was probably the first time the number of songs the band played outnumbered the number of degrees on the thermometer.

Eddie solidified the show's place in Pearl Jam history when he greeted the shivering crowd of 25,000 with, "Welcome to 'The Ice Bowl.'" Coauthor Bernie Corbett was in the house that night. Even he, a veteran New York Giants season ticket holder, still shivers at the thought of that show. He dressed for the occasion as though he were preparing for a late season trip to Giant Stadium. Because of the extreme weather conditions, watching Pearl Jam on that cold Wisconsin stage was a surreal experience for fans, as one could clearly see the breath coming out of the band members' mouths. As Bernie noted, the fact that Eddie Vedder had the presence of mind and sense of place to reference "The Ice Bowl"—the nickname for the 1967 NFL Championship Game featuring the Dallas Cowboys versus the Green Bay Packers at Lambeau Field—is indicative of the band's passion for sports and the depth of their collective knowledge. All things considered, even though the running time of this show was somewhat shorter than usual, the fact that they took to the stage in the first place was incredibly impressive. It was almost as though they were approaching the show with an NFL team's mentality. The show must go on, just as football games must go on, no matter the weather.

"The Experiment" and the Band That Would Not Leave

Friday, July 11, 2003. The Tweeter Center. Boston, Massachusetts. This was the third in a non-sequential series of shows at the Tweeter Center (July 2, 3, and 11) that came to be known as "The Experiment." Bernie Corbett was in attendance at the first two shows. At the July 3 show, the band announced that they would be adding a third show, on July 11. Upon hearing this news, Bernie and his friends ran right outside and got on line for tickets at the Tweeter Center box office. Their quick thinking landed them second row seats, front and center for the third show on July 11. The gist of the experiment was that they would play their entire catalog of songs over the course of the three nights without repeating one.

On this night Pearl Jam must have been channeling their inner Bruce Springsteen or Grateful Dead, because they turned in a show for the ages. The truly surreal aspect of this show, according to Bernie, was seeing the band onstage playing acoustic instruments in broad daylight, as though they were sitting around at a picnic, just having fun. The opening song, "Long Road," may have been a cryptic clue of what was to come. That twelve-song, all acoustic pre-set ended with "Indifference," at which point Pearl Jam gave up the stage for their "opening act," Sleater-Kinney. Normally, of course, "opening acts" *open* the shows, but Pearl Jam is nothing if not unpredictable.

The second set, post-Sleater-Kinney, began with "Can't Keep" and ended with the twenty-first song, "Blood." In the middle they performed their fabled "man trilogy": "Leatherman," "Better Man," and "Nothing Man." Man, oh man.

You may as well have added "sweat and tears" to that "Blood," because they were just getting warmed up. The first encore set featured seven songs, ending with the *Ten*-era classics "Black" and "Jeremy." The second set of encores featured five songs, including a cover of Creedence Clearwater Revival's "Fortunate Son" and their old favorite, "Rockin' in the Free World." The icing on the cake was a *third*, one-song encore of "Yellow Ledbetter." Yes, they had already played it as an encore during the July 3 show, but when the fired-up July 11 crowd showed no signs of leaving, they were forced to air it out once more. When all was said and done, they had played eighty-two original songs and eleven covers. The July 11 show has also been Pearl Jam's longest show to date, as they went way past the 11:00 p.m. curfew, costing them $7,500 in fines. The show weighed in at a whopping three hours and just shy of twenty-five minutes (204:47, to be precise), and made for one impressive three-disc official bootleg when it was released on September 16 of that year. It was a noble experiment indeed. As to whether it was a success, or whether the repeat of "Yellow Ledbetter" rendered it a failure, we'll let you be the judge. In our experience, another encore is *always* a win.

Wrigley Field: This Is Your Hometown, Ed

July 19, 2013. Wrigley Field. Chicago, Illinois. Pearl Jam's appearance at Wrigley Field became, for all intents and purposes, "PJ22." During their career, the band has marked a number of its milestones through its appearances in Eddie's hometown. Playing first at the Metro, then at Chicago Stadium (the predecessor of the United Center), and then at the iconic 1995 Soldier Field show (on the Grateful Dead's stage) are just some of the rites of passage Pearl Jam marked on the Windy City's rock and roll scene. Until July 19 of 2013, only Wrigley Field, the home of Vedder's beloved (and long-suffering) Chicago Cubs remained. The buzz surrounding the one-show-only appearance was epic. Pearl Jam fans from around the world planned months in advance to meet in Chicago.

The night soon took on a life of its own. As a result of a souvenir T-shirt that revealed the show's prepared set list, there was no question that Pearl Jam had a special night in mind. They were aiming to reward their fans and make the most of appearing on the hallowed diamond at the "Friendly Confines." The band opened their first set with "Release" and managed to get in seven songs before Mother Nature took over. With thunderstorms rolling in, Vedder announced a "rain delay" a half hour into the show. After torrential downpours, and a two-hour break, the band returned to the stage with "Mr. Cub" himself, Hall of Famer Ernie Banks. The Chicago crowd went wild as Banks greeted the audience and welcomed them to "his house." The show went on until 2:00 a.m. "'Let's play two' became 'Let's play 'til 2,'" said Vedder, who honored the Cubs at the beginning of the post-rain delay set by playing the song he had written for the team, "All the Way," much to the delight of the hometown crowd. It was an historic, unprecedented night of camaraderie between grateful artists and adoring fans.

What struck attendee Bernie the most about this show is how well-behaved the crowd was in the face of this unprecedented delay. Beer sales continued unabated as fans wandered about the Friendly Confines during the rain delay, meeting new people and making new friends. The communal spirit of the assembled was a testament to the pervasive camaraderie of the Pearl Jam community; this truly was, and still is, an extended family. Unbeknownst to the fans, there was no scheduled rain date for the show. While the fans made the most of the rain delay, Pearl Jam and their representatives were busy backstage. The first order of business was getting the curfew lifted in anticipation of resuming the show once the rain passed. And resume they did, playing until 2:00 a.m. What really blew Brendan O'Brien away that night was the fact that, despite the late hour, nobody left. All of the fans stayed to watched their heroes bring it on home. And by all accounts, all of the fans were orderly and well-behaved, in spite of the somewhat unusual circumstances.

Pearls of Wisdom from Bernie Corbett

Lifetime rock and roll fan Bernie Corbett attended his first Pearl Jam concert on September 29, 1996, and he hasn't looked back since. As of this writing, he is a veteran of seventy-five Pearl Jam concerts and counting. As fate would have it, he was there for many of the band's most historically significant moments. His first show, at Randall's Island, New York, was the band's longest show up until that point. Right out of the gate, the band made an indelible impression on the concert veteran, who quickly learned his first lesson that day: stay on the edge of the mosh pit and not *in* it.

Previously, Bernie had been scheduled to see Pearl Jam at Boston Garden on April 10, 1994, but a conflict arose, which involved the Boston University alumnus and Terriers' broadcaster being hungover and depressed following his team's 9–1 loss in the national championship game the week before. In retrospect, turning down that ticket is one of Bernie's few regrets from his forty year plus history of attending rock concerts. What was he thinking? Not only did he miss what would turn out to be his favorite band, but those were also historically significant shows, coming on the heels of Kurt Cobain's untimely demise—a poignant moment in Pearl Jam's history, as discussed elsewhere in this narrative.

But Pearl Jam had encroached on Bernie's territory even earlier, when they played a show at Walter Brown Arena on November 1, 1991, with the Red Hot Chili Peppers and the Smashing Pumpkins. Walter Brown Arena, of course, was the home of Boston University Hockey from 1971 to 2005. But on the night of the show in question, Bernie and the Terriers were in Hamilton, New York, to open their season against Colgate University. Time and sports wait for no man, particularly when you're the man calling the game; Pearl Jam would have to wait.

On the day of the Randall's Island show in 1996, Bernie, in his typical fashion, traveled directly to the show from Giants Stadium, where the season ticket holder had spent the afternoon watching Big Blue beat the Minnesota Vikings, fifteen to ten. He scalped a ticket on the bus to Randall's Island for fifty bucks, and he was on his way. The concert, of course, was legendary, a lengthy, high-energy affair that featured Vedder, at one point, wrapping himself with duct tape and leaping into the crowd. That will certainly make an impression. To cap off an eventful day, Bernie stopped into the famed Carnegie Deli after the show to fill his belly for the bus ride back to Boston. There would be many similar days to come. This was only the beginning.

On Tuesday, November 18, 1997, Bernie traveled cross-country to catch the Rolling Stones on their *Bridges to Babylon* Tour at Alameda County Coliseum. The Stones' opening act was, of course, Pearl Jam. In the course of one evening, Bernie got to see his two all-time favorite bands in the same venue; the ultimate double bill.

On June 29, 1998, at the United Center in Chicago, Bernie saw Pearl Jam just one month after losing his beloved father. He wound up sitting in a box with diehard Pearl Jam fan Chris Chelios, the legendary Chicago Blackhawks' Hall of Fame defenseman. The two were joined by New York Rangers' 1994 champion and fellow Jammer Brian Noonan, and the legendary Chicago bluesman Sugar Blue, best known for his harmonica part on the Rolling Stone's hit "Miss You." As one would expect, hockey was just as much a topic of conversation as rock and roll that night. It was a night that Bernie needed at the time, as he experienced the healing effects of good company and great music.

During a single nine-day period in 2003, Bernie enjoyed his most memorable stretch of Pearl Jam shows to that point, beginning with the first two shows of "The Experiment," July 2 and 3, continuing down into New York city, where he attended the Red Sox-Yankees series between the Fourth of July and July 7, before hitting Madison Square Garden on the eighth and ninth to witness Pearl Jam's triumphant, building-shaking return to the "World's Most Famous Arena." The highlight of this little New York City adventure came in the midst of the Yankees-Red Sox series, when Bernie left during the eighth inning of the July 6 game, and then made his way, via public transportation, over to Camden, New Jersey, scalping a ticket on the ferry from Penn's Landing along the way, and found himself at the Tweeter Center on the Waterfront for the Pearl Jam show that night. Just another day in the life of a Pearl Jam fan. And yes, he did it make it back to Yankee Stadium in time for the next day's game. This stretch of shows, of course, culminated back on Bernie's home court in Boston, for the third show of "The Experiment." His own experiment was attending six of the seven possible Pearl Jam shows during that nine-day stretch. Now surely there are Pearl Jam fans out there who saw all seven, but how many of them can also boast of seeing the entire four-game Yankees-Red Sox series? Not many, we'll wager.

In 2006, Bernie attended the legendary July 22 and 23 shows at the Gorge, which formed the basis for two-thirds of the voluminous boxed set that followed. He had gone from the Ice Bowl to the Inferno, as the temperature for both shows reached into the triple digits (and yes, in case any of you were wondering, he *did* attend all three Red Sox-Mariners games that weekend, in spite of the heat; talk about dedication).

In 2007, Bernie made up for his past disappointment at missing out on Lollapalooza 1992 by attending Pearl Jam's headlining turn at Lollapalooza 2007, which is documented elsewhere in this narrative. At one point during this show, Bernie wondered aloud, "Was that Dennis *Rodman*?" He wasn't the only one. (It was.)

In 2008, during Pearl Jam's thirteen-show tour of the East Coast, Bernie enjoyed his longest string of Pearl Jam concerts to date. He and his buddy, Dave, were on the road from June 17 through 26. As fate would have it, Pearl Jam's itinerary just happened to coincide with the Boston Red Sox' road schedule, so the pair enjoyed equal parts rock and roll and baseball during their travels. Bernie hit the two shows in Camden, New Jersey; one in Washington, D.C.; the back-to-back at Madison Square Garden in New York City; one in Hartford, Connecticut; and, finally, the back-to-back on his home court, at Mansfield, Massachusetts. The next day, he headed south to attend the Robin Hood Foundation Fundraiser at the Beacon Theater in New York City. All told, he had made it to nine shows out of a possible thirteen. Not too shabby. A highlight of his year was attending the *VH1 Rock Honors: The Who* show at the Pauley Pavilion on July 12.

One of Bernie's highlights of 2009 was heading out to see Pearl Jam in their own backyard at Seattle's KeyArena during the *Backspacer* Tour, on September 21 and 22.

Like all of his fellow Ten Clubbers and Pearl Jam collectors, Ryan Byrne spends a *lot* of time attending Pearl Jam concerts. Here are just a few of his voluminous collection of ticket stubs and wristbands. All indications are that this collection will only continue to grow in the years to come. *Ryan Byrne*

The other highlight of 2009, owing to Bernie's broadcasting responsibilities, was one of the four closing shows at the Philadelphia Spectrum, on Tuesday, October 28. He would have liked to have had attended all four (particularly the final night, the Halloween show), but responsibility reared its ugly head; he had to work.

During 2010, Bernie caught the *Backspacer* Tour stop in Cleveland on May 9 before truckin' up to Buffalo the next day for the show at the HSBC Arena on the tenth. Five days later, he was back on the road at the Hartford show on the fifteenth and at Boston's TD Garden show on the seventeenth. He skipped Newark on the eighteenth but hit Madison Square Garden on the twentieth and twenty-first. Through his numerous contacts in the sporting world, Bernie found himself in the star-studded MSG VIP section, where he soon found himself in possession of a backstage pass. That pass led him, as one might expect, backstage after the show, where he was fortunate enough to have a conversation with Mike McCready. Bernie broached the subject of McCready's "Lost Dog" song "Down," which was written about Howard Zinn—a noted political activist, author, and Boston University professor—who also happened to be one of Bernie's teachers during his undergraduate years. The sportscaster and the guitarist bonded over their shared musical tastes. At one point, Bernie looked McCready right in the eye and said, "Mike, I grew up with the Stones and the Who. When I got to college, I embraced the Clash and the Ramones. Now I'm forty-nine years old. It's up to you guys to take me the rest of the way." McCready looked at him, nodded his head, and said, "We're gonna try."

Apart from the thrill of meeting the Pearl Jam guitarist for the first time, one of the key highlights of Bernie's 2010 Pearl Jam adventures was attending the Bridge School Benefit concert on Sunday, October 24. He would have been there both days, but naturally he was busy calling a hockey game on Saturday.

Pearl Jam knows that oftentimes it is the rarity of a given item that makes it so special. Here we see a Pearl Jam singles collection, one of only 1,500 such sets in existence. No doubt there are plenty of fans out there would love to get their hands on a copy. *Ryan Byrne*

During the 2011 *Pearl Jam Twenty* Tour, Bernie was in attendance for both days at Alpine Valley and the big twentieth anniversary celebration. What a weekend that was. No self-respecting hockey fan is afraid to go north of the border, so Bernie followed the tour to Canada for the show in Montreal on the seventh, with members of the NHL's Montreal Canadiens in tow. Next up was the back-to-back on the eleventh and twelfth in Toronto, dates which coincided with the Toronto Film Festival, which featured a debut screening of Cameron Crowe's *Pearl Jam Twenty*.

In Bernie's profession, one can only hope for spring and summer tours, with June being the optimal month. During 2013, however, Bernie only hit the aforementioned Wrigley Field show and then the back-to-back at Worcester's DCU Center on the fifteenth and sixteenth. The rest of Pearl Jam's shows clashed with scheduled Harvard Football and Boston University Hockey games, but the allure of attending just *one* more show proved too great for him to bear. On Wednesday, December fourth, Bernie hopped a flight to Vancouver's Rogers Arena, where he enjoyed a marathon three-hour-and-ten-minute, thirty-seven song masterpiece of a Pearl Jam show before turning right around and flying back home to work.

During 2014, Bernie worked around his sports schedule (and his coauthor duties) to catch Pearl Jam at the Austin City Limits Music Festival on Saturday, October 4, and later, at St. Paul and Milwaukee on October 19 and 20. For the St. Paul show, Bernie and his friend Mike, a veteran of more than a hundred Pearl Jam shows by that point, enjoyed seats right on the rail, front and center in front of Mike McCready. The last time we checked, he was getting his passport in order in case the urge strikes him to light out for South America.

My Favorite Pearl Jam Concert: The Fans Remember

For our money, nothing will ever beat hearing the experiences of Pearl Jam's most ardent fans as they relate their concert experiences. Along the way, several of them shared their fondest memories with us. Here is a sampling of some of our favorites.

From Jeff Wilder, of Sunrise, Florida:

> The best was in 1998. Partly because I got to see them at a time of personal upheaval, and this provided a way to escape for a couple hours, and also because it came at a point when they had fallen out of the mainstream, and the people there were the dedicated fans. I'd previously tried to get tickets to see them in 1996 with no luck. I realized if I had seen them then, the place would be packed with people going to see them because it was the "in" thing. Now it was the dedicated fans only.

Matt Spitz, guitarist for the Lost Dogs: A Tribute to Pearl Jam, told us:

> Pearl Jam played on Halloween on the *Binaural* Tour. It was the first concert I'd ever been to, and it was amazing. For the second encore, the band came back dressed as the Village People, and halfway through "Yellow Ledbetter," McCready turned around and revealed that he wasn't wearing anything under his chaps!

Ten Clubber Terri McNelly says:

> St. Louis, 2014. I live in Dallas, but I'm from St. Louis originally. This was my first time in GA [General Admission], [and I] rode the rail, saw everything up front and personal. Just an amazing night, and made some great friends standing in the GA line all day, listening to the Cardinals' playoff game and then Eddie Vedder begrudgingly giving us updates on the score, and the Cards won!

John Cafarella of Maynard, Massachusetts, says his first Pearl Jam concert, April 6, 1992, in Lowell, Massachusetts, also remains his favorite. He says:

> This was my first experience [of] moshing. It was an out-of-body experience seeing Eleven and then Pearl Jam. And when they sang "Garden" as the last song I went crazy! I still have the poster from the show hanging up in my house. It is my most prized Pearl Jam item. If I could ever get it signed that would make my life complete.
>
> In the years since, Cafarella has returned to see Pearl Jam more than twenty times and is eager for more. "I love that no two shows are the same," he says. "That's why I usually go to see them multiple nights when they come around."

Jeremy Mahn of Kitchener, Ontario, Canada, says:

> My biggest and most amazing concert experience would be PJ20, without a doubt. After refreshing my Internet browser for over eight hours to score tickets I posted a message on the Ten Club message board, looking for

people to go with me over ten hours from Kitchener, Ontario, Canada. A bunch of people replied, and I chose three guys that I had never met. They arrived at my house Thursday night before PJ20, and we left for our great adventure. We stayed at Scenic Ridge Campground in a cabin on a lake. After ten hours of driving I had a two-hour catnap. We went to the venue to get our tickets, then to an amazing pre-party. Day one it rained all day, but we had an amazing day, followed by a killer show that opened with "Release." There were guest singers and a Temple of the Dog reunion; I was on cloud nine. Night two was just as incredible. Opened with "Wash" and ended the weekend with "Yellow Ledbetter" and "The Star Spangled Banner." Being from Canada, I would have never experienced an ending like that again. There were guests and a Temple of the Dog Reunion. We all got tons of merch and early Monday morning made the ten hour drive home; four strangers with a love for Pearl Jam. I talk to them via Facebook as often as our schedules allow and have caught a couple Pearl Jam shows with them since; memories that will last a lifetime. I have seen the band thirteen times and that weekend will go down as the best concert event to date.

27

Under the Covers

Pearl Jam Plays Songs by Their Favorite Bands

Why Do Bands Play Covers?

There are a variety of reasons why bands play songs by other artists. The most common, particularly for bands just starting out, is that they don't yet have any of their *own* to perform. Anyone who has ever been in a band, or has grown up with a band, can relate. All rock and rollers, no matter their age or what stage of development their band is at, are fans at heart. They started playing music because they were inspired by the music they heard as children. They wanted to emulate their musical heroes and to make their own contributions to the ongoing "great conversation" of rock and roll. Cameron Crowe touches upon this idea in *PJ20*, when he suggests that because of the dodgy nature of Seattle's weather, kids there tended to spend a lot of time indoors listening to music, and that these self-guided musical educations were later reflected in the music that they made. We agree wholeheartedly with this assessment, which at least partially helps to explain the prolific nature of the Seattle music scene. All of the members of Pearl Jam, from Seattle native Stone to fair-weather San Diego friend Eddie, have always unabashedly celebrated their fandom, and to this day they continue to treat their idols with a respect bordering on reverence.

Pearl Jam Plays . . . Who?

Between pearljam.com, *Two Feet Thick*, and speaking with assorted Pearl Jam fanatics over the course of this project, I think we can say safely say that Pearl Jam began slipping cover songs into their sets as early as August 23, 1991. By our calculations, this was the band's thirty-fifth show (including those they played as Mookie Blaylock), and it took place at the Mural Amphitheater in Seattle. Best of all, it was *free*. That night they played Soundgarden's "Outshined" (from their soon-to-be-released album *Badmotorfinger*), and they would go on to play it at least another sixteen times.

It is easy enough to point out possible motivations for Pearl Jam playing "Outshined." Soundgarden's Chris Cornell, after all, had been a towering presence in the band members' lives from day one, from sharing his grief for Andy Wood's passing with Stone, Jeff, Mike, Matt Cameron (and Eddie) in the *Temple of the Dog* project, to being a de facto mentor/big brother figure for Eddie Vedder. Or maybe they just had more time to fill in their set, and they happened to dig Soundgarden's music; who knows for sure? All we know for certain is that from the perspective of an audience member, there are few things more exhilarating than seeing a rock concert where the featured band surprises everyone with a few carefully chosen cover songs. It serves as a reminder that we are *all* fans. Here, in alphabetical order, we will look at the bands whose songs Pearl Jam has covered.

Afterward, we will consider the "One-and-Done" category, which consists of songs that Pearl Jam has played only once, from bands they have only covered once. We offer no "partial credit" for cover songs. Like most guitarists with a head full of music, Mike McCready has been known to spontaneously peel off brief runs of whatever tunes might be floating through his mind at any given moment, often during breaks in the action or when waiting for someone else to tune up. Stone and the others have been known to do the same. Such quick riffs cannot be considered "covers" of a song, precisely, though they do tend to catch the attention of the most focused audience members. This explains why you will often see these riffs—"snippets," "partials," "tags," or "improvs"—mentioned in places like the notes section of *Two Feet Thick*'s "Concert Chronology" feature or on other fan sites, but you won't find them listed on the band's official website. Our goal is not to provide you with an exhaustive accounting of every single familiar chord that the band has struck over the years, but rather to present a healthy overview of the material Pearl Jam has covered. Doing so should provide us with compelling insights into the band members' tastes and knowledge of music history.

AC/DC

None of AC/DC's songs ever became a part of Pearl Jam's repertoire, but clearly they liked them, as evidenced by their one-off takes on "Highway to Hell" on May 3, 1993; "Dirty Deeds Done Dirt Cheap" on May 5, 1993; and—more than sixteen years later—"If You Want Blood (You've Got It)," on November 25, 2009.

Aerosmith

The "Bad Boys from Boston" may seem a little too mainstream for the punk rock sensibilities of Pearl Jam, but then again, Pearl Jam always seems to know when to show their respects to the elders of the rock and roll tribe. They have played Aerosmith's smash hit "Sweet Emotion" on three occasions, all of them on the veteran rockers' home turf in Massachusetts.

Anonymous

"Romanza," "Romance," or "Spanish Romance." Yes, *anonymous*. By whichever title, no one seems to be able to trace this song's origins. Hard to believe, especially in a world where we can trace the history of "Happy Birthday," but that is the story. Eddie has used "Romanza" as an intro to "Better Man" fourteen times so far.

Arthur Alexander

Not exactly a household name, we know, but there is a Beatles connection. Arthur Alexander recorded "Soldier of Love (Lay Down Your Arms)" and released it as the B-side of his single, "Where Have You Been (All My Life)," in 1962, making it older than everybody in Pearl Jam (except Boom!). The song was plucked from certain obscurity when the Beatles recorded it the following year. Both of the aforementioned Alexander songs had been a regular part of the Beatles' early live repertoire. Down the road, Pearl Jam would not only cover the song twenty-one times in concert, they also recorded it and released it.

The Avengers

San Francisco punk band the Avengers came to life in 1977. As protest songs go, you can't do much better than "The American in Me," an indictment of mindless jingoism and hyper-patriotism. As such, it was a natural fit for Pearl Jam, who have covered it eleven times since 2004.

Bad Radio

Yes, Eddie's old band from San Diego. You know our rule: you can't "cover" yourself. Apparently, Eddie must have reached the same conclusion after Pearl Jam played five renditions of the unfortunately named Bad Radio tune "Sick of Pussies." Guess they got sick of playing the song, too.

The Band

An act closely associated with Bob Dylan, the Band has many amazing songs and albums to their own credit. Pearl Jam covered one of our personal favorites, "It Makes No Difference," on six occasions.

The Beatles

Pearl Jam's favorite Beatles' tune (during the twentieth century, at least) had to be "I've Got a Feeling," from 1970's *Let It Be*. The wacky thing about this tune is that it is really *two* tunes: Paul's upbeat "I've Got a Feeling" layered on top of John's curmudgeonly "Everybody Had a Hard Year." This song, the perfect antithesis of collaboration, was one of the last songs the Beatles performed live, during their fabled rooftop concert. Beginning in September 1991, Pearl Jam has performed the song live nearly thirty times. They also tagged it onto the Japanese version of *Ten* as a bonus track.

The clear runner-up is the moving, almost Dylanesque folk ballad from 1965's *Help*, "You've Got to Hide Your Love Away," which Pearl Jam has performed twenty-seven times since 2003.

The B-side from the 1966 "Paperback Writer" single, "Rain," was recorded during the studio sessions for *Revolver*, but it didn't make the cut; think of it as a Beatles-style "Lost Dog." Pearl Jam first covered it, somewhat tentatively, during their 1992 Pinkpop Festival appearance. Five years later, they broke it out again in Oakland, only to shelve it for another fifteen years. Who knows, maybe playing "Rain" at Isle of Wight 2012 planted a seed of some kind because they went on to play it *four* times during the summer and fall of 2014. Good luck finding a pattern in any of this, but we have a hunch the "Rain" may fall again.

During 1993 and 1994, Pearl Jam played "Across the Universe" a total of five times. The spacy Lennon composition, rife with the spirit of India and Hindu yogis, and mildly psychedelic in tone, provided a marked contrast to the aggressive energy of early Pearl Jam shows.

"Don't Let Me Down" is another song that began life as a B-side (to 1969's "Get Back"); it didn't make the cut for the final album, *Let It Be*, but it is in the film. Pearl Jam covered it just twice, both times as part of the first encore during shows in August of 1998.

As for Beatles' cover one-offs, Ed sang "I've Just Seen a Face" a cappella at Red Rocks during June of 1995, and the band has also played "Eleanor Rigby."

Beck

Pearl Jam covered Beck's "Beautiful Way" three times during 2000.

David Bowie

Patron of Iggy Pop, David Bowie is a rock and roll icon. Fame, the old adage goes, is fleeting, particularly in the music industry. And while this may hold true for the majority of musical acts, it proves true here in the case of a song with the same title. Pearl Jam has played David Bowie's hit song "Fame" (cowritten with John Lennon, incidentally) a grand total of nine times, all within a single year, 1996. Go figure. They've also played Bowie's hit "Golden Years" twice.

Bruce Springsteen and the E Street Band

Pearl Jam has also covered "The Boss" himself, though not as often as you might imagine. We've only found one instance of them covering Springsteen's coming-of-age masterpiece "Growin' Up," which was erroneously listed as a "PJ Original" on the official band website last time we checked. They also did a one-off of Springsteen's "Open All Night" and another of "No Surrender."

The Buzzcocks

The Buzzcocks were another 70s-era English punk band. Pearl Jam covered their hit "Why Can't I Touch It?" five times, four of them during 2003. They've since revisited the song during 2012, and who knows when it will pop up again?

The Clash

We know that one of Eddie's most treasured possessions is a framed photograph of him with the late Joe Strummer, and that he and his bandmates are well acquainted with Strummer's work in the seminal English punk band, the Clash (long before Joe Strummer and The Mescaleros!). "Know Your Rights" is a Clash classic that certainly seems to fit within the whole Pearl Jam ethos. To date, they've played it twenty-one times, eighteen times during 2003 alone, beginning just after Strummer passed away suddenly and unexpectedly three days before Christmas of 2002, and then again three times during 2012. Don't be surprised if you hear it again one day.

Wayne Cochran

We've told the story of Wayne Cochran's "Last Kiss" in some detail already elsewhere in this narrative—and it's a good one—so we'll just stick to the numbers here. Pearl Jam has covered the tragic song 125 times so far, and, as gambling men, we wager you'll hear it again.

Cheap Trick

Like Pearl Jam, we are big fans of Cheap Trick, though the cover songs have been limited. Pearl Jam has performed one-offs of "Surrender" and "I Want You to Want Me."

George Clinton

Pearl Jam honored the Parliament-Funkadelic legend by covering his "Atomic Dog" at least nine times, beginning on May 6, 2006, though this particular dog hasn't been unleashed since November 13, 2011.

Creedence Clearwater Revival

Even though it dates back to the Vietnam War era, "Fortunate Son" is one of those timeless anti-war rallying cries that seem appropriate during any era. The song is tailor-made for Pearl Jam, who've covered it twenty-one times, mostly between 2003 and 2006, and as recently as 2012.

The Dead Boys

They didn't come much "punkier" than the Dead Boys on their 1977 debut album, *Young, Loud and Snotty*. The title sums them up fairly well, actually. One song in particular caught the attention of Pearl Jam, a little tune called "Sonic Reducer," which they've played over seventy times since 1992. They also played "Ain't Nothin' to Do" at a gig in Las Vegas's Alladin Theater. However, since Mark Arm and Steve Turner had joined them on stage that night, along with Urge Overkill's drummer Chuck Treece, this was more like a Green River reunion jam than a Pearl Jam rendition per se. Still, it bears mentioning.

The Dead Kennedys

The Dead Kennedys are punk rock royalty, as Pearl Jam knows all too well. They've played "Bleed for Me" eight times thus far.

Dead Moon

The Oregon punk rockers' career predates that of Pearl Jam by a few years, but they are more or less contemporaries. Pearl Jam has covered their song "It's Ok" from the 1994 album *Crack in the System* two dozen times and counting.

The Doors

As we've noted elsewhere, Eddie Vedder gave the Rock and Roll Hall of Fame Induction Ceremony speech for the Doors and then joined them onstage to perform Doors' classics. But Pearl Jam has test driven a couple of Doors songs as a band, too, including "Love Me Two Times," which they whipped out in Spain back in 2000, and "Roadhouse Blues," which they performed in France, the final resting place of the Doors' legendary lead singer, Jim Morrison.

Bob Dylan

We all know that Bob Dylan is an icon among icons, and Pearl Jam has always shown a healthy respect for the legend. In fact, to this day, many people still say that Eddie and Mike stole the show when they appeared at Dylan's thirtieth anniversary concert, singing his classic "Masters of War" with the legendary and ubiquitous G.E. Smith on mandolin.

That performance was early on in the Pearl Jam story, on October 16, 1992, at Madison Square Garden, but the band was already receiving critical acclaim to match their robust album sales. Let's face it, when Dylan knows who you are, you've arrived.

Eleven years later, on October 22, 2003, Pearl Jam dusted off "Masters of War" and played it as a band for the first of sixteen times and counting. About a year later, on October 4, 2004, they expanded their Dylan repertoire with "All Along the Watchtower," a favorite of the late Dylan fan, Jimi Hendrix. A dozen plays later and counting, we wager you will hear "Watchtower" again. During a May 24, 2006, show in Boston, they did a one-off of "Forever Young" as a lead-in to "Masters of War" during the first encore. Playing solo at a Ralph Nader rally in 2000, Eddie covered "The Times They Are a-Changin'," but thus far Pearl Jam hasn't covered it as a group.

The English Beat

On rare occasions, a song will really capture Pearl Jam's imaginations, and they will play it repeatedly until the point where it seems like the song is of their own creation. One such song is the English Beat's "Save It for Later." To date, Pearl Jam has played this song an impressive 107 times.

The Frogs

Milwaukee's most unusual band formed in 1980, and while visiting the area in 1995, Pearl Jam played their "Star Boy" on two occasions. We further discuss the Frogs elsewhere in this narrative.

Fugazi

Fugazi burst onto the scene a few years earlier than Pearl Jam, and the guys in Pearl Jam were always impressed with Fugazi's way of doing things, particularly with their DIY ethos. Pearl Jam covered Fugazi's song "Suggestion" a total of thirty-seven times, beginning at the I-Beam in San Francisco on September 30, 1991. The only other full cover of a Fugazi song they played was "We Want Control of Our Bodies," which they played only twice.

Peter Gabriel

The former Genesis front man turned world music ambassador and chart-topping solo artist, Peter Gabriel seems an odd choice for a Pearl Jam cover. Pearl Jam tested the waters with Gabriel's apocalyptic "Red Rain" twice, both times during shows in November 2011.

Green River

When Mark Arm, Steve Turner, and Urge Overkill's Chuck Treece joined Pearl Jam onstage at the Aladdin Theater in Las Vegas on November 30, 1993, the ensemble became a de facto Green River reunion and was no longer Pearl Jam . . . exactly. But they played the Green River tunes "Swallow My Pride" and "Jazz Odyssey," the latter of which Pearl Jam would go on to play on three other occasions.

The Guess Who

Randy Bachman (of Bachman Turner Overdrive)'s early band from Winnipeg, Manitoba, eh? Pearl Jam, apparently ever mindful of their whereabouts while playing live, played the Guess Who's "Running Back to Saskatoon" three times, all of them *in* Saskatoon.

Ben Harper

The eclectic, multi-talented musician and activist Ben Harper is certainly a kindred spirit of Pearl Jam's. Pearl Jam has covered Harper's "With My Own Two Hands" on four occasions between 2003 and 2006. They also did a one-off of "Walkaway" at the "A Drop in the Park" gig in 1992.

Jimi Hendrix and the Jimi Hendrix Experience

"Little Wing," from the Jimi Hendrix Experience's 1967 album *Axis: Bold as Love*, is a favorite of guitar players everywhere, and Mike McCready is no exception. Pearl Jam has covered this gem two dozen times since 1992, and it provides Mike with an opportunity to show off his chops. They did a one-off of "Dolly Dagger" at a June 1992 gig in Sweden. Pearl Jam also once whipped out "Voodoo Chile" for a jam at a gig in New Orleans, where we suspect "voodoo" was more of the point than Hendrix.

Hunters and Collectors

As a nineteen-year-old fan, so the story goes, Eddie Vedder talked his way backstage after a Hunters and Collectors show. Who could ever have figured that a few years down the road Eddie would be a rock star in his own right, the lead singer of one of the biggest bands on the planet, and that his idols would be serving as the opening act? It is a small world indeed. Pearl Jam has covered Hunters and Collectors' "Throw Your Arms Around Me" some twenty times since 1992.

Iggy and the Stooges

All fans of punk rock revere Iggy Pop, and the members of Pearl Jam are no exception. They've played Iggy and the Stooges' "Search and Destroy" on four occasions since 2010.

Michael Jackson

Say this for the members of Pearl Jam, they are quick to pay tribute to fellow musicians who are ill, or who have passed away, whether they were controversial figures or not. So, it made perfect sense that Pearl Jam would append Michael Jackson's "Ben" (yes, it was a song from the film of the same name, and it concerns the titular *rat*) to their own song, "Rats," in the wake of Jackson's fatal 2009 overdose.

Jane's Addiction

Jane's Addiction pre-dates Pearl Jam, of course, and they had already completed the first phase of their career before Pearl Jam ever came into existence, but the two bands were forever bonded by Lollapalooza 1992. Pearl Jam has covered their "Summertime Rolls" on three occasions. They've also done a one-off of "Mountain Song."

(Sir) Elton John

The rock legend needs no introduction, though Pearl Jam has barely tested the waters of the Elton John-Bernie Taupin catalog, with one-off covers of John's "Candle in the Wind" and "Philadelphia Freedom," which they played in Camden, New Jersey, just a stone's throw from Philadelphia.

Daniel Johnston

The schizophrenic Johnston captured the imagination of the late Kurt Cobain around the same time Pearl Jam took notice of him. Pearl Jam first broke out Johnston's "Walking the Cow" at the 1994 Bridge School Benefit concert but then shelved it for a dozen years. All told, the band has only played it three times, but Eddie Vedder apparently really embraced the song. He used it as the opening number for his entire 2008 solo tour.

Israel Kamakawiwoʻole

Surfing and ukulele aficionado Eddie has a special place in his heart for Hawaii. In fact, he owns a place in Hawaii, and that's where he found Pearl Jam's keyboard player, Boom Gaspar. Israel Kamakawiwoʻole was a noteworthy Hawaiian singer, musician, and activist, who passed away young due to complications from morbid obesity. Pearl Jam has covered his "Hawaii 78" as a tribute to the late musician twice while playing in Honolulu.

The Kinks

The Kinks were another early influence on the punk rock sensibilities that Pearl Jam would come to embody, though they have not covered the British legends very extensively. Pearl Jam covered "Better Things" twice, both times in Europe during summer 2012.

Kiss

Like the late Andrew Wood and many of their contemporaries, the guys in Pearl Jam are proud members of the Kiss Army (especially Mike and Matt). Though they've only covered the Kiss "Klassic," "Black Diamond," twice—once on Kiss' home turf at Madison Square Garden—we wouldn't be at all surprised to hear more songs from New York City's most famous band if the occasion is right.

The La's

The La's was an English band that was finishing up its career right around the time Pearl Jam's was gaining some momentum. The La's were best known for their 1990 hit, "There She Goes." Pearl Jam covered The La's "Timeless Melody" ten times, beginning at a Wembley Stadium show on May 29, 2000.

Led Zeppelin

While Led Zeppelin's music would seem to be more in Soundgarden's wheelhouse than in Pearl Jam's, Pearl Jam did in fact cover a couple of the legendary band's songs, including "Fool in the Rain," "Thank You," and "Going to California." They've also performed a one-off of one-time opening act Robert Plant's "In the Mood."

John Lennon

Pearl Jam's love affair with the Fab Four extended beyond the Beatles proper to include John Lennon's solo work, though, curiously, nothing by Paul McCartney, George Harrison, or Ringo Starr. John Lennon's "Mother" debuted in 1998 and has recurred frequently—twenty times and counting—in recent years.

"Gimme Some Truth" made its first appearance soon after the September 11 terrorist attacks. Pearl Jam played it sixteen times over the next five years. They played "Imagine," arguably one of Lennon's most famous compositions, seven times, but only in recent years, beginning on Friday, October 3, 2014, at the Scottrade Center in St. Louis, Missouri.

Pearl Jam's Lennon "one-offs" include his first post-Beatles hit with the Plastic Ono Band, "Instant Karma"; "Hard Times Are Over," from 1980's *Double Fantasy*, which is, to be fair, a Yoko Ono song; and an audience sing-along of "Give Peace a Chance."

Bob Marley

Everyone—well, *most* everyone, we'll wager—loves the late reggae legend Bob Marley, who was as much an activist and a champion of the people as he was a musical legend. Pearl Jam has covered Marley's "Three Little Birds" three times, and the amazing, "Redemption Song," three times, most recently as an Eddie Vedder duet with Beyoncé at the Global Citizen Festival in Central Park (see chapter thirty for more details). They've also done a one-off of "No Woman, No Cry."

The MC5

"MC" as in "Motor City," or Detroit. The proto-punk quintet dates all the way back to 1964 but didn't start putting out albums until 1969's *Kick Out the Jams*. The title track from this album became an anthem of the counterculture and remains a favorite of ours to this day. Pearl Jam clearly dug it, too, and they have played it more than two dozen times.

Don McClean

Don McClean was another popular singer from the folk-rock tradition, and he was most famous for "American Pie," his often-parsed historical lament. Appropriately enough, Pearl Jam covered this song, with its "The day the music died" refrain, three times, beginning on the day they discovered Kurt Cobain had taken his life.

Midnight Oil

The Australian band had a huge commercial hit with 1987's "Beds Are Burning." Pearl Jam covered the song twice over the course of four days during a trip to Australia during the Fall 2006 Tour.

The Monkees

The so-called "Pre-Fab Four." The comedy quartet had a hit with Boyce and Hart's "Steppin' Stone," and Pearl Jam covered it three times during the summer 1995 West Coast Tour.

Mother Love Bone

Okay, so it *was* a special occasion. In honor of their tenth anniversary, Pearl Jam played tribute to Stone and Jeff's earlier work with the late Andy Wood, playing

"Crown of Thorns." They have played it again since that day, twenty-eight plays and counting. They've also played "Chloe Dancer" more than a dozen times, and more often in recent years, post-2011.

Mudhoney

As Seattle as they come, Mudhoney is sort of the alternate universe Pearl Jam, featuring Stone and Jeff's former Green River colleague, Mark Arm. Pearl Jam has played Mudhoney's "Suck You Dry" on eight occasions since 1993.

Nirvana

Pearl Jam honored their quasi-rivals Nirvana by playing their hit "Smells Like Teen Spirit" five times during the fall of 1991, beginning on September 28 at the Satyricon in Portland, Oregon.

Phil Ochs

Pearl Jam covered the troubled, late folk troubadour on "Here's to the State of Mississippi" three times between 2004 and 2006.

Pink Floyd

Eddie has performed Pink Floyd songs with founding Floydian Roger Waters in recent years, and Waters is a kindred spirit. Of all the songs in the Pink Floyd canon, it is the psychedelic instrumental "Interstellar Overdrive" which most captured Pearl Jam's attention. To date they've played it fifty-three times. While hit songs were something of a rarity for the concept-album-oriented veterans, "Another Brick in the Wall (Part II)," from 1979's *The Wall*, enjoyed significant airplay, reaching number one on the charts in the UK, US, and Norway. Pearl Jam clearly loves this song, and the band has played it forty-four times. When Pearl Jam performed Pink Floyd's "Brain Damage" on the legendary band's home turf in Hyde Park, London, it was one of the most geographically appropriate one-off covers of all time.

The Pixies

Pearl Jam has played the Pixies' "Monkey Gone to Heaven" on five occasions since1994, and the song's decidedly environmentalist perspective is a clear selling point for the band. They have also performed a one-off of "I've Been Tired."

The Police

Another British band that enjoyed phenomenal success, and whose leader, Sting, has gone on to a rich solo career. Pearl Jam has covered the post-punk power trio's "Driven to Tears" a dozen times. Ten Club member John Cafarella caught a July 3, 2003 show in Mansfield, Massachusetts, that featured one of these performances and said, "It is such a different song for Pearl Jam to cover that I went nuts when they played it. I don't think a lot of people know the song but I certainly did and I was singing very loud [sic] during it. And I never thought they would sing the entire song, but they did."

Elvis Presley

At one point or another during their careers, every band seems to cover something by "The King." For Pearl Jam it was "Little Sister," which they've covered three times. Pearl Jam has covered "(I Can't Help) Falling in Love with You" twice. They also once covered Elvis's "Suspicious Minds" during a gig in Memphis.

The Ramones

The Ramones, of Forest Hills, Queens, in NYC, were a band long admired by the members of Pearl Jam, and they honored the punk pioneers by covering several of their songs, most prominently "I Believe in Miracles," which they played an impressive seventy-five times, beginning at Veteran's Coliseum in Phoenix, Arizona, on September 13, 1995. They played the ever-popular "Blitzkrieg Bop" twenty times, beginning on December 15, 1991, in Salt Lake City, Utah. "I Wanna Be Your Boyfriend" is another popular Ramones tune, and Pearl Jam covered it eight times. "Daytime Dilemma" and "I Remember You" were just one-offs. A particularly proud one-off moment found Pearl Jam doing "The KKK Took My Baby Away" for an encore, with Johnny Ramone on the stage at the Forum in Inglewood, California, on July 14, 1998.

The Red Hot Chili Peppers

Pearl Jam played the Red Hot Chili Pepper's "Funky Crime" twice early on, first at NYC's Roseland Ballroom on November 15, 1991, several years before founding Pepper Jack Irons became a member of Pearl Jam.

R.E.M.

The Atlanta, Georgia group long ago achieved critical acclaim, and Pearl Jam respects them a great deal. Among the R.E.M. tunes they've covered are "The Wrong Child," which they've performed ten times; "Talk About the Passion," which they've performed twice; and a one-off of "It Happened Today."

The Rolling Stones

Though none of their songs ever found a regular place in their live rotation, Pearl Jam first revealed their affinity for the Rolling Stones on February 25, 1992, when they played a short improvisational jam of "Sympathy for the Devil." Appropriately enough, this occurred in England, the Stones' native land. A careful analysis of Pearl Jam's cover song choices over the years indicates that they tend to put some thought into the matter, and that there is often some kind of logic behind the timing and location of the cover songs that they play. That pattern seems to have been established during this week in England, and it continues to this day. About a month later, Pearl Jam test-drove "Angie" when they were at the studios in Queens, New York, filming their episode of *MTV Unplugged*, and they went on to play it twice more. And that seems to have remained their pattern when it came to Stones' songs: try them out and play them a handful of times. Other examples include "Beast of Burden," and "Ruby Tuesday," which they broke out during their next trip to London in 1993, and "Gimme Shelter," which first saw the light of day in Manitoba, Canada. The following year they broke out "Street Fightin' Man" on two occasions. And that was it for more than a decade. "Waiting on a Friend" was one song that seemed poised to become a regular when they broke it out in 2006, but they only played it four times. In 2010, Eddie did a pre-opener acoustic version of "Dead Flowers" at a gig in Ohio, but this would prove to be just a one-off.

The Rollins Band

The charismatic Henry Rollins is another veteran performer revered by Pearl Jam. The tattooed and heavily muscled former lead singer of Black Flag is more often seen on the History Channel than on a stage these days, but when Pearl Jam first hit the scene, Rollins was still a vital force to be reckoned with. They've covered Rollins's "Tearing" nearly thirty times since 1992. They've also done a one-off of "Shine."

The Sonics

Formed as far back as 1960, the Sonics are among the founding fathers of "garage rock," a genre generally considered to be a forerunner of punk rock. On two occasions in December of 2002, Pearl Jam played the Sonics' "Don't Believe In Christmas."

Shel Silverstein/Johnny Cash

No matter which artist gets the credit for this song or for inspiring Pearl Jam to cover it, they've performed the humorous "25 Minutes to Go" on three occasions.

Patti Smith

To many, she is the high priestess of punk rock. And it seems only natural that Pearl Jam has covered Smith's rallying cry, "People Have the Power," five times, dating back to 2003. They've also done a one-off of "Dancing Barefoot."

Edwin Starr

It seems like the late soul singer's 1970 protest song "War" has been covered by just about everyone, including Bruce Springsteen and the E Street Band. The song is right up Pearl Jam's alley, and they've played it thirteen times, so far, between 2002 and 2008.

Shudder to Think

Pearl Jam played Shudder to Think's song "Pebbles" from their 1992 album, *Get Your Goat*, on just two occasions during March 1998.

Sleater-Kinney

The riot-grrrl act from Washington State is a favorite of Pearl Jam's, and they've frequently shared the stage with them during the many shows where Sleater-Kinney opened the bill. Pearl Jam really took a liking to Sleater-Kinney's "Modern Girl," and they've covered it forty-four times in just the last ten years. They've also done a one-off of "Dig Me Out."

The Smashing Pumpkins

The Smashing Pumpkins were given the Pearl Jam treatment when the band covered "Window Paine," from May 1991's *Gish*, at NYC's Roseland Ballroom on November 12, 1991. It was the first of seven performances.

Sonic Youth

No matter the many genre labels they were tagged with over the years, Sonic Youth is, to our way of thinking, a punk rock band. Pearl Jam knew their work and played "Androgynous Mind" nearly two dozen times. They've also played "Bull in the Heather" three times.

Soundgarden

Soundgarden holds the distinction of being the first band Pearl Jam covered. As mentioned earlier, the song was "Outshined," from their breakthrough *Badmotorfinger* album. The album would not be released until October 8, 1991, but Pearl Jam offered the world a preview of sorts when they first played "Outshined" on Friday, August 23, 1991, at Seattle's Mural Amphitheater. They would go on to cover the song sixteen more times.

The Split Enz

The genre-spanning New Zealanders scored a hit with 1980's "I Got You," and Pearl Jam has covered it five times during the current millennium, though only once in the United States. The first go-around was in Italy, but they went on to play twice in Australia, and, finally, in the Split Enz' stomping grounds in New Zealand. They've also done their "Stuff and Nonsense" four times.

Stereolab

The British band Stereolab came into being back in 1990, making them contemporaries of Pearl Jam's. Pearl Jam took a shine to Stereolab's "Noise of Carpet" and played it fifteen times between 1996 and 1998.

Cat Stevens

On two occasions, Pearl Jam covered the 1970's folk troubadour Cat Stevens, who has been known as Yusuf Islam since converting to Islam back in December of 1977. Pearl Jam twice used the classic Cat track "Where Do the Children Play" as a lead-in to "State of Love and Trust," first on March 12, 1992, at Batschkaap in Frankfurt, Germany. The band has also covered Stevens's "Don't Be Shy" four times since 2000, usually in the form of Eddie playing solo to begin the band's encore set.

Joe Strummer and the Mescaleros

Pearl Jam has covered Strummer's post-Clash band on "Arms Aloft" twelve times so far.

The Talking Heads

New York City's the Talking Heads first burst upon the scene in 1975, when most of Pearl Jam's members were still in grade school. By 1991, the Talking Heads were calling it a career, just as Pearl Jam was getting started. Pearl Jam first covered one of their tunes on their second trip to Europe, when they played "Pulled Up" in Oslo, Norway, on June 27, 1993. This song was the final track on the Talking Heads' 1977 debut album: *Talking Heads: 77.* This was the only full Talking Heads song that Pearl Jam covered.

James Taylor

Pearl Jam has covered the Bostonian bard's "Shower the People" and "Millworker," but both songs were one-offs, never to be heard again.

Tom Petty and the Heartbreakers

Often introduced to their live audiences as "the last great American rock and roll band," Tom Petty and the Heartbreakers have to be on the radar of any serious student of American rock and roll. They seem to follow in the time-honored tradition of Bob Dylan and the Byrds. Pearl Jam has covered Tom Petty's solo effort "I Won't Back Down" at least a dozen times. They've also done a one-off of Petty's "You Tell Me."

Temple of the Dog/Chris Cornell

Chris Cornell's solo song "Can't Change Me" qualifies as a cover, though Pearl Jam has performed it just once. As for the Temple of the Dog songs, like "Hunger Strike," at twenty-eight plays and counting, they really do belong in a category all by themselves. Check out our "Pearls Before Dogs" chapter for more details on the early Seattle supergroup and their eponymous tribute to the late Andrew Wood.

That Dog

An estrogen-heavy Los Angeles band, That Dog hit the scene in 1991, right around the same time that Pearl Jam was getting started. But for their lone male band member, they might even have been labeled a riot-grrrl group, too. Pearl Jam covered their "This Boy" three times.

Thin Lizzy

Pearl Jam has performed one-offs of the Irish hard rockers' "Cowboy Song" and "The Boys are Back in Town," both during shows in Dublin, Ireland.

U2

U2 is another monster band that Pearl Jam has opened for and clearly respects. Yet Pearl Jam covers of U2 songs are few and far between. They've covered U2's "MLK" only twice, so far, with a five-year gap between plays. They've covered "Bad" twice, once with Bono and The Edge in the audience. During that show, they also tagged on one-offs of "Yahweh" and "A Sort of Homecoming."

Van Halen

"Eruption," from Van Halen's eponymous 1978 debut album, is another favorite of fleet-fingered guitarists everywhere, and Mike McCready has enjoyed playing it a dozen times, mostly in recent years, post 2012. Also in recent years (since 2010), Pearl Jam has covered another track from Van Halen's debut, "Ain't Talkin' 'Bout Love," on three occasions.

A Couple of American Standards

"Happy Birthday." Yes, you read that correctly, "Happy Birthday." It is a song that *every* artist has been asked to perform at least once during his or her lifetime. Pearl Jam has sung the perennial favorite—credited to Patty and Mildred Hill, in case anyone was wondering—at least sixteen times so far in their storied career.

"The Star Spangled Banner." Talk about your "American standards," eh? Officially, Pearl Jam has performed the national anthem of the US seven times in concert, in the spirit of Jimi Hendrix, but this figure does not include the band members' occasional appearances at Seattle sporting events, singing and/or playing the anthem for the home crowds of the Seahawks, Mariners, and Supersonics.

Steven Van Zandt

Whether you know him as "Little Steven" or "Miami Steve" or even "Silvio Dante"—his Mafioso character on HBO's hit series, *The Sopranos*—the E Street Band veteran and disc jockey is a walking encyclopedia of rock and roll lore. Pearl Jam seems particularly fond of Van Zandt's "I Am a Patriot," which they've covered eighteen times since 1992.

The Velvet Underground

Every self-respecting punk rock fan in the world knows and cherishes the work of Lou Reed and his early bandmates in the Velvet Underground. Pearl Jam played "After Hours" seven times and "Beginning to See the Light" five times. They've also done one-offs of "Waiting for the Man" and "Sweet Jane."

Tom Waits

Many people in the music industry respect the gravel-voiced bard. Pearl Jam was taken with Waits's "Hold On," which they've given a dozen spins since 2000, beginning on May 10 at the Mount Baker Theatre in Bellingham, Washington. They've also covered his "Picture in a Frame" on four occasions. They've done "It Rains on Me" twice as a "Daughter" tag. Finally, as anyone might have predicted, they whipped out the Waits favorite, "Jersey Girl," on two occasions while playing shows in the Garden State.

Victoria Williams

Though slightly older than most of the band members, Victoria Williams is a contemporary of Pearl Jam's as a performer, and one who has inspired a great deal of loyalty and support, too. When Williams was diagnosed with multiple sclerosis, Pearl Jam recorded Williams's hit "Crazy Mary" as a part of the benefit album *Sweet Relief*, which we discuss in detail elsewhere. To date they've performed the song a whopping 155 times in concert. While Williams's illness was certainly a catalyst for the sheer number of plays, Pearl Jam had been playing the song in concert since before Williams's diagnosis.

The Who (nee the High Numbers)

Pearl Jam have long covered the Who, beginning with a rendition of "Baba O'Reilly" at the Moore Theatre in Seattle during January 1992. This was the first of 142 renditions to date, and you may rest assured you will hear it again. They first broke out "My Generation" during that first go-around in England, in February 1992, but have only played it a comparatively modest six times thus far; likewise the Who's early hit, "Can't Explain," which they've only covered thrice. Pearl Jam debuted "The Kids Are Alright" in 1993 and have done it nineteen times thus far. "The Real Me," a ferocious tune from Eddie's favorite album, *Quadrophenia*, clearly struck a chord with the boys, and they've played it forty times. They've played the majestic finale of *Quadrophenia*, "Love, Reign O'er Me," twenty-three times thus far, and this is a favorite of Ten Clubber Terri McNelly, who says, "The instrumental on this song is just so beautiful. And then you add the lyrics and EV's passionate voice; it's the perfect storm of lovely." "Young Man Blues" is another early Who song, and many say the definitive version is featured on the *Live at Leeds* album, yet Pearl Jam only took this gem for a walk four times. On three occasions apiece, they broke out "I'm One," a "mod" anthem from *Quadrophenia*, "The Seeker," and "Blue, Red And Grey". They've also been known to do the Pete Townshend solo songs "Let My Love Open the Door," which they've done five times, and "Sheraton Gibson," which they've played once. Finally, how about a cover *of* a cover? Pearl Jam has played the old Eddie Holland Motown song "Leaving Here" about seventy-two times so far, most likely because it was also covered decades earlier by the High

Numbers, whom many of you will recognize as an early incarnation of the Who. One-offs thus far include "Magic Bus," "Behind Blue Eyes," "I'm a Boy," "Naked Eye," and Keith Moon's "Girl's Eyes."

X

Another group Pearl Jam holds in high esteem is X, the L.A. punk band. They've performed X's "New World" a dozen times, at least once with X member John Doe sharing the stage for an encore jam. They've also done a one-off of X's "White Girl."

Yes

At first glance, it might seem odd for a group of self-styled punk rockers to cover a song by Yes, the English progressive rock studio rats. But Yes's "Owner of a Lonely Heart" enjoyed some real commercial success and radio play, and let's face it, it does have that infectious Christopher Squire bass line. Pearl Jam covered the song twice, which is enough to tell you that they are fans.

Neil Young

When they refer to him as "Uncle Neil," it is with perfect sincerity and all due respect. Pearl Jam's most ubiquitous Neil Young cover, indeed their most ubiquitous cover song *period*, is Neil Young's anthem "Rockin' in the Free World." They first played it at the Loft in Berlin, Germany, on March 9, 1992, and to date have played it 276 times and counting. They've played it with Neil and without him, on television, at award shows, and just about anywhere else you can think of. They have, in a sense, practically made the song their own, and people have come to associate the song as much with Pearl Jam as they do with Neil Young. Clearly, the song embodies many of the values that the band holds dear. Next, in order of frequency, is "Fuckin' Up," at sixty-seven plays. Young's classic "Hey Hey, My My" weighs in at a dozen plays, "Harvest Moon" at nine, "Cinnamon Girl" at five, and "Tonight's the Night" at four. Another four-timer is the haunting "The Needle and the Damage Done." Appropriately enough, the first time they covered it—on March 10, 1995, in Sydney, Australia—Flea, a man who knows a thing or two about the song's grim subject matter, was their special guest; a very poignant performance indeed.

Our usual motto is: you can't cover yourself. But we will break our own rules and offer partial credit for "Act of Love," because it is a track from 1995's *Mirror Ball*, which, of course, featured the members of Pearl Jam as Neil's backing band and studio collaborators. They've played that one nine times. Finally, Neil Young one-offs include "Sail Away," "Cortez the Killer," and "Old Man."

One-and-Done

Many of the cover songs Pearl Jam has played over the years have been of the one-and-done variety, which we often refer to as "one-offs." Why is that? Well, in some cases, the songs were clearly selected for a specific location or occasion. In other cases, the band just seemed to be taking a given song for a test drive, perhaps to gauge the audience's reactions. The first of these one-offs that stood out for us was a cover of Alice Cooper's "School's Out," which they performed at Portland, Oregon's Roseland Theater on May 17, 1992. There doesn't seem to have been any rhyme or reason behind them playing it so we guess they were just giving it a whirl to cap off the first encore that night.

A personal favorite of ours is Arthur "Guitar Boogie" Smith's "Dueling Banjos," from the soundtrack of the infamous 1972 film *Deliverance*. Pearl Jam whipped this gem out in Birmingham, Alabama, of all places, even though the film was shot in Georgia.

At one show in Zurich, Switzerland, Pearl Jam covered the Pretenders' "Brass in Pocket." Perhaps Europe is just a comfortable place to workshop potential new additions to the repertoire. Who can say for sure? A week later, during the same tour, Pearl Jam broke out the Beach Boys' "Help Me, Rhonda" in Sweden, a place not exactly known for surf music!

Curiously, the one time Pearl Jam played Louis Armstrong's "When the Saints Come Marching In," they were in Italy, of all places. From a purely secular, musical perspective, New Orleans would

It is the "Holy Grail" of concertgoers everywhere. Behold, the fabled "backstage pass." These two coveted items belong to master clothier and artisan Jeremy "Crash" Crowley, of Crashious Roadside fame. If you play your cards right, you just might be able to secure a backstage pass yourself.   *Jeremy "Crash" Crowley*

have made more sense. However, when you consider that saints have historically been canonized at the Vatican in Rome, the connection becomes a little clearer.

Pearl Jam honored the memory and passing of beloved comedian John Candy by playing Roy and Dale Evans Rogers's "Happy Trails." Recall that *Wagon's East!* was Candy's final film, and he passed away before it was released in theaters.

Considering all of the basketball they played with Ice Cube backstage during Lollapalooza 1992, it should come as no surprise that Pearl Jam performed NWA's controversial "Fuck Tha Police" as a jam during the August 25 stop on that legendary tour.

It really is extraordinary when you stop and consider the sheer breadth of the artists Pearl Jam has covered in the "one-and-done" category, and you may rest assured that there are more stories behind some of these covers than time or space will allow. As one reads the names of the artists and the song selections, one can almost visualize a *really* big record collection, owned by someone with an incredibly wide range of taste in music. Doing so also provides further insight into the musical educations of Pearl Jam's members. The results are a veritable smorgasbord: the Bee Gees' "If I Can't Have You," Kodaline's "Take Control," Cindy Lauper's "Girls Just Want to Have Fun," Lynyrd Skynyrd's "Sweet Home Alabama," Otis Redding's "Dock of the Bay" (a jam with Steve "The Colonel" Cropper), Nick Cave and the Bad Seeds' "The Ship Song," Eddie Hazel's "Maggot Brain," Sly and the Family Stone's "Everyday People" (with producer Brendan O'Brien manning the keyboards!), Gerry and the Pacemakers' "Don't Let the Sun Catch You Crying," Madonna's "Ray of Light," Suicidal Tendencies' "Institutionalized," The B52's "Roam," Celine Dion's "My Heart Will Go On," Rancid's "Time Bomb," Buddy Holly's "Everyday," and the Trogg's "Wild Thing." During one Mexico City show on July 19, 1993, Pearl Jam unleashed a torrent of Spanish language one-offs, including the traditional birthday song, "Las Mañanitas" (sung with local trio Chucko y Los Clasicos), José Fernandez's "La Guantanamera," and, of course, the late Richie Valens's "La Bamba." The one-offs continued with the Germs' "Lion's Share," Suicide's "Dream Baby Dream," Barret Strong's oft-covered classic, "Money (That's What I Want)," The Knack's "My Sharona," Chris Knox's "Not Given Lightly," Crowded House's "Better Be Home Soon," a jam with Jay-Z on his "99 Problems," Raffi's "Baby Beluga," Oasis's "Falling Down," Neil Diamond's "Forever in Blue Jeans," Bobby Vee and Carole King's "Go Away Little Girl," John Doe's (of X fame) "Golden State," Jack Sheldon's "Grammar Rock" (from the old children's TV program *Schoolhouse Rock!*), Larry Vincent's "I Used to Work in Chicago," Simon Townshend's "I'm the Answer," Robert Pollard's "Love Is Stronger Than Witchcraft," Giovanni Capurro and Eduardo di Capua's Italian classic, "'O Sole Mio" (performed in Italy, as you might expect), the Fastbacks' "Old Address of the Unknown," Papa Roach's "Take Me," Devo's "Whip It," and the Yeastie Girlz' "Yeastie Girlz Rap." Any way you slice it, that is an awe-inspiring collection of cover songs.

28

And, Opening For

Everyone has to start *somewhere*. And even though many of the members of Pearl Jam were seasoned music professionals by the time they came together as a band, they still had to pay their dues by serving as the opening act for dozens upon dozens of other bands, many of which have been lost to history, and many of which continue to thrive to this very day. I think you all know where this story begins. It was back in the early days—the Mookie Blaylock days—and the boys were paying their dues on their own home court, the Off Ramp Café, and other small clubs. Here, without further ado, are the bands that Pearl Jam has opened for. Wherever possible to do so, we have included the date and the place of the show where Mookie Blaylock/Pearl Jam first opened for the bands in question.

Inspector Luv and the Ride Me Babies

October 22, 1990. Off Ramp Café. Seattle, Washington. Inspector Luv and the Ride Me Babies formed in Tacoma, Washington in 1989, but quickly evolved into the Seattle-based Green Apple Quickstep by 1992. And here you thought "Pearl Jam" was a weird name for a band. But they were still "Inspector Luv" when Mookie Blaylock opened for them (and Bathtub Gin) at Seattle's Off Ramp Café on October 22, 1990. The band featured Tyler William on vocals, Steve Ross and Dan Kempthorne on the guitars, Eric Munday on bass, and Bob Martin on drums. They actually released an EP in 1989 called *Another World*, but only 700 copies were pressed; a humble and brief chapter in the annals of rock and roll.

This was Mookie Blaylock's rookie debut, so it will always remain a special show.

Bathtub Gin

October 22, 1990. Off Ramp Café. Seattle, Washington. The second act on the bill that same night was a band called Bathtub Gin, a name that is more well-known today as the title of a Phish song (or an illegal, Prohibition-era libation) than it is for ever having been a band.

El Steiner

December 19, 1990. The Vogue. Seattle, Washington. Larry Steiner, leader of the novelty rock band El Steiner, was/is what one might refer to as "a character." A throwback hippie and artist fond of vintage day-glo painted school buses, Steiner is also reputed to have been a major pot dealer back during the days when that sort of thing was frowned upon.

Alice in Chains

December 22, 1990. Moore Theater. Seattle, Washington. For a more detailed accounting of Alice in Chains, check out our sidebar on the band in chapter two. The point to emphasize here is that Alice in Chains were already well established on the Seattle scene by the time Mookie Blaylock came along, and they were in the perfect position to give the fledgling band the road workout it needed. The early whirlwind tour the band took in support of Alice in Chains primed the pump for the high-energy Pearl Jam live performances to come.

Green Jellö/Green Jellÿ

February 8, 1991. God Save the Queen. Long Beach, California. Green Jellö began life in 1981 as a comedy/punk band from upstate New York and was started by a guy named Bill Manspeaker, whose dream it was to form the world's *worst* band. Kraft Foods, the makers of Jell-O™, were grumbling about filing suit over the trademarked name, so they changed Jellö to Jellÿ. In a stroke of comic genius, the accent mark means that both spellings are pronounced the same anyway! Their outrageous live act got them banned so often that they resorted to using fake names just to get back into playing in places from which they'd been banned.

By sheer luck, the novelty of their act, or both, they were still around when Pearl Jam was going through its larval, Mookie stage. In one of those oddball twists of fate, they would later become popular in Seattle when radio station "The X," KXRX 96.5 FM, began playing their punk version of the children's classic, "The Three Little Pigs." The video, readily available on YouTube, is also worth a look. Through the decades and numerous personnel changes, Green Jellö/Jellÿ has endured and, frighteningly enough, still exists to this day, in one form or another.

Love on Ice

February 20, 1991. Melody Ballroom. Portland, Oregon. Love on Ice hailed from Portland, Oregon, which we suppose makes them a "southern" band from a Seattle native's perspective. At the time of this show they were gigging on the strength of a four-song demo they had recorded at London Bridge Studios, and they actually went on to record a full album, titled *Nude*, for Interscope Records in 1992. Like many bands, their ambition far outstripped their sales figures, and when they went back into London Bridge to record another album, Interscope basically dropped the ball on them, and the project was abandoned. Poetically speaking, Love on Ice was now . . . well, *iced*.

Yellow Dog

Friday, March 1, 1991. The Off Ramp Café. Seattle, Washington. Apart from a 1970s British band by this name, a modern Brooklyn, New York, band called Yellow Dogs, and, of course, the band's name written on the concert poster, we can find no record of this band's existence. We need a dogcatcher for this one!

Cherry Poppin' Daddies

Date unclear: The W.O.W. (Woodmen of the World) Union Trade Hall in Eugene, Oregon. Here's a fascinating case study for you. Cherry Poppin' Daddies were a local Eugene, Oregon band that formed in 1989. Like Journey before them, they had a lead singer named Steve Perry. And there the similarities end. Cherry Poppin' Daddies were no pop act; they were (and remain) one of those genre-straddling groups that drive music collectors trying to properly categorize them absolutely *crazy*. They have, at different times, been described as funk, rock, punk, ska, swing, jazz, rockabilly, R&B, and soul—labels which many would consider to be mutually exclusive. Fittingly, Cherry Poppin' Daddies also featured a horn section, in an age when horns, sadly, (outside of the E Street Band and Billy Joel's band) were becoming something of a rock and roll anachronism. When the young Pearl Jam came to town, Cherry Poppin' Daddies' greatest commercial success was still years in the future. Their big hit, album and single, *Zoot Suit Riot*, came in 1997, selling in excess of two million copies, but they never reached those heights again. But give them credit for perseverance. At the time of this writing, the band is still plugging away, having released an album of originals in 2013 and a tribute to Frank Sinatra and his infamous Rat Pack in the summer of 2014.

The Lemonheads

July 10, 1991. Citi Boston, Massachusetts. Evan Dando formed the Lemonheads in Boston, along with two high school classmates, and they've been famous in punk rock circles ever since their 1986 EP, *Laughing All the Way to the Cleaners*. Apparently the boys were bursting at the seams with creativity, because when they were signed to a local Boston label, Taang! Records, they released *three* LPs over the span of three consecutive years. *Hate Your Friends, Creator,* and *Lick* came out in 1987, 1988, and 1989, respectively, which garnered them some national and international attention, which, in turn, led to their signing with the prestigious Atlantic Records in 1990 and the subsequent release of album number four, *Lovey*. By the time Pearl Jam came around, the Lemonheads were firmly established as a prolific band; even if the lineup lacked stability, Evan Dando was the real focal point of the band (a la Lemmy, of Motörhead!). In 1991, the Lemonheads went off on a world-hopping tour that would lead them to a whole other phase of their careers. Though the band appears to be dormant at the time of this writing, a lifetime of studying rock and roll history tells us never to write *anyone* off!

Buffalo Tom

July 10, 1991. Avalon. Boston, Massachusetts. It should come as no surprise that several of the acts on the bill this July night in Boston were local bands. Like the Lemonheads, Buffalo Tom hailed from Boston and even formed during the same year, 1986. Perhaps indicative that they shared some of the same musical tastes as Eddie Vedder & co., the band's name was inspired by Neil Young's old band, Buffalo Springfield (plus "Tom," being the first name of their drummer, Tom Maginnis!). But Buffalo Tom was a college band, not a high school band, formed at UMASS Amherst by Chris Colbourn, Bill Janovitz, and the aforementioned Mr. Maginnis. On this night the bulk of their work still lay ahead of them, and they had only two albums under their belts, including their 1988 debut, *Buffalo Tom*, and 1990's *Birdbrain*. Though ostensibly still in existence, Buffalo Tom haven't released an album since 2011's *Skins*, and the most recent gig listed on their official website is a June 21, 2014, show on their home turf at the Paradise in Boston. Stay tuned.

7 League Boots

July 10, 1991. Avalon. Boston, Massachusetts. One of those proverbial "shooting star" bands, 7 League Boots was formed in Boston by a restless musical spirit named Bobby Sullivan, in the wake of the demise of his earlier band, Soulside. The concept of the band was a fusion of reggae and rock and roll, and they released two 7-inch singles and one album, released, fittingly enough, by a label called Constant Change/Cargo Records. After that, the band broke up and Sullivan was on to his next musical project.

Venus Beads

July 10, 1991. Avalon. Boston, Massachusetts. On a rockin' night in *New* England, comes a band formed in *old* England, Venus Beads. This simple three-piece featured Rob Jones on vocals and rhythm guitar, Anthony Price on lead guitar, and Mark Hassall on drums. Following a four-track 1990 EP, *Transfixed*, they only released two full albums during their brief career, *both* of them during the year of this show, 1991: the debut, *Incision*, on Roadrunner Records, and the follow-up, *Black Aspirin*, on Emergo. For some reason, they just never really took off, and we have a theory as to why. Let this be a lesson to aspiring bands. The Doors notwithstanding, never underestimate the value of a good *bass* player to your overall sound.

Stress

July 10, 1991. Avalon. Boston, Massachusetts. Another one of those fleeting bands; one might say that 1991 was Stress's year—as in their *only* year. The neo-psychedelic outfit released their self-titled debut album on the respectable Reprise/Warner Bros. Records label, and even charted a number seven single, "Beautiful People." The sunny optimism of the song, with its "Beautiful people, beautiful world" refrain and its lyrical homage to *Sgt. Pepper*, strikes us as being perhaps a tad too optimistic for the grim and dour music scene emerging at the time. Sure enough, Stress—featuring Wayne Binitie, Ian Mussington, and Mitch Amachi Ogugua—soon succumbed to the stresses of the music business and disbanded.

Rev. Horton Heat

July 13, 1991. The Marquee Room. New York, New York. At the time of this writing, the Reverend Horton Heat was still a living, breathing, and viable act, with a full slate of live performances scheduled for 2015, which is its thirtieth anniversary, in case anyone is counting. To specify, "Rev. Horton Heat" is both the stage name of main man, Jim Heath, *and* his band, who fall under the "psychobilly" genre. Though they hailed from Dallas, Texas, and formed in 1985, Heath, along with bassist Jimbo Wallace and drummer Bobby Baranowski, wound up in Seattle, signing a record deal with none other than Bruce Pavitt and Jonathan Poneman, of Sub Pop Records fame. By this time, Baranowski was gone, drummer Kyle Thomas had come and gone, and Patrick "Taz" Bentley was manning the skins (sounds familiar, doesn't it?). Heath, Wallace, and Bentley comprised the lineup on this July night when Pearl Jam honed their craft as opening act. Their first of many NYC gigs, as it turned out. Given the attrition rate for rock and roll bands, it is really quite remarkable that Rev. Horton Heat continues to tour and record after thirty years. And while we don't have a crystal ball, we confess that we expect the same from Pearl Jam.

Afghan Whigs

July 13, 1991. The Marquee Room. New York, New York. This independent minded band from Cincinnati, Ohio, released its debut album, 1988's *Big Top Halloween*, on its own label, Ultrasuede. Somehow or other, the band soon found itself on the west coast, signing with Sub Pop Records for album number two, *Up in It*.

Gorilla

July 13, 1991. The Marquee Room. New York, New York. Gorilla, as near as we can figure, were most likely a Hungarian rockabilly trio. Many of these early bands have disappeared without leaving behind much of a trace. In some cases, archived concert posters are the only evidence we have of their existence.

Beasts of Bourbon

July 13, 1991. The Marquee Room. New York, New York. Any way you slice it, New York City is a long way from Pearl Jam's home base in Seattle. And, though not quite as far, it is also a good long ways away from Kentucky, home state of bourbon (the beverage). But if you want to talk about a *real* road trip, consider that the cleverly named Beasts of Bourbon hailed from Sydney and New South Wales in Australia, halfway across the planet. The down-under rockers have been labeled both "alternative rock" and "blues rock," and though we are not overly fond of such categorizations when it comes to rock and roll, one could also make a case for the term "supergroup." Beasts of Bourbon formed in 1983 from the detritus of several defunct (or soon-to-be defunct) bands, including the Scientists, Dum-Dums, the Johnnys, and Hoodoo Guns. With the exception of guitarist Spencer P. Jones and vocalist Tex Perkins, the band's lineup was often in a state of flux, with at least a dozen members to date. On the night of this NYC gig, Beasts of Bourbon were still touring on the strength of their third album, *Black Milk*, though album number four, *The Low Road*, would hit the shelves before year's end.

Codeine

July 13, 1991. The Marquee Room. New York, New York. Codeine was a local New York City band formed in 1989. They were barely two years old on this night and were touring on the first of their two albums, 1990's *Frigid Stars*. The Seattle connection here is that the *Glitterhouse* (German) album was rereleased by Sub Pop in the spring of 1991, so it was fresh in people's minds. Codeine's claim-to-fame—fleeting though their fame may have been—is that they are credited with pioneering yet another two entries in a never-ending list of sub-genres: indie "slowcore" and "sadcore"; labels which seem appropriate enough, given the effects of the drug, codeine, and the sounds of the eponymous band.

Naked Raygun

July 21, 1991. Cabaret Metro. Chicago, Illinois. Local Chicago band Naked Raygun was a seasoned outfit by this point, having been formed in 1980 by singer Jeff Pezzati and supported by a revolving cast of band members over the ensuing years. By the time Pearl Jam were making their first supporting appearance in Eddie's home town, Naked Raygun was on the cusp of beginning a fourteen-year hiatus. They would later regroup in 2006, and at the time of this writing, they had new shows scheduled through 2015.

Urge Overkill

July 21, 1991. Cabaret Metro. Chicago, Illinois. Fellow Chicago group Urge Overkill was also on the bill that night, a slightly greener outfit that formed in 1985 out of Northwestern University. They must have made a positive impression on the young Pearl Jam this night, because their respective roles would reverse a couple of years later when Urge Overkill opened for Pearl Jam during the *Vs.* Tour. In a real pop culture quirk, their chief claim to fame would be a cover version they did of Neil Diamond's "Girl, You'll Be a Woman Soon" for the soundtrack of Quentin Tarrantino's 1994 cult movie classic, *Pulp Fiction*.

Ned's Atomic Dustbin

July 21, 1991. Cabaret Metro. Chicago, Illinois. This five-piece from Stourbridge, England, distinguished itself from their competition by featuring *two* bass players, Alex Griffin and Matt Cheslin. Essentially Cheslin was playing bass the traditional way, while Griffin was playing guitar leads on a bass. As admirers of bassists as diverse as John Entwistle and Lemmy, we think this is a great concept for a band. Their odd name comes from an episode of an old British radio comedy program called *The Goon Show* (the name of which was inspired, in turn, by the "Goons" from the old *Popeye* cartoons). To borrow a term from Mel Brooks's *Spaceballs* character, Yogurt, they were also quite adept at "moichendizing." Legend has it that they produced nearly *ninety* unique T-shirt designs during their first three years of existence. And last we checked, they are still making music—and new T-shirts—to this very day!

The Jayhawks

July 21, 1991. Cabaret Metro. Chicago, Illinois. One of the more recognizable names on the bill that night, the Jayhawks had been around for six years at the time, having formed in Minneapolis, Minnesota, back in 1985. By the time of this gig, they were already on their third drummer, perhaps giving Pearl Jam a glimpse of their own future. While they would go on to become one of the most respected "alt country" bands on the planet, at this point they were still a year away from their major label debut. They were touring on the merits of *Blue Earth*, essentially a collection of demos released on a small Minnesota label called Twin Tone. As we all know now, there was *potential* in those demos. The Jayhawks have undergone their share of lineup changes over the years, but they celebrated their thirtieth anniversary in 2015—"still alive," as Pearl Jam might say.

Soul Asylum

July 21, 1991. Cabaret Metro. Chicago, Illinois. Like the Jayhawks, Soul Asylum hails from Minneapolis, Minnesota. Their origins go back to 1981, when they evolved out of an earlier band called Loud Fast Rules. On the night of this show they were already five albums into their career (three on the local label, Twin Tone, and two on the major label A&M) without a breakthrough. Their hard work would pay off about a year later, when their album *Grave Dancers Union* would hit triple-Platinum, bolstered by the smash single "Runaway Train" (which would go on to earn a Grammy). At the time of this writing, the band was rumored to have completed recordings for a new album.

Trip Shakespeare

July 22, 1991. First Avenue Club. Minneapolis, Minnesota. The very next night after the Chicago gig, Pearl Jam hits Minneapolis, and opens for yet another band from the twin cities area. Trip Shakespeare featured a pair of Wilson brothers, Matt and Dan (which worked out pretty well for the Beach Boys, we should point out), along with John Munson and Elaine Harris. Padding their resume further, both Matt Wilson and Harris were students at Harvard University (a noted New England institution of higher learning featuring a colorful football radio broadcaster named Bernard M. Corbett). Sadly, neither the name Wilson, nor its Ivy League pedigree, was enough to sustain the unusual band on the cusp of "grunge" mania. They disbanded later that same year. One might say it was a "*short*, strange trip." Dan Wilson and John Munson went on to form Semisonic, who recorded the hit single "Closing Time."

John Eller & the DTs

July 22, 1991. First Avenue Club. Minneapolis, Minnesota. John Eller & the DTs were new at the time themselves, with only one album, 1990's *All These Reasons*, under their belts.

Walt Mink

July 22, 1991. First Avenue Club. Minneapolis, Minnesota. Walt Mink hailed from the *other* "twin city," St. Paul. Like a lot of bands, the indie rock power trio formed at college, in this case Macalester College in St. Paul in 1989. They pulled the Lynyrd Skynyrd-esque move of naming the band after one of their favorite professors (hey, at least it wasn't some rookie NBA player they had never met before). At the time of this summer gig, the only recordings they had to their credit were a pair of full-length cassette demos, but they were building a respectable following. A few months later, in October, Janet Billig would see them in NYC and would sign them to a deal with Caroline Records.

The Smashing Pumpkins

October 16, 1991. Oscar Mayer Theater. Madison, Wisconsin. Wow, what a lineup, huh? Pearls, Pumpkins, and Peppers. This is one of those shows where people who there probably *love* to brag about it, saying things like, "You had to be there." Also, notice how the names of the bands on the bills are becoming more prominent as we move forward in time. Like our man, Eddie, the Smashing Pumpkins hail from Chicago, Illinois. The original lineup of Billy Corgan, James Iha, Jimmy Chamberlain, and D'arcy Wretzky first came together in 1988. The unusual-looking and unique-sounding quartet was still more than a year away from their breakthrough sophomore album, *Siamese Dream* (1993), on this October night. They were touring solely on the merits of their 1991 Wisconsin-recorded debut, *Gish*, and a brand-new EP with Caroline Records called *Lull*. So things were on the upswing for them, but their glory years still lay ahead. Also ahead were the realization that Corgan was a bit of a perfectionist and a control-freak in the studio, and that infighting, broken relationships, frequent lineup changes, and drug addiction would befall the Pumpkins, but those are stories for another time and place.

Red Hot Chili Peppers

October 16, 1991. Oscar Mayer Theater. Madison, Wisconsin. Yet another case study in rock and roll excess and a walking cautionary tale in their own right, the Red Hot Chili Peppers are, along with Soundgarden's Chris Cornell, arguably the professional musicians most responsible for midwifing the unlikely birth of Pearl Jam. Or Jack Irons is, at any rate, though Flea *was* present during the fabled "Crazy Eddie" Yosemite backpacking trip. The original lineup—featuring Flea, Anthony Kiedis, Hillel Slovak, and our man, Jack Irons—came together back in 1983 on a mission to bring the funk back to Los Angeles. One oddity we'd like to mention is that neither Irons nor Slovak played on the band's debut album, *The Red Hot Chili Peppers* (1984), due to commitments to other bands. Slovak played on the second album, 1985's *Freaky Styley*, but Irons did not make his album debut until the *third* album, 1987's *The Uplift Mofo Party Plan*. As discussed elsewhere in this narrative, Slovak passed away the following year (1988) from a heroin overdose, and the shock of Slovak's passing caused Irons to leave the band. P-Funk's DeWayne McKnight subbed for Slovak temporarily until John Frusciante came onboard. D. H. Peligro, of the legendary punk band Dead Kennedys, filled in for Irons until Chad Smith came along, and at this point the lineup entered a prolonged period of stability. It also heralded the start of a highly productive and creative period. The band released *Mother's Milk* in 1989, signed a deal with Warner Brothers in 1990, and released a killer album, the Rick Rubin-produced *Blood Sugar Sex Magik*, the following year, 1991. That was the album that broke them wide open, and this was clearly their stage on this night. Against the odds, at thirty-two and counting, the Peppers are still going strong. They appeared during the Super Bowl XLVIII Halftime Show with Bruno Mars in 2014 and have a new album scheduled for release in 2015.

Nirvana

December 27, 1991. Sports Arena. Los Angeles, California. The Red Hot Chili Peppers may have been the headliners at this show, but Nirvana's star was clearly ascendant at this point. The band originated in the town of Aberdeen, Washington, eighty-two miles southwest of Seattle. Krist Novoselic and Kurt Cobain first met in 1985 and played in a few bands, including one with the boastful name, Stiff Woodies. By the end of 1987, the pair, along with drummer Aaron Burckhard, formed the original lineup of Nirvana. And then . . . man, what *is* it with drummers? At one point, Cobain and Novoselic moved to new homes and *lost track of* Burckhard altogether, so they jammed at practices with the Melvins' drummer, Dale Crover, who sat in for the demos. They recorded a demo in January of 1988 with respected Seattle producer Jack Endino, the original "Godfather of Grunge," before the nickname became attached to Pearl Jam patron Neil Young. Jonathan Poneman liked what he heard from the three-piece and struck a deal to release a single. In the meantime, Dale Crover moved down to San Francisco and recommended a guy named Dave Foster to man the drums in his stead. Then (and we are *not* making this up) Foster landed himself in *jail*, just in time for the reappearance of . . . Burckhard. This reunion was tearless and short-lived, however, as a hungover Burckhard essentially bailed out on the band one day at practice, never

The iconic Irish quartet U2 befriended Pearl Jam early on, booking them to open four shows in Italy during their 1993 Zoo TV Tour. The bloated excess of that tour didn't agree with the mercurial and idealistic young Vedder, but the two bands have remained close. Thirteen years later, just a week after wrapping up their own "Avocado" Tour, Pearl Jam returned to open for U2 at Aloha Stadium in Honolulu, as the Irish legends closed out the fifth leg of their *Vertigo* Tour.   *Author's collection*

to return. Things grew so desperate for a while that Cobain and Novoselic actually placed an ad for a drummer in the *Rocket*. The ad never panned out, but in the meantime a friend introduced them to Chad Channing, who began to play gigs with the band in May of 1988, and just kind of stuck around . . . for a while. *Bleach* was released by Sub Pop Records on June 15th of the following year, 1989. It contains the popular tune "About a Girl," along with a dozen other quality tracks. The band is off and running, gigging across the country. The guy who laid out the money for the *Bleach* sessions, Jason Everman, joined the band on guitar, making them a quartet, temporarily (he didn't even last through their first tour). Late 1989 found the boys in the studio with Steve Fisk to record an EP, *Blew*. During studio sessions for the follow-up to *Bleach*, Cobain and Novoselic realized they weren't digging Channing's drumming; Channing, in turn, resented being left out of the creative process. So, they parted ways. In the collaborative spirit of the area, Mudhoney's Dan Peters fills in on drums for the single "Silver." By September of 1990, the group took on a more familiar appearance when drummer Dave Grohl— alumnus of the recently defunct hardcore punk band Scream—joined, at the recommendation of the Melvin's Buzz Osbourne. Grohl may have been a long way from Scream's Washington, D.C. home base, but he fit right in with Cobain and Novoselic. With Dave onboard and their classic lineup finally in place, the band headed over to England with L7 for a few gigs. Early in 1991, at the urging of Sonic Youth's Kim Gordon, Nirvana landed a major label record deal with DGC Records. They spent part of that summer supporting Sonic Youth on a European tour, causing something of a sensation with their performance—captured on film—at the Reading Festival. With momentum building, their landmark album, *Nevermind*, was released in September and became certified Gold within a few weeks. MTV released the video for "Smells Like Teen Spirit" and played it *ad nauseam* while the band headed back to Europe for a tour during November and the first half of December. By the time the band returned stateside and took the stage for this post-Christmas gig, Nirvana was the biggest band in the country, and their lead singer, Kurt Cobain, was the unwitting (and unwilling) voice of his generation. Suffice it to say that this was *not* a role he would handle gracefully. He would be dead, by his own hand, within two-and-a-half years. But as you will read elsewhere in this account, his impact on the evolution of Pearl Jam, and on the entire landscape of popular culture, was profound—so much so that one could argue that his presence looms large to this day, as we embark on the third decade since his passing.

Soundgarden

April 28, 1992. The Coliseum. Austin, Texas. If Jack Irons can be considered the Patron Saint of Pearl Jam for playing matchmaker, then Soundgarden's Chris Cornell was the band's spirit guide. And how about drummer, Matt Cameron? Eventually he would end up having the best of both worlds when he found himself playing drums for both Pearl Jam and Soundgarden. While tales of their friendships, collaborations, and sense of communal spirit appear elsewhere in this

The "World's Greatest Rock and Roll Band" at Roseland, New York City, on October 1, 2002. Left to right: the "Core Four," Ronnie Wood, Mick Jagger, Keith Richards, and Charlie Watts. Let's face it, folks, they just don't come any bigger than the Rolling Stones, and Pearl Jam first opened for the living legends during their 1997 *Bridges to Babylon* Tour.   *Photofest*

narrative, it is important that we mention Soundgarden's origin story here. The band's history stretches back to Seattle, 1984, when Chis Cornell, Kim Thayil, and Hiro Yamamoto first got together, out of the ashes of their earlier band, the Shemps. Originally, Cornell was planning to pull double-duty as lead singer *and* drummer, but that construct was abandoned the following year when Scott Sundquist was brought on board to man the skins, and Cornell was free to roam the stage as a proper front man. Matt Cameron, an alumnus of Skin-Yard, replaced Sundquist on drums in 1986, giving Soundgarden its classic lineup. The band released their Grammy-nominated (Best Metal Performance, 1990) 1988 debut, *Ultramega OK*, and hit the road in support of it. The success led to a major label signing with A&M Records and a tour in support of Guns N' Roses (coauthor Tom Harkins was there with his siblings for one of those shows at Madison Square Garden). With the A&M signing and support tour came the predictable grumblings among the fan base about the band's direction, and internal squabbling, all while preparing for their sophomore recording, 1989's *Louder Than Love*. The album charted at 109, so it was a solid step in the right direction for the band. Just before the tour started, Yamamoto bailed out, paving the way for Nirvana's former friend, Jason Everman, to join the lineup on bass—temporarily. After they toured America and then Europe, they canned Everman (who now holds the dubious distinction of being bounced out of *two* of the biggest bands ever to come from the Pacific Northwest). Enter bass player number three, Ben Shepherd, who was part of the lineup that recorded Soundgarden's landmark third album, *Badmotorfinger*, in October of 1991. *Badmotorfinger* earned a 1992 Grammy nomination for Best Metal Performance, and on the night of this late April show—in spite of pretty much *everyone* being overshadowed by Nirvana's *Nevermind* at the time— Soundgarden would have been riding high on that album's success and their successful support tour(s) in America and Europe.

The Cult

June 6, 1992. Finsbury Park Festival. London, England. The Cult are a British hard rock band with roots dating back to either 1981, when Ian Astbury formed Southern Death Cult, or 1983, when he joined forces with Billy Duffy and they shortened the band's name to Death Cult. By January of the following year, they were known simply as the Cult. They were often categorized as a "goth" band. With principal members and chief songwriters Ian Astbury on vocals and Billy Duffy on guitar, they've enjoyed quite a bit of longevity, despite a couple of hiatuses, and are still a viable entity as this is written. They were already a veteran outfit with several records under their belts by the time Pearl Jam opened for them at this London festival gig. It is worth noting that when Astbury organized 1990's A Gathering of the Tribes Festival in San Francisco and Los Angeles, he planted the seeds of inspiration for Lollapalooza, the legendary second incarnation of which kicked off soon after this Finsbury Park Festival. As we write this, the Cult is alive and well, with new material expected in 2015.

Keith Richards and the X-Pensive Winos

December 31, 1992. The Academy. New York, New York. A New Year's Eve with "Keef," what could be cooler than *that*? The legendary Rolling Stone, known in some circles as "the human riff," Keith Richards first formed his side project, "The X-pensive Winos" with Steve Jordan back in 1987, when Mick Jagger was off doing his own solo thing. The band featured Bobby Keys (the longtime Stones' sax man), Ivan Neville, Charley Drayton, and Waddy Wachtel. They released their debut album, *Talk Is Cheap*, in 1988. On the night of this show, Keef and the boys were touring in support of their second album, 1992's *Main Offender*.

Neil Young

June 27, 1993. Isle of Calf Festival (Kalvoya). Oslo, Norway. In our circles, the two-time Rock and Roll Hall of Fame Inductee needs little introduction, but given his importance in the lives of Pearl Jam's members, a few highlights bear mentioning. The Canadian legend began playing in bands by age fifteen and headed south to California in 1966, where the stars aligned to give us Buffalo Springfield. The seminal band featured Dewy Martin and fellow legends Stephen Stills and Richie Furay (later of Poco). Young released his self-titled debut in 1968, and then joined Stills, Graham Nash (the Hollies), and David Crosby (the Byrds) in 1969 to form "supergroup" Crosby, Stills, Nash & Young (aka CSNY). Already a certified legend on this night in 1993, Young must have taken note of the young Pearl Jam and liked what he saw. As you will read elsewhere in this narrative, he would soon become a fixture in their lives and careers, leading, as always, by example. For more insight on Neil, check out Glen Boyd's 2012 offering, *Neil Young FAQ: Everything Left to Know About the Iconic and Mercurial Rocker.*

U2

July 2, 1993. Stadio Marc' Antonio Bentegodi. Verona, Italy. For an example of true unity in rock and roll, one need look no further than the Dublin, Ireland quartet who formed in 1976. Bono, The Edge, Larry Mullen, Jr., and Adam Clayton first came together as a band back at the Mount Temple Comprehensive School and have stayed together through thick and thin ever since. The four teens with punk rock sensibilities were much longer on ambition than they were on musical talent at the time, but they worked hard at it, and four years later released their debut album, *Boy*, in 1980. And the rest, as they say, is history. By the time Pearl Jam crossed the pond to open for them during this Italian stop on the Zoo TV Tour, U2 had long since passed the dues-paying point of their career. Like Neil Young, they had reached the stage where they could afford to take creative chances and were happy to do so, even if the results were sometimes mixed. Pearl Jam were beginning to garner some real respect by this point; they weren't the first band on the bill this night; that distinction went to An Emotional Fish, a young band from Dublin, Ireland. Things were looking up.

Van Morrison

July 10, 1993. Slane Castle. Slane, Ireland. Van the Man, in Ireland, with Neil Young as the headliner. And while we're on the subject of Irish rock and roll royalty, here's a living legend, contemporary in age with Neil Young, who made his musical bones at a time when the members of U2 were barely out of diapers. Belfast-born Van Morrison roared onto the scene with his band, Them, in 1964, snarling the lyrics to the punkish classic rocker "Gloria." He went solo in 1966, and his debut album, *Blowin' Your Mind!* was released in 1967, much to the surprise of Morrison (to make a long story short, his shady recording company took the eight songs he'd intended for release on singles (45s) and then packaged and released them as an LP). He wasn't happy about it. But some good did come out of those early sessions in the form of "Brown Eyed Girl," which went on to become one of the most popular rock songs of all time, and it remains so, nearly half-a-century later. Morrison forged a sonic masterpiece with his sophomore release, 1968's *Astral Weeks*, still considered by many to be one of the greatest albums of all time.

He broke through commercially and critically with the success of his third album, 1970's *Moondance*. By the time Pearl Jam rolled into town, sowing the seeds of their own legendary career, Morrison was already twenty-four albums into his solo career and counting. That count is scheduled to hit forty-one in 2015, as "The Man" releases the first album under his new record deal with RCA. As for Pearl Jam, they were now comfortably in the driver's seat and would not serve as an opening act again for nearly four-and-a-half years. You'll understand why, once you read the next entry.

The Rolling Stones

November 14, 1997. Oakland Stadium. Oakland, California. Talk about needing no introduction. As Pete Fornatale, Peter Thomas Fornatale, and (our very own) Bernard M. Corbett phrase it at the beginning of their comprehensive 2013 publication, *50 Licks: Myths & Stories from Half a Century of the Rolling Stones,* "July 12, 1962, was the first time that an entity publicly described as 'Mick Jagger and the Rolling Stones' took the stage." That means that when the Stones rolled into Oakland in November of 1997 for their *Bridges to Babylon* Tour, they had already celebrated their thirty-fifth anniversary. And Pearl Jam, lest we forget, had become one of the biggest bands in the world by this point. This was during the Jack Irons era, in between *No Code* and *Yield.* But let's face it; *no one* is bigger than "The World's Greatest Rock and Roll Band."

Cheap Trick

October 10, 1998. Crocodile Café. Seattle, Washington. Turnabout is fair play, particularly where your idols are concerned. Recall that Cheap Trick had already opened three shows for Pearl Jam during August 1998, beginning at the Molson Centre in Quebec on the twentieth. The boys in the band were definitely a little star-struck that night, and apparently they decided to return the favor and open for their idols. This was the first time Pearl Jam served as an opening act since the Rolling Stones' *Bridges to Babylon* Tour back in 1997 (see preceding item). A wonderfully classy show of respect from a group of guys who have always been reverent of and deferential to their musical forbears. And Cheap Trick was, and are, certainly worthy of that respect. Cheap Trick hails from Illinois, a town called Rockford, to be precise. In 1977, they released their debut album, *Cheap Trick*, on Epic Records. Critics dug it, but it didn't sell. Oddly enough, the album began to catch on in Japan. In an ambitious move, the follow-up, *In Color*, came out later that same year, with largely the same result in the USA. Even the band didn't care for the album's production, and American music fans basically said, "meh." But Japan was ahead of the curve on this one, as the singles "I Want You To Want Me" and "Clock Strikes Ten" burned up the charts there. Third time's the charm? They were determined to keep going until they got it right. The third Cheap Trick album, 1978's *Heaven Tonight*, finally garnered them some respect stateside, as the single "Surrender" hit the charts. Back in the flower of our youth, when we were prolific concertgoers, we used to tease other kids who professed to like a certain band with the snarky retort, "They're much better *live!*" Evidently this must have been the case with Cheap Trick, because when the late 1978 Japanese release *Cheap Trick at Budokan* finally hit the shelves in the USA in early 1979, it seemed like the whole musical world exploded. The album—a double live album, let us not forget—went triple Platinum that year, a feat rivaled only by Peter Frampton's earlier (1976) *Frampton Comes Alive. Cheap Trick at Budokan* proved to be the pinnacle of the band's commercial success, of course, but Cheap Trick remains a popular touring attraction to this day. Like us, the members of Pearl Jam no doubt harbor fond memories of this

album, which makes it easy to see why they brought their idols to their home turf in Seattle to share those memories with their friends and fans; a lovely gesture, on many levels.

Tom Petty and the Heartbreakers

June 26, 2006. Xcel Energy Center. St. Paul, Minnesota. Nearly eight years after the Cheap Trick gig in Seattle, Pearl Jam once again assumed the role of opening act, this time for the legendary Tom Petty and the Heartbreakers, who were celebrating their thirtieth anniversary at the time. The Gainesville, Florida quintet began making music together back in 1976, with the eponymous *Tom Petty and the Heartbreakers.* Like Cheap Trick, Tom Petty and the Heartbreakers first gained traction overseas—in this case, England—before the blowback effect helped to break them wide open stateside. The single "Breakdown" was their first charting single in the USA, after it was rereleased in 1978. Hey, those Brits are *onto* something here! This was just in time for the sophomore release, 1978's *You're*

American legends in the tradition of Bob Dylan and the Byrds, Tom Petty and the Heartbreakers are often introduced at concerts as "the last great American rock and roll band." While their fans may take issue with the finality of this characterization, Pearl Jam has always had a deep respect for Petty and his band. During the 2006 tour in support of its own eponymous eighth album, Pearl Jam served as the opening act for six dates on Petty's *Highway Companion* Tour.   *Photofest*

Gonna Get It!, which went Gold and yielded the hit singles "I Need to Know" and "Listen to Her Heart." The ball was rolling. In yet another example of the third time being the proverbial charm, 1979's *Damn the Torpedoes* propelled the band into the Platinum stratosphere. More hit albums and an appearance at 1985's Live Aid soon followed. In a foreshadowing of Pearl Jam's later backing of Neil Young, Tom Petty and the Heartbreakers toured as Bob Dylan's backing band during his *True Confessions Tour* during 1986.

The boys opened up for "The Last Great American Rock and Roll Band" a total of six times during the run, and this June 26 gig was the first. Perhaps fittingly, it was also, at press time, the *last* time Pearl Jam, now firmly established in the pantheon of rock and roll legends, has opened for anyone else.

29

For Openers

Bands That Have Opened for Pearl Jam

G iven the fact that Pearl Jam enjoyed a rapid ascendency to fame early in their storied career, they assumed the mantle of headlining act while they were still honing their own chops. This led to a scenario where many of the bands opening for *them* early on were bands they would have been thrilled to open *for* just a few months earlier.

Over the ensuing years, the incidence of Pearl Jam serving as an opening act have grown fewer and farther between; but occasionally, as we learn in the preceding chapter, they do make exceptions in the case of industry giants and legends like the Rolling Stones or Tom Petty and the Heartbreakers. It should come as no surprise that many of these bands, particularly those opening acts that supported Pearl Jam in its infancy, seem to have vanished without a trace. Others have enjoyed enormous success, critical acclaim, and careers spanning decades. Any attempt to give a detailed accounting of all of the bands that have opened for Pearl Jam over the years would by necessity become a book length project in its own right. So we won't do that, but we will take a look at the parade of opening acts tour by tour, and point out some of the bright lights and compelling figures along the way.

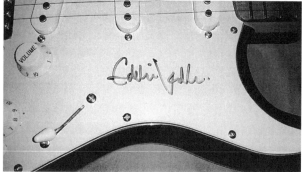

An Eddie Vedder-autographed guitar. As Pearl Jam evolved, Vedder's decision to add a third guitar to Stone and Mike's tandem created an unprecedented layer of depth and complexity in the band's overall sound. As a bonus, it helped the notoriously adventurous front man to keep his feet firmly planted on the stage.
Ryan Byrne

Pre-Tens: On the Road in 1991

Early on during Pearl Jam's career, back when they were still known as Mookie Blaylock, the overwhelming majority of their shows were played in small clubs, before crowds of a few hundred fans, at best. In those contexts, the notion of an "opening act" is slightly different than the notion of an opening act in the context of a show at a larger venue. Club managers tend to determine their featured bands' order of performance based upon their own evaluations of audience reaction and attendance. Nevertheless, it is still fascinating to take a look at some of the bands that shared a bill with Mookie Blaylock and Pearl Jam in the early days. If nothing else, it tells us that rock and roll is not an easy game to play. Not too many bands survive to enjoy the type of success that Pearl Jam enjoys today. Some toil away in relative obscurity, and others have disappeared with nary a trace.

Luv Mule

It was May 17, 1991, at the Off Ramp Café in Seattle, when Pearl Jam's show featured their *first* official opening act, the rather unfortunately named Luv Mule. For the record, Luv Mule seems to have disappeared without a trace.

Carnival of Souls and Mellow Vibe

A few months later, during a brief East Coast tour, Pearl Jam had not one but *two* supporting acts for a show at Philadelphia's legendary South Street rock bar, JC Dobbs on July 12: Carnival of Souls and Mellow Vibe. If you are asking, "Who?" we understand perfectly.

Sweet Water

Not to be confused with Woodstock veterans Sweetwater or, for that matter, with the fictional band, Stillwater, from Cameron Crowe's critically acclaimed 2000 film, *Almost Famous*. Local Seattle band Sweet Water would go on to record five albums, but on the night of this show, August 3, at Seattle's RCKNDY, they were still a year away from their C/Z Records debut album, *Ter*.

Bathtub Gin

The local blue collar and blues-based Bathtub Gin didn't have much more than a demo tape, *Mash*, and a modest-but-loyal local following when they supported Pearl Jam at RCKNDY on August 29. It was Molasses, Regan Hagar's post-Malfunkshun band, not Pearl Jam, who headlined the show that night, but there were several other ASCAP (the American Society of Composers, Authors, and Publishers) bands preceding Pearl Jam on the roster, including the Odds, Hungry Crocodiles, Ramadillo, and Best Kissers in the World. Bathtub Gin's closest brush with fame would come later on, when Mike McCready wore a T-shirt bearing their name on television.

The Odds

The Odds hailed from Vancouver, British Columbia, Canada. They formed in 1987 and paid their dues for a few years on the circuit as a cover band. By the time of this RKCNDY gig, they had come south of the border and released their 1991 self-produced debut album, *Neopolitan* (yes, spelled *that* way!). Among their claims to fame—or perhaps *infamy*, depending upon your own moral or aesthetic sensibilities—was their third single, "Wendy Under the Stars," which features the straightforward and—in an odd way—charming lyrics, "I was fucking Wendy under the stars, the night that Elvis died."

Hungry Crocodiles

Another local Seattle band, Hungry Crocodiles was clearly influenced by the work of the Red Hot Chili Peppers. They put forth a sound that was a fusion of rock, punk, and funk, at times flirting with rap/hip-hop.

Ramadillo (featuring Pete Droge)

Local Seattle boy Pete Droge was just four years old when he embarked on his musical journey by playing the ukulele, a distinction he shares with the legendary Neil Young, who also started off by playing the ukulele. According to Carol Brennan, in her entry on Droge in *Contemporary Musicians* at Encyclopedia.com:

> As a young adult, Droge worked in a pizza place and befriended Mike McCready, who would later go on to fame as the lead guitarist for Pearl Jam. By the time the Seattle-based group achieved massive success in the early 1990s . . . Droge had his own roots-rock outfit called Ramadillo. "We didn't have the attitude, 'Let's get it perfect,' so it was 'alternative,'" Droge told *Rolling Stone's* Kim Ahearn, and said Ramadillo was just part of a "subscene" at the time that "the Artist and Repertoire (A&R) people who were flocking [to Seattle] didn't pick up on."

Best Kissers in the World

According to William Ruhlmann's *AllMusic.com* bio of the band:

> Best Kissers in the World [were] a Seattle-based rock quartet . . . They released a self-titled EP through Sub Pop in 1991 before inking a deal with MCA. Two albums were then issued in 1993, *Puddin'* and the band's sole full-length, *Been There*. The latter record spawned the single "Miss Teen U.S.A.," which found some airplay on college radio. Best Kissers in the World disbanded in 1995.

The *Ten* Tour

Though they were still essentially an opening act in their own right as they toured the world in support of *Ten*, Pearl Jam did feature opening acts at many of their shows. Here they are, in descending order of appearances.

Eleven

Eleven opened one show on November 11, in the Student Union Ballroom at the University of Massachusetts: Amherst, MA, and appropriately enough would go on to open for Pearl Jam *eleven* times during the *Ten* Tour; more than any other act. It may not have been the Red Hot Chili Peppers, but founding Pepper Jack Irons was the drummer for this LA-based trio, itself an early offshoot of the Peppers, with roots dating back to their tumultuous formative years. Eleven is a favorite of Ten Clubber John Cafarella, who told us, "I got their first album in 1991, *Awake in a Dream*, and loved it. It was my first 'grunge' album. A friend had seen Eleven and told me I needed to get the album. When I found out they were opening for Pearl Jam I was elated."

I Love You

I Love You opened nine shows. They were a Hollywood, California band that formed in 1988 and toured on the merits of their self-titled debut album, released earlier in 1991 on the prestigious Geffen label. Alas, the sentiment inherent in the band's name was unreciprocated by the cold and often cruel world of the music business. They would go on to release just one more full-length album, *All of Us*, in 1994, before disbanding the following year.

Clayton Troupe

Clayton Troupe opened for a week straight at shows in England and Scotland, from February 21 through 28. They were a local band from Bristol, England, who had been playing since 1984. According to Clayton Troupe's origin story, lead singer Christian Riou formed the band at the urging of a local psychic, who thought it might be a good idea. Apparently, it was *they* who initially invited Pearl Jam over to open for *them*, but their roles were reversed due to Pearl Jam's rapid ascendency with the success of *Ten*. They put out a couple of albums (1989's *Through the Veil*, on Island, and 1991's *Out There*, on EMI), a half dozen singles that charted, and enjoyed moderate success, not to mention great longevity; they are still together to this day.

Tribe After Tribe

Tribe After Tribe hailed from Johannesburg, South Africa, and formed back in 1984. Once they released their debut album, 1985's *Power*, on EMI Records, they moved their base of operations to California. At the time of these four shows with

Pearl Jam (including one with Rage Against the Machine), they were touring on the strengths of their eponymous 1991 release on Atlantic, *Tribe After Tribe*. They have released five albums since then, are still active to this day, and are considered one of South Africa's truly legendary bands.

The Smashing Pumpkins

Finally, a name you are sure to recognize. The Smashing Pumpkins opened for Pearl Jam on March 27 and 28, at Marquette University Alumni Hall in Milwaukee and Cabaret Metro in Chicago, respectively. The band is described in great detail in the previous chapter.

Follow for Now

Follow for Now, from Athens, Georgia, also opened twice, once at Ritchie Coliseum at the University of Maryland in College Park on April 13, and again at Legion Field at the University of Georgia in their hometown of Athens. But, sadly, they were already on their way out. Their debut album, *Follow for Now*, was released in 1991 on the Chrysalis label, to mixed reviews. Though renowned for their energetic live performances and musically ambitious sound, they were unable to capture that essence in the recording studio. Though they would survive until 1994 on the strength of their performances alone, *Follow for Now* would prove to be their only album. The rest of the opening acts on the *Ten* Tour opened one show each.

Mystery Machine

Young Vancouver, British Columbia, Canada band Mystery Machine really *was* still something of a mystery when they opened for Pearl Jam to close out the third leg of the tour (second leg in North America) on May 21 at the Plaza of Nations in Vancouver, Canada. They had released an EP, titled *Stain*, in 1992, but they were still about a year away from releasing their 1993 debut album, *Glazed*. Local music fans already loved them. Through lineup changes, they would go on to record a total of three albums during the nineties, before going on hiatus in 1999. Though they technically reformed in 2004, they wouldn't release their fourth album, *Western Magnetics*, until 2012. By all indications, at the time of this writing, they are dormant once more.

Zoo Gods

This mysterious band, lost in the annals of rock and roll history, opened for Pearl Jam at the Blind Pig, a small club in Ann Arbor, Michigan, on November 21.

Captain Nemo

On March 1, 1992, Captain Nemo opened for Pearl Jam in Groningen, the Netherlands, at a place called Vera. Unlike their heroic literary namesake, the reputed discoverer of Atlantis, this band was evidently lost at sea.

The Swamp Babies

The first band to open for Pearl Jam on the European, or second, leg of the *Ten* Tour was the Swamp Babies, who opened at a place called Alaska, in Oslo, Norway, on February 8, 1992. While we can find no trace of *this* band, as so often happens in rock and roll history, there is a young American band currently using the same name in Jackson, Mississippi.

Swervedriver

Soundgarden was the headliner at this April 28, 1992 gig at the Coliseum in Austin, Texas, with Pearl Jam featured third on the bill, but there were two bands coming on before them: Swervedriver and Monster Magnet. Swervedriver, for their part, were here on a road trip from their hometown of Oxford, England, UK. At this time they were in their fourth year of existence, with founding members Adam Franklin and Jimmy Hartridge as the two mainstays hosting an otherwise revolving lineup of sideman. Though they would endure a series of lineup and record label changes over the ensuing decades, as well as an eight-year hiatus from 1999 to 2007, Swervedriver has proven to be remarkably resilient. The resurgent band remains active and released a new album, *I Wasn't Born to Lose You*, on March 3, 2015, on the Cobraside label.

Monster Magnet

Like Swervedriver, Monster Magnet formed in 1989, but from this side of the proverbial pond. They hailed from the fertile rock and roll breeding grounds of Red Bank, New Jersey, and their sound was—and still is—often described as "Stoner Rock," a label they cultivated with ubiquitous drug references and iconography on their early demos and EPs. The band enjoyed the European release of their critically acclaimed debut LP, *Spine of God*, on Caroline Records in 1991, and subsequent stateside release in February 1992. The disc was still hot off the presses on this night in Austin, and their association with the surging Soundgarden on this early tour led them to a major label signing with A&M. In a remarkable, Lemmy-esque" career, founder, lead vocalist and guitarist Dave Wyndorf has kept Monster Magnet viable to this very day, aided and abetted by an ever-shifting cast of sidemen.

Rage Against the Machine

Rage Against the Machine has enjoyed a fascinating and, at times, controversial history. And although that history dates back to 1987, at the time of this May 13, 1992 gig at the Hollywood Palladium, they were still six months away from the release of their self-titled, chart-topping debut album for Epic Records, *Rage Against the Machine*. The band, with just four studio albums to its credit during their initial thirteen year run (and *none* since their 2007 reunion) could never be considered prolific, but there's something to be said for quality over quantity.

Redd Kross

The origins of Redd Kross date back to 1978. The incarnation of the band that played Finsbury on this night was touring in support of their 1990 Atlantic Records release, *Third Eye*, and included Pearl Jam patron and future member Jack Irons on drums. The following tidbit of rock and roll trivia is not for the squeamish. They changed their name to Red Cross in 1980, for the release of their eponymous EP, *Red Cross*. The name was inspired by an infamous scene in *The Exorcist*, in which Linda Blair's demonically possessed twelve-year old character, Regan MacNeil, masturbates violently with a bloody crucifix while spewing blasphemous profanities. The band released their self-titled debut EP in 1980, much to the displeasure of the long-established charity/rescue organization, the Red Cross, which threatened legal action, which in turn led to the band's rebranding as Redd Kross (note the homage to comedian Redd Foxx).

L7

L7 formed in 1985 and hailed from Los Angeles. The rebellious and, at times, controversial all-girl ensemble served as something of a prototype for the Riot Grrrl movement of the 1990s. The L7 that hit the stage at Finsbury Park that day were a seasoned group of veterans, touring in support of their third studio album, *Bricks Are Heavy*, released barely two months earlier. They would later go on an extended hiatus from 2001 until December 2014. At the time of this writing, they have a full slate of appearances scheduled for 2015.

Therapy?

Therapy? hails from the Finsbury side of the proverbial pond and first roared to life onstage in Belfast, Northern Ireland, during the summer of 1989. The ambitious Irish metal-punks released two albums in rapid succession on the local Wiiija Records label: first *Babyteeth* in the summer of 1991, and then *Pleasure Death* the following January, 1992. By the time of this Finsbury Park Festival, they had already caught the attention of major label A&M and inked a recording contract. Against all odds, Therapy? is still going strong to this day.

Bad Religion

On the day of the 1992 Go Bang Festival, on June 13 in Wuhlheide, Berlin, Germany, Bad Religion was already creeping up on its fifteenth anniversary, plugging along thanks to a small but loyal cult following of punk rockers. Interestingly enough, despite being well into its second decade by the time of this festival, the band had been toiling in relative obscurity and wouldn't achieve real commercial success until two years later, in 1994, with the release of their eighth studio album, *Stranger Than Fiction*. They would go on to become one of the best selling punk rock bands of all time, moving in excess of five million albums worldwide. Bad Religion continues to tour and record and are just a few years shy of their fortieth anniversary.

Sisters of Mercy

Formed in 1977, Sisters of Mercy is an even older band than their Go Bang Festival cohorts, Bad Religion. Like Bad Religion, Sisters of Mercy revolves around one guy, in this case, singer and songwriter Andrew Eldritch. We must admit we find it rather amusing that the only other steady "member" of the band over the years has been a series of anthropomorphized drum machines Eldritch calls "Doktor Avalanche." The Sisters of Mercy who hit the stage on this day were going through a tumultuous time, flat broke, feuding with their record company, and firing their manager. This state of turmoil seems to be the band's default position, actually. And though they haven't recorded an album in over twenty-five years, Eldritch still manages to dust off the latest incarnation of Doktor Avalanche every year, and take his weird, enduring act on the road.

Post-Ten

Immediately following the official end of the *Ten* Tour, Pearl Jam embarked on Lollapalooza 1992, which kept them busy until September, when they finally pulled off their free hometown concert, A Drop in the Park. Though a number of other artists joined in the fun at Warren G. Magnuson Park that day (among them Pete Droge, Cypress Hill, Lazy Susan, Shawn Smith, Seaweed, and the Jim Rose Circus Sideshow), this was a festival, so they aren't considered "opening bands" per se.

Once they had completed their studio work for the *Vs.* album, Pearl Jam made plans to head to Europe for a couple of dozen shows, after a couple of hometown warm-ups, of course.

Orgone Box

Orgone Box was a fledgling one-man band at the time, in the person of England's Rick Corcoran. They (he) opened the warm-up show in Missoula.

Lazy Susan

A relatively obscure band, Lazy Susan opened the warm-up gig at the Met in Spokane. They had just one album at the time, 1992's *Twang*, and have since released half a dozen more.

1993 Europe

Of the fifteen shows Pearl Jam played in Europe during 1993, they were an opening act *themselves* for nine of them. Returning friends Tribe After Tribe opened five of these. Red Fun opened one of them, and James, Teenage Fanclub, and 4 Non Blondes joined Pearl Jam and Neil Young at Finsbury Park for one big party.

Red Fun

While opening for Neil Young at the Sjöhistoriska Museet in Stockholm, Sweden on June 28, Pearl Jam had its own opening act, Red Fun. They were a short-lived

Swedish band that had just formed at the time and would be gone by 1995. Their legacy is a single album, 1993's *Music for Nations*.

Finsbury Friends: James, Teenage Fanclub, and 4 Non Blondes

Neil Young headlined the Finsbury Festival at London's Finsbury Park on July 11, 1993, leaving Pearl Jam as the fourth act on the bill that night. The opening acts were mostly local.

James

A Manchester, England band already in their eleventh year of existence at the time, James would enjoy its greatest commercial success during the 1990s. At the time of the festival, they had four albums under their belts and were just months away from the October 1993 release of their fifth album, *Laid*, which enjoyed some success in the States among the college radio crowd. They subsequently broke up and later reunited, and they remain active as of this writing.

Teenage Fanclub

A band of Scotsmen from Bellshill, Teenage Fanclub had been around for about four years by this point and had been painted by the broad brush of the "alternative" label. They were quite prolific early on, with a *fourth* album already waiting to drop a few months after Finsbury. Ten albums on, they remain active, and recently (2015) opened for the Foo Fighters.

4 Non Blondes

Though they were not at all prolific, or very successful, this all-female San Francisco quartet is arguably the most recognizable on this bill (the name was catchy). They, too, were in their fourth year of existence at the time of Finsbury 1993, touring on the merits of their one-and-only studio album, 1992's *Bigger, Better, Faster, More!*, featuring their only major hit song, "What's Up?" A live album and some singles would follow, but (with the exception of a one-off reunion in 2014) they were done by 1994.

1993 North America

During the 1993 North American Tour in August and September, Pearl Jam featured six different opening bands across eight shows, while opening three for Neil Young themselves. Three of those bands opened two shows apiece.

Cadillac Tramps

Much to Pearl Jam's delight, Cadillac Tramps was a hardcore punk band formed in the mid-1980s and hailing from California. Eddie Vedder was an early fan. The

Cadillac Tramps were on the road supporting their second album, 1993's *Tombstone Radio*, at the time. They would go on to release another, *It's Allright*, the following year, before splitting up in 1995. They were on and off for a few years after that, but these Cadillacs are currently gathering rust.

Blind Melon

To "Bee" or not to "Bee"? *That* is the question. Los Angeles-based Blind Melon, featuring the ill-fated vocalist Shannon Hoon, opened the final two shows for Pearl Jam on the North American leg of the 1993 tour. They only had one album under their belts, 1992's *Blind Melon*, but they were riding a wave of popularity because of their hit single, "No Rain," the video of which features the now-iconic "Bee Girl," a little girl dancing around in a bee costume. The character, if not the band itself, captured Pearl Jam's imaginations to the degree that they wrote the song "Bee Girl" in her honor. As for Hoon, he would shuffle off this mortal coil on October 21, 1995, as the result of a cocaine-induced heart attack in New Orleans at age twenty-eight. The band tried to regroup with another singer but could never recapture that early spark.

Doughboys

Canada natives, Doughboys were already halfway through their lifecycle with six albums under their belts when they opened for Pearl Jam during two gigs in Canada (one in Hull, one in Montreal). They would be broken up by 1997 after releasing just one more album.

Blues Traveler

The throwback band hailed from the Ivy League streets of Princeton, New Jersey, and formed back in 1987. Led by the corpulent and affable lead vocalist and harmonica master John Popper, Blues Traveler almost inadvertently got lumped in with the so-called "Jam Band" phenomenon, a direct consequence of the exploding late-career success of the Grateful Dead, the resiliency of the Allman Brothers Band, and their disciples, such as Phish. Blues Traveler was then three albums into their career and remains active to this day.

Soundgarden

Soundgarden needs no introduction. Pearl Jam's fellow Seattle titans were supporting Pearl Jam on this day, along with Blues Traveler, and everybody took second place to headliner Neil Young.

The Darling Buds

Though they hailed from Newport, in South Wales, with a history dating back to 1986, the Darling Buds were nevertheless stuck with the "alternative" label. At the time of this show, they were still touring on the strengths of their 1992 album,

Erotica, but they were apparently frustrated that commercial success had eluded them, and they disbanded soon thereafter. Predictably, they reunited twenty years later and are considered active today, in spite of having released no new music.

The *Vs.* Tour

Between the two warm-up shows and the first leg of the *Vs.* Tour in North America, Pearl Jam featured ten opening acts, including one repeat customer, Jack Irons' band, Eleven. The reigning champion this time around was Urge Overkill.

Urge Overkill

The most common opening act on the first leg of the *Vs.* Tour, Chicago based Urge Overkill opened eleven shows. They had released their fourth album, *Saturation*, on Geffen back in June, and they were riding high on the album's hit single, "Sister Havana." The following year they would achieve greater acclaim with a cover version of Neil Diamond's "Girl, You'll Be a Woman Soon." That was the pinnacle. The ensuing years were filled with breakups, reunions, a new album, and a live album, but nothing to match the early 1990s.

American Music Club

American Music Club opened the second tour warm-up show, held at the Catalyst in Santa Cruz, and four more on the tour itself. They were an indie band from San Francisco that had already been around since 1981 and would be broken up by the following year, until a 2004 reunion. They were on the road with their sixth studio album, 1993's *Mercury*. They would go on to release another, *San Francisco*, in September of 1994, and then another *four* following their 2004 reunion. They are still considered active, though they have released no new music since 2008.

The Butthole Surfers

The very first time that Pearl Jam performed, Eddie Vedder was sporting a Butthole Surfers T-shirt. Given the sheer number of T-shirts that the members of Pearl Jam evidently go through, you wouldn't think they'd be sentimental about them, but later in his career, during his first-ever solo show, Eddie wore the very same T-shirt. This must be one special band to Eddie.

The oddly named Butthole Surfers hailed from Texas and had been around since 1981, when most of the Pearl Jam members were in high school. They were a hardcore punk band with an outrageous live act that appealed to the sensibilities of the nascent superstars. By the time they opened for Pearl Jam on these five shows, they were showcasing their sixth studio album, 1993's *Independent Worm Saloon*, and were still three years away from the only commercial success they would ever enjoy, 1996's *Electriclarryland*, which yielded them a hit single, "Pepper." Ostensibly, they still exist, though they haven't released an album since 2001 and have been dormant since the fall of 2011.

The Rollins Band

Henry Rollins' post-Black Flag band opened the first three shows on this tour. The members of Pearl Jam had always had a great deal of respect for the burly, tattooed Washington D.C. native, Henry Rollins. During the *Vs.* Tour, the Rollins Band was showcasing their most recent release, 1992's *The End of Silence*. The band went through several phases until going on a three year hiatus in 2003. And while Rollins reunited the band for a brief run in 2006, he is more often seen on television or heard doing voiceover work these days than he is performing on stage.

Mudhoney

In what would soon become a Pearl Jam tradition, Mudhoney opened five shows on the *Vs.* Tour. The band featured Stone and Jeff's former colleagues from Green River, Steve Turner and Mark Arm, along with their rhythm section, bass player Matt Lukin (later of "Lukin" fame) and drummer Dan Peters. Mudhoney had been busy since their 1988 inception and were now touring in support of their 1992 album, *Piece of Cake*. And they are still going strong today, nine albums into it, in spite of Lukin's 1999 departure.

Bill Miller

Though his "Americanized" name belies his Native American heritage, Bill Miller may not be the *last* of the Mohicans, but he is arguably among the fabled tribe's most talented. He recorded his first album, *Bill Miller and Native Sons* in 1983, and by the time of the *Vs.* Tour he was showcasing his fifth studio album, 1993's *Red Road*, which came hot on the heels of a live album, 1992's *Reservation Road: Live*. People were beginning to take notice, and he opened for Tori Amos prior to opening twice for Pearl Jam. He has released no new music since 2004, but did recently contribute to a Johnny Cash tribute album.

The remaining acts on this leg of the tour opened one show apiece.

Weapon of Choice

Weapon of Choice opened the show at the Empire Polo Club in Indio, California, on November 5, taking the stage after American Music Club and before Jack Iron's Eleven. The genre-spanning band was virtually unknown at the time and still a year away from their debut album, 1994's *Nut-Meg Sez "Bozo the Town."* They have since released seven more albums and are still honing their funky craft.

Six in the Clip

A paragon of intercultural harmony, Seattle-based hip-hop pioneers Six in the Clip was the result of a merger between two earlier bands: the Movement, an African-American band, and a band of white guys called Major League Players. The pioneering group was a bit of a novelty on the Seattle scene, and they longed for critical acclaim from the larger rap community. They opened the show on

December 7 at the Seattle Center Arena, just before Urge Overkill took the stage. Alas, they soon faded into obscurity.

Hater

Hater opened the December 9 show at the Seattle Center Arena, warming the crowd up for Urge Overkill, as Six in the Clip had done two days earlier. They were a new band, but this was no squad of rookies. They were a Soundgarden side project, featuring Matt Cameron on drums and Ben Shepherd on guitar and vocals, with Brian Wood, brother of the late Andrew, on lead vocals, John McBain (formerly of Monster Magnet and later of Wellwater Conspiracy) on guitar, and John Waterman. The makeshift group had just released an album, *Hater*, in September. As so often happens with side project bands, Hater would not release a second album for twelve years.

Vs. Second Leg 1994

The second leg of Pearl Jam's *Vs.* Tour featured return engagement opening acts like Mudhoney, who opened seven shows, L7 and Follow For Now, who *together* opened the March 9 show at Pensacola's Civic Center, and Urge Overkill, who opened at Chicago Stadium on March 10, right after new friends, the Frogs.

King's X

King's X was the reigning champs on this leg, opening seven shows. This was a vintage band, dating back to 1979, a progressive metal band that played around with a variety of genres and styles. The *Vs.* Tour found King's X during a period of renewal. They had recently moved to the prestigious Atlantic Records, and released their fourth studio album, 1992's eponymous *King's X*. Since then the workingman's band has gone on to change record labels twice and release *fifteen* more albums. They are still at it today.

The Frogs

This leg of the *Vs.* Tour got hopping with the Frogs, who opened six shows, including the first two at Denver's Paramount Theatre on March 6 and 7. The Wisconsin brother band, founded by siblings Jimmy and Dennis Flemion, had existed since 1980. Kurt Cobain was a fan of the group, which certainly didn't hurt their stature on the Seattle scene. They were only two albums into their career at the time. Dennis Flemion later toured as part of the Smashing Pumpkins, and Jimmy as a part of Sebastian Bach's solo band. The Frogs recorded a critically acclaimed cover of Pearl Jam's "Rearviewmirror," which Pearl Jam released as a B-side on their "Immortality" single. The Frogs were mostly inactive from 2001 to 2012, when they released two new albums in digital format. Dennis met an untimely yet oddly poetic end on July 7, 2012, at Wisconsin's Wind Lake; his body was recovered there days later.

Grant Lee Buffalo

Grant Lee Buffalo hailed from Los Angeles, and took two-thirds of their name from guitarist and vocalist Grant Lee Philips. They had just released their debut album, 1993's *Fuzzy*, and they opened five shows for Pearl Jam during this run. They would go on to release three more albums, but the only commercial success they enjoyed was "Truly Truly," the single from their fourth and thus far final album, 1998's *Jubilee*, which hit number eleven on *Billboard*'s U.S. Modern Rock Tracks.

Magic Slim and the MGs

Last but not least, the somewhat obscure blues act Magic Slim and the MGs opened one show, at Chicago's New Regal Theater on March 13, 1994. The prolific musician had sixteen or seventeen albums under his belt by 1994 and had been playing music since the early 1950's.

The *Vitalogy* Tour Warm-Ups 1995

Two out of the three warm-up shows for the *Vitalogy* Tour featured new opening acts, Magnog and Shangri-La Speedway.

Magnog

Washingtonian native band Magnog was on hand for Pearl Jam's infamous February 6 Moore Theater show, when they appeared under the assumed identity, Piss Bottle Men. Opening act Magnog was one of two bands (the other being Hovercraft) to break off from the band Space Helmet. At this time, the spacy, quasi-psychedelic trio (wherein the guitarist, drummer, and bass player all also played keyboards and sang) had only demo tapes to market themselves. Though virtually unknown at this time, Magnog would return to Pearl Jam's orbit a few years down the road.

Shangri-La Speedway

Shangri-La Speedway hails from Jeff Ament's native Missoula, Montana, and features none other than the Ten Club's President (and Ament's childhood friend), Tim Bierman, on guitar. They were about as local as a local band can get and opened the show at the University of Montana Missoula's Adam's Fieldhouse on February 8.

Vitalogy: Pacific/Oceania Leg

Old friends, Mudhoney, opened four of these winter 1995 shows but there were also some new faces, including the Dead Flowers, Cosmic Psychos, and the Meanies.

The Meanies

The Meanies dominated the opening slot, working ten of the sixteen shows that featured an opening act. It should come as no surprise that they were an Australian punk rock band, and had been playing since 1988. Their lead singer, Link, was every bit as manic on stage as the young Eddie Vedder had been, throwing himself about with a reckless abandon that landed him on the injured list on several occasions.

Cosmic Psychos

On one occasion, on March 14 in Canberra, Australia, Cosmic Psychos joined the Meanies as openers. An even older local punk band than the Meanies, Cosmic Psychos, in spite of plying their craft on the other side of the planet, also had a tremendous influence on the Seattle scene. Everyone from the Melvins, Pearl Jam, L7, and Nirvana held them in high esteem.

The Dead Flowers

No one loves a good Rolling Stones homage as much as we do, and what could be cooler than naming your band after one of the greatest Stone's tunes of all time? This mysterious band opened the two final shows of the leg, at Auckland's Mt. Smart Super Top. We can only assume they were another local band, as they seem to have been lost to the annals of rock and roll history, buried beneath an avalanche of Rolling Stones tribute bands.

Vitalogy North America, First Leg

The summer 1995 leg of the *Vitalogy* Tour featured the return of opening acts the Frogs, who opened on two occasions, July 8 and 9, and Bad Religion, who dominated the opening slot with eight appearances. As you will recall from the *Vitalogy* chapter, seven of these dates were cancelled. But there were a handful of new faces, including the Scollywags, Crash and Brittany, and Otis Rush.

The Scollywags

The Scollywags preceded Bad Religion on the opening date of the summer leg on June 16, 1995. Regrettably, no one seems to know much about them, apart from the fact that are evidently dozens of bands using some form of the name (Scallywags, Skallywags, etc.).

Crash and Brittany

The obscure Crash and Brittany preceded Bad Religion on stage at the infamous Pearl Jam "food poisoning" show at Golden Gate Park in San Francisco on June 24. The trio consisted of Kelly Slusher, Mike Thiemann, and Huy Ngo. We know this because there is video on YouTube of their performance. Originally filmed in Super 8 format, the existing film makes the Zapruder film seem like IMAX by comparison.

Otis Rush

Otis Rush opened the show at Chicago's Soldier Field, the final date on this leg. Born in Mississippi and relocated to Chicago as a teenager, his slow, note-bending style was a huge influence on the guitar heroes of the 60s and 70s, including Eric Clapton and Carlos Santana. Led Zeppelin fans will recognize Rush's contributions in the form of his 1956 single (written by Willie Dixon), "I Can't Quit You, Baby," which Zep covered on their 1969 debut album. Dixon is still with us, but, sadly, health issues have rendered him unable to play his guitar. He was sidelined by a debilitating stroke in 2004, but his legacy lives on.

Vitalogy North America, Second Leg

Pearl Jam is honored to have yet another one of their favorite acts open six of the nine dates on the second North American leg of the *Vitalogy* Tour, NYC's very own punk rock royalty, the Ramones. The Ramones joined the Fastbacks, who opened three shows, and Ben Harper, who appeared along with the Fastbacks at one of the shows.

The Ramones

From their humble 1974 beginnings in Forest Hills, Queens, Joey, Johnny, Dee Dee, and Tommy Ramone went on to define and embody the punk rock genre over twenty-two years and more than 2,200 shows. At this time, the Ramones were nearing the end of their run, and they were eleven months away from breaking up for good.

The Fastbacks

Punk rock veterans, the Fastbacks formed in Seattle back in 1979 and burst into the public eye at the dawn of the 1980s. Like their East Coast forebears the Ramones, they lasted almost exactly twenty-two years (though they did reunite for a one-off performance in 2011). The Fastbacks featured *so* many different drummers over the years that no source can give us a definitive number. We know that it's somewhere between a dozen and twenty, including a stint by fifteen-year-old multi-instrumentalist Duff McKagan, who went on to play bass for Guns N' Roses. This was the Fastbacks' first foray as a Pearl Jam opening act. They would later support the band for virtually *all* of their 1996 shows, opening more than thirty gigs in all.

Ben Harper

Ben Harper joins the Fastbacks for the San Jose show on November 4. Harper may be the perfect example of why it can prove beneficial to introduce children to music and the arts at an early age. His grandparents owned a renowned music store, the *Folk Music Center and Museum*, in Claremont, California, where the youngster was exposed to a steady parade of musicians, including many esteemed professionals. His family furthered his musical education by taking him to concerts, so it should come as no surprise that he was playing shows by the age of twelve and gigging regularly soon thereafter. On this night in San Jose, Harper was still a decade away from earning accolades and prestige at the Grammy Awards, but he was already earning the respect of his peers, gigging and recording with the likes of the legendary Taj Mahal and Tom Freund. He also had two solo albums under his belt by this time. His debut, *Welcome to the Cruel World*, came out in 1994, followed soon thereafter by 1995's *Fight for Your Mind*. He has averaged one album every two years ever since. Multitalented and socially conscious, Harper is Pearl Jam's kind of guy, and he is still going strong to this day.

No Code Tour Warm-Ups 1996

Pearl Jam prepared for the *No Code* Tour with a warm-up show at the Showbox on the home court in Seattle. This one show would feature a most unusual opening act.

Gus

On September 14, 1996, at the Showbox in Seattle, Pearl Jam featured Gus as an opening act. "Gus" isn't a band, he's a *guy*; a guy who *isn't* named Gus. His real name is Anthony Penaloza, and today he goes by the stage name Gus Black. By whatever name you call him, he's a pretty eclectic guy and also a Los Angeles-based director and producer who also happens to play music. At this time, he had just released his 1996 debut album, *Gus*, and he would go on to release six more in between producing and directing music videos for other bands.

No Code North America 1996

The Fastbacks opened all twelve full-length concerts on the abbreviated North American leg of the *No Code* Tour. Ben Harper joined the bill for two of the shows.

No Code Europe 1996

The Fastbacks opened eighteen of the twenty shows scheduled for the European leg of the *No Code* Tour. They were scheduled to open the Munich show on November 10, but it was cancelled, and there was no opening act for the Prague show on November 15.

Yield Tour Warm-Ups 1998

Pearl Jam's warm-up show for the *Yield* Tour was a clandestine affair indeed, as the band would appear under an assumed identity. Knowing what we now know about the band's musical tastes, their choice of opening act should come as no surprise.

The Odd Numbers

When Pearl Jam played the Catalyst in Santa Cruz on November 12, in preparation for the *Yield* Tour, the Odd Numbers opened the bill. This was another one of those "on the down low" shows that only a few people knew about. Pearl Jam, preparing for their own turn as openers for the Rolling Stones, used the pseudonym "Honking Seals." Opening act Odd Numbers were another somewhat obscure band. A trio of self-styled California "mods" (yes, *mods*, complete with the scooters, like something straight out of *Quadrophenia*) whose music became popular in skateboard culture (which certainly explains the attraction for Eddie Vedder), the Odd Numbers featured a pair of guys named Dave (Maisa, guitar/vocals; and Miller, bass), and John Cummings on the drums. By the time of this gig at the Catalyst, they had released their fourth album, 1997's *A Guide to Modern Living*. There would be a fifth album forthcoming in 2001, titled *The Trials and Tribulations of the Odd Numbers*, but after that the trail grows cold.

Yield Hawaii/Oceania

Old friends Mudhoney opened the two Maui shows, but a new face, Shudder to Think, joined the tour for *all* thirteen New Zealand and Australia dates.

Shudder to Think

We're not sure if anyone was actually shuddering at the thought, but opening act Shudder to Think was in the final throes of its first phase of existence during this tour. Within months, the members would go their separate ways (though the future held a number of reunions of varying duration). By this point in their career, Shudder to Think had gained the respect of their musical peers, if not the life-altering superstardom of bands like Pearl Jam. They had already served as opening act for the Smashing Pumpkins and Pearl Jam favorites, Fugazi, so their appearance on this tour was part of a natural progression. In the words of *Spin*'s Peter Gaston, "While the band's cocktail of tricky time changes, aggressive guitar bursts, and Craig Wedren's effeminate falsetto proved inaccessible for the mainstream, many musicians found it utterly compelling." Illustrative of this point, Pearl Jam would actually cover one of STT's songs, "Pebbles," at their Melbourne, Australia gig on March 5, just a week later.

Yield **North America, First Leg**

With Pearl Jam back on the road in America post-Ticketmaster War, they featured some fresh faces in the opening slot, including Frank Black, the Murder City Devils, Spacehog, X, Goodness, Zeke, Tenacious D, the Wallflowers, and Sean Lennon.

Frank Black

Frank Black's chief claim to fame is as the leader of Boston's alternative rock legends, the Pixies (wherein he is billed as Black Francis), but he appeared as a solo opening act at eight of these shows, because the Pixies were on hiatus at the time. His most recent album at the time was 1998's *Frank Black and the Catholics.*

The Murder City Devils

The Murder City Devils, which sounds much more like an outlaw motorcycle gang than it does a band, opened the shows on July 2, 3, and 5. They were a garage rock band, relatively new to the scene at the time. They had recently released their sophomore album, 1998's *Empty Bottles, Broken Hearts,* on Sub Pop Records, which explains their connection to Pearl Jam. They have released five more albums in the years since and continue to tour and record.

Spacehog

Here's a multicultural puzzle. Spacehog, an *English* band, was formed in New York City back in 1994. When they opened three shows for Pearl Jam on this leg of the tour, they were showcasing their sophomore effort, 1998's *The Chinese Album.* Little did they know it, but they had already peaked. The single, "In the Meantime," from their 1996 debut album, *Resident Alien,* was a number one single on *Billboard*'s US Mainstream Rock chart. They've barely made a ripple since.

X

In the introductory words of Eddie Vedder, as quoted on *Two Feet Thick*'s "Concert Chronology" entry for the July 16 show, X is "one of the greatest bands to ever write, sing and play." The veteran American punk rock band had the Vedder seal of approval, and they opened three shows on this leg, already on their second reunion. Their recording days were already behind them, but X clearly embodies the punk rock ethos that the members of Pearl Jam have long admired.

Goodness

Another partial "side dish," Goodness was comprised mainly of future members of Mike McCready's side project, the Rockfords. But at this stage, opening for Pearl Jam at Washington Grizzly Stadium in Missoula and the Canyons in Park City, Utah, to kick off this leg on June 20 and 21, Goodness was just one album into a career that began in 1995. That was the year they released their self-titled debut, and their 1998 follow-up, *Anthem*, wasn't scheduled for release until mid-October. Note to aspiring rock and rollers: that's why it pays to have friends in high places.

Zeke

Seattle hardcore punk rockers Zeke also opened two dates, July 11 in Las Vegas, and later at the first of the two Seattle shows that closed out this leg on July 21. Zeke had been around since 1993 and were currently touring behind their fourth album, 1998's *Kicked in the Teeth*. They are still considered extant, though they haven't released an album since 2007.

Tenacious D

We're not sure if Tenacious D is an example of life imitating art or vice versa, but actor/comedian/musician Jack Black and Kyle Gass's band is a lot of fun. They joined X in support of Pearl Jam at this back-to-back at the Forum in Inglewood, California, on July 13 and 14. Though they had been together as an act since 1994, the duo was still three years shy of their 2001 debut album, *Tenacious D*.

The Wallflowers

The Wallflowers, featuring rock and roll legacy and Bob Dylan progeny Jakob Dylan, joined Zeke on the bill at Seattle's Memorial Stadium on July 21 and 22. The Wallflowers had been at it since 1989 and were currently riding high on the strength of their sophomore release, 1996's *Bringing Down the Horse*, featuring the band's only number one hit single, "One Headlight."

Sean Lennon

The next night continued the theme of rock and roll legacies, as Sean Lennon (son of the Beatles' John Lennon and Yoko Ono, on the outside chance that someone out there is unaware) joined the Wallflowers as an opener for Pearl Jam at Seattle Memorial Stadium on July 22 to wrap up this leg of the tour.

Yield North America, Second Leg

Old friends Mudhoney and Ben Harper opened eight and seven shows, respectively, but more new faces, including some legendary ones, also filled the opening slots on the second North American leg of the *Yield* Tour, including Pearl Jam idols Cheap Trick and Iggy Pop.

Iggy Pop

Punk rock royalty kicks off the August 17 and 18 shows, as the indefatigable Iggy Pop took the stage in support of Pearl Jam at shows in Indiana and Michigan. Iggy, nee James Newell Osterberg Jr., was one of the architects of punk rock, being the leader of the Stooges since 1967. At the time of his four appearances on the *Yield* Tour, Iggy was touring on his *eleventh* solo album, 1996's *Naughty Little Doggie*. In

Like many of us, the members of Pearl Jam grew up listening to and loving the bright, optimistic music of Cheap Trick. After Cheap Trick opened three shows for Pearl Jam during August of 1998, Pearl Jam returned the favor by opening for their childhood idols at Seattle's Crocodile Café later that same year on October 10.   *Author's collection*

later years, the "Lust for Life" legend would reunite the Stooges in 2007 and 2013 to record and tour.

Cheap Trick

Cheap Trick opened for Pearl Jam on three occasions during this leg, including the Molson Centre gig on April 20, the big outdoor festival at Molson Park in Barrie, Canada, on April 22, and the Palace of Auburn Hills on April 23. Cheap Trick had some additional help on the supporting act front as All Systems Go!, Hayden, Cracker, and the Matthew Good Band joined them at the Molson Park Festival. For more, look back at what we wrote in Chapter 28.

Rancid

Rancid was a California punk band of more recent vintage. They formed in 1991, making them contemporary with Pearl Jam. Like Pearl Jam, two of the founding members were veterans of a successful earlier band. Tim Armstrong, the lead singer and guitarist, and Matt Freeman, the bass player, were once members of

Operation Ivy. Rancid opened the shows at West Palm Beach's Coral Amphitheatre on September 22 and 23 to help Pearl Jam close out the *Yield* Tour in style. At the time, they were on the road in support of their fourth studio album, 1998's *Life Won't Wait*.

Hovercraft

Yet another keep-it-in-the-family opening act, Hovercraft consisted of Ryan Shinn on guitar and various sound effects, and bass player Beth Liebling, better known at the time as Mrs. Eddie Vedder. But in the context of Hovercraft, they used stage names. Beth was "Sadie 7" and Ryan was "Campbell 2000." Their act was purely instrumental, highly experimental, and garnered favorable critical acclaim. Their close association with Pearl Jam was a classic catch-22. On the one hand it gained them exposure; on the other they took a lot of flak and heard a lot of grumbles about nepotism. They opened just one show on the tour, at Washington D.C.'s DAR Constitution Hall.

Binaural Tour 2000: Warm-Ups and European Leg

At the dawn of the new millennium, Pearl Jam welcomed some new friends, and some older friends, to open for them on the *Binaural* Tour. C Average, a quasi-side project of Eddie's, opened the two warm-up shows. During the first leg, the Vandals opened eight shows, and the Dismemberment Plan opened a dozen.

The Vandals

A California punk rock band formed back in Pearl Jam's high school days, the Vandals opened eight shows on the European leg of the tour in support of their ninth studio album, 2000's *Look What I Almost Stepped In*. It had taken nine years for their classic lineup to emerge, and they have enjoyed remarkable stability ever since. As with their contemporaries the Beastie Boys, humor is a key element in the Vandals' material. They continue to tour today, though they have released no new material since 2004.

The Dismemberment Plan

The Dismemberment Plan picked up where the Vandals left off and opened twelve shows on the pre-Roskilde European leg. This Washington D.C.-based indie band had been around since 1993, and they were touring on the strengths of their third album, the well-reviewed *Emergency & I*. They were kindred spirits of Pearl Jam who loved Fugazi and were leery of fans getting hurt in aggressive mosh pits.

The Monkeywrench

The only other band to open on the European leg was the Monkeywrench, who opened the two shows at Wembley Arena in London on May 29 and 30. The Monkeywrench weren't exactly *new* faces. They were a 1990 side project of old

Green River/Mudhoney buddies Steve Turner and Mark Arm, who wanted to collaborate with Poison 13's Tim Kerr, and that's how the Monkeywrench came to be.

Binaural North American Leg 2000

By this point, Pearl Jam was falling into the pattern of featuring one opening act for the duration of a single leg of a given tour, or else splitting a leg between two different acts. In this case, they were clearly giving back to their own sense of rock and roll community by employing one of their own favorite acts. The fans had become the employers, and they hadn't forgotten the bands they loved during their own early days.

Sonic Youth

The opening slot belonged to New York rock icons Sonic Youth for the duration of this leg of the tour. The band dates back to 1981 and has been called every adjective in the name-that-genre lexicon: alternative, post-punk, noise, no-wave, experimental, independent, hardcore, blah, blah, blah. Pearl Jam were, first and foremost, fans of Sonic Youth, but the veterans also appealed to them because, like Fugazi, they favored the DIY approach to the rock business. On this tour, Sonic Youth was showcasing their 2000 album, *NYC Ghosts & Flowers*, its eleventh of fifteen to date in their storied career. During the final show, at the Post-Gazette Pavilion in Burgettstown, Pennsylvania, only three members of Sonic Youth appeared: Lee Ranaldo, Steve Shelley, and Jim O'Rourke. Thurston Moore and Kim Gordon were not in attendance.

Binaural North American Leg Two, 2000

Pearl Jam's single-opening-act approach continued on the next leg of the *Binaural* Tour. In retrospect, we can appreciate the wisdom of their ways here. Pearl Jam had long since become a destination act in its own right. By this we mean that Pearl Jam fans were no longer content to wait for the band to come around and visit their town. Now, like the Deadheads of yore, Pearl Jam fans were following the band from city to city, racking up as many shows as they could afford. Given that, it made a great deal of sense for them to feature a single opening act for the duration of a tour leg; it provided a sense of continuity for the increasingly nomadic fan base, not to mention some economic stability for the opening acts, which is always appreciated.

Supergrass

If the grass is always greener on the other side of the fence, the Supergrass must be greener on the other side of the pond. The band hailed from England and opened every show on the second leg of the tour, except the last one. They were a brother act, featuring Roy and Gaz Coombes, who played keyboards and guitar, respectively. Gaz was the lead vocalist, while Roy and the rhythm section of bassist

Few bands did more to introduce Pearl Jam to a wider audience than their original patrons, the Red Hot Chili Peppers. Founding Pepper Jack Irons manned the skins for Pearl Jam and helped to ground them during a particularly tumultuous phase of their development. And yes, in later years, the veteran Peppers proudly served as an opening act for Pearl Jam.

Author's collection

Mick Quinn and drummer Dan Goffey sang backup. The harmonious quartet was then showcasing their third, self-titled album, 1999's *Supergrass*, and the Top Ten single "Moving."

The Red Hot Chili Peppers

The Red Hot Chili Peppers joined Pearl Jam for the final two shows at Seattle's KeyArena on September 5 and 6. This is another of those "circle of life" moments for the band. When you consider the role of founding Pepper Jack Irons in Pearl Jam's history, this was truly an amazing moment. For the final show, they also brought along a side dish: the Wellwater Conspiracy.

The Wellwater Conspiracy

The ominous sounding band was another Matt Cameron side project, as discussed in the "A Little Something on the Side" chapter.

Riot Act Tour Warm-Ups

During the two sets of back-to-back warm-up shows—two at the Showbox and two at KeyArena—Pearl Jam gave the opening slots to NEO, the legendary Steve Earle, Stone's side project, Brad, and old friends, Mudhoney.

NEO

NEO was a Hungarian electronic band in their fourth year of existence. They were showcasing their second album, 2002's *Low-Tech Man, Hi-Tech World*. As fans of the classic Peter Sellers movies, we feel that the coolest thing about NEO was their interpretation of Henry Mancini's "The Pink Panther Theme," which they released as their first single in 1988.

Steve Earle

Steve Earle is a formidably talented singer, songwriter, producer, actor, and published author, whose music covers a wide swath of folk, rock, and country. At the time he joined Pearl Jam in Seattle, he was more of an honored guest than an opening act, and he was showcasing his ninth solo album, 2002's *Jerusalem*.

Riot Act Oceania/Asia 2003

Johnny Marr and the Healers

The opening slot on this leg belonged to English musicians Johnny Marr and the Healers. You may know Marr better as the lead guitarist for the Smiths, the legendary alternative band that also launched Morrissey. Apart from session work with the likes of Sir Paul McCartney and a brief stint in another legendary band, the Pretenders, Johnny Marr and the Healers was Marr's first serious post-Smiths band and featured Zak Starkey (son of Ringo) on the drums (when he wasn't busy with the Who). Their debut album, 2003's *Boomslang*, was hot off the presses. During the three shows in Sydney, Australia, Marr and his band were joined by another opening band, Betachadupa.

Betchadupa

Betchadupa was a New Zealand rock band dating back to 1997. On one level, they are a rock and roll legacy band. Guitarist and vocalist Liam Finn is the son of Neil Finn, and nephew of Tim Finn, who fronted Split Enz. At the time of these Sydney gigs, Betchadupa were pushing their 2002 debut album, *Alphabetchadupa*, which hit number two on the local New Zealand charts. They would release one more album before Liam Finn struck out on his own to begin his solo career.

Riot Act North America, First Leg

Opening slots on the first North American leg were divided between Sleater-Kinney, who opened eleven of the first twelve shows, and Sparta, who opened the final eleven.

Sleater-Kinney

Riot-grrrl group Sleater-Kinney marks their first appearance as Pearl Jam's opening act. The Washingtonian trio of Corin Tucker, Carrie Brownstein, and Janet Weiss formed in 1994. They soon became musical and sociopolitical kindred spirits of Pearl Jam, often joining them onstage for jams. They had recently released their critically acclaimed sixth studio album, 2002's *One Beat.*

Sparta

Down in the west Texas town of El Paso, there was born a band called Sparta. Formed in 2001 by members of At the Drive-in and Engine Down, Sparta had recently released their debut album, 2002's *Wiretap Scars.*

Riot Act North America, Second Leg

As on the first leg, the second leg opening slots were divided between Idlewild, who opened the first fifteen shows, the Buzzcocks, who opened the next thirteen, and a return engagement by Sleater-Kinney, who opened the final eight.

Idlewild

The indie act Idlewild hailed from Edinborough, Scotland, and formed back in 1995. At the time of the *Riot Act* Tour, they were touring on the merits of their third album, 2002's *The Remote Part.* Though they had no way of knowing it at the time, the third time was the charm, and this would be their most commercially successful album. Pearl Jam loved them and even had them come out on stage with them at the United Center for a jam.

The Buzzcocks

The Buzzcocks, too, hailed from across the pond and were formed in Bolton, England. The proto-punk band dates back to 1976 and had previously opened for Nirvana near the end of their run in 1994. At the time of the *Riot Act* Tour, the British veterans were resurgent, having just released their seventh studio album (their first in four years), 2003's eponymous *Buzzcocks.*

No Openings/Old Friends

The brief 2004 Vote for Change Tour featured *no* opening acts. Nor did Pearl Jam feature opening acts during the thirty-four shows on their between-albums 2005 North American and Latin American Tours. The final show on the first leg was a Hurricane Katrina Benefit, held at the Chicago House of Blues, and featured Led Zeppelin's legendary front man, Robert Plant, who was not an "opening act" per se. The Latin American leg of the tour, Pearl Jam's first foray south of the border, kicked off on November 22 in Santiago, Chile, and then hit Argentina and Brazil before winding up in Mexico City on December 10. Old friends Mudhoney opened all nine of these south-of-the-border shows.

Pearl Jam 2006 World Tour

Opening acts continued to be sporadic as Pearl Jam hit the road in support of their self-titled album, *Pearl Jam* (aka the "Avocado Album"), in the spring of 2006. Though there were no opening acts on most of the first leg, My Morning Jacket opened the first two shows at the Air Canada Centre in Toronto. Old friends Sonic Youth returned to open the majority of dates on the second leg.

My Morning Jacket

My Morning Jacket hails from Louisville, Kentucky, a town whose previous claim-to-fame had been the legendary Louisville Slugger baseball bats. Kentucky was a state better known for its bourbon than its bands. The quintet, the brainchild of singer/songwriter Jim James, formed back in 1998. At the time they opened these Toronto shows, My Morning Jacket was still riding on the strengths of its critically acclaimed fourth studio album, 1995's *Z*.

Europe 2007: A Dozen, Cousin

Pearl Jam played a dozen shows of a scheduled thirteen (the Heineken Jammin' Festival was cancelled on June 15). Several of these shows featured opening acts; the other dates were festivals. On June 12, the Futureheads opened the third show of the tour in Munich. They would return on June 21, joined by Interpol, and again on June 26. On June 13, Linkin Park and Coma opened at Selesian Stadium in Katowice, Poland. On June 28, Incubus, Kings of Leon, and Satellite Party opened at Goffertpark in Nijmegen, the Netherlands.

The Futureheads

Hailing from Sunderland, England, the Futureheads were a post-punk four-piece band of college buddies who got together in 2000. When they opened for Pearl Jam, they were showcasing their second studio album, 2006's *News and Tributes*. Though the album garnered good reviews, it did not sell particularly well.

Linkin Park

Linkin Park hail from Agoura Hills, California, and got together in 1996. An "alternative" band, they've also been tagged with labels like "nu-metal," "rap-rock," and "alternative metal," *none* of which manage to effectively capture the band's compellingly heavy sound. By 2007, they were showcasing their new *Minutes to Midnight* album, which debuted at number one in the United States, the UK, and more than a dozen other countries, eventually going triple Platinum. Half of the critics hated it, but it sold eighteen *million* copies. Go figure.

Coma

Local Polish rock band Coma joined Linkin Park in opening for Pearl Jam and were in their ninth year of existence at the time. We're not fluent in Polish, but at the time of this show, they were showcasing their second album, 2006's *Zaprzepaszczone siły wielkiej armii świętych znaków*.

Interpol

Interpol hailed from New York City and joined the Futureheads in opening the June 21 show in Düsseldorf, Germany. Formed in 1997, it was, and remains, a four-piece rock band commonly lumped in with the so-called "New York Indie scene." At this time, they were on the cusp of releasing their third studio album, 2007's *Our Love to Admire*.

Incubus

Incubus hails from the San Fernando Valley city of Calabassas, California, and had been around as long as Pearl Jam by this point. At the time of the June 28 show, they were still riding high on 2006's *Light Grenades*, which started out strong but dropped like a stone, failing to attain the Platinum status of its three predecessors.

Kings of Leon

Kings of Leon joined Incubus that day. The Followill brothers—Caleb, Nathan, and Jared—along with cousin, Matt, hail from the holy land of country music, Nashville, Tennessee, but they are rock and rollers by trade. Seven years into their careers on this day, they were showcasing their third album, *Because of the Times*, and were in the midst of their period of greatest commercial success.

Satellite Party

Rounding out the party on June 28 was an old friend in a new guise. Perry Farrell of Jane's Addiction (and Lollapalooza) fame formed this post-Jane's band with his wife, Etty Lau Farrell, and bass player Carl Restivo. They were showcasing their one and only album, 2007's *Ultra Payload*.

Pearl Jam United States Tour 2008

Returning friends, Kings of Leon opened the first four dates from June 11 though June 17, with the exception of the Bonnaroo Music Festival on June 14, while some new faces, Ted Leo and the Pharmacists, opened the final nine dates.

Ted Leo and the Pharmacists

A Washington D.C. band dating back to 1999, the neo-punk band consists of main man Ted Leo and a revolving door cast of "Pharmacists" over the years. At the time of this tour, they were working out 2007's *Living with the Living*.

Backspacer Tour 2009–2010

The *Backspacer* Tour would feature Gomez opening the bulk of the European dates, as well as the return of Ted Leo and the Pharmacists for one show. Bad Religion opened four; old friend Ben Harper with his new band, the Relentless7, played ten; and old Betchadupa friend Liam Finn, now solo, opened all seven of the Oceania dates. Band of Horses ruled the opening slot on the North American leg, with the exception of May 20, when the Black Keys opened.

Gomez

Gomez is an English "Indie" band dating back to 1997. At the time of the *Backspacer* Tour, they had released their sixth studio album, *A New Tide*, and opened all five of the shows on the European leg of the tour.

Social Distortion

Social Distortion is the real deal—a punk rock band from Fullerton, California, dating back to 1978—that continues to record and perform as of this writing. They opened the October 27 and 28 shows on this tour. At this time, they were about eight months away from the release of their seventh studio album, 2011's *Hard Times and Nursery Rhymes*.

Band of Horses

Band of Horses opened twelve of the thirteen 2010 North American shows; The Black Keys subbed for them on May 20. The young Seattle band formed in 2004 and was now a part of Pearl Jam's home team. During this tour, they had a brand new album (their third), *Infinite Arms*, hot off the presses, which would garner a Grammy Award nomination for Best Alternative Album.

The Black Keys

Hailing from Akron, Ohio, the Black Keys are a two-man band consisting of childhood buddies Dan Auerbach on the guitar and Patrick Carney on the drums.

And to think it all began with that legendary camping trip, when Eddie astounded Flea, Jack Irons, and their friends with his daredevil, "Crazy Eddie" antics. They don't come much raunchier or funkier than the Red Hot Chili Peppers, still going strong to this day.   *Author's collection*

They first started playing bluesy rock together back in 2001. Their debut album, *The Big Come Up*, was released in 2002, but they really caught a wave during 2010 with the album, *Brothers*, which featured their infectious hit "Tighten Up." The album hit number three on the *Billboard* 200, so this was a perfect time to make a live appearance with Pearl Jam.

The Pearl Jam Twenty Tour 2012

On this celebratory twentieth anniversary jaunt, old friends Mudhoney opened all of the North American dates, except for those in Costa Rica and Mexico. Those dates, plus all of the South America shows, were covered by old friends X.

The Pearl Jam 2012 Tour

Once again, old friends X covered all ten of the non-festival dates on the European leg of the tour, while neighborhood friends Mudhoney opened the one non-festival show in North America at Missoula's Adams Centre.

Lightning Bolt Tour 2013–14

Support acts were once again sporadic on the *Lightning Bolt* Tour. Mudhoney opened four dates in North America, and Midlake opened a pair. Black Rebel Motorcycle Club and Off! opened the festive July 11 gig at the Milton Keynes Bowl in England.

Midlake

A new face on this tour, Midlake opened two shows, Dallas and Oklahoma City. The location was appropriate for the six-piece band of folk-rockers, who hail from Denton, Texas. Formed in 1999, they had *just* released their 2013 album, *Antiphon*, in time for these opening slots. And that was it for North American opening acts. On the European leg, Black Rebel Motorcycle Club and Off! opened the festivities at the Milton Keynes Bowl.

Black Rebel Motorcycle Club

Not to be confused with Zakk Wylde's Black Label Society (though they often are), Black Rebel Motorcycle Club took its name from one of the gangs in the iconic 1953 Marlon Brando and Lee Marvin biker film, *The Wild One*. At the time of the Milton Keynes gig, BRMC had just released their seventh studio album, 2013's *Specter at the Feast*.

Off!

Joining BRMC in opening for Pearl Jam on this night was Off! Off! may have been a new name, but the 2009 act was the brainchild of Keith Morris, Henry Rollins' predecessor as Black Flag vocalist and former member of hardcore punk icons, Circle Jerks. They had just released their third album, 2014's *Wasted Years*, earlier that spring.

Pearl Jam 2015 Latin American Tour

As we went to press, there had been no announcements made about opening acts for Pearl Jam's (then) forthcoming 2015 Latin American Tour.

30

Global Citizens

Heading into the Future

A Bolt of Inspiration as *Lightning Bolt* Strikes

The ideas and conversations that led to the book you are now holding in your hands began during the winter of 2014, just as Pearl Jam was coming off the third leg of their *Lightning Bolt* Tour in Oceania. As we embarked on this journey, Pearl Jam enjoyed three-and-a-half months off the road, and then headed to Europe for the fourth leg of the tour on June 16. Our work continued as the band returned stateside after a big outdoor concert at England's Milton-Keynes Bowl on July 11.

As this book took shape, Pearl Jam, too, continued to take shape. Our muse was, and remains, a living, breathing entity, and did not simply sit still and strike a pose as we constructed a narrative around it. No. This eclectic assemblage of musicians remained dynamic and went on being Pearl Jam. Indeed, it is entirely likely, given the band's current set of circumstances, and barring any unforeseen circumstances, that their journey will continue long after you have finished reading this book and placed it upon your shelf. As fans, that is what we desire most. This was never meant to be an epitaph; it was meant to be a celebration of an extraordinary band with a compelling story. That story continued to unfold all throughout the writing and production of this book.

Autumn 2014

Roughly five weeks after we signed our contract and began this journey, Pearl Jam took off on another leg of its own journey. On October 1, 2014, they embarked on the fifth leg of the *Lightning Bolt* Tour in North America, their *third* North American leg on this particular tour. Though we chronicle that entire tour in detail in chapter twenty-three, "*Lightning Bolt* Strikes," it bears repeating that Pearl Jam wrapped things up with back-to-back appearances at the Bridge School Benefit in Mountainview, California, on October 25 and 26, capping the tour with a rousing rendition of "Throw Your Hatred Down." Nothing captures the ethos of Pearl Jam more perfectly than the idea that they would wrap up a major world tour with a pair of charity concert appearances. They could easily have sold out the biggest stadium in the country and ended the tour in grand style. Instead they continue to show great humility and an innate awareness of the things that are truly important. The journey continues.

Anyone for Tennis?

On November 17, 2014, we were surprised to pick up a copy of the *New York Daily News* and read an Eli Rosenberg piece detailing a supposed controversy between competing factions of Pearl Jam fans. A guy named Dan Sheffer is part of a group of East Coast Pearl Jam fans who were trying to get the band to play at the historic Forest Hills Tennis Stadium in Forest Hills, Queens. Rosenberg claims Pearl Jam fans from the Wishlist Foundation have attempted to thwart his crowdsourcing efforts. This West Coast faction wants the band to play closer to Seattle, at the Gorge Amphitheater, the site of many of the band's greatest in-concert moments, as we have seen. Hmmm. We may not possess Solomonic wisdom, but what exactly is the issue here? Couldn't the band, at this stage in its career, play pretty much wherever the mood strikes them? It seems like a non-issue to us. Oh, and as far as Forest Hills Tennis Stadium is concerned, for all of its many charms and storied history (Tom has seen Yes, Peter Gabriel, and the Further Festival there), it does have one or two flaws. Essentially it sits on one side of a residential street, and in deference to its location, shows have a 10:00 p.m. curfew—not very "rock and roll."

The Ice Bucket Challenge

The Ice Bucket Challenge, more properly known as the ALS Ice Bucket Challenge, was a cultural phenomenon during the summer of 2014. The idea behind the challenge is simple: those people who are challenged have twenty-four hours from the moment they receive the challenge to film themselves having a bucket of ice water dumped over their heads and to pass the challenge on to three (or more) others. If they fail to make good on the challenge, they have to make a charitable donation to ALS research.

Mike McCready was challenged by his friend, Steve Gleason, and passed along the challenge in grand style. He challenged *all* of his Pearl Jam bandmates, plus Ben "Macklemore" Haggerty, former Guns N' Roses bassist Duff McKagan, Stefan Lessard, and Mike Wells, all at the same time. Then, while riding his skateboard, he had a bucket of ice water thrown directly in his face by his friend as he rolled by. Duff McKagan stepped up to the challenge, as did Eddie Vedder—who challenged Tim Robbins, Bruce Springsteen, and, at his daughter's behest, Niall Horan from boy band du jour, One Direction—before having a beer tub of icewater poured over his head by a friend. Jeff Ament, surfboard in hand, challenged his surfer bros Brent Barry, Frank Brickowski, and Kenny Mayne, and then took the challenge in dramatic fashion, taking a bucket of ice water in the face as he surfed in the wake of a boat. Stone made sure to show his check for $5,000 to ALS, and challenged Josh Freese, along with "all Pearl Jam fans," before taking a beer cooler full of icewater over the head (oddly, he was still holding the check, which got wet). Last but not least, Matt Cameron accepted the challenge. He enlisted his son, Ray, to pour water over his head after challenging John Tempesta, Neil Hunt, and assorted members of the Cameron family. After a brief consultation with Ray, he added Josh Evans to his list. Even Boom Gaspar, Pearl Jam's "sixth man" off the bench, stepped up to the plate for ALS, taking a bucket of icewater over the head while sitting on a rock by the seaside; he may even have challenged someone else, but his accent makes it difficult for us to tell for certain. Good work, guys.

The Global Citizen Festival

Central Park. New York City. September 26, 2015. In July 2015, it was announced that Pearl Jam would join Beyoncé, Coldplay, and Ed Sheeran in headlining the 2015 Global Citizen Festival, to be held on the Great Lawn in Central Park. Tickets became available in mid-July. "Became available," as opposed to, "went on sale." There was a catch with this festival.

One couldn't simply call or go online to purchase them (the expensive "VIP tickets," available through our old friend Ticketmaster, being the exception to the rule). Rather, one had to register online at globalcitzen-festival.com and commit to taking an "Action Journey" to earn tickets to the festival. All of the required actions were geared towards attaining the festival's overarching goal, which is captured succinctly on the festival's posters: "Take Action/Earn Tickets/See Impact: Launch the Global Goals and Join the

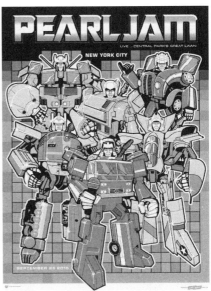

Manager Kelly Curtis has served the Global Citizen Festival in an advisory capacity since its 2012 inception, so it was inevitable that Pearl Jam would eventually headline the annual Central Park event. On the weekend of September 26, 2015, Pearl Jam fans from all over the world converged on the Big Apple to experience their heroes' triumphant return to the stage. Upon their arrival, posters, such as this Transformers-themed specimen, adorned the city to greet them.   *Ryan Byrne*

Movement to End Extreme Poverty." Toward that end, one could volunteer, man the phones, or personally lobby the State Department to commit funding or allocate half of its foreign aid budget to impoverished nations. Among the Global Goals was bringing electricity to underserved parts of Africa, providing educational opportunities, ending polio, aiding refugees, and spreading the word to others who might be able to help.

The window of opportunity to obtain tickets closed on September 16 after the "draw" was held. Naturally, as one might expect, the "secondary market" (a clever euphemism for legalized scalping, in our opinion) was flooded with tickets the very next day.

Pearl Jam, as civic minded and charitable a group of guys as you are apt to find, first became involved with Global Citizen Festival back in 2012, when their manager, Kelly Curtis, signed on to the nonprofit in an advisory capacity; so it's about time that they took the stage. That first iteration of Global Citizen Festival was a great show, too. Held on September 29, 2012, it featured performances by some of Pearl Jam's old friends, including Neil Young and Crazy Horse, the Foo Fighters, the Black Keys, Band of Horses, K'naan, and John Legend. The following year's lineup wasn't too shabby either. On September 27, 2013, the Great Lawn hosted the likes of Kings of Leon, Stevie Wonder, Alicia Keys, Elvis Costello, and John Mayer. The Saturday, September 27, 2014, lineup featured Carrie Underwood, No Doubt (with a cameo by Sting), Fun, hometown hero Jay-Z (with an appearance by Beyoncé), Tiësto, and the Roots.

Once the lineup was announced, it became a foregone conclusion that Global Citizen Festival 2015 would at least live up to the legacy of its predecessors, if not surpass it. But, true to form, Pearl Jam strove to keep fans' minds on the *real* purpose for their appearance there. *Billboard*'s Andrew Hampp quoted Stone Gossard as saying:

> We hope Pearl Jam fans will sign up to become Global Citizens—not just to earn tickets to the show—but to be part of a movement that encourages leaders of nations with the greatest wealth to apply aid, trade, and governance policies in support of nations and communities in the greatest need. People living on less than $1.50-a-day deserve the opportunity to lift themselves up out of extreme poverty.

A wide array of corporate, nonprofit, and civic sponsors lent their support to the 2015 festival, among them Citi Band, YouTube, Gucci, Chime for Change, Google, T-Mobile, MSNBC, the Bill & Melinda Gates Foundation, and the New York City Parks Department.

Live, from the Great Lawn in New York City's Central Park

The weather gods were clearing smiling for the Global Citizen Festival on September 26. At a comfortable high of 72°F, it was neither too hot, nor too cold. There was no rain, but just enough intermittent cloud cover to mute the effects of the sun's rays. Pearl Jam fans had come from across the country to enjoy the sights, sounds, and smells of New York City, many making a long weekend of it. With the U.N. General Assembly in session, and both Pope Francis and the Obamas in and out of town, this was an exciting weekend to be in the Big Apple (provided one wasn't driving a car, of course!).

The Festival kicked off with a performance by Chris Martin and his band, Coldplay, who had the presence of mind to debut a new song, the aptly titled (if presumptuous) "Amazing Day," which was well received by the appreciative crowd. As it turned out, Martin would be proved correct; this *was* an amazing day.

Ed Sheeran, this generation's answer to the classic singer/songwriter, wrung as much power out of his modestly sized acoustic guitar and vocals as he could muster, and he clearly had the audience in his thrall.

Beyoncé, something of a local celebrity in New York City, gave a typically larger-than-life performance, kicking it off with "Crazy in Love." But this was not all empty-headed pop music frivolity. Beyoncé understood the importance of the occasion and offered a healthy dose of feminist sensibility to the otherwise all-male lineup. Snippets of Maya Angelou's poetry readings punctuated her performances, as did a reading from Chimamanda Ngozi Adichie, a critically acclaimed writer from Nigeria whose repertoire grew from poetry to short stories to novels. At one point, Ed Sheeran joined "Queen Bey" for a duet on "Drunk in Love."

As at Live Aid, thirty years earlier, the transitional periods between bands featured many speeches, ostensibly tailored to remind the assembled why they were there. Co-hosts Stephen Colbert and Hugh Jackman did their best to keep the crowd focused on the business at hand, with a little help from Bono, First Lady Michelle Obama, Vice President Joe Biden, Leonardo DiCaprio, and Nobel Prize laureate Malala Yousafzai. Then, there were the obligatory speeches from the corporate bigwigs and visiting governmental dignitaries.

Finally, after what seemed an interminable wait for the faithful, Pearl Jam took to the stage and delivered a dozen songs. They got things off to a roaring start with "Mind Your Manners," a ferocious punk rocker that reminded the audience of the band's aggressive early days. "Do the Evolution" seemed aptly suited for the occasion, evoking images from the video, which chronicled some of the darker periods of human history. "Given to Fly," the number one single from *Yield*, never fails to inspire, and this occasion was no different: as evidenced on Facebook's many Pearl Jam fan pages, at least one young lady visited a tattoo parlor that weekend to

From the personal collection of Ten Clubber Jen Manlove, here is a Pearl Jam-themed, St. Christopher-style medal bidding its owner "Safe Travels." The backdrop incorporates familiar elements of the Great Seal of the United States, with the arrows and olive branch representing the continuing dialectic tension between war and peace. The sentiments expressed herein are particularly poignant as the band hits the road to begin the next phase of its legendary career.

Jen Manlove

have the words "Given to Fly" tattooed on her forearm. The fourth song, "Elderly Woman Behind the Counter in a Small Town," mellowed out the crowd, who dutifully sang along on the chorus. Meanwhile, those watching at home on MSNBC were fuming at a lengthy tape delay and an on-the-fly rearrangement of the set list, which omitted fan favorites like "Elderly Woman Behind the Counter in a Small Town" and "Daughter."

"Lightning Bolt," the title track from the band's most recent album, was fifth, followed by the beautiful yet disturbing "Daughter." True to form, Eddie tagged "Daughter" with a tribute to New York legends the Ramones by intoning softly, "Hey Ho, Let's Go." The thought-provoking "Unthought Known" followed, and they closed out the regular set with the one-two punch of their classics, "Better Man" and "Alive," which whipped the crowd into a frenzy of joy, as always.

The encore set began in mellow fashion, with Eddie solo on acoustic guitar, paying homage to one of Central Park's long lost legends, John Lennon, on "Imagine," as the crowd sang along. Next up was a duet for the ages, as Beyoncé once more took to the stage to join Eddie on a beautiful rendition of Bob Marley and the Wailers' "Redemption Song," while Nelson Mandela's image spoke in the background, "Overcoming poverty is not a gesture of charity. It is the protection of a fundamental human right."

The grand finale of the festival found Pearl Jam tearing into Neil Young's "Rockin' in the Free World" while just about every other performer and speaker who had graced the stage that day returned to help them bring it on home. It was earnest, manic, and joyous all at once, which is perhaps the perfect way to describe Pearl Jam. At one point, Eddie, in his own inimitable way, summed up the spirit of the event by invoking his guiding metaphor, the ocean. Looking out at the crowd and deeming them to be "one hundred percent activists," he said, "We just want to thank you for making this wave of hope, that can rise and it can grow. And I hope it smashes on the shore of cynicism and apathy." We hope so, too.

Selected Bibliography

American Red Cross. http://www.redcross.org/

Ankeny, Jason. Arthur Alexander. Artist Biography by Jason Ankeny. http://www .allmusic.com/artist/arthuralexandermn0000931202/biography

Artists for Peace and Justice. www.artistsforpeaceandjustice.com

Bad Religion. http://www.badreligion.com/

Boyd, Glen. *Neil Young FAQ: Everything Left to Know About the Iconic and Mercurial Rocker.* Montclair, NJ: Backbeat Books, 2012.

Brad. http://www.bradcorporation.com/

Brennan, Carol. "Droge, Pete." *Contemporary Musicians,* 1999. Encyclopedia.com. (February 21, 2015). http://www.encyclopedia.com/doc/1G2-3494200023.html

Bridge School, The. https://www.bridgeschool.org

Buchanan, Brett. "Screaming Trees Look Back At 'Nearly Lost You' 20 Years Later." Alternative Nation. http://www.alternativenation.net/screaming -trees-look -back-at-nearly-lost-you-20-years-later/

Budnick, Dean, and Josh Baron. *Ticket Masters: The Rise of the Concert Industry and How the Public Got Scalped.* New York: Penguin, 2012.

Buffalo Tom. http://www.buffalotom.com/

Bulgakov, Mikhail. *The Master and Margarita.* Paris: YMCA Press, 1967.

Bush, John. Artist Biography: Shudder to Think. AllMusic.com. http://www .allmusic.com/artist/shudder-to-thinkmn0000752635/biography

Cabrera, Luis. "Grunge Rockers Work Days to Play Nights." *Free-Lance Star,* July 5, 1993.

Caraeff, Ezra Ace. "The Best Kissers in the World Are Still a Band, Now Based in Portland." http://www.portlandmercury.com/endhits/archives/2010/05/03/ tbest-kissers-in the-world-are-still-a-band-now-based-in-portland

Cascade Land Conservancy (now Fortera): http://forterra.org/

Cedars-Sinai. Samuel Oschin Comprehensive Cancer Institute: Louis Warschaw Prostate Cancer Center. http://research.csmc.edu/acad/cancer?

Cheap Trick. http://www.cheaptrick.com/

Clarke, Martin. *Pearl Jam & Eddie Vedder: None Too Fragile.* London: Plexus, 1998.

Coalition of Independent Music Stores (CIMS). http://www.cimsmusic.com/

Codeine's "semi-official" website. http://www.heartofthunder.com/codeine/who .htm

Cohen, Jonathan and Mark Wilkerson. *Pearl Jam Twenty.* New York: Simon & Schuster, 2011.

Conservation International: http://www.conservation.org

Cornell, Chris. Interviewed by Damon Stewart. KISW. April 14, 1991.

Crohn's & Colitis Foundation of America (CCFA). http://www.ccfa.org/

Crohn's & Colitis Foundation of Canada (CCFC) http://www.crohnsandcolitis.ca/site/c.dtJRL9NUJmL4H/b.9012407/k.BE24/Home.htm

Crowe, Cameron. "Five Against the World." *Rolling Stone*, October 28, 1993.

Crowe, Cameron. *Pearl Jam Twenty*. DVD. Directed by Cameron Crowe, 2011.

Cult, The. http://www.thecult.us/

Deming, Mark. Artist Biography: The Fastbacks. http://www.allmusic.com/artist/fastbacks-mn0000174582/biography

Distance Between Cities: Distance from Seattle, WA to San Diego, CA. http://www.distance-cities.com/distance-seattle-wa-to-san-diego-ca

Doyle Patrick. "Q&A: Eddie Vedder on West Memphis Three, New Pearl Jam Music." *Rolling Stone*, January 2, 2013.

Dunn, Sam and Scot McFadyen (Dir.). *Grunge. Metal Evolution*. VH1 2011 documentary series. Original Broadcast Date: January 7, 2012.

Eleven. Elevenworld. http://www.elevenworld.com

Enter the Soul Asylum. http://enterthesoulasylum.com/

Erlewine, Stephen Thomas. About J. Frank Wilson. http://www.mtv.com/artists/j-frank-wilson/biography/

———Artist Biography: The Ramones. http://www.allmusic.com/artist/the-ramones-mn0000490004/biography

Exonerate the West Memphis Three Support Fund. http://www.wm3.org/

Fastbacks, The. Sub Pop. https://www.subpop.com/artists/fastbacks

Folk Music Center Museum & Store. http://folkmusiccenter.com/

Food and Agriculture Organization of the United Nations (FAO): http://www.fao.org/about/en/

Food Lifeline. https://foodlifeline.org/

Fornatale, Pete, Peter Thomas Fornatale, and Bernard M. Corbett. *50 Licks: Myths & Stories from Half a Century of the Rolling Stones*. New York: Bloomsbury, 2013.

Fornatale, Pete. *Back to the Garden*. New York: Touchstone, 2009.

Fortera (aka: Cascade Land Conservancy): http://forterra.org/

Fricke, David. "Nine Dead at Pearl Jam Concert." *Rolling Stone*, August 17, 2000.

Gaston, Peter. "Listen: Five Bands Inspired by Shudder to Think." *Spin*, October 3, 2008.

Gateway Battered Women's Services. http://www.gatewayshelter.org/

Graff, Gary. "Pearl Jam's Jeff Ament Talks New Project, Tres Mts." *Billboard*, March 15, 2011.

Green Party of the United States. http://www.gp.org/index.php

Greene, Andy. "Reader's Poll: The Ten Best Pearl Jam Deep Cuts." *Rolling Stone*, June 15, 2015.

Greenpeace. http://www.greenpeace.org/usa/en/

Habitat for Humanity. https://www.habitat.org

Hampp, Andrew. "Beyoncé, Coldplay, Pearl Jam to Headline New York's 2015 Global Citizen Festival." *Rolling Stone*, July 9, 2015.

Harper, Ben. Ben Harper.com. http://www.benharper.com/

Heaney, John. (of the Missoulian) "A Team Player: What Might Have Been for Jeff Ament." *Seattle Threads*, 2008. http://webspace.ringling.edu/~hclark/seattle_threads/interviews_story.php

Hiattposted, Brian. "The Second Coming of Pearl Jam: A Decade After Turning Their Backs on Fame, Seattle's Grunge Survivors Are Ready for Act Two." *Rolling Stone*, June 16, 2006.

Home Alive. http://www.teachhomealive.org/

I Love You. http://www.discogs.com/artist/1436854-I-Love-You-4

Jayhawks, The. http://www.jayhawksofficial.com/

Jazz Foundation Of America. azzfoundation.org

Kaufman, Gil. "R.E.M., Pearl Jam, Nine Inch Nails Join Campaign to Close Guantanamo Bay." *MTV News*, October 22, 2009 http://www.mtv.com/news/1624448/rem-pearl-jam-nine-inch-nails-join-campaign-to-close-guantanamo-bay/

Kloke, Joshua. "I Don't Want to Be a Soldier: An Interview with Pearl Jam's Mike McCready." *PopMatters*, April 2, 2013.

L7. http://l7theband.com/

Lemonheads, The. http://www.thelemonheads.net/

Letkemann, Jessica, and John Reynolds. "How Did Mookie Blaylock Become Pearl Jam?" *Two Feet Thick* (http://www.twofeetthick.com/2011/03/how-did-mookie-blaylock-become-pearl-jam/), March 10, 2011.

Locey, Bill. "L.A. Band Re-Creating Own 'Stoned Age Rock' Sound: I Love You Will Give Its Debut Performance Friday at the Metro Bay Club in Ventura." *L.A. Times*, February 17, 1994. http://articles.latimes.com/1994-02-17/news/vl-23993_1_stoned-age-rock

Maryville Academy. http://www.maryvilleacademy.org/

McDonough, Jimmy. *Shakey: Neil Young's Biography*. New York: Knopf Doubleday Publishing Group, 2003.

Monkees, The. http://www.monkees.com/

Monster Magnet. Official Monster Magnet Headquarters. http://www.zodiaclung.com/

Moss, Corey. "U2, Coldplay, Pearl Jam Added to MTV Disaster Relief Show: ReAct Now: Music & Relief airs Saturday at 8PM." *MTV News*, September 9, 2005. http://www.mtv.com/news/1509254/u2-coldplay-pearl-jam-added-to-mtv-disaster-relief-show/

Mount Graham Coalition: http://www.mountgraham.org/

Murder Victims' Families for Reconciliation. http://www.mvfr.org/

Music Masters. *Pearl Jam: The Story of America's Last Rock 'n' Roll Band*. Amazon, November 15, 2014.

Nader, Ralph. Ralph Nader. https://nader.org/

Naked Raygun: The Official Site. http://www.nakedraygun.org/

National Campaign to Close Guantanamo. http://www.fitzgibbonmedia.com/national-campaign-to-close-guantanamo-2/

Ned's Atomic Dustbin. http://www.nedsatomicdustbin.com/

Neely, Kim. *Five Against One: The Pearl Jam Story*. New York: Penguin, 1998.

Newton, Sir Isaac. A Letter to Robert Hooke. February 5, 1676. www.isaacnewton.org.uk/essays/Giants

NFL Kick Hunger Challenge. http://support.tasteofthenfl.com

Nirvana. http://www.nirvana.com/

Northwest School, The. http://www.northwestschool.org

O'Donnell, Kevin. "EXCLUSIVE: Pearl Jam's Ament Debuts Tres Mts." *Spin*, March 4, 2011.

Open Secrets.org. The Center for Responsive Politics: https://www.opensecrets .org/pacs/lookup2.php?strID=C00388876

Pareles, Jon. "Review: Global Citizen Festival, Including Beyoncé and Pearl Jam, Mixes Music and Activism." *New York Times*, September 27, 2015.

Powers, Ann. "It's a lot to live up to: But Eddie Vedder pulls it off. As he begins his first solo tour, he comes across as thoughtful and sociable." The *Los Angeles Times*. April 4, 2008.

Quinn, Daniel. *Ishmael: An Adventure of the Mind and Spirit.* New York: Bantam, 1992.

Rage Against the Machine. http://www.ratm.com/

Ramones, The. Biography. *Rolling Stone.* http://www.rollingstone.com/music/ artists/the-ramones/biography

Red Hot Chili Peppers. http://redhotchilipeppers.com/

Redd Kross. http://reddkross.com/

"Retired Generals, Veterans Group and Former Congressman Launch Campaign to Close Gitmo." Common Dreams: Breaking News & Views for the Progressive Community, October 20, 2009. http://www.commondreams.org/ newswire/2009/10/20

Reverend Horton Heat. http://www.reverendhortonheat.com/

Robb, Robbi. Robbirobb.com. Tribe After Tribe Bio. http://www.robbirobb.com/ tribeaftertribe/index.html

—— Robbirobb.com. Three Fish Bio. http://www.robbirobb.com/threefish/ index.html

Robin Hood Foundation. https://www.robinhood.org/

Rock for Choice. Feminist Majority Foundation. http://www.feminist.org/rock4c/

Rock the Vote. http://www.rockthevote.com/

Rodriguez, Robert. *Fab Four FAQ 2.0.* Montclair: Backbeat Books, 2010.

Roe v. Wade – Case Brief Summary. http://www.lawnix.com/cases/roe-wade.html

Rolling Stones, The. http://www.rollingstones.com/

Rosenberg, Eli. "Fans in a Jam: Group's Backers in Tiff Over Concert Venue." *New York Daily News*, November 17, 2014.

Ruhlmann, William. Biography: Best Kissers in the World. http://www.allmusic .com/artist/best-kissers-in-the-world-mn0000052523

Rush, Otis. 20111123/otis-rush-20111122—Otis Rush.net. http://www.otisrush.net/ OtisRush18_home.html

Rolling Stone's 100 Greatest Guitarists. http://www.rollingstone.com/music/lists/ 100-greatest-guitarists-

Santana, Carlos, Ashley Kahn and Hal Miller. *The Universal Tone: Bringing My Story to Light.* New York: Little, Brown and Company, 2014.

Santana.com. The Official Website of Carlos Santana. http://www.santana.com/

Schulz, David. "Screaming full-on punk the way it should be!" Amazon.com, May 1, 2001. http://www.amazon.com/review

Seattle Seahawks, The. http://www.seahawks.com/

September 11th Fund, The. http://www.september11fund.org/

Siamese Dream (1993; The Smashing Pumpkins)

Silver Lake Conservatory of Music: http://www.silverlakeconservatory.org/

Sisters of Mercy. http://www.the-sisters-of-mercy.com/

Smashing Pumpkins Nexus. http://www.smashingpumpkinsnexus.com/

Smith, Shawn. http://www.shawnsmithsinger.com/

Soul Asylum. http://www.soulasylum.com/

Soundgarden World. http://soundgardenworld.com/

Stout, Gene. "Pearl Jam Thrills Benaroya Throng." *Seattle Post-Intelligencer*, Wednesday, October 22, 2003. http://www.seattlepi.com/ae/music/article/Pearl-Jam-thrills-Benaroyathrong-1127743.php#photo-635128

Surfrider Foundation, The. http://www.surfrider.org/

Sutton, Michael. Venus Beads: Biography by Michael Sutton. http://www.allmusic.com/artist/venus-beads-mn0000841679/biography

Swervedriver.com. http://www.swervedriver.com/

Teenage Cancer Trust. https://www.teenagecancertrust.org/

Teen Cancer America. https://teencanceramerica.org/

Therapy? http://www.therapyquestionmark.co.uk/

Tibetan Freedom. Free Tibet. http://freetibet.org/

Tom Petty and the Heartbreakers. http://www.tompetty.com/

Travel Math. http://www.travelmath.com/flying-distance/from/Aberdeen,+WA/to/Seattle,+WA

Trip Shakespeare. http://www.tripshakespeare.com/

U2. http://www.u2.com/index/home

"Uncut Artist Interview: Pearl Jam's Eddie Vedder." *Uncut*. August 6, 2009.

Urge Overkill. http://urgeoverkill.com/

US Senator for Montana: John Tester. http://www.tester.senate.gov/

Van Morrison. http://www.vanmorrison.com/

Vedder, Eddie. "Reclamation." *Spin*, November 1992. http://www.freewebs.com/pearljamstudy/992spinmagazinereclamati.htm

Vedder, Eddie. "100 Greatest Artists. No. 29: The Who." *Rolling Stone*, December 2, 2010. http://www.rollingstone.com/music/lists/100-greatest-artists-of-all-time-19691231/the-who-20110420

Vitalogy Foundation. http://pearljam.com/activism/vitalogy-foundation

Voters for Choice—Feminist.com. http://www.feminist.com/voters.htm

Vozick-Levinson, Simon. "Pearl Jam Reward Fans with Epic Two-Day Festival." *Rolling Stone*, September 6, 2011.

Weidman, Rich. *The Doors FAQ: All That's Left to Know About the Kings of Acid Rock.* Montclair, NJ: Backbeat Books, 2011.

Weisbard, Eric, et al. "Ten Past Ten." *Spin Online*, August 2001.

White, Richard T. "The Art of the Deal: How Mother Love Bone Got One of the Biggest Record Deals of the Rear." The *Rocket*, January, 1989

Wilson, MacKenzie. Ben Harper Biography. AllMusic.com. http://www.allmusic
.com/artist/ben-harper-mn0000792733/biography

Wishlist Foundation: A Pearl Jam Fan Nonprofit Organization. http://wishlist
foundation.org/

Yarm, Mark. *Everybody Loves Our Town: An Oral History of Grunge.* New York: Three
Rivers Press, 2011.

YouthCare. http://youthcare.crchealth.com

Index

THE FAQ SERIES

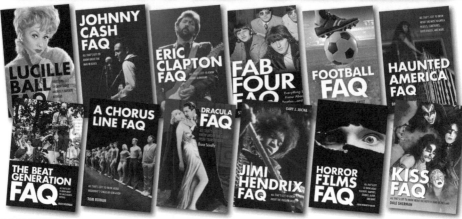

AC/DC FAQ
by Susan Masino
Backbeat Books
978-1-4803-9450-6.......... $24.99

Armageddon Films FAQ
by Dale Sherman
Applause Books
978-1-61713-119-6................. $24.99

Lucille Ball FAQ
by James Sheridan
and Barry Monush
Applause Books
978-1-61774-082-4................$19.99

The Beach Boys FAQ
by Jon Stebbins
Backbeat Books
978-0-87930-987-9...........$22.99

The Beat Generation FAQ
by Rich Weidman
Backbeat Books
978-1-61713-601-6 ....$19.99

Black Sabbath FAQ
by Martin Popoff
Backbeat Books
978-0-87930-957-2.............$19.99

Johnny Cash FAQ
by C. Eric Banister
Backbeat Books
978-1-4803-8540-5......... $24.99

A Chorus Line FAQ
by Tom Rowan
Applause Books
978-1-4803-6754-8 ....$19.99

Eric Clapton FAQ
by David Bowling
Backbeat Books
978-1-61713-454-8................$22.99

Doctor Who FAQ
by Dave Thompson
Applause Books
978-1-55783-854-4.............$22.99

The Doors FAQ
by Rich Weidman
Backbeat Books
978-1-61713-017-5................ $24.99

Dracula FAQ
by Bruce Scivally
Backbeat Books
978-1-61713-600-9 ....$19.99

The Eagles FAQ
by Andrew Vaughan
Backbeat Books
978-1-4803-8541-2 .... $24.99

Fab Four FAQ
by Stuart Shea and
Robert Rodriguez
Hal Leonard Books
978-1-4234-2138-2................$19.99

Fab Four FAQ 2.0
by Robert Rodriguez
Backbeat Books
978-0-87930-968-8...........$19.99

Film Noir FAQ
by David J. Hogan
Applause Books
978-1-55783-855-1................$22.99

Football FAQ
by Dave Thompson
Backbeat Books
978-1-4950-0748-4 .... $24.99

Prices, contents, and availability
subject to change without notice.

The Grateful Dead FAQ
by Tony Sclafani
Backbeat Books
978-1-61713-086-1............... $24.99

Haunted America FAQ
by Dave Thompson
Backbeat Books
978-1-4803-9262-5.............$19.99

Jimi Hendrix FAQ
by Gary J. Jucha
Backbeat Books
978-1-61713-095-3...............$22.99

Horror Films FAQ
by John Kenneth Muir
Applause Books
978-1-55783-950-3.............$22.99

James Bond FAQ
by Tom DeMichael
Applause Books
978-1-55783-856-8............$22.99

Stephen King Films FAQ
by Scott Von Doviak
Applause Books
978-1-4803-5551-4 .... $24.99

KISS FAQ
by Dale Sherman
Backbeat Books
978-1-61713-091-5................$22.99

Led Zeppelin FAQ
by George Case
Backbeat Books
978-1-61713-025-0 ....$19.99

Modern Sci-Fi Films FAQ
by Tom DeMichael
Applause Books
978-1-4803-5061-8............ $24.99

Morrissey FAQ
by D. McKinney
Backbeat Books
978-1-4803-9448-3........... $24.99

Nirvana FAQ
by John D. Luerssen
Backbeat Books
978-1-61713-450-0............ $24.99

Pink Floyd FAQ
by Stuart Shea
Backbeat Books
978-0-87930-950-3...........$19.99

Elvis Films FAQ
by Paul Simpson
Applause Books
978-1-55783-858-2............ $24.99

Elvis Music FAQ
by Mike Eder
Backbeat Books
978-1-61713-049-6............ $24.99

Prog Rock FAQ
by Will Romano
Backbeat Books
978-1-61713-587-3............. $24.99

Pro Wrestling FAQ
by Brian Solomon
Backbeat Books
978-1-61713-599-6............. $29.99

Rush FAQ
by Max Mobley
Backbeat Books
978-1-61713-451-7............... $24.99

Saturday Night Live FAQ
by Stephen Tropiano
Applause Books
978-1-55783-951-0............. $24.99

Prices, contents, and availability
subject to change without notice.

Seinfeld FAQ
by Nicholas Nigro
Applause Books
978-1-55783-857-5............. $24.99

Sherlock Holmes FAQ
by Dave Thompson
Applause Books
978-1-4803-3149-5............ $24.99

The Smiths FAQ
by John D. Luerssen
Backbeat Books
978-1-4803-9449-0.......... $24.99

Soccer FAQ
by Dave Thompson
Backbeat Books
978-1-61713-598-9............. $24.99

The Sound of Music FAQ
by Barry Monush
Applause Books
978-1-4803-6043-3........... $27.99

South Park FAQ
by Dave Thompson
Applause Books
978-1-4803-5064-9.......... $24.99

Bruce Springsteen FAQ
by John D. Luerssen
Backbeat Books
978-1-61713-093-9..............$22.99

Star Trek FAQ
(Unofficial and Unauthorized)
by Mark Clark
Applause Books
978-1-55783-792-9..............$19.99

Star Trek FAQ 2.0
(Unofficial and Unauthorized)
by Mark Clark
Applause Books
978-1-55783-793-6..............$22.99

Star Wars FAQ
by Mark Clark
Applause Books
978-1-4803-6018-1............. $24.99

Quentin Tarantino FAQ
by Dale Sherman
Applause Books
978-1-4803-5588-0.......... $24.99

Three Stooges FAQ
by David J. Hogan
Applause Books
978-1-55783-788-2..............$22.99

The Who FAQ
by Mike Segretto
Backbeat Books
978-1-4803-6103-4........... $24.99

The Wizard of Oz FAQ
by David J. Hogan
Applause Books
978-1-4803-5062-5........... $24.99

The X-Files FAQ
by John Kenneth Muir
Applause Books
978-1-4803-6974-0........... $24.99

Neil Young FAQ
by Glen Boyd
Backbeat Books
978-1-61713-037-3.................$19.99

HAL•LEONARD®
PERFORMING ARTS
PUBLISHING GROUP

FAQ.halleonardbooks.com

0815